The Post-Soviet Handbook

A Guide to Grassroots Organizations
and Internet Resources in the Newly Independent States

The Post-Soviet Handbook

*A Guide to Grassroots Organizations
and Internet Resources in the Newly Independent States*

M. Holt Ruffin
Joan McCarter
Richard Upjohn

Foreword by S. Frederick Starr

Center for Civil Society International
Seattle

in association with

University of Washington Press
Seattle and London

Library of Congress Cataloging-in-Publication Data
Ruffin, M. Holt.
  The post-Soviet handbook: a guide to grassroots organizations and Internet
resources in the newly independent states / by M. Holt Ruffin, Joan McCarter,
Richard Upjohn; foreword by S. Frederick Starr.
    p. cm.
  ISBN 0–295–97534–2 (alk. paper)
    1. Associations, institutions, etc.—Former Soviet republics—Directories. 2.
Pressure groups—Former Soviet republics—Directories. 3. Former Soviet
republics —Computer network resources—Directories. 4. Internet (Computer
network)—Directories. I. McCarter, Joan. II. Upjohn, Richard. III. Title
HS71.F6R84   1996   95–53198
067'.025—dc20   CIP

The paper used in this publication meets the minimum requirements of American
National Standard for Information Sciences—Permanence of Paper for Printed
Library Materials, ANSI Z39.48–1984. ∞

Cover illustration: St. Petersburg, 1991. Photograph by Holt Ruffin.

For Lucy Dougall

Free institutions, public service and active civic spirit deployed
to social ends are the lifeblood of the properly-ordered
commonwealth, the fundamental preconditions for
peace, harmony and material progress.

–Edward Gibbon
The Decline and Fall of the Roman Empire

Special Thanks to Handbook Donors

The Post-Soviet Handbook is the outgrowth of work in 1994 and 1995 that was supported by The Eurasia Foundation, which receives funding from the United States Agency for International Development; an anonymous member of the Rockefeller Family; and the Stewardship Foundation.

Without the substantial financial contributions that the individuals named below made to *The Post-Soviet Handbook*, this project could never have been completed nor this book produced. Center for Civil Society International gratefully acknowledges their generous donations.

Anthony Arnold

Ronald and Michelle Bemis

Robert W. Blake

Allan Blackman

Robert Bowie

Mark D'Anastasio

R. T. Davies

Lucy Dougall

Esther Dyson

Paul Ekman

H. Walter Emori

Michael D. Evans

James Finn

Albert M. Franco

Kurt Taylor Gaubatz

William and Joyce Gleason

Janet Gray

Martin L. Greene

Richard and Beth Greene

John and Heidi Hamer

James E. Harnish

John and Karyl Hughes

Linda Jaech

George E. Kenny

Judith S. Kleinfeld

Frank S. Letcher

Donald R. Marsh

Mary Ann Mason

Richard John Neuhaus

Roy L. Prosterman

William and Jean Rosen

Bradley Rind

Takako Satoh

Witold S. Sulimirski

George E. Taylor

Lilya Wagner

Virtus ad beate vivendum se ipsa contenta est.
–Cicero, *De Finibus*

Contents

Appendices

Foreword

This volume, prepared by Holt Ruffin and his staff at the Center for Civil Society International, is in many respects remarkable. On the one hand, *The Post-Soviet Handbook* is the best available practical guide to the independent sector in the countries carved from the former Soviet Union. It consists of two parts, the first profiling "third sector" organizations in the newly independent states and American organizations interacting with them, and the second consisting of a useful compendium of Internet resources in those same countries.

Soaring far above these issues in importance is this volume's second identity, namely, as an insightful report on the state of civil society in Russia and other countries of the former Soviet Union, developed by an organization devoted to fostering and monitoring developments in this area. Thanks to this dual identity, *The Post-Soviet Handbook* offers something for everyone, no matter how practical and specific or how theoretical and general one's interest may be.

It needs scarcely be said that the editors have had to be highly selective. *The Post-Soviet Handbook* describes only a few hundred of the tens of thousands of NGOs active in the NIS today. Only a small fraction of not-for-profit groups in Western Europe and Japan, which have found their own points of interaction in the newly independent states, are listed here. Most difficult to document are the many independent groups in Russia and elsewhere that are not interacting with Western counterparts. It is hoped that indigenous researchers will soon begin detailing such groups. But until then, this volume will remain the standard reference.

Anyone connected with the Internet is *ipso facto* part of the new societal sector worldwide that exists outside the ready control of governmental organs; any guide to independent sector activity in the former Soviet Union must therefore include Internet users. Like airline pilots' associations or ham radio operator networks, Internet users constitute a kind of supra-national society in "cyberspace" whose links with each other are often as close as their ties with their local communities. Inevitably, even as substantial a guide to Internet resources as *The Post-Soviet Handbook* will not be comprehensive—so rapidly are these resources growing. The editors have wisely provided for regular updating through e-mail and through CCSI's World Wide Web site. In keeping with the democratic and participatory character of civil society, readers are encouraged to help update this site and perfect this compendium.

As the independent sector in the NIS grows and comes to include an ever greater number of increasingly diverse organizations, it would be very helpful if *The Post-Soviet Handbook* spawned additional, more specialized guides to important subsectors. Four possibilities stand out.

ix

First are scientific and technical fields. Highly organized and interactive, such disciplines have moved swiftly to participate both in third sector activity generally and in the Internet. Second and third are the many religious and ethnic-based organizations that exist within Russia and other newly independent states and which in many cases maintain close ties with kindred groupings abroad. It is worth noting that in Soviet times the vast majority of so-called "dissident" writings emerged form religious and national groups. Since the fall of the USSR such groups have greatly expanded their activity and have extended their reach into the political realm as well.

The fourth sphere that deserves a special compendium consists of local and provincial organizations. Relatively few such bodies maintain links with Moscow or Petersburg, let alone with counterpart organizations abroad. Having grown up "from below," these essential elements of civil society are the hardest to document. It is to be hoped that over time some readers will carry *The Post-Soviet Handbook* idea forward in all four of these areas.

∅

It is impossible to overstate the importance of the present guide to third sector organizations and Internet users in Russia and the other newly independent states. The astonishing proliferation of businesses and financial institutions in the former Soviet Union is well documented elsewhere, thanks to reports by the U.S. Department of Commerce, Deutsche Bank and various business groups. The independent sector has been far less accessible, however.

Perhaps it is too much to be hoped that those researching the rise of civil society in the former Soviet Union will adequately utilize a handbook like this. They should do so, however, for *The Post-Soviet Handbook* provides as revealing an index to this phenomenon as any in existence. More than three decades ago the MIT political scientist Karl Deutsch assessed the likelihood of political community embracing North America and Western Europe by counting the number of telephone calls and the amount of first-class mail between those two regions. The present volume provides the raw material for a similar study of civil society and it is worth drawing here some of the obvious conclusions.

So rapidly does the past slip from our consciousness that we must pause to recall the situation as it existed only a decade ago. Soviet law permitted no truly independent organizations whatsoever. True, nominally "societal" (*obshchest-vennyi*) groups existed, but only under the tutelage of a governmental or Communist Party patron. Even in the case of these governmentalized entities, the state exercised a monopoly of communication, both domestic and international. Unauthorized communications both within the USSR and with independent entities abroad was banned. The receipt of funds from foreign bodies, whether public or private, was grounds for stern legal action.

The political underpinnings of this unnatural order traced directly to Marxism-Leninism, with its ideal of the totally organized society, and also to notions of autarky that permeated the official ideology. All these traced in turn to an earlier era when the major channels of communication–the printed word, mail, and film–were readily controlled by the state. Such control was all the easier if the state was prepared to use force, as was certainly the case in the USSR.

Beginning in the 1960s, however, the willingness of the Soviet state to employ force to achieve its ends diminished. Meanwhile, the spread of education in the USSR created a growing number of men and women who were eager to participate directly in the leading cultural movements worldwide. Beginning in the realm of religion and movements for national identity and rapidly extending into such diverse realms as popular culture, jazz, ecology, and the arts, truly self-organized and independent initiatives sprouted throughout Soviet society. Long before the Internet, these hearty bands of enthusiasts exploited 35 mm film, tape recordings, telephone, and xerox to advance their cause and forge links with like-minded groups both locally and abroad.

By this process, a true civil society began to re-emerge even during the "golden age" of Brezhnev's rule. *Glasnost'* existed long before Gorbachev's *glasnost'*, and voluntary associations existed long before the state acknowledged them as legal.

Whence came this effervescence of independence in the very heart of the Marxist-Leninist state? Contrary to the claims of Soviet officialdom and Western kremlinology, Russians, Ukrainians and many other peoples of the USSR possessed a strong tradition of self-organization. The progenitors of today's not-for-profits in the newly independent states are the thousands of self-help and philanthropic societies that existed prior to the Bolshevik revolution. The fact that the Soviet government had to exert so much brutal force in order to wipe out these groups in the 1920s and 1930s attests to their vitality. Nor did the spirit of self-initiative stay dead for long. Obliterated by 1937, the volunteeristic urge in Russia reappeared like Lazarus in the 1960s, a mere quarter-century later. As the spirit of self-initiative came once more to the fore, it revealed the absolute limits of absolute power in the USSR, thus contributing directly to the system's downfall.

What, then, is the state of volunteerism and the independent sector in Russia today? Besides the mere fact of their reappearance after so many years, the two most important features of the present situation are, first, that the new associations and groupings are far more closely interlinked with counterpart groups in Europe and America than were their predecessors, and second, that they are yet to obtain the solid legal basis that is essential if they are to be viable for the long term.

It is easy to be cynical about American and Western aid to the independent sector in Russia. Far too much of that aid–estimates range up to 90 percent–has ended up in the pockets of American and European organizations rather than of the

Russian groups they purport to champion. Nonetheless, wherever the money ends up, American assistance under USAID has helped forge close personal links between independent sector activists in the NIS and the U.S. Such ties are more enduring than any financial support, and over time they are bound to affect the "culture" and mentality of the third sector in Russia and neighboring countries.

Second, for all the vitality of voluntary initiatives in Russia and elsewhere, they have yet to gain the firm basis in law that is essential for their long-term viability. Only in May 1995 did the first body of legislation in this area pass the Duma. Supplementary legislation validating foundations and political parties has, at this writing, yet to be approved.

Skeptics may find evidence in this of a kind of "Soviet hangover," i.e., the resistance of the new Russian government to true voluntarism and pluralism. For the time being, however, the evidence does not support this conclusion. On the contrary, the legislative delays are attributable not to opposition but to the serious effort of Russian legislators to "get it right," i.e., to produce legislation that is solid, enduring, and grounded in the best experience of other countries. The first section of the new Civil Code, approved early in 1995, is a solid piece of legislation based on the Napoleonic tradition. There is every reason to expect that subsequent legislation based on volunteerism will have an equally serious character, and will meet the needs of a modern society as Russians perceive them.

This leaves unanswered only one question, but a crucially important one. Already, there are many men and women of wealth in Russia. Thousands of other fortunes are bound to be made in the vast and increasingly privatized energy sector, the burgeoning service sector, in banking, and even in the manufacturing sphere. Will those who possess such fortunes place them in the public good? Will they, in other words, adopt a philosophy akin to Andrew Carnegie's *Gospel of Wealth*, which would obligate them to devote the fruits of their good fortune to civic uplift and the public's welfare?

It is too early to judge whether this will occur. However, public discussion of this issue within Russia henceforth will no longer be a purely Russian affair. Thanks to the channels of communication with many organizations described herein, and to the great river of transnational dialogue that is the Internet, this issue can be thoroughly aired not only by Russians alone, but by friends of the independent sector everywhere. If this dialogue fosters the further effervescence of volunteerism in Russia, as one might hope and even expect, then the present volume will soon be obsolete. One can pay no higher compliment to it than this!

S. Frederick Starr
Distinguished Fellow
Senior Advisor, International Programs
The Aspen Institute

Acknowledgments

Many people and organizations assisted Center for Civil Society International in producing *The Post-Soviet Handbook.* We would first like to thank the numerous third sector organizations based in the NIS who received our e-mail notice of the project and promptly e-mailed back to us profiles of their organizations. We incorporated virtually all of these submissions. They further confirmed the power of the Internet for grassroots communication and collaboration between citizens of the U.S. and the newly independent states.

ISAR's executive director, Eliza Klose, and her staff in Washington and in the NIS, lent important support to the project. Of the various ISAR[1] offices, we would like to thank especially Michael Clayton (Tbilisi), Alyson Ewald and Karen Smallwood (Kyiv), Todd Karl (Washington, DC) and Amy McVey (Moscow).

Wim Aspeslagh of the Armenian Assembly of America's NGO Training and Resource Center in Yerevan shared his organization's extensive database of NGOs. Zoya Khotkina, a leading figure in the Russian women's movement, manages the Women's Database Archive project in Moscow. She e-mailed us information on a number of important women's organizations in Russia. For most of the material on NGOs in Tajikistan, we are indebted to Eric Sievers, who was working on a legal reform project in Central Asia at the time he sent it to us.

Colleen F. Halley, now working for IREX (International Research & Exchanges Board) in Rostov-on-Don, provided us with almost all our information on NIS human rights organizations. Elena Belova, manager of the NGO Resources Center in Moscow (part of Save the Children's Civic Initiatives Program), provided helpful research assistance during a visit to the center last November. Sheila Scott of Winrock International supplied us with an extensive list of the NIS-U.S. Women's Consortium member organizations and individuals. COUNTERPART sent information from databases they have been compiling on NGOs in the Russian Far East and Central Asia.

Newsletters and other materials produced by the Interlegal organization in Moscow, United Way International and World Learning all proved to be excellent sources of information on third sector developments in the NIS. The Center for International Private Enterprise provided their list of grantees in the business institutions development sector in Ukraine and Russia.

Without the support over the past two years of Greg Cole and Natasha Bulashova, whose Friends and Partners site on the World Wide Web we have used as a platform

---

[1] ISAR was formerly known as the Institute for Soviet-American Relations.

for our own CivilSoc electronic mailing list and Web site, we might never have experienced lift-off, as far as the Internet is concerned. Similarly, without many instances of assistance and support from Professor Daniel Waugh, chair of the Russian, East European and Central Asian Studies department of the University of Washington's Jackson School of International Studies, the *Handbook* could not exist.

Parts of the Internet sections benefited from the knowledge or know-how of Max Pyziur, Garth Coogan, Brenden West, and Alan Boyle. Tatiana Savenkova of Relcom (Moscow) helped us to understand how to convert from Latin characters to Cyrillic, and back, and generously donated some utilities for this purpose.

At different points in time Irina Carnevale, Anne Flueckiger, and Laura Hjerpe, all made contributions to *The Post-Soviet Handbook*. In the final month of the project, Deirdre Shelly arrived as if by providence and gave us scores of hours of help, so that we could complete the project in a timely fashion.

We are grateful to the University of Washington Press–in particular Pat Soden, general manager, and Michael Duckworth, acquisitions editor–for the opportunity they have given us to do this project together. It has been a pleasure to work with them.

Finally, CCSI wishes to acknowledge the thousands of "civil society builders" in the NIS, of all nationalities, only a small fraction of whose creative work we could document in *The Post-Soviet Handbook*. History too seldom recognizes the important contributions of such people.

Needless to say, Center for Civil Society International is alone responsible for whatever shortcomings are to be found in *The Post-Soviet Handbook*.

–The Editors

Guide to Foreign Words and Abbreviations

Foreign words

A/ya (abonementnii yashchik)	Post Office Box
Bulvar, bul. or boul.	Boulevard
Dom, d.	Building
Etazh	Floor
Indeks	Zip code
Kabinet, kab.	Office
Komnata, kom.	Room
Korpus, korp.	Section
Krai	Territorial area, comparable to oblast
Kvartira, kv.	Apartment
Naberezhnaia, nab.	Embankment
Oblast, obl.	Province (more or less equivalent to a U.S. state)
Pereulok, per.	Lane or alley
Ploshchad, pl.	Square
Pochtamt, Glavnii Pochtamt	Post Office, General Post Office (GPO)
Podezd, pod.	Entrance, doorway
Prospekt, pr.	Avenue
Proyezd	Passageway, thoroughfare
Raion	Municipal district
Shosse	Highway
Ulitsa, ul.	Street
Vulytsya, vul.	Street, in Ukrainian

Abbreviations

CEE	Central and Eastern Europe
FAQ	Frequently Asked Questions, the name given to a type of document found on World Wide Web sites. E.g., a "Ukraine FAQ" will contain basic facts about Ukraine.
FSU	Former Soviet Union
NIS	Newly Independent States (of the former Soviet Union)
NGO	Nongovernmental organization
PVO	Private voluntary organization, used interchangeably with NGO
RFE	Russian Far East

USAID   United States Agency for International Development
USIA   United States Information Agency
USIS   United States Information Service, the services provided
                                   overseas by the USIA
URL   Uniform Resource Locator, the address of a file on the
                                   Internet

Notes to *Handbook* users

1.   Addresses in Russia and the NIS are written in the reverse order from the U.S.
Russians first give the city, then the street, then the individual's name. The zip code
(*indeks*) precedes the name of the city, and the building number usually follows the
street name. Also, since people commonly live in large apartment complexes, there
are often three numbers in a street address: the building (*dom*), the section (*korpus*)
of the building, and the apartment *(kvartira)* or room (*komnata*) number. Thus, a
typical Russian address might read in this order:

> 194156   St. Petersburg
> Nevski pr., d. 93, korp. 4, kv. 203
> Assotsiatsia Nadezhda

Alternatively, the street address can be written:

> Nevski pr., 93-4-203

or

> Nevski pr., 93/4/203

They all mean the same thing: that the association Nadezhda is located in
apartment 203 in section 4 of the building at 93 Nevski Prospect.

2.   If you intend to send snail mail, i.e. a letter, to an organization and have a
choice between post office box and street address, use the post office box. It is
reputedly more secure.

3.   A few telephone numbers have a special area code. An example is the
International Press Center and Club in Moscow, which has a telephone and fax line
with a 4481 prefix, instead of the standard Moscow prefix of 095. Use the prefix
that is given. In this case, it probably represents a special high quality line that is
being leased from a telecommunications service provider.

4.   In the sections on NIS organizations, we have grouped organizations by city. If
an organization is in a village or small town that is part of a larger region identified
with a city, we classified it by that city's name. Thus, the Gaia organization, in the
town of Zapadnaya Dvina in the Tver region, will be found under Tver–not
Zapadnaya Dvina.

Map 1. Western NIS

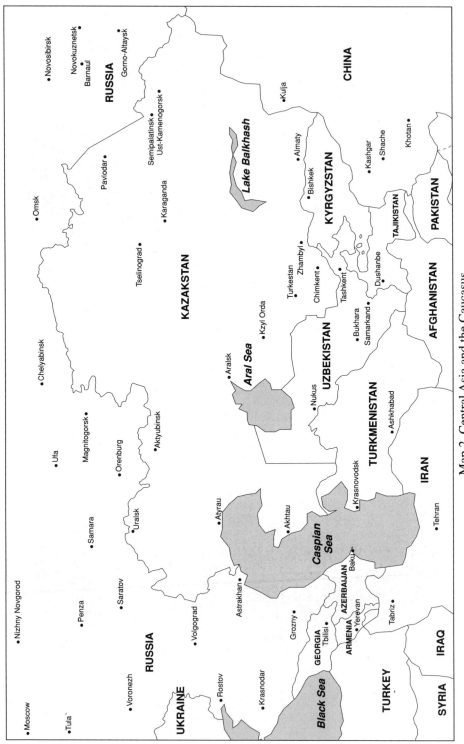

Map 2. Central Asia and the Caucasus

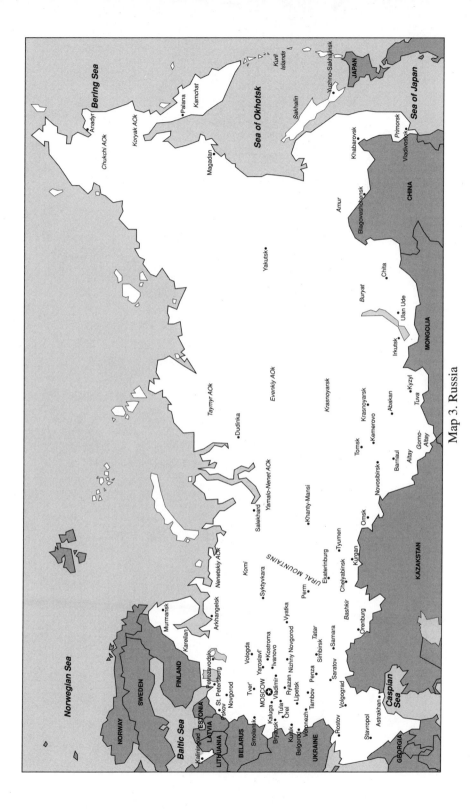

Map 3. Russia

The Post-Soviet Handbook

*A Guide to Grassroots Organizations
and Internet Resources in the Newly Independent States*

Introduction

Where institution building (and not mere constitution writing) is concerned, time is measured in decades. This was true of the German Länder, it has been true of the Italian regions and of the communal republics before them, and it will be true of the ex-Communist states of Eurasia, even in the most optimistic scenarios.[1]

–Robert Putnam
Harvard University

It is easier to make fish soup from an aquarium, than to make an aquarium out of fish soup.

–Popular Eastern European aphorism

What is the purpose of *The Post-Soviet Handbook*? For more than a year Center for Civil Society International has operated an electronic information service, named CivilSoc, routinely posting information of the type found in the *Handbook* to a list that now numbers almost 1,000 subscribers. After a post to the list earlier this year, describing the interesting work of the Moscow-based Social Center for Assistance in Reforming Criminal Justice, a longstanding CivilSoc subscriber responded with this message:

> *My problem is that it is not obvious to me what to do with all the information. Is money wanted? Are volunteers wanted? Or is this a consoling confirmation that someone is trying to do <u>something</u> about human nature?*

It was a puzzling question. Was it not clear what could be done with such information? Or was the message intended as a little splash of cold water...not over the idea of changing human nature, but the idea that grassroots organizations could

---

[1] Robert D. Putnam, *Making Democracy Work: Civic Traditions in Modern Italy*, (Princeton, 1993), p. 184.

3

help build civil society and democracy in Russia or any of the other newly independent states (NIS)[2] ?

Put in these terms, the question was reminiscent of the view afforded of Russia by the Western press over the past two or three years. Crime, corruption, and anarchy have been the themes most likely to interest news editors, leaving readers to conclude that greater freedom has only made life different, not better, since the fall of communism.

That there is great disorder today in Russia and the other countries of the NIS is undeniable. But it is by no means the whole story. Side by side with the Russian mafia, forces are also at work that represent a future democratic order, a dynamic market economy, and a functioning civil society. Their success is not assured, but neither is their failure. The story of some of these forces is contained in *The Post-Soviet Handbook*. It is not a human interest or a human nature story, but in many ways a more interesting one. It is the story of myriad independent groups and organizations, often spanning national borders in their membership, which are successfully creating new social values and structures for a multinational population of 200 million to 300 million people, heirs to the empty legacy of "actual socialism."

Grassroots Social Innovators in the NIS

So the first purpose of the *Handbook* is to recognize the significant and growing forces of social change in the NIS today: specifically, the thousands of grassroots innovators active throughout this vast territory. Their work is creative; much of it deserves international support, and in many cases they are receiving it–in ways that go far beyond money or volunteering, as will be seen below.

According to a statement drafted at a 1993 meeting in Moscow by leaders of 50 charitable and nonprofit organizations, Russia's third sector[3] contained more than 50,000 organizations at that time.[4] One may debate the exact number because such estimates are based upon government lists of registered organizations, which always

---

[2] NIS refers to states in the area that used to be the USSR. As some states included in this term come to be identified more with other regions, e.g. Central Asia, the term may fall out of use. For the time being, however, it seems superior to the alternatives: Eurasia, the former Soviet Union, or the Commonwealth of Independent States (CIS). The latter is the political entity which Moscow created to supersede the USSR. So far it has achieved no significant authority, primarily because of the misgivings of newly independent member states such as Ukraine.

[3] The term "third sector" refers to voluntary organizations, associations, and other nonprofit enterprises, such as religious, service and charitable institutions. The two other sectors are business firms and government agencies.

[4] Interlegal International Foundation (Moscow), *Third Sector*, no. 1, 1994, p. 4.

contain inactive or defunct ones. What is indisputable is that tens of thousands of independent grassroots organizations are now active in Russia and other nations of the NIS, less than five years after the failed August 1991 *putsch* that sealed the fate of the Soviet Union.

Today in the NIS an independent third sector is rendering social services to those who would otherwise be without them and articulating the concerns of sectors of society hitherto voiceless. From feeding the poor and elderly through privately funded soup kitchens, to representing the interests of small businesses, to dealing with the environmental legacy of Soviet-style industrialization, independent voluntary organizations are showing the power of activism, public education, advocacy and cooperative behavior.

Whether such activities exist on a scale large enough to be building in their societies what Alexis de Tocqueville called "the habits that freedom forms" remains to be seen.[5] But day in and day out the spreading tapestry of grassroots organiza-tions and independent associations in Russia and the NIS is giving thousands of citizens the authentic experience of democracy in action.

A good example is the Soldiers' Mothers Committees, established in 1989 to curb abuses such as hazing in the Russian military. Over the past year and a half, the savage war in Chechnya has redirected their considerable energies toward public education and lobbying for change in Moscow's policy. The Soldiers' Mothers group–which now has branches in many cities of Russia and 14 former Soviet republics–has not only collected statements from others opposed to the war, organized meetings and demonstrations, and lobbied the government. In early 1995 hundreds of women travelled to Grozny from Moscow in the Mothers' March for Life and Compassion. The march generated a great deal of publicity about the war. In Grozny the mothers from Moscow shared their sorrow with Chechen mothers; together they helped negotiate the release of military men held by Chechen forces.[6] Since then they have

---

[5] "If an American," de Tocqueville wrote, "were condemned to confine his activity to his own affairs, he would be robbed of one half of his own existence; he would feel an immense void in the life which he is accustomed to lead, and his wretchedness would be unbearable. I am persuaded that if ever a despotism should be established in America, it would be more difficult to overcome the habits that freedom has formed than to conquer the love of freedom itself." *Democracy in America*, vol. 1 (New York: Vintage Books, 1945), p. 260.

[6] Organizations in Germany and Switzerland, such as the International Peace Bureau based in Bern, are launching a worldwide campaign to award the 1996 Nobel Peace Prize to the Soldiers' Mothers Committee. If the prize is awarded to the group, it will be well-deserved. The organization is truly committed to nonviolence, supporting neither the military actions of Yeltsin, nor those of Dudayev. If Soldiers' Mothers do not receive the prize, one hopes the publicity generated by the campaign will at least help the organization and the cause of peace in Chechnya.

continued to press for an end to the war, assisted soldiers unwilling to participate in the conflict, and provided shelter and relief to many refugees from the war zone.

Transferring and Building Social Capital

If the first purpose of *The Post-Soviet Handbook* is to recognize a vibrant third sector in the NIS, the second major aim is to demonstrate the power of international collaborations between independent nongovernmental organizations in projects designed to build new social institutions.

At root, the problem Russia and its neighbors face is how to create in a short period of time institutions that have evolved in unbroken fashion over decades or even centuries in other societies: schools of law and business, commercial banks, securities markets, watchdog organizations which protect the environment or consumers from unscrupulous business practices, trade and professional associations, foundations dedicated to the needs of children or adults with disabilities, etc.

Despite the pleas one used to hear for a "Marshall Plan for Russia," the problem of the newly independent states has not been one of insufficient capital to rebuild a shattered economy. The central problem has been one of creating independent institutions–economic, social, political, religious–out of a 70-year void. Never in history have nations faced such a challenge.

It is a towering challenge, and one in which Americans and other citizens of the world community are rightly seeking to offer assistance. But how best to help? To return to our subscriber's question, is it simply a matter of sending money or volunteers?

At a general level, both money and volunteeers can be very helpful, of course. But in the *The Post-Soviet Handbook* the reader will find a wide variety of well-considered, long-term projects that are addressing discrete, specific aspects of the civil society puzzle that the NIS presents. Cumulatively, these collaborations represent an unprecedented effort by the U.S. to transfer and help create *social capital* in Russia and the other nations of the NIS.

Social capital refers to certain norms, as well as organizations and institutions, that make government, the economy, and the entire national community work better. Like other forms of capital, it is a form of wealth, an aspect of development. Destroy the American Institute of Architects and you have destroyed a form of capital as surely as if you had bombed an office building. Unlike physical capital, which depreciates with use, social capital grows with use. Also unlike physical capital, which can be either a public good (a park) or a private good (a yacht), social capital is by its very nature a public good.

Trust and Cooperation

Trust and cooperation between citizens are important aspects of social capital. If trust is low in a society, people will think twice before joining any voluntary organization to pursue shared goals. As a simple example, Ivan Ivanovich, vice president of a bank in Omsk, may ask himself: should I attend the meeting next Thursday of a local group concerned about the shortage of safe play areas for the children in our neighborhood? I care about this issue, but I don't know who else will be there. Associating with strangers has its risks. Next thing I know, I'll be hearing that so-and-so, with whom I chatted for three minutes at the meeting, is calling me to insist on a meeting to request financing for a personal business venture of his. I don't want to have such problems, so I think I'll not attend.

Voluntary cooperative behavior in civil society depends on people trusting one another enough such that fears like that of Ivan Ivanovich don't prevent people-as-citizens (i.e., essentially anonymous individuals) from attending meetings or engaging in other public activities with one another. While "distrust of the public" is not a syndrome exclusive to the NIS, it is a real legacy of communism that remains alive and slows the pace of reform there.[7]

One of the most effective ways to change such patterns of thinking it is to show or model alternatives. This is why exchange programs which give individuals the opportunity to observe and experience differences in trust and cooperative behavior between different societies can have such a powerful impact.

Independent Organizations and Institutions

Another aspect of social capital consists of the myriad nongovernmental organizations and institutions which give shape to so many interactions among citizens in civil societies and to their interactions with government. Professional associations such as the American Bar Association play an important role in setting and maintaining professional standards and providing for the continuing education of members–among other important functions. Debate societies are instruments of civic education, sustaining the values of reason and persuasion as the basis for democratic governance and training the political leaders of the future. Trade groups such as the Washington Software Association, based in Seattle, help members stay abreast of developments in technology and markets in this very dynamic industry. Cause

---

[7] A related attitude that retards civic engagement is the belief that things only get accomplished through personal connections in high places. It dismisses the idea of a public square or social contract, since it does not believe that the opinions of ordinary citizens, even if well-organized and well-articulated, can change public law or behavior.

organizations such as the Anti-Defamation League of B'nai B'rith fight political extremism and intolerance in society through public education campaigns, historical exhibits, annual awards programs, etc. Humanitarian organizations such as the Red Cross have years of experience dealing with natural disasters such as floods or earthquakes.

All of these activities happen essentially at the initiative of each organization's members and leaders. They are not programs initiated or commanded by government. Sometimes, as in the case of the ABA or the Red Cross, programs work in close coordination with government. But they are essentially the work of independent social institutions, making fundamental contributions to the functioning of our society, our economy and our government.

Some critics argue that the spirit of self-reliance and the village meetings of de Tocqueville's day long ago gave way to a plethora of "special interest" groups which today simply lobby Washington incessantly on their own behalf.

This is a matter of debate, and a debate of importance–which cannot be settled here. Suffice it to say, however, that an equally strong case can be made that major advances in American legislation have been achieved precisely because of the unflagging efforts of "special interest groups." In addition, such criticisms often ignore the role of associations and voluntary organizations in assuming responsibi-lities which in other countries are either assumed by no group, public or private, or monopolized by the state. A case in point is the nongovernmental Underwriters' Laboratories, whose product certification program makes a major contribution to household and consumer safety in the U.S.[8]

The Power of Citizen Engagement

This, then, is social capital. But if we grant that it is a good thing, and responds to an essential need of the transitional societies comprising the NIS, the question remains: How is social capital created in countries emerging from 70 years of institutional amnesia? Can it be transferred between societies as different as the U.S. and the 15 newly independent states? The answer, or many answers, will be found in *The Post-Soviet Handbook*. It contains the story of an engagement between societies which– despite large differences of language and geography–seems to be working. This broad engagement represents a novel and exciting approach to "foreign aid" that sidesteps old approaches and familiar pitfalls. Vice President Al Gore has stated that within five

---

[8] Putnam's *Making Democracy Work* has a chapter devoted to the idea of social capital, including a refutation of the charge that "associationism" is anti-democratic. See pp. 163-185, *op. cit.*

years the U.S. government plans to channel nearly half of its foreign aid through private voluntary organizations rather than governments.[9] Certainly, it is an approach that seems worth trying, given the instances of USAID loans to governments in less developed countries that have terminated not in infrastructural investments, as intended, but in officials' private bank accounts in Grand Cayman or Geneva.

In the case of the NIS, this approach appears to be working well for two reasons. First, of course, it is because sizable funding has been provided for it by the government of the United States, by a remarkable philanthropist named George Soros, and by a host of voluntary organizations, foundations, educational institutions and individuals that have contributed smaller amounts.[10] Of equal importance, it is working because tens of thousands of private citizens on both sides, East and West, working through nonprofit organizations, have *wanted* to engage with one another and endure all the frustrations, headaches and difficulties that many of these projects entail.[11]

Forms of Engagement

The 150-plus projects described in the two sections that immediately follow (*Clearinghouse Organizations* and *Special Focus Organizations*) illustrate the

---

[9] See "President's Letter" in COUNTERPART Foundation's 1994-1995 Program Summary and Annual Report.

[10] According to David Evans, Senior Advisor to the Commission on Security and Cooperation in Europe (CSCE), U.S. assistance to East-Central Europe and the NIS for the period 1990-95, including food and nuclear weapons reduction programs, amounted to more than $9 billion. A large fraction of the $9 billion Evans cited–perhaps as much as 50%–has supported programs to help in the destruction of nuclear weapons and intercontinental rockets in the NIS. The balance has supported programs involved in democratic institution-building, market reform and restructuring, health care improvement, energy efficiency, environmental policy and housing sector reform.

The amount President Clinton requested for the NIS for fiscal year 1996 was $1.4 billion. See *Briefing on U.S. Assistance to Central and Eastern Europe and the NIS: an Assessment*, U.S. Congress: Commission on Security and Cooperation in Europe (February 17, 1995), p. 2.

The total amount that the 24 national Soros Foundations and related entities (e.g., the International Science Foundation) spent in 1994, the last year for which figures are available, was approximately $300 million. See *Building Open Societies: Soros Foundations 1994* (New York: Open Society Institute, 1995).

[11] Whether a predisposition exists on the part of Americans toward engaging with other regions of the world comparable to the way we seem to feel about Russia and other countries of the NIS is an open question. If it doesn't exist, this is an argument for developing programs, for example, that would increase student enrollments at our universities in those language and area studies (e.g., Arabic and the Middle East) which perhaps lack the allure that Russian and Soviet studies enjoyed for many years.

astonishing range of activities made possible when the desire for mutual engagement is strong between different societies. The range is geographical as well as functional, for many of the projects are located in remote parts of Russia and other countries of the NIS.

What are some of the forms this engagement can take? There are many, as *Handbook* users will discover, but a common aspect is organizational partnerships through which exchanges of people, internships, trainings, and joint program development take place. One example is USAID's Institutional Partnerships Project which is funding 22 discrete projects under a cooperative agreement with the International Research & Exchanges Board (IREX).

This project, begun in late 1994, aims to "strengthen the institutional bases of civil society" by helping educational institutions, professional associations, and trade organizations in the Russian Federation and Ukraine improve the services they provide their own members. Three examples of these partnerships are as follows:

- The American Road and Transportation Builders Association is working with the Russian Association of Territorial Bodies of Highway Administration (RADOR) to strengthen RADOR as a transportation development trade association in the Russian Federation, provide training in free-market industry operations, and promote joint venture activities between association member organizations.
- The World Institute on Disability, based in Oakland, CA, is working with the All-Russian Society of the Disabled, based in Moscow, to develop seven centers that will offer employment training and other skills that will support the integration of the disabled into society.
- The Carl Vinson Institute of Government at the University of Georgia is working with Ukraine's Uzhhorod State University' Center for Public Administration Reform and Assistance in a program targeted at providing training and technical assistance to local governments in the Transcarpathia region.

Using the same partnership concept, USAID also funded the so-called PVO/NIS Project between 1992 and 1996. This was led by World Learning and eventually supported 46 initiatives by American private voluntary organizations (PVOs) working with social service organizations in 12 of the 15 newly independent states. Save the Children and COUNTERPART are other organizations which are currently serving as lead managers of teams of American PVOs in projects focused on strengthening the NGO sector in the NIS.

An additional feature of projects such as these in the past two years–as well as the work of ISAR, the Soros foundations, the Eurasia Foundation and other foundations– has been a growing number of small grants programs which distribute grants ranging in size from a few hundred to a few thousand dollars directly to Russian and other NGOs in the region.

"It Isn't Necessary To Wait Until Everything Is In Order"

What is the cumulative impact of these projects, or their rate of success? Anyone who has traveled to the region and met the talented and dedicated Americans working side-by-side with Russians, Ukrainians, Uzbeks or Georgians to carry out the projects described in the *Handbook* finds it easy to believe in their effectiveness and importance. Objectively, on the other hand, it is difficult to measure their accomplishments, especially when so many variables are at play and goals are defined as broadly as "strengthening the institutional bases of civil society."

It is also important to remember that a significant number of projects and relationships exist between NGOs in the NIS and partners in Canada, Germany, the UK, Scandinavia and other regions of the world, including East Asia. This makes it even more difficult to analyze the uniquely "American contribution" to civil society in the NIS.[12] Nevertheless, for those who like to keep score, as well as for those who care about the ability of the U.S. to launch comparable NGO-based development initiatives in the future, it would be helpful if USAID were to make widely available any independent analyses or evaluations that are done as to the effectiveness of the many NIS-based third sector projects they have funded.

It would be helpful, too, if USAID–or some other institution–carried out some analysis and evaluation of U.S.-based third sector projects in the NIS that have *not* been entirely or primarily funded by USAID. These are often smaller projects, often inadequately funded, but sustained by the strong personal commitment and enthusiasm of their leadership. Such projects are sometimes staffed by individuals with a special spirit–of dedication, enterprise, and desire to be of service–that can have a strong impact on Russians and other colleagues in the NIS.

An example of such a project is Serendipity. Its founder, Ron Pope, a professor of political science at Illinois State University, first became active in 1990, when he took a group of officers from his local police force to Vladimir, using substantial amounts of personal funds to accomplish this. Within a short space of time Pope and his organization's members had accomplished a great deal more–including the construction, together with their Russian partners, of a wooden ranch house in the

---

[12] For information on the organizations from Western Europe active in the NIS, see Brian Harvey, *Networking in Eastern and Central Europe: A Guide to Voluntary and Community Organizations*, published in late 1995 by Community Development Foundation, 60 Highbury Grove, London N5 2AG, England. Tel: (0171) 226-5375. Fax: (0171) 704-0313. Price: £17.95 plus postage and handling. 304 pp.

center of Vladimir. (The project is described in detail in the section, *Special Focus Organizations*.)

What motivated Pope and his team? Not a USAID contract, but a spirit of service, a sense of empathy for the Russian people, and no doubt a drop or two of desire for adventure. To judge from an editorial in the local newspaper, *Molva*, written in July 1993 (upon the first anniversary of the completion of the house), the demonstrated personal values and attitudes of the Americans involved in Serendipity may have made as great a contribution to the people of Vladimir as the construction of the *dom amerikanskii* itself. In an editorial titled, "The American Home Has Stood for a Year and Not Collapsed," *Molva* expressed admiration for Serendipity's special approach:

> *to complete in Russia small but concrete projects. The professor's motto: It isn't necessary to wait until everything here is in order–we need to work now.*

Here was a project that created physical capital, but over time the returns on the "social capital" that Serendipity has also created will dwarf the value of the physical structure. Projects like Serendipity are occurring in many cities and regions of the NIS, thanks to the can-do spirit of their leaders and staff and their willingness to engage with the problems of the NIS. They instill a sense of confidence about the future in nations where, for long periods in the past, feelings of hope and trust were exceedingly difficult to sustain. If *The Post-Soviet Handbook* contributes to the strengthening of projects such as these, our work will have been richly rewarded.

What Is Not In The Handbook

Ideally a volume such as *The Post-Soviet Handbook* should be as inclusive as possible. But in fact, there are too many projects and too many organizations for a single volume to encompass. From the start, we knew we had to set limits on what the *Handbook* would include, to keep the project manageable. Directories already exist for religious projects[13]; moreover, for persons especially interested in this area, religious institutions and organizations in the NIS are by and large easy to identify and find. Therefore, with a few exceptions, we have not included projects or organizations of a religious character–indispensable though they may be to a healthy civil society.

---

[13] See, for example, *East-West Christian Organizations: A Directory of Western Christian Organizations Working in East Central Europe and the Newly Independent States Formerly Part of the Soviet Union*, edited by Sharon Linzey, M. Holt Ruffin, and Mark R. Elliott. (Evanston, IL: Berry Publishing Services, 1993.)

Political parties and organizations are also not represented in *The Post-Soviet Handbook*. They have been well documented elsewhere. Likewise most clubs, sports organizations, and fraternal societies have been omitted.

Professional associations and trade organizations are a very rapidly growing sector of civil society in the NIS. Examples of these will be found in the *Handbook*, but perhaps not as many as there should be. A directory of just this class of organizations would be a very useful thing for somebody to produce.

After all these limitations, we still have a book which by no means includes all the organizations or institutions in the remaining categories: advocacy groups, service and charitable organizations, health organizations, new and experimental educational institutions, women's organizations, youth groups, etc. Because we knew in advance that we would inevitably have to leave out organizations that in principle should be included, we made a special effort to do a good job with the section titled *Clearinghouse Organizations*. The reader who reviews this section of the *Handbook* will find organizations in it which can serve as excellent reference points to many of the other organizations and sectors of civil society not represented in the *Handbook*. We encourage readers to contact any of the clearinghouse organizations profiled in the *Handbook*, including ourselves, Center for Civil Society International, if their curiosity about any particular field of activity isn't satisfied in the pages that follow.

A Special Note on the Baltic States

The *Handbook* also includes few organizations dealing primarily with the Baltic states, for the reason that Baltic organizations have produced excellent resources like this one, and we would only be duplicating that work by reproducing it here. Three of these resources are described below.

• The U.S.-Baltic Foundation in 1994 produced *U.S.-Baltic Partnerships*, described as a "directory of American private sector, non-governmental organizations which have made an express commitment to become active partners with the Baltic peoples as they rebuild and retrain their society." It is a comprehensive resource, also featuring a very helpful indexing system. It can be obtained from:

The U.S.-Baltic Foundation	Tel:	(202) 986-0380
1211 Connecticut Avenue NW, Suite 506	Fax:	(202) 234-8130
Washington, DC 20036	E-mail:	63855648@mcimail.com

• The *Estonian Foundation Centre Directory 1994* provides information about 68 Estonian foundations working in the areas of education, culture, environment and philanthropy and who are members of the Estonian Foundation Centre. Entries are in English and include: name, address, phone number, director's name, founders

and date founded, purpose, annual expenditure and publications. For further
information, contact:

Ingrid Veinmann, Information Officer   Tel/fax: (372 2) 448 884
Eesti Fondide Keskus
Lai 34/ Vaimu 3
EE0001 Tallinn, Estonia

• The *Directory of Non-Governmental Organizations in Lithuania* ("Lietuvos
Nevyriausybiniu Organizaciju Rodykle"), published in 1995, contains information
about approximately 125 NGOs that are working to improve the quality of life in
Lithuania through a range of socio-economic and humanitarian activities. Included
are affiliates of international NGOs with a socio-economic or humanitarian agenda,
but not political parties. NGO profiles include: name, address, phone and/or fax,
contact person(s), objectives, sources of funding, affiliations with other
organizations and publications, if any. In Lithuanian and English. UNDP, the
publisher of the *Directory*, indicates that there will be future updates, and requests
that NGOs wishing to be included (or updated) in future editions, send their most
current information to the address below.

Jorgen Lissner, United Nations Resident   Tel: (370 2) 223-111
Coordinator and UNDP Representative   Fax: (370 2) 224-274
J. Tumo-Vaizganto 2
LT-2600 Vilnius, Lithuania

April 1996   *M. Holt Ruffin*
Seattle, WA   Center for Civil Society International

U.S.-Based Organizations

Clearinghouse Organizations

A clearinghouse, says Webster, is "a central agency for the collection and distribution of materials, information, etc." The organizations below have been grouped in this section because they do work that routinely puts them in touch with numerous other organizations active in third sector work in the NIS; or they publish newsletters or directories, or maintain databases of information, about the work of other third sector organizations active in the NIS. As such, clearinghouse organizations can serve as helpful "first stops," referring individuals with particular interests in NIS third sector work to the appropriate organizations in a specific field or geographic location.

American Association for the Advancement of Slavic Studies

8 Storey Street
Cambridge, MA 02138
Tel: (617) 495-0677
Fax: (617) 495-0680
E-mail: aaass@hcs.harvard.edu
Contact: Carol R. Saivetz, Executive Director; Tracie Vanz, NewsNet Editor

AAASS is the leading American professional association for scholars and others concerned with the region comprised by Eastern Europe and the NIS. Its quarterly journal, *The Slavic Review*, is the major scholarly journal in the field. The AAASS *Newsletter* is an excellent source of information on language study programs and academic exchange and travel opportunities. It sometimes carries information about organizations in the NIS that are looking for staff and volunteers. Likewise, its *Directory of Programs* and *Directory of Members*, each published bi-annually, are useful resources for locating academic centers engaged in projects in the NIS.

American International Health Alliance

1212 New York Avenue NW, Suite 750
Washington, DC 20005
Tel: (202) 789-1136
Fax: (202) 789-1277
E-mail: aiha@igc.apc.org
Contact: F. Curtiss Swezy, NIS Program Director

The American International Health Alliance, an alliance of major hospital associations and hospital-related organizations, describes itself as "the U.S. hospital sector's most coordinated response to health care issues in the Newly Independent States of the former Soviet Union and Central and Eastern Europe." AIHA manages eight hospital partnerships between the U.S. and the CEE region, and 24 such partnerships with health care institutions in eleven nations of the NIS. In addition, with the active sup-port of national health ministries, AIHA has established four Emergency Medical Services training centers in the NIS and anticipates four additional centers within the next year. The AIHA also sponsors a number of related activities, including conferences, workshops, and a clearing-house for information concerning health care in the NIS and CEE.

Much of AIHA's information is available in both print and electronic form. Among the useful resources AIHA has produced is a *Directory of Health-Related Assistance Projects in the NIS*. It pub-lishes a quarterly journal, *CommonHealth*, containing interesting,

17

non-technical articles about the wide variety of activities AIHA is involved with in the NIS and CEE region. Those interested in the AIHA Clearinghouse or in obtaining Russian or English language copies of *CommonHealth* (available free of charge) should send an e-mail message to *jneuber@igc.apc.org*.

AIHA has regional offices in Moscow, Almaty, Kyiv, and Tallinn. The organ-ization operates under a cooperative agree-ment with USAID.

Armenian Assembly of America
122 C Street NW, Suite 350
Washington, DC 20001
Tel: (202) 393-3434
Fax: (202) 638-4904
Contact: Ross Vartian, Executive Director

50 North La Cienega Blvd., Suite 202
Beverly Hills, CA 90211
Tel: (310) 360-0091
Fax: (310) 360-0094
Contact: Gassia Apkarian

The Armenian Assembly of America is a nationwide nonprofit organization which promotes public understanding and awareness of Armenian issues. Since 1988, the Assembly has become increasingly active in Armenia, through its Yerevan office, and it is now focus-ing much of its effort on development projects there.

In 1988 AAA funneled significant resources to earthquake-ravaged Spitak and Leninagan (now Gyumri). The Assembly, according to Board Chair-man Hrair Hovnanian, was the "first Western organization allowed to set up operations in Armenia, and the extreme emergency situation dictated that."

With support from USAID AAA manages 15 microprojects, including

two village water systems, the repair of a school's sanitation system, road re-construction, demolition of condemned buildings, and the renovation of a clinic in Geghashen.

AAA also provides technical assis-tance to the Armenia Social Investment Fund staff , capitalized by a World Bank loan.

AAA supports a nine-person office in Yerevan, including an NGO clearing-house.

Center for Citizen Initiatives
3268 Sacramento Street
San Francisco, CA 94115
Tel: (415) 346-1875
Fax: (415) 346-3731
E-mail: cciedp@igc.apc.org
Contact: Sharon Tennison, President; Dale Needles, Executive Director

CCI has implemented a wide range of citizen-based initiatives in the former Soviet Union since its founding in 1983. A pioneer in "citizen diploma-cy," CCI took thousands of Americans to the USSR during the eighties as "citizen ambassadors."

With the superpower thaw in 1985, CCI began longer-term program work, first in the field of alcoholism addic-tion. As a result, Alcoholics Anony-mous was established in eight Repub-lics. The Soviet Meet Middle America program brought 400 Soviet citizens in groups of four to 265 American cities in 1988 and 1989. CCI's Environ-mental Program began in 1989 and centered on an environmentally sensi-tive land use program for the Lake Bai-kal region. Numerous other exchanges involving psychologists, educators, law enforcement officers, medical profes-sionals, etc., were carried out during the 80's.

In the 90's CCI runs six multi-year programs in Russia:

• The Economic Development Program has four components: (1) Business management internships for Russian business persons in U.S. firms, (2) U.S. business specialists consulting on-site in Russian firms, (3) the creation of "Business Service Centers" in six Russian cities, and (4) a Media project which produces television programs on the market economy. American business consultants volunteer two-weeks at a time, three times a year to provide free consultations to small business owners on a wide range of business and management issues.

• The Productivity Enhancement Program is an internship program for non-English speaking Russians who are key figures in small or medium-sized private companies. Industry specific delegations are brought to the U.S. for one month, during which they study and train in 8-10 U.S. production sites. PEP includes daily documentation of production site experience. A workbook is compiled which becomes a training tool for presentations upon return to the NIS. Graduates become members of a follow-up Fellows Program.

• The Russian Initiative for Self Employment is a microenterprise development training program, primarily for women. RISE runs a "business incubator," a loan program, and offers classes in business development and self-employment.

• The Agricultural Initiative promotes small-scale and sustainable and organic agriculture in Russia. AI has helped Russians establish the Farmers Development service based on U.S. extension services, which is becoming the model for 37 agricultural regions in Russia. It promotes inner-city rooftop gardening and has worked with the All-Russian Agriculture College to develop and distribute agricultural education materials and courses.

• The Environmental Program supports the development of NIS environmental NGOs, especially those which work on nuclear energy (and alternatives to nuclear energy) issues. The program holds conferences, oversees exchanges, and assists citizens to address nuclear issues. CCI organizes one-month internships in the U.S. for leaders of NIS environmental groups led by women. The program also works with water quality issues in the Black Sea region.

• The Non-Profit Management Program identifies and trains charity organization managers through seminars, personal counseling, and training internships in the U.S. NPMP also awards small grants to improve organizational capacity.

CCI is funded by a range of U.S. foundations and private memberships. It receives full support from USAID for EDP and PEP, and partial support for RISE, EP and AI.

CCI has offices in San Francisco and Chicago and six Russian offices: St. Petersburg, Volgograd, Voronezh, Dubna, Ekaterinburg, Rostov-on-Don, Moscow. It has 25 full-time U.S. staff and 60 in Russia. CCI works collaboratively with numbers of U.S. PVOs to support Russian individuals and private sector institutions in the former Soviet Union.

Center for Civil Society International
2929 NE Blakeley Street
Seattle, WA 98105-3120

Tel: (206) 523-4755
Fax: (206) 523-1974
E-mail: ccsi@u.washington.edu
URL:
http://solar.rtd.utk.edu/~ccsi/ccsihome.
html
Contact: Holt Ruffin, Executive Director

CCSI promotes the growth of civil and democratic societies by publishing resources and materials that foster relationships and the sharing of experiences between leaders of private voluntary associations in the U.S. and Eastern Europe and the NIS. It publishes a monthly newsletter, *Civil Society . . . East and West*, which reports on new projects, organizations, resources and announcements with relation to third sector activities in the NIS. It also makes this information available at no charge electronically to users of the World Wide Web and those with e-mail, by offering an electronic mailing list known as *CivilSoc.* (See the section on Electronic Mailing Lists.)

CCSI has published *Internet Resources for the NIS*, and *Civil Society: USA*, which describes in detail the operations of more than 150 diverse American third sector organizations. This resource will be expanded, translated, and published in Poland in 1996. For information about these publications, contact CCSI.

CCSI also maintains a database of some 2,000 American third sector organizations with experience and expertise relevant to the transition challenges in the NIS.

COUNTERPART Foundation, Inc.

910 17th Street NW, #328
Washington, DC 20006

Tel: (202) 296-9676
Fax: (202) 296-9679
E-mail: cpfsp@igc.apc.org
Contact: Stanley W. Hosie, Executive Director

Founded in 1965 as the Foundation for the Peoples of the South Pacific, COUNTERPART's central organizational purpose is "to support the creation and development of strong, sustainable local institutions and nongovernmental networks capable of ad-dressing local and regional needs."

In 1992, in cooperation with USAID, COUNTERPART launched the Volunteer Executive Service Team Initiative. Among the objectives for the program were the design of sector-specific strategies for developing and strengthening indigenous NGO capacity and service delivery and for fostering partnerships between U.S. PVOs and indigenous NGOs.

Since 1992, COUNTERPART has provided training and technical assistance to women entrepreneurs and has provided basic business skill training seminars for over 250 military wives from Moscow to Vladivostok. In partnership with Russian Care, a Moscow-based voluntary organization headed by Irina Kozyrev (wife of former Russian Foreign Minister Andrei Kozyrev), COUNTERPART has developed small enterprise pilot projects which develop marketable skills and income generating opportunities for unemployed military wives.

COUNTERPART Service Centers serve as regional resources for local and international NGOs, and provide training in management and leadership, strategic planning, fiscal management, fundraising and project design. The first CSC was established in Kyiv,

Ukraine in 1993 and the program has expanded since then to include satellite centers in Moldova, Belarus and Kyrgyzstan. These CSCs maintain databases of over 1000 local NGOs interested in linkages and partnerships with foreign private voluntary organizations.

COUNTERPART's Humanitarian Assistance Program coordinates the provision of U.S. Department of Defense excess property for humanitarian purposes to vulnerable groups in the region. COUNTERPART estimates that the program has provided more than $8 million in aid to a broad range of social service providers. CHAP pro-vides material assistance such as medical supplies, clinical furniture, school furniture and supplies, sleeping bags, bedding, clothing, appliances and vehicles. CHAP staff also maintains a stock of emergency relief supplies.

In the Russian Federation, COUNT-ERPART manages the training and information services component of the USAID funded Civic Initiatives Program led by Save the Children Federation. Please see the Save the Children Federation entry for more information on this project.

The COUNTERPART Consortium NGO Support Initiative for Central Asia is intended to foster the development of NGOs in sectors critical to the economic, political and social development of the region by: a) providing training to local NGOs; b) promoting and facilitating information exchange among NGOs locally and internationally; and c) implementing a regional Grant Program. Consortium members Aid to Artisans, Citizen's Network for Foreign Affairs, and Goodwill Industries International provide assistance in such fields as crafts-based microenter-prises, vocational training for special needs populations, and small businesses.

COUNTERPART has offices in Belarus, Georgia, Kazakstan, Kyrgyz Republic, Moldova, Russia, Tajikistan, Turkmenistan, Ukraine and Uzbekistan.

The Eurasia Foundation

1527 New Hampshire Avenue NW
Washington, DC 20036
Tel: (202) 234-7370
Fax: (202) 234-7377
E-mail: eurasia@eurasia.org
Contact: William B. Bader, President

The Eurasia Foundation was established in 1993 as a privately managed, nonprofit grantmaking organization with funding from USAID to support economic and democratic reform in the NIS. In its first 19 months, EF made a total of 375 grants to 205 U.S. organizations working with NIS partners and to 170 NIS organizations. The percentage of EF grants made directly to NIS organizations grew from less than 10% in the first six months to nearly 75% for the last quarter of 1994.

The foundation focuses its grantmaking in three areas:
• Economic Reform, including management training, business and economic education, development of free market institutions, private sector development and policy advice;
• Governmental Reform and the Nonprofit Sector, including public administration reform, public policy advice, law, and assistance to NGOs;
• Media and Communications, including projects in print, broadcast, electronic media and electronic communication.

EF encourages grant seekers to submit proposals at any time. It also manages special grant competitions for NGOs in specific geographic regions and for specific kinds of projects such as sister-city projects, support for local media, and e-mail related projects. Most Eurasia Foundation grants are small. The average grant to a U.S. based organization is $40,000, and for NIS organizations the maximum is usually $25,000.

A sample of Eurasia grants includes:
• A grant to print and distribute a catalogue of Russian-language economics and business texts.
• A short-term management training seminar for more than 50 plant managers, government administrators, and university faculty.
• Establishment of a Center for Business Development in Saratov that provides counseling, information, and communications to the local business community.
• A series of seminars organized by the Ukrainian Association of Local and Regional Authorities to familiarize local officials with their new responsibilities.
• A grant to the Independent Law Research Agency in Minsk to provide ongoing legal consultation to Belarussian NGOs on such issues as legal registration, taxation, and personnel policies.
• Funding for three senior managers of the Russian National Orchestra to intern with the San Francisco Ballet.
• A grant to *Novy Styl* to increase its distribution so that it could become the first local newspaper in Saratov to become adequately funded by advertisements.
• Support for television journalists in Ukraine to study economic reforms in Eastern Europe–which resulted in a series of television programs improving

the level of public debate on Ukraine's fledgling economic reform program.

The Eurasia Foundation has offices in Moscow, Vladivostok, Saratov, Kyiv, Tashkent, Almaty, Yerevan, and Tbilisi.

Institute for Democracy in Eastern Europe

2000 P Street NW, Suite 400
Washington, DC 20036
Tel: (202) 466-7105
Fax: (202) 466-7140
E-mail: idee@dgs.dgsys.com
Contact: Irena Lasota, President and Director of Programs

The institute was established in 1985 to support the growing independent opposition movements in Eastern Europe seeking peaceful democratic change and an end to communism. IDEE provided financial and technical assistance and also published information and analysis in Eastern European media on world affairs, democracy and market economics. Its journal *Uncaptive Minds* established an English-language forum in the West for a broad range of East European opposition voices.

Through its Eastern European Democracy and Publishing Program, IDEE has administered over $3 million in assistance to nearly 2,000 independent publications, civic organizations, human rights groups, and opposition movements in Belarus, Bulgaria, the Czech and Slovak Republics, Estonia, Hungary, Latvia, Lithuania, Mongolia, Poland, Romania, Russia, Serbia and Ukraine.

In 1992, IDEE began its Centers for Pluralism Program. Centers have been established in Bucharest, Bratislava, Simferopol, Sofia, Tallinn, Vilnius,

Warsaw, Split and Belgrade, with additional centers planned for Belarus, Azerbaijan, Ukraine, and the Czech Republic. Each center conducts its own civic, educational, and publishing programs, and supports a network of individuals and organizations dedicated to principles of democracy and pluralism. The coordinating hub of the Centers for Pluralism program is the IDEE office in Warsaw.

IDEE–Warsaw publishes the quarterly *Centers for Pluralism Newsletter*, which is distributed to over 2,000 individuals and groups, and provides basic information on the activities and needs of democratic and independent organizations in the region, helping these organizations to communicate and to cooperate within and across borders. *Uncaptive Minds* has a distribution of over 5,000 in Eastern Europe and the U.S. It is a key resource for democrats in Central and Eastern Europe and the former Soviet Union to learn about other countries' transitions from communism. The journal's readership includes government officials, academics, journalists, newspaper editors, business people, NGO leaders, and private citizens. Its articles are regularly translated and republished in independent newspapers throughout the region and the U.S.

Institute for East-West Christian Studies

Billy Graham Center
Wheaton College
Wheaton, IL   60187-5593
Tel: (708) 752-5917
Fax: (708) 752-5555
E-mail: iewcs@david.wheaton.edu
Contact: Dr. Mark Elliott, Director

This institute was formed in 1986 and used to be called the Institute for the Study of Christianity and Marxism. It publishes a respected quarterly newsletter, the *East-West Church & Ministry Report*, and distributes other books and resources, including *The East-West Christian Organizations Directory*. (Ask for the Institute's Resource Catalog.) Dr. Elliott is a professor of history at Wheaton College and author or editor of numerous books and articles.

InterAction

1717 Massachusetts Avenue NW, Suite 801
Washington, DC 20036
Tel: (202) 667-8227
Fax: (202) 667-8236

InterAction, the American Council for Voluntary International Action, is a coalition of more than 150 U.S. private voluntary organizations that work overseas in development, disaster response and refugee assistance. Many InterAction member agencies have projects in the NIS.

InterAction publishes *Monday Developments*, a bi-weekly newsletter with articles of interest to the international development community. It contains sections on publications and events as well as job listings. It also publishes *Member Profiles*, a directory of InterAction member agencies. In addition to names, addresses, phone numbers and financial data for each agency, it includes information on which agencies are working in each country, what activities they sponsor and which local groups they collaborate with. It is indexed by geography, pro-grams and personnel.

Interlegal USA

c/o The Samuel Rubin Foundation
777 United Nations Plaza, Suite 10D
New York, NY 10017
Tel: (212) 697-8945
Fax: (212) 682-0886
Contact: Ms. Cora Weiss

This is the U.S. representative office of
the Moscow-based organization.

International Center for Foreign Journalists

11690-A Sunrise Valley Drive
Reston, VA 22091
Tel: (703) 620-5745
Fax: (703) 620-6790
E-mail: editor@cfj.org
Contact: Don Lippincott,
Clearinghouse Manager

Founded in 1984, ICFJ has organized
training workshops for nearly 7,000
journalists and media officials from 172
countries. It helps establish sister newspaper exchanges, administer internships
for foreign journalists in the U.S., and
publishes resources for journalists, including an *Environmental Sourcebook,
Interviewing Techniques, Tips on Edit-
ing,* and the *Newsroom Management
Handbook.* In September 1991 it established the Clearinghouse on the Central
and East European Press, which maintains a computerized database of more
than 1,800 media organizations in Eastern Europe and the NIS.

The Clearinghouse can provide lists of
newspapers and broadcast media in the
NIS which would-be volunteer journalists can contact. It has been ICFJ's experience that American journalists who
want to volunteer with an NIS media
outlet should be prepared to commit to a
stay of 4-6 months. Fluency in the language of the country is highly recom-

mended. ICFJ also compiles information
on English-language newspapers in the
region that can utilize the skills of professional journalists, journalism students, and Americans with good writing
skills.

ICFJ administers the Knight International Press Fellowship Program, which
sends American journalists overseas on
long-term media assistance projects.

IREX–International Research & Exchanges Board

1616 H Street NW,
Washington, DC 20006
Tel: (202) 628-8188
Fax: (202) 628-8189
E-mail: irex@info.irex.org
Contact: Keith Burner, Public Informa-
tion Officer

IREX was founded in 1968 by a consortium of U.S. colleges and universities to administer academic and
research exchanges between the United
States and Soviet Union. IREX's activities have expanded both geographically
and topically in the past 27 years. They
now encompass not only scholarly
exchanges, but also professional
development, technical assistance, and
policy programs dealing with the Newly
Independent States, Central and Eastern
Europe, and Mongolia.

IREX grants to American specialists
for long- and short-term study of the region cultivate expertise that will inform
U.S. policy in the future. At the same
time, IREX research and training programs for specialists from the region
serve to reinforce indigenous capabilities
and help the region overcome a legacy of
international isolation. These programs
draw on the resources of American policy and academic communities to provide emerging leaders with opportunities

for developing skills in local governance, journalism, curriculum development, finance and entrepreneurship, parliamentary democracy, and ethnic conflict resolution.

• Scholar Programs form the core of IREX's activities. They include long- and short-term research and study opportunities for advanced scholars and graduate students from the United States, CEE, the NIS and Mongolia.

• The Institutional Partnerships Project is a major initiative linking educational and professional associations in Russia and Ukraine with counterpart institutions in the U.S.

• Professional Training Programs provide policy makers, entrepreneurs, and other specialists from CEE, the Baltics, and the NIS opportunities to hone skills that are immediately applicable in their home countries.

• Policy Programs bring the results of basic research to bear on issues of topical concern. Each year IREX convenes forums and roundtables where scholars and policy makers discuss research findings and thrash out solutions to political, economic, and social problems.

• Library and Archival Programs support collaborative activities in the field of library and information science, provide professional training for individuals, and assist in developing e-mail networks to facilitate professional and scholarly contacts.

• Communications Programs address the relative isolation that is a legacy of the Cold War period by providing the equipment and training necessary to establish computer linkages throughout CEE, the Balkans, and the NIS.

• The IREX International Alumni Network is an initiative to link over 3,000 international alumni of IREX programs, many of whom occupy positions of authority in government, business and academia. The Network will also provide them with professional development opportunities and cultivate their support for IREX's current work in the region.

• Publications include the bi-monthly *News in Brief*, as well as a variety of conference reports, research guides, and directories.

• Sixteen Field Offices throughout CEE and NIS conduct outreach for IREX programs and provide services to U.S. scholars, as well as to candidates, participants, and alumni from the regions they serve.

ISAR: A Clearinghouse on Grassroots Cooperation in Eurasia

1601 Connecticut Avenue NW
Washington, DC 20009
Tel: (202) 387-3034
Fax: (202) 667-3291
E-mail: isar@igc.apc.org
Contact: Eliza Klose, Executive Director

ISAR (formerly the Institute for Soviet American Relations) was founded in 1983 as part of the "citizen diplomacy" move-ment that sought to reduce the threat of war by promoting personal contacts between the people of the Soviet Union and the U.S. It was an important clearing-house organization for that movement and continues to be one for a large number of grassroots collaborations between the U.S. and NIS today.

In the current era, ISAR main focus is on "gathering and distributing information and offering technical assistance and financial support to nongovernmental environmentalists in the former Soviet Union." Other areas of emphasis are small business development, civil society, and the growth of women's organizations in the NIS.

ISAR organizes conferences in the region, manages small grants program for projects in the NIS, and publishes *Surviving Together: A Quarterly on Grassroots Cooperation in Eurasia*, which has regular sections on "sustainable economics," agriculture, the environment, women and civil society. A Russian-language digest of *Surviving Together* is also published in Moscow and is available free of charge to individuals and NGOs throughout the former Soviet Union. To receive the Russian edition of *Surviving Together*, see ISAR-Moscow in section *Russia: West of the Urals*.

ISAR also publishes or distributes a variety of other useful resources, such as a *List of NGOs Involved in Environmental Activities*. ISAR's Kyiv office maintains a database of over 400 environmental NGOs in Belarus, Moldova and Ukraine and intends to publish the second edition of its *NGO and Ecology* directory in early 1996.

ISAR has regional offices in Tbilisi, Almaty, Moscow, Nizhny Novgorod, Vladivostok, and Kyiv.

Network of East-West Women

1601 Connecticut Avenue NW
Washington, DC 20009
Tel: (202) 332-4840, 265-3585
Fax: (202) 322-4865, 265-3508
E-mail: newwdc@igc.apc.org
              neww@igc.apc.org
Contact: Shana Penn

The Network of East-West Women (NEEW) is a communication network that links over 700 women's advocates in more than 20 countries in the former Soviet Union (FSU) and Central and Eastern Europe (CEE). NEWW members are writers, students, health care workers, journalists, lawyers, parliamentarians, professors, artists, union organizers and feminist activists. Members of the Board of Advisers and International Steering Committee are "leaders in the effort to include women in the building of democracy."

NEWW's primary goal is to support the establishment of independent women's movements in the region. It seeks to increase the capacity of women and women's NGOs to effectively advocate on policy regarding women's lives. It coordinates projects, ad hoc committees, training workshops, consultations, conferences, and information exchanges that reflect the programmatic areas its members have identified. These areas include: law and policy, employment, reproductive rights, health and environment, violence against women, communication, gender scholarship and the ongoing conflict in the former Yugoslavia.

In 1995 NEWW and the Moscow Center for Gender Studies received a grant to increase the capacity of local NGOs/PVOs to participate in the formation and enforcement of laws while monitoring the legal status of women in the provinces and regions of Russia, Ukraine and Kyrgyzstan.

The organization also maintains NEWW On-Line, an electronic communications network that links women's NGOs in the FSU, CEE, Western Europe and the U.S. The network allows for information exchange, development of technical and institution building skills, and coordination of research and activist projects.

Open Society Institute– New York

888 Seventh Avenue, 31st Floor
New York, NY 10106
Tel: (212) 757-2323
Fax: (212) 974-0367
E-mail: osnews@sorosny.org
URL: http://www.soros.org
Contact: George Soros, Chairman;
Aryeh Neier, President

The Soros Foundations, now known as the Open Society Institutes, began operating in the NIS in 1987 with the establishment of the Cultural Initiative Foundation in Moscow. The institutes are sponsored by George Soros who was born in Hungary in 1930 and emigrated first to England in 1947 and later to the U.S. in 1956, where he has made his fortune as an international investment manager.

Open Society Institutes operate in 26 countries across Central and Eastern Europe, the NIS, as well as South Africa and Haiti. Each national institute or foundation operates independently with its own staff and board. However, all are "committed to certain common goals, such as the rule of law, a democratically elected government, a vigorous, diverse civil society, respect for minorities, and a free market economy."

Under their mandate to "foster the development of open societies," the national foundations have established programs and supported projects by other organizations in a wide variety of fields. OSIs in the NIS have support numerous projects in the fields of science and higher education, media, the arts, and fostering civil society.

One of the major projects supported in each NIS country by its respective national foundation has been the Trans-

formation of the Humanities Program. This awards grants for the writing and printing of new textbooks and for the development of new pedagogical methods. (George Soros pledged $10 million for education reform in Russia in 1993.) In 1994 the Ukrainian OSI, called the International Renaissance Foundation, awarded grants to more than 500 authors writing new textbooks. The IRF also supported two academic institutes–the Kyiv-Mohyla Academy and the International Management Institute–plus a business education program for high schools run by Junior Achievement, and projects in management education, health education for teenagers, and preschool development.

In the field of the media, OSI national foundations have awarded grants to support independent radio and television broadcast stations. In Russia OSI established a Production Competition Fund to support the production of television programs and public service announcements which promote public understanding of democratic values. Other OSI projects have included supporting an Institute of Public Administration and Local Government and a project in Ukraine that offers training and job placement services for former members of the armed forces.

The Soros network of foundations also includes region-wide specialty foundations such as the International Science Foundation (see U.S.-Based Organizations). In 1992 Mr. Soros pledged $100 million in direct research grants to keep scientists in the former Soviet Union working and thus avoid a "brain drain." At the time Mr. Soros's grant was equal to about 20% of the entire Russian budget for science. The

ISF has also played a major role in extending the infrastructure for the Internet in the NIS.

The Open Society Institute in New York acts as a coordinating and support organization for the OSI foundations in the region. While the New York office can provide some information about what national foundations are doing, it is best to contact them directly. Grant inquiries should also be made directly to the national foundation offices, a listing of which can be found at the Soros World Wide Web site on the Internet. The OSI office in New York publishes *Open Society News*, a quarterly newsletter which reports on the work of the various Soros-sponsored foundations and projects.

Peter Deyneka
Russian Ministries

P. O. Box 496
Wheaton, IL
Tel: (708) 462-1739
Fax: (708) 690-2976
E-mail: rmusa@mcimail.com
              rmmoscow@mcimail.com
Contact: Peter Deyneka, Jr., President

Deyneka, son of a Russian immigrant, served for 17 years as head of Slavic Gospel Association, before founding this organization in 1992. It has a staff of 40, evenly divided between Russians and Americans, and is active in many areas of work: Christian education, training of ministers, media, social service, "church planting," etc. It assists or works with a large number of both Western and indigenous Christian organizations active in the NIS, most of which would call themselves non-denominational.

Save the Children Federation

54 Wilton Road
PO Box 950
Westport, CT 06881
Tel: (203) 221-4000
Fax: (203) 221-4210
Contact: Nora Bazzy, Regional Director of NIS; Shannon Moncrief, Desk Officer for Russia

Save the Children heads a consortium of organizations conducting a five-year, $30 million USAID program for assistance and development of the Russian nonprofit sector. The program, the Russian Civic Initiatives for Democratic & Economic Reform Program (CIP), was announced in September 1994 as an effort to support "the transition to democracy and the emergence of a new sector of civil society in the Russian Federation."

Save the Children manages and provides overall leadership and direction in establishing the program and in implementing CIP activities. It is responsible for coordinating a network of technical resources, and awarding grant funds to Russian nonprofits and U.S. organizations working in the area.

The Center for Democracy is responsible for programs that encourage the development of a better legislative and regulatory environment for NGOs, both at the federation and regional levels.

COUNTERPART Foundation offers training programs directly to Russian NGOs and also works to enhance indigenous NGO training capacities. It is responsible for operating a clearinghouse of information about Russian NGOs and will seek to catalyze "creative partnerships" between and among U.S.-based and Russian NGOs.

The Education Development Center is working with Russian NGOs to help them correct some of the unfavorable perceptions of NGOs in Russia and to "market" themselves more effectively. EDC's focus will be on NGOs in five sectors: education, health, public advocacy, social services, and civic/trade/professional organizations.

The final member of the CIP consortium, the Institute for Policy Studies at Johns Hopkins University, is running a "train the trainers" project and doing research and evaluation for the program.

These organizations, led by Save the Children, comprise the project's Moscow Coordinating Office (MOSCOR). Also at MOSCOR headquarters is an NGO clearinghouse, library and conference facility.

There are also two regional components of the CIP. The Citizens Network for Foreign Affairs is responsible for the Black Sea region, with a center in Krasnodar and satellites in Stavropol and Rostov. Its goal is to bring 150 NGOs to "self-sustaining status" by the end of the project, but it will focus its assistance primarily on 25 strategic ones. The Fund for Democracy and Development, working with a local group, ECHO, is responsible for the regional program in Siberia, with a center in Novosibirsk. It anticipates that its work will eventually reach 200 NGOs in that region.

See also the profile for the Civic Initiatives Program (Moscow Coordinating Center) in the section, *Russia: West of the Urals.*

Sister Cities International

120 South Payne Street
Alexandria, VA 22314
Tel: (703) 836-3535
Fax: (703) 836-4815
E-mail: sgorev@sister-cities.org

Contact: Alexander Gorev, NIS Program Officer

SCI is the coordinating body for more than 1,040 U.S. communities that are paired with over 1,800 partner cities in 113 nations around the world. There are more than 150 U.S.-NIS sister city relationships. SCI helps organize a biennial U.S.-NIS sister city conference and supports efforts by unpartnered cities to create new sister city relationships.

Union of Councils for Soviet Jews

1819 H Street NW, Suite 230
Washington, DC 20006
Tel: (202) 775-9770, ext. 18
Fax: (202) 775-9776
E-mail: 4201773@mcimail.com
Contact: Pamela Cohen, National President; Micah Naftalin, National Director

The Union of Councils, as it is more commonly known, continues to pursue its founding mission: to provide for the freedom, security and welfare of the Jews of the former Soviet Union. UCSJ, with 100,000 members and local councils in 30 American cities, is the oldest and largest independent , grassroots Soviet Jewry and human rights organization in the world.

Two million Jews still live in the 15 successor nations of the Soviet Union and, according to UCSJ, "their survival is no less threatened today than in 1970, when [the] organization was founded."

UCSJ's program for 1996 is designed to respond to the following "critical dangers" facing Jews in the NIS today:

- economic deprivation, hunger and illness;
- growing antisemitism, fascism, inter-ethnic tension and xenophobia;
- religious and spiritual deprivation, lack of Jewish knowledge and education;
- lack of freedom of movement, emigration refusals and separated families.

The major programs of UCSJ respond to each of these problems.

- Human Rights Bureaus. UCSJ sponsors bureaus in Moscow, St. Petersburg, Almaty and Bishkek. Additional ones are planned for Lviv, Ukraine, and Tbilisi, Georgia. These bureaus focus primarily on Jewish emigration, general human rights and rule of law, monitoring and confronting antisemitism, xenophobia and other anti-democratic values. The Central Asian bureaus are also especially active in mentoring other local NGOs.
- *Yad l'Yad* Jewish Partnership Program. *Yad l'Yad* (Hand to Hand) is a program that promotes the twinning of congregations, organizations and communities in North America with emerging Jewish communities and organizations in the NIS. More than 60 such partnerships, involving hundreds of organizational leaders, have been created so far.
- Anti-Fascist Campaign. UCSJ's Moscow office has forged an Anti-Fascist Coalition to monitor and confront racism and extremism in Russian society.
- Humanitarian Aid. During 1995 $500,000 of food and other assistance was delivered to poor Jews of Ukraine and Georgia. Additionally a medical aid program, coordinated out of UCSJ's Chicago office working through Yad l'Yad partnerships, delivered hundreds

of thousands of dollars of medicine through doctors and clinics within the NIS treating needy Jews.
- Prisoners' Commission and Electronic Emergency Response Network. UCSJ continues to investigate allegations of human rights violations in the NIS, particularly those involving charges of antisemitism.
- Emigration/Immigration Advocacy. UCSJ advocates for Jews denied the right to emigrate from the NIS and lobbies for liberal and humane policies by the U.S. toward Jewish applicants from the NIS for immigration.

UCSJ's Director of International Bureaus and Activities, Dr. Leonid Stonov, works out of the organization's Chicago office:

555 Vine Avenue, Suite 107
Highland Park, IL 60035
Tel: (708) 433-4325
Fax: (708) 433-5530
E-mail: 4201773@mcimail.com

United Way International
701 North Fairfax Street
Alexandria, VA 22314-2045
Tel: (703) 519-0092
Fax: (703) 519-0097
E-mail: uwi@igc.apc.org

UWI seeks to develop civil societies worldwide by promoting voluntary initiatives and development of the nonprofit sector. It aims to establish "community-wide, self-sufficient and self-sustaining organizations to meet human needs." Established in 1974, UWI has more than 275 affiliates in 31 countries on six continents.

UWI activities in the NIS have included: establishment of a Volunteer Center in Moscow that trains Russian and foreign volunteers and matches them with charitable organizations in Russia; training for nonprofit managers to more effectively operate their organizations; coordination of special events, such as "Make A Difference Days" in which many volunteers work with charitable organizations in Moscow providing services to children. UWI has also consulted with the Russian Parliament on the drafting of laws concerning charitable organizations which would include tax exempt status for them and tax deductibility of contributions to them.

In Belarus and Ukraine, UWI conducted research on the status of charitable activity and published a directory of charitable organizations in these countries. In 1994, UWI opened the United Way of Belarus in Minsk. It intends to open another United Way office in Naryan-Mar, Russia.

UWI has published a *Directory of Russian Charitable Organizations* which includes a full description of the 75 most active charities in Russia and contact information on the approximately 700 registered charities in Moscow and St. Petersburg at the time.

This directory has been computerized in order to make contact and program information readily available to Russian and international users.

All inquiries about UWI programs in the NIS should be directed to executive director Nancy Galloway in Moscow.

U.S.-Ukraine Foundation

1511 K Street NW, Suite 1100
Washington, DC 20005
Tel: (202) 347-4264
Fax: (202) 347-4267
E-mail: ukraine@access.digex.net
Contact: Nadia McConnell,
President.

The U.S.-Ukraine Foundation was founded in 1991 to strengthen ties between the U.S. and Ukraine and to promote the development of democratic institutions and a market economy in Ukraine. It develops its programs in consultation with key democratic leaders of the Ukrainian government and private organizations. The Foundation has organized a number of study trips by Ukrainian leaders to the U.S. and has provided logistical support for numerous programs in Ukraine by U.S. nongovernmental organizations, government agencies, the media, and private firms.

In 1992 the Foundation established a U.S.-Ukraine Center in Kyiv with a permanent staff of 12. The Center houses the Pylyp Orlyk Institute for Democracy, named after Hetman Pylyp Orlyk who drafted Ukraine's first democratic constitution in 1710. The Institute, whose Executive Policy Committee is composed of members of the Ukrainian legislature, government, and academic community, prepares analyses of legislation and option papers for Ukrainian policy-makers, translates and publishes Western books, and provides training and internship opportunities for Ukrainian legislative staff. In 1995 it became a subcontractor to Indiana University's three-year Parliamentary Development Project.

The Institute's Democracy Hotline maintains an e-mail link between Kyiv and Washington. It uses it to give Ukrainian government officials the most up-to-date reports on how the U.S. media is covering Ukraine. A print publication, *The West: Window on Ukraine*, is distributed to 1,500 individuals in Ukraine and provides translations of important American Congressional hearings, U.S. government policy statements, etc., that relate to Ukraine. (In Washington, DC, the U.S.-Ukraine Foundation distributes *Update from Ukraine* to important American policy-makers on a regular basis.) The Center also houses the U.S.-Ukraine Biblioteka Resource Center which is a reference library for members of Parliament. The Biblioteka holds over 1,500 volumes on public policy issues.

The Pylyp Orlyk Institute has also translated, published and distributed 10,000 copies of Bernard Siegan's *Drafting a Constitution for a Nation or Republic Emerging Into Freedom.* It has also translated Henry Hazlitt's *Economics in One Lesson* and Charles Epping's *Guide to the World Economy.*

The Foundation's Talent Bank is a database of Americans who would like to volunteer their services in Ukraine. Candidates are matched with organizations in Ukraine that submit requests for volunteers to the Foundation's Kyiv office. To become registered in the Talent Bank, send a resume and a cover letter. Include information on language ability and length of time available for service. Ukrainian language skills help but are not essential. Volunteers are responsible for travel and living expenses.

VOICE International

2904 N. Greencastle Street
Arlington, VA 22207
Tel: (703) 241-0148
Fax: (703) 533-9412
E-mail: voiceintl@igc.apc.org
Contact: Nancy Pettis

VOICE International is an information clearinghouse and technical assistance network which operates a program of research, information dissemination,

and referrals for NGOs in Central and Eastern Europe and the NIS. Over the past three years, VOICE has supplied over 1,400 pieces of material to request-ing organizations in nine countries in the region, and has provided an addi-tional number of referrals to informa-tion and technical assistance sources in the U.S. and other Western countries.

Materials relating to policy, practice, programs and institution-building are provided to Central and East European and NIS information centers and NGOs for free and to U.S. organizations for a fee. Examples of the materials that VOICE has provided to requesting or-ganizations are listed below by cate-gory.

- Exemplary law on adoptions (U.S.)
- Gender equity law (Sweden)
- Law on the education of handicapped children (U.S.)
- Family and medical leave law from around the world
- Voter education projects
- How to operate a homeless shelter
- Programs for juvenile offenders
- Description of a national phone service for children in need
- Articles on fundraising, proposal writing, the operation of Boards of Directors, strategic planning and fi-nancial management

VOICE also distributes selected books. One of them is *The Legal Status of Women in the New Independent States of the Former Soviet Union* (May 1994), by Janet Hunt-McCool and Lisa Granik.

World Learning Inc.

1015 Fifteenth Street NW, Suite 911
Washington, DC 20005
Tel: (202) 408-5420

Fax: (202) 898-1920
E-mail: 0005663077@mcimail.com
Contact: Marguerite Mininni,
Program/Information Officer

World Learning Inc. was founded in 1932 as The U.S. Experiment in International Living, dedicated to strengthening inter-national understanding and peace by giving young people the opportunity to learn the culture and language of another country by living as a member of one of its families. It is one of the oldest private, nonprofit, international educational ex-change services in the world, and the oldest of its kind in the U.S.

Today World Learning employs over 1,200 people and offers a broad range of programs, including a School for Inter-national Training. In May of 1992, WL was selected to administer a new funding initiative sponsored by USAID in support of U.S. private voluntary organizations (PVOs) working in the NIS. The "core component" of this project was to solicit and review proposals leading to the award of grants to implement "humanitarian and development activities in the NIS" through "a network of indigenous organizations able to sustain these activities." The ultimate aim was to "encourage the growth of voluntarism" in the ex-com-munist societies of the NIS.

Among World Learning's first group of PVO/NIS subgrantees were Access Exchange International, the Aga Khan Foundation U.S.A., Aid to Artisans, American Red Cross, Goodwill Industries International, International Orthodox Christian Charities, ISAR, Planned Parenthood of Northern New England, the Salvation Army World Service Office, United Ukrainian American Relief Committee, Wheeled Mobility Center, World Institute on Disability, and the YMCA of the U.S.A.

World Learning has held conferences, workshops and PVO training sessions in various parts of the NIS and has gathered and distributed information about its third sector. It does this through a monthly newsletter published out of its Moscow office, titled *Infohelp*, and a newsletter published in Washington, DC, titled *Initiatives in the New Independent States*.

Initiatives tends to focus each issue on a specific theme–e.g. women's issues, NGO law, public health, nonprofit training programs–and often publishes useful lists of names and addresses of important NIS third sector organizations.

World Learning has assembled a *Training Book* in Russian for use by its subgrantees, with sections on public education through the media, advocacy work, NGO-business sector interaction, NGO-government sector interaction, and Board development. It also intends to publish a compendium of all the program resources it has featured in past issues of *Initiatives*. The Moscow office also has developed a database of several hundred NIS third sector organizations. As a rule, WL makes all the resources it produces publicly accessible at no cost.

Special Focus Organizations

Academy for Educational Development
NIS Exchanges & Training Project
1875 Connecticut Avenue, Suite 900
Washington, DC 20009-1202
Tel: (202) 884-8129
Fax: (202) 884-8419
E-mail: rkaplan@aed.aed.org
Contact: Ron Kaplan

The NIS Exchanges and Training Project (NET) is a USAID-funded short-term technical assistance project managed by the AED. The goal of NET is to provide NIS leaders and professionals with the practical knowledge and technical skills needed to create policies, programs and institutions which will support the transition to democratic governance and free market economies. Since 1993, AED has brought more than 6,000 mid- and senior-level professionals from the NIS to the United States for three to six-week training sessions in such fields as: agriculture, business development, democratic initiatives, economic restructuring, energy, health, housing, and PVO/NGO development and management.

The NET project includes in-country follow-up training. In Central Asia AED has established NET Alumni Centers which include resource libraries and offer e-mail and Internet access for NET alumni. There are centers in: Ashkabad, Turkmenistan; Bishkek, Kyrgyzstan; Dushanbe, Tajikistan; and Tashkent, Uzbekistan.

Access Exchange International
112 San Pablo Avenue
San Francisco, CA 94127
Tel: (415) 661-6355
Fax: (415) 661-1543
Contact: Tom Rickert, Executive Director

Access Exchange International promotes accessible transportation for the disabled. The organization was founded in 1990 by Tom Rickert, who played a key role in developing accessible transit in San Francisco in the 1980s. Working with the engineering departments at San Francisco and Oregon state universities, AEI developed a low-cost platform enabling wheelchair users to board buses and trams.

AEI began its activities in the then-USSR in 1990 and in 1993 USAID awarded it a two-year grant to assist the Moscow Charity House develop a paratransit program to provide thousands of door-to-door trips each year for disabled people. In late 1995 AEI and MCH expected that the project would provide 100,000 paratransit trips during the course of 1995.

AEI's strategy is to develop both paratransit and accessible fixed-route services in Moscow. To pursue this goal, they are working with Moscow's 10,000 vehicle transportation system, Mosgortrans, to develop a prototype project demonstrating access for wheelchair users to buses at key stops. AEI and its Moscow consultant, Valeria Sviatkina, have also established a relationship with the disabled community and transit officials in St. Petersburg.

An important element of AEI's long-term strategy is to bring leaders of disability organizations and transit agencies from the NIS into the international network of professionals who work on transportation access issues. It has conducted workshops on accessible transportation and NGO management in Russia and arranged training programs in social service public administration for Russian participants in the U.S.

AEI maintains a roster of transportation professionals who are available to donate their services to international projects. Any potential volunteers are encouraged to contact them.

AEI has produced a variety of publications, including:

- *Access for Disabled Persons to Public Transit: Some Practical Steps.* AEI's pamphlet for social service and transit agencies; available in Russian, Spanish and English.
- *Accessible Transportation Issues in Moscow and St. Petersburg.* A report of an AEI fact-finding trip to Russia in February 1994.
- *Accessible Transportation Around the World.* AEI's semi-annual newsletter.

ACTR/ACCELS

1776 Massachusetts Avenue NW
Suite 300
Washington, DC 20036
Tel: (202) 833-7522
Fax: (202) 833-7523

The American Council of Teachers of Russian/American Council for Collaboration in Education and Language Study is a professional association of university and secondary school instructors of Russian. It was established in 1974 "to advance research, training, and materials development and to strengthen communication within the profession."

ACTR/ACCELS coordinates exchanges of high school, undergraduate, and graduate students as well as language instructors between the U.S. and NIS. It also organizes conferences and delegations of school and university administrators and education specialists to encourage educational cooperation between the U.S. and the NIS.

ACTR/ACCELS assisted in the development and implementation of several U.S.-Soviet and U.S.-NIS governmental exchange initiatives in the past several years, including the High School Academic Partnerships exchange, the Presidential Expanded Undergraduate Exchange, the Muskie Fellowship Program, the Freedom Support Act and the Regional Scholars Exchange. ACTR/ACCELS also provides academic advising and testing services in the NIS to place students from the NIS in U.S. universities.

Since 1992, ACTR/ACCELS has worked with the Soros Foundations and the Ministries of Education of Belarus, Estonia, Kyrgyzstan, Lithuania, Russia and Ukraine in the development of educational reform initiatives in the social sciences and humanities. ACTR/AC-CELS maintains offices and educational advisory centers throughout the NIS.

Advocates International

7002-C Little River Turnpike
Annandale, VA 22003
Tel: (703) 658-0070
Fax: (703) 658-0077
E-mail: sam.ericsson@gen.org
Contact: Samuel Ericsson, Executive Director

AI places experienced lawyers and legal professionals in government offices (usually at the national level) to act as advisors and consultants for various legal projects. It focuses on legal issues which in the U.S. would be consi-dered First Amendment rights–freedom of religion, freedom of association, freedom of expression. Many of the legal experts placed in the NIS have been involved in the drafting of new legislation relating to these issues.

AI uses volunteers in the legal field for its work in the NIS. Lawyers, judges, and other legal professionals who have a considerable amount of experience are preferred, since volunteers will very often be working hand-in-hand with top governmental officials in the process of drafting laws. While Advocates International works mainly with those whose specialties are in the fields of civil rights and related legal theory, professionals with other interests are welcome as well. Dura-tion of the projects varies depending on individual project demands, but a one-month commitment is usually the minimum.

Aga Khan Foundation USA

1901 L Street NW, Suite 700
Washington. DC 20036
Tel: (202) 293-2537
Fax: (202) 785-1752
E-mail:
     71075.1561@compuserve.com
Contact: Igbal Noor Ali, Chief Executive Officer; Patricia Scheid, Program Officer

In 1994 AKF received a grant from USAID to work with the Pamir Relief and Development Program in Khorog, Tajikistan to organize rural development projects. In the course of the project AKF worked with and provided technical assistance to a variety of NGOs in the region.

Agricultural Cooperative Development International

50 F Street NW, Suite 1100
Washington, DC 20001
Tel: (202) 638-4661
Fax: (202) 626-8726
E-mail: acdi-hq@mcimail.com

Contact: Michael J. Moran, Executive Director, New Independent States Programs; James Phippard, Vice President

Founded in 1963, ACDI is a private, nonprofit organization that provides educational and management assistance and technical development expertise to farmers worldwide. Its membership in-cludes 50 regional agricultural supply, marketing and manufacturing co-operatives, national farmer associations, and farm credit banks. Its five program divisions are: Agribusiness and Trade Development; Credit Systems; Food for Development; Natural Resource Man-agement; Training and Exchange.

ACDI is affiliated with the National Council of Farmer Cooperatives and the Farm Credit Council.

Under the USAID-funded Farmer-to-Farmer program, ACDI had fielded more than 150 volunteers throughout the NIS by late 1995. A number of volunteers worked with agricultural credit banks in Central Asia, helping them to find ways to extend agricultural credit terms for longer periods of time. Among other things, volunteers have helped farmers develop better record-keeping systems that in turn make it easier for them to obtain credit. ACDI volunteers have also contributed to the development of legislation in Russia on cooperatives and on land title registration.

With support from USAID, ACDI is also one of several organizations administering a "reverse Farmer-to-Farmer" pilot project: bringing NIS nationals to the U.S. to study in more depth what they have learned through the Farmer-to-Farmer project. ACDI has organized programs in the U.S. for NIS visitors in the fields of rural credit and agricultural cooperative management.

ACDI's average volunteer assignment is one month. ACDI will cover travel and living expenses. Language skills may be required, depending on the assignment. ACDI has offices in Moscow and Almaty.

Al-Anon/Alateen Family Groups

E-mail: odat@ccnet.com
URL: http://solar.rtd.utk.edu/~Al-Anon/
Contact: Don R.

This is a recovery program for the families and friends of alcoholics. It is self-supporting, with no dues or fees. Currently there are approximately 32,000 Al-Anon Family Groups worldwide, including 60 in Russia.

Alliance of American and Russian Women

PO Box 328
Washington Depot, CT 06794
Tel: (203) 868-9089
Fax: (203) 868-9768
E-mail: sashaaarw@aol.com
Contact: Ms. Alexandra Chalif, President; Yulia Yamova, Resource Director

The Alliance of American and Russian Women (AARW) was established in 1991 as a nonprofit membership organization whose objective is to "encourage, equip and support Russian women to succeed and flourish in a market economy." It publishes a newsletter, *Russian Exchange*.

Current projects include the development of a "small business incubator," primarily for women-led businesses in the city of Volkhov; the Druzhba Awards, which publicly recognize Russian and American women whose leadership has advanced the position of women generally, and businesswomen particularly; Round-table Conferences that bring American and Russian businesswomen together in Russia; and mentoring relationships, via e-mail, whereby Russian nonprofits can learn how to strengthen their organizations, both from Americans living and working in Russia and through e-mail connections between the two countries. These projects extend from Moscow, St. Petersburg and Volkhov to cities and towns as far east as Krasnoyarsk.

Americans wishing to participate in an e-mail mentor program, or join a Roundtable delegation, may call Yulia Yamova at AARW for referrals.

Alliance of Universities for Democracy

East European Center
Glocker Bldg., Suite 9
1000 Volunteer Blvd.
Knoxville, TN 37996-4170
Tel: (423) 974-6110
Fax: (423) 974-3100
E-mail: dknief@utkvx.utk.edu
dhake@utkvx.utk.edu
Contact: Dr. David A. Hake
Director, East European Center, Univesity of Tennessee

AUD is a consortium of universities in Eastern and Western Europe, the NIS, and U.S. that was formed in 1990 to "enhance the role of education in promoting democratic institutions, economic development including technology transfer, decentralized decision making, human health, sustainable habitation of the earth, and common moral and social values." AUD's primary program is a four-day annual conference held in Europe beginning the first Sunday of November. (The 1996 conference is scheduled to be held in Prague.) At the conference members share information about projects and discuss ways in which similar issues are dealt with at member institutions. Papers presented at the Annual Conference are collected and published in AUD's journal *Perspectives in Higher Education Reform.* Papers presented at the 1995 conference included: "How Urban Universities Interact with Regional Businesses;" "A Two-University Cooperative Agreement;" and "Problems of Science Research in Central and Eastern European Universities in the Transition Period."

American Bar Association
Central and East European Law Initiative (CEELI)
1800 M Street NW, Suite 200 South
Washington, DC 20036
Tel: (202) 331-4070
Fax: (202) 862-8533
Contact: Mark S. Ellis, CEELI
Executive Director

CEELI is a public service project of the ABA to support the process of legal reform in Eastern Europe and the former USSR. Of special interest is the degree to which CEELI utilizes the pro-bono ser-vices of the ABA's more than 350,000 members. CEELI offers four major pro-jects in which lawyers and judges have volunteered their services.
• Liaison Placements. Liaisons are American attorneys who work independently with both government offices and nongovernmental organ-izations in host countries for 6-12 months in order to prioritize and coordinate CEELI's activities in the region. Liaisons also seek to facilitate communication between government and civic organiz-ations involved in the legal reform process. To date, CEELI has placed over 90 liaisons in the region.
• Workshops and Training Seminars. At the request of NIS and Eastern

European countries, CEELI organizes in-country seminars and training sessions. Seminars, usually one week long, are run by 4-6 American lawyers and judges. Work-shops provide a forum where volunteers can interact with legal professionals and parliamentary committees to discuss the drafting of new legislation. Workshop topics have included: "The International Sale of Goods;" "Criminal Law;" "Constitutional Drafting;" and "Judicial Re-structuring."
• Legal Advisors. Advisors are assigned to government ministries, parliamentary committees and NGOs to work on specific projects, including assisting with legal administration, drafting legislation and judicial reform. Projects vary in duration. CEELI has placed over 115 legal specialists in host countries to date.
• Legal Assessments. Lawyers and legal specialists in the U.S. can participate in CEELI's program from home through the draft law review program. Draft legis-lation from abroad is circulated within the U.S. for comments. 220 such assessments have been made on topics ranging from antitrust laws to land use codes.

Participants in these programs have a variety of legal specialties. A minimum of five years experience in legal practice is re-quired. All expenses for these pro-grams are covered.

CEELI has a variety of other projects in Eastern Europe and the NIS. CEELI's Sister School Program has helped to es-tablish cooperative relations between 140 U.S. and 47 Eastern European law schools, and is currently being expanded to include schools in five NIS countries. The program includes the exchange of educational ideas as well as professors and law school administrators. In 1995

CEELI received a grant through USAID to work with attorneys in Ukraine who wish to establish a Ukrainian Bar Association. CEELI will conduct seminars throughout the country to explain the functions of a bar association and will organize internships for Ukrainian lawyers abroad.

America's Development Foundation

101 North Union Street, Suite 200
Alexandria VA 22314
Tel: (703) 836-2717
Fax: (703) 836-3379
Contact: Michael Miller, Director

ADF was established in 1980 and is "dedicated to assisting the international development of democracy and respect for human rights." It was worked in the fields of civic education, human rights, and NGO development in the NIS.

American Institute of Business and Economics

216 Bliss Lane
Great Falls, VA 22066
Tel: (703) 759-2507
Fax: (703) 759-3389
E-mail: aibec@knight-hub.com
URL: http://www.knight-hub.com/aibec
Contact: Edwin G. Dolan, President

AIBEc operates a two-year, evening business school in Moscow that specifically targets undergraduate students with scientific and technical backgrounds who want to make a career switch into business. The curriculum is taught in English by American faculty. AIBEc generally has a need for experienced teachers of English during its fall semester, September to December. In addition, in both fall and spring, AIBEc sometimes has a need for teachers of business and economics

subjects: marketing, accounting, finance, business law, etc. AIBEc will provide international airfare, a housing allowance, and a modest stipend.

American Russian Center

Business Education Bldg. 203
3211 Providence Drive
Anchorage, AK 99508-8356
Tel: (907) 786-4300
Fax: (907) 786-4319
E-mail: ayarc@acad2.alaska.edu
Contact: Charles B. Neff, Director

The American Russian Center at the University of Alaska works in the Russian Far East (RFE) to promote small business development through training and technical assistance; to enhance Russian-American business connections; to facilitate educational and cultural exchanges between Alaska and the RFE; and to build institutional relationships between universities in Alaska and educational institutions in the RFE.

ARC was established in May 1993 with a grant from USAID. That fall, ARC opened small business development branches in Yakutsk and Yuzhno-Sakhalinsk, and a year later opened additional centers in Khabarovsk and Magadan. These branches offer basic courses in small business management and operations taught by visiting experts and permanent staff. Individuals are chosen from the graduates of these courses for further study in Alaska and internships with Alaska businesses. In addition, ARC offers technical assistance seminars for a variety of professional groups as well as for women interested in establishing small businesses. ARC maintains a business information library in the Anchorage office and consults with American businesses interested in joint ventures with

Russian companies or investing in the RFE.

Between 1994 and 1996, with funding from USIA, ARC has conducted 32 separate projects involving exchanges between Alaskan cultural and educational groups and their counterparts in the RFE. These exchanges involved Natives, women, students, professors, journalists, local government officials and representatives of specialized groups from virtually all geographic areas of Alaska and the RFE.

ARC is currently sponsoring a program to develop more direct relationships between the campuses of the University of Alaska around the state and several RFE educational institutions. These projects involve exchanging professors and developing joint curricula in the areas of business, education and journalism, and will operate over a two-year period commencing in the spring of 1995.

ARC occasionally hires business trainers, particularly those with small business experience, for periods of six weeks to three months. They also welcome Russian-speaking individuals, preferably with Northern experience, who can provide administrative leadership in one of the four branch centers in the RFE for a minimum of one year. Volunteers with business skills are welcome, and ARC can provide travel expenses, some local support and, in a few cases, housing.

American-Ukrainian Advisory Committee

c/o Center for Strategic and International Studies
1800 K Street, NW Suite 400
Washington, DC 20006
Tel: (202) 887-0200

Contact: Dr. Zbigniew Brzezinski, Chairman

The committee unites a prestigious group of diplomats, national leaders and experts to offer periodic policy recommendations–the latest communique was based on a meeting held in New York City in November 1995–and consult informally with the Council of Advisors to the Presidium of the Parliament of Ukraine. Committee members have included Henry Kissinger; George Soros; former Defense Secretary Frank Carlucci; Westinghouse CEO Michael Jordan; Geoffrey Howe, former minister of foreign affairs in the UK; Shirley Williams, former leader of the Social Democratic Party of Great Britain; and a distinguished number of leaders from Ukraine. The international experts on the U.S.-Ukrainian Advisory Committee all offer their consulting services at no cost.

Aral Sea International Committee
Pacific Environment and Resources Center

1055 Fort Cronkhite
Sausalito, CA 94965
Tel: (415) 331-5122
Fax: (415) 332-8167
E-mail: perc@igc.org
Contact: William T. Davoren, Executive Director

ASIC was formed in Moscow in March 1991 as a bilateral US/USSR organization. Now the committee is a cooperative venture involving Americans and activists of five new Central Asian nations–Uzbekistan, Turkmenistan, Tajikistan, Kyrgyzstan, Kazakstan–plus Uzbekistan's Republic of Karakalpakstan. The committee's primary goal is to assist NGOs of

Central Asia in bringing about reform of land and water use in the Amu Darya and Syr Darya river basins–severely damaged by USSR irrigation developments of the past 35 years. These rivers have supported life and nature over a vast area and fed the Aral Sea for thousand of years.

According to William Davoren, the Aral Sea is now only 25% of its 1960 volume. All of its 24 fish species have been extirpated, its rich wide river deltas have dried up, and its exposed sandy seabed is now the source of toxic salts and chemical residues that blow over thousands of square miles of desert and steppe. For the 3- to 5-million residents of the sub-region near the Sea–in three new nations on the lower reaches of the two rivers–the problems are urgent. They need clean water for drinking and new health services to assure survival, sustenance and sustainability. Drinking water supplies have been destroyed or polluted, only a few cities have wastewater treatment plants, and health and economic problems abound.

ASIC has plans to create a clearinghouse of credentialed experts for international planning teams and missions. Experienced agronomists, economists, hydrologists, hydrogeologists, biologists, meteorologists, lawyers and zoologists are invited to inquire. This would be part of a ten-project program working towards the restoration of the Aral Sea and developing a sustainable economy in Central Asia.

The Committee's principal Central Asian cooperating NGO is the Union for Defense of the Aral and Amu Darya in Nukus, Karakalpakstan, Uzbekistan.

ARD/CHECCHI Rule of Law Consortium

1819 L Street NW, 5th Floor
Washington, DC 20036
Tel: (202) 861-0351
Fax: (202) 861-0370
E-mail: 73744.2312@compuserve.com
Contact: Robert Sharlet, Coordinator–Institution Building

Under contract from USAID, this joint venture between two consulting firms, ARD (Associates in Rural Development) and Checchi and Co., Inc., is involved in a three-year, multi-national legal reform project in the NIS. In cooperation with the Interparliamentary Assembly of the Commonwealth of Independent States, it has helped to draft a Model Civil Code, which in turn is recommended to member states by the Interparliamentary Assembly.

The Rule of Law Consortium (ROLC) has also created an electronic mail network linking civil legislation drafters throughout the NIS with one another, and with experts in Western Europe and the U.S. In Western Europe, much of this communication centers around the Center for International Legal Cooperation at the University of Leiden in the Netherlands.

In Ukraine, a major focus of the Rule of Law Consortium has been the institutions of legal education, particularly in Kharkiv, Odessa, Kyiv and Lviv. At each law school the ROLC has helped to develop new curricula, teaching methods and course materials. This has involved not only collaborations with leading Western legal educators and law school administrators, but also the donation of printing equipment to Ukrainian law schools so that they can produce their own law texts.

Finally, ARD/Checchi has administered a "Small Grants

Program," through which it makes grants ranging from $5,000 to $100,000 to third parties through a competitive bidding process. Among the recipients of grants under the first round of this program were the Network for East West Women, the League of Women Voters, the Moscow Center for Gender Studies, the Social Science Research Council, the International Tax and Information Center, the Environmental Law Institute, and the Ukrainian Legal Foundation.

ARD/Checchi publishes a quarterly newsletter which includes articles about various rule of law issues in the NIS and reports of ARD/Checchi programs and projects in the region.

Arizona Russian Abroad
University Of Arizona

UA Department of Russian,
Mod Lang 340
Tucson, AZ 85721
Tel: (520) 621-7341
Fax: (520) 749-2163
E-mail: dphil@ccit.arizona.edu
Contact: Professor Del Phillips, Director
or
Study Abroad Office
University of Arizona
Harvill 147, PO Box 11
Tucson, AZ 85721
Tel: (520) 621-4819
Fax: (520) 621-2757

The UA program is one of several offered by American colleges and universities to individuals interested in learning Russian and having a chance to live and work in the culture. According to Professor Phillips, Russian Language Coordinator at the UA and veteran of over 25 years of experience leading student groups to Russia, the Department of Russian and Slavic Languages is "acknowledged as one of the premiere Russian language training programs in the USA." More than 1,100 students from more than 100 institutions in the U.S. and abroad have participated in a UA program.

UA's programs began initially with summer travel programs and have expanded to the current eight programs per year, which include both summer and semester language and business internship programs. UA Russian Abroad Business Internship programs in Moscow allow students to study Russian for the purpose of business communication and to utilize this knowledge directly on the job by interning in one of the many companies which receive UA interns.

For business internships, each student submits a resume along with an application for the program. On the basis of this resume and telephone interviews, participants are placed in an internship with a firm or NGO operating in Moscow. The internship usually occupies about 20 hours per week.

UA has placed interns in companies and organizations such as: First Russian Real Estate; Greenpeace; Abbott Laboratories; US West; Allied Signal Aerospace; Xerox; The Moscow Tribune; IMF; Prestige Radio International; Pepsi; American Chamber of Commerce; Boeing; Cargill Enterprises; Radio Maximum; Reebok; Price Waterhouse; Coca Cola; Amnesty International; Digital; General Electric; Ernst & Young; Master Foods; Philip Morris; Project Hope; Moscow Tribune; Moscow Conservatory; and Junior Achievement.

Program participants have the option of homestays or staying at the Hotel Metallurg in Moscow. Housing in St. Petersburg is available at the dormitory for foreign students at St. Petersburg State University, located on Vasilevsky Island on the shore of the Gulf of Finland.

Armenian-American Health Association of Greater Washington

1160 Varnum Street NE, Suite 308
Washington, DC 20017
Tel: (202) 529-3756
Fax: (202) 529-5474
Contact: Hayk Kaftarian, M.D.

AAHA is a voluntary association of Armenian-American physicians, dentists, nurses, psychologists, social workers, pharmacists, and other health care professionals in the DC area. AAHA members have engaged in a variety of projects in Armenia, including efforts to: improve the health care delivery system; train health care providers; do general public education on health care; and provide biomedical and technical information. AAHA has also been able to collect and distribute medical supplies in Armenia.

Armenian National Committee of America

888 17th Street NW, Suite 904
Washington, DC 20006
Tel: (202) 775-1918
Fax: (202) 775-5648
E-mail: anca-dc@ix.netcom.com
Contact: Elizabeth S. Chouldjia

The ANC works to promote public understanding of the history of Armenia and the issues facing the country today. It organizes programs on human rights in Armenia, the conflict in Karabagh, and the need for increased foreign assistance to Armenia.

ANC is a worldwide grassroots organization, and maintains full-time staffed offices in Glendale, California, Washington, DC, and Watertown, MA. Other staffed and volunteer chapters exist in at least 13 other states of the U.S.

Armenian National Committee Massachusetts Chapter

80 Bigelow Avenue
Watertown, MA 02172
Tel: (617) 923-1918
Fax: (617) 926-1750
E-mail: 76443.1011@compuserve.com
Contact: Siran Tamakian, Executive Director

Like southern California, the Boston area is a center of Armenian-American activism in the U.S.

AzerAid

Downington, PA
Tel: (610) 942-3022
Contact: Nermin Cox, Director

AzerAid has delivered thousands of pounds of clothing and blankets donated by Mennonites in Pennsylvania to refugees in Baku. The Mennonites also collected several hundred thousand dollars used to purchase food for refugees in Imishli.

Biointensive for Russia

831 Marshall Drive
Palo Alto, CA 94303-3614
Tel: (415) 856-9751
Fax: (415) 424-8767
E-mail: cvesecky@aol.com.
Contact: Carol Vesecky

Biointensive for Russia grew out of an effort to provide translated copies of "one of the most authoritative books on 'bio-intensive' gardening and mini-farming–John Jeavons' *How to Grow More Vegetables*–to friends in Russia." The project has grown to include training sessions for Russians who are now teaching biointensive methods to gardeners and farmers in Russia, and exchanges with representatives of Ecodom, Inc., based in Akademgorodok (near Novosibirsk) in Siberia.

Ecodom is a project of Russian architects, engineers, and scientists, to build self-sufficient single-family dwellings that have "minimum impact on the local environment," outside of existing towns and cities in Russia. Ecodom's educational director, Larissa Avrorina, traveled to California in late 1994 to study resource-conserving biointensive gardening techniques, which are now being incorporated into the Ecodom program. (For more on Ecodom, see Novosibirsk section in *Russia: East of the Urals*.)

Additionally, Biointensive for Russia is seeking funds to translate selected publications of John Jeavons' Ecology Action into Russian, and is exploring the possibility of translating other U.S. environmental books into Russian as well as Russian-language books on similar topics into English (e.g. Galina Shatalova's *Formula for Health and Long Life*).

Biointensive for Russia's newsletter provides information on environmental projects in the former Soviet Union, Biointensive exchange programs, workshops and activities.

Boston University
Office of International Programs
232 Bay State Road, PO Box CSI
Boston, MA 02215
Tel: (617) 353-9888
Fax: (617) 353-5402
E-mail: abroad@bu.edu

In 1993 BU began its Moscow Internship Program. The semester-long program includes eight weeks of language and culture study at European University and eight weeks of on-the-job internships in such fields as art and architecture, business, media, advertising and public relations, law, and politics.

Internship placements have included: managing sales and marketing for two new private radio stations; working with clients at an employment agency that places Russians in positions at foreign firms; doing research at United Way International's Moscow office on private voluntary associations in Russia; and other placements with a diverse group of organ-izations, including: AIDS Infoshare Russia; MacArthur Foundation; Poly-Gram Russia; Salvation Army; Pratt and Whitney; National Democratic Institute; and Ernst and Young.

Applicants must have completed six or more semesters of college-level Russian or the equivalent. Those with less than six semesters of Russian spend one month in intensive language study in St. Petersburg prior to joining the program in Moscow. The deadline for the Fall semester is March 15; for the Spring semester the deadline is October 15. The cost for the 1995-6 program was $8,400, which included tuition, room and board, and internship. Financial aid is available.

Boy Scouts of America
1325 West Walnut Hill Lane
PO Box 152079
Irving, TX 75015-2079
Tel: (214) 580-2401
Fax: (214) 580-2413
E-mail: tbooth@glas.apc.org
Contact: Tony Booth, B.S.A.-SibAS Project Director

Scouting in Russia began in 1908 and grew rapidly following a visit from the founder of Scouting, Lord Baden-Powell in 1910. By 1922, however, independent scouting organizations were officially prohibited and remained so until 1990, when the World Organization of the Scout Movement was asked for assistance in re-establishing Scouting in Russia.

Dr. Alexander Bondar, a Russian with extensive experience in the International Red Cross, has helped to organize Scouting in Russia and arranged the translation of both *The Leader's Handbook* and *The Scout Handbook* into Russian. The first Russian Congress of the Federation of Scouts of Russia was held in November 1991.

As of 1995, there were in excess of 25,000 Scouts in 40 cities throughout Russia, from St. Petersburg to Vladivostok.

Most recent U.S.-Russian Scouting exchange activity has been between Boy Scouts of America and the Siberian Association of Scouts (SibAS), under a three-year project led by Tony Booth and aimed at helping Scouts in Siberia become financially and organizationally self-sufficient.

Exchanges between Scouts and Scout Leaders from the Boy Scouts of America and members of SibAS have occurred regularly over the past three years and further exchanges, pen pals, and other interactions with the Siberian Scout organization are strongly encouraged. Those interested in pursuing any possibilities should contact the International Division at the address above, or send e-mail to: *boyscouts@igc.apc.org*.

Besides the *Leader's Handbook* and the *Scout Handbook*, various brochures on Scouting have been translated into Russian. Support for some of these projects has come from the United States Foundation for International Scouting (USFIS).

A Call to Serve International

895 Kifer Road
PO Box 60788
Sunnyvale, CA 94088-0788
Tel: (408) 245-4905
Fax: (408) 245-4907
Contact: Anthony DePalms,
Vice President of Operations

ACTS gives training and technical assistance to their affiliate organization in Georgia, leading to self-sufficiency and creating local management expertise.

The Carnegie Endowment for International Peace

2400 N Street, NW
Washington, DC 20037
Tel: (202) 862-7900
Fax: (202) 466-6007
E-mail: ceip@igc.apc.org

The endowment, founded in 1910 by industrialist Andrew Carnegie, is a tax-exempt operating (not a grant-making) foundation. It conducts its own programs of research, discussion, publication, and public education.

Associates of the Carnegie Endowment bring to their work substantial firsthand experience in government, journalism, universities, international organizations, and the law. Through media appearances, consulting, and conference participation worldwide, CEIP staff address the major policy issues of the day in ways that reach both expert and general audiences. The Endowment publishes books, monographs, and *Foreign Policy*, a leading U.S. international affairs magazine.

In 1993 Carnegie launched an ambitious program in Russian and Eurasian affairs. CEIP not only expanded its team of Washington-based specialists working in the field, but also established the Carnegie Center in Moscow. The activities of the Center–including seminars, publications, and working groups–present a range of views on the problems and opportunities that confront the postcommunist world. Together, the two halves of the program provide a forum for collaboration among Americans, Russians, and others–especially citizens from states of the former Soviet Union. One of the first accomplishments of the Moscow office was to produce, together with IREX, a *Directory of Foreign Affairs Research Organizations in Russia.*

CEC International Partners

12 West 31st Street
New York, NY 10001-4415
Tel: (212) 643-1985
Fax: (212) 643-1996
E-mail: cecny@igc.apc.org
Contact: Michael Brainerd, President

CEC International Partners, formerly the Citizen Exchange Council, was founded in 1962. The organization today describes itself as "the largest non-academic, nonpartisan American organization dedicated to reciprocal exchanges between the U.S. and the former Soviet Union."

As it enters its fourth decade of activity, CEC's new mission is "helping the peoples of the former Soviet Union to rebuild their shattered societies." CEC offers individuals and groups the opportunity to be involved in any of three initiatives in education, the arts, and the environment.

In education, CEC has paired 14 U.S. colleges and universities with partner institutions in six of the newly independent states. The centerpiece of the environmental focus is the EcoBridge program, a partnership between Rostov-on-Don Region and Tennessee Valley. This program was launched in 1991 between government agencies and universities to improve teaching on the environment and management of natural resources.

CEC, in partnership with the St. Petersburg Mayor's Committee on Culture and Tourism and Russian arts organizations, is organizing American support for St. Petersburg 2003. This program is an effort to revitalize the arts and culture in preparation for St. Petersburg's tercentennial.

CEC has recently expanded its highly successful ArtsLink program with the nations of Eastern Europe and the NIS. In 1995 nearly 50 artists and arts managers from the NIS came to the U.S. for 5-week residencies and CEC sent more than 33 individuals or arts groups to 11 Eastern European countries.

U.S. nonprofit organizations wishing to host an ArtsLink Fellow will receive from $3,500 to $5,000 to support the residency. It is expected that matching funds or in-kind support will be required to cover full residency costs.

CEC also sponsors ArtsLink Collaborative Projects for U.S. artists (individ-uals or small groups) wishing to undertake collaborations with colleagues in Eastern Europe or the NIS. Stipends for these grants will generally range between $1,500 and $3,500, with a cap of $6,000.

This program is a partnership between CEC, the National Endowment for the Arts, Open Society Institute, Soros Foundations/Soros Centers for

Contemporary Arts, the Trust for Mutual Understanding and other institutions.

Center for Democracy
1101 15th Street NW, Suite 505
Washington, DC 20005
Tel: (202) 429-9141
Fax: (202) 293-1768
Contact: Allen Weinstein, President; Thomas B. Reems, Program Director

Programs of the Center for Democracy (CFD) in the NIS focus on rule-of-law issues, legal reform, and environmental improvement. CFD assists officials, lawyers, and NGOs with legal reform issues by coordinating seminars and conferences and sending U.S. lawyers and environmental professionals to the NIS as advisors and trainers. CFD also arranges informal visits and exchanges for U.S. and NIS leaders. One of CFD's long-term projects is leading the legal reform division of the Civic Initiatives Program (see Moscow section in "Russia: West of the Urals"), designed to promote the growth and sustainability of Russian NGOs.

CFD has also organized conferences and training seminars dealing with judicial development in Central Asia and with environmental issues throughout the NIS. CFD has sent U.S. environmental and legal specialists to the NIS to conduct these various seminars and colloquies.

An ongoing CFD project is it annual conference "Courts of Ultimate Appeal" which brings together high court officials from throughout the NIS, Eastern and Western Europe, and North America to discuss common issues and problems with the goal of strengthening judicial indep-endence and operations in the NIS and Eastern Europe. CFD

publishes tran-scripts of its seminars and conferences. It has an office in Moscow.

Center for Economic Initiatives
PO Box 234
Terrace Park, OH 45174
Tel: (513) 831-6771
Fax: (513) 831-6741
E-mail: leecole@tso.cin.ix.net
Contact: Leland M. Cole, President

The Center for Economic Activities is involved in the following activities in the NIS:
• organizing and conducting Technical Assistance study tours based on the approach used by James Silberman who conceived and ran the original Marshall Plan program;
• supporting a Productivity Center to be located in Kharkiv, Ukraine;
• providing training for companies in the NIS on business and manufacturing related topics;
• fostering economic growth and development by bringing together parties with different resources.

Center for International Environmental Law
1621 Connecticut Avenue NW
Suite 200
Washington, DC 20009-1052
Tel: (202) 332-4840
Fax: (202) 332-4865
E-mail: cielus@igc.apc.org
URL: http://www.econet.apc.org/ciel/
Contact: Durwood J. Zaelke, President; Barbara Finamore, Russia Counsel

CIEL was founded in 1989 "to bring the energy and experience of the public interest environmental law movement to the critical task of strengthening and developing international and comparative national law, policy and

management throughout the world." The Center works with NGOs, international institutions and government bodies in the NIS, providing policy research and advice, education and training, and institutional development services. CIEL has programs worldwide in the following issue areas:
• Biodiversity and Wildlife
• Climate Change
• Environmental Law Education
• Intellectual Property
• International Financial Institutions
• NGO Development
• Ozone Depletion
• Ocean Governance
• State of Environmental Law
• Trade and the Environment

Center for International Networking Initiatives

The University of Tennessee System
UT Conference Center, Suite 313
Building 600 Henley Street
Knoxville, TN 37996-4137
Tel: (615) 974-2908
Fax: (615) 974-6508
E-mail: gcole@solar.rtd.utk.edu
Contact: Greg Cole, Director
URL:
http://solar.rtd.utk.edu/friends/home.html

The center was established in 1995 by the University of Tennessee to further the work Greg Cole, formerly with the university's Research Services, has done together with Natasha Bulashova of Pushchino State University in Russia. Cole and Bulashova are responsible for the widely-visited World Wide Web site "Friends and Partners," often cited as a model for how the Internet can assist U.S.-NIS citizen collaborations. (See section on *NIS-Related Internet Sites.*)

Center for International Private Enterprise

1615 H Street NW
Washington, DC 20062-2000
Tel: (202) 463-5901
Fax: (202) 887-3447
E-mail: cipe@cipe.org
URL: http://www.cipe.org
Contact: Stephen Deane, Program Officer for the NIS

The Center for International Private Enterprise, one of the organizations created under the National Endowment for Democracy and sponsored by the U.S. Chamber of Commerce, works directly with foreign business organizations, think tanks and other business-oriented private sector organizations, assisting them to function as national entities supportive of free enterprise. It publishes a monthly magazine, *Economic Reform Today*, which is distributed through USIA to policy makers in governments around the world.

CIPE has recently embarked on a two-year, $1.7 million program of training and grants with the Russian Federation Chamber of Commerce and Industry (RCCI). This program is funded by USAID and administered by IREX. The mission is to help the RCCI develop into a nationwide, voluntary, non-state business association that provides services to its members and supports the transition to a market-based democracy.

The program has a three-pronged strategy:
• Training Program. CIPE expects to train about 100 leaders and key staff members of the national and regional Russian Chambers in up to five cities each year. Training topics include: an overview of Chamber activities, public policy advocacy, communication tech-

niques, ethics, and small business development.
• An Accreditation Program based on the U.S. Chamber program. This is a diagnostic and management tool that enables chambers to identify their own weaknesses and strengths, develop a concrete plan for improvement, and recognize and maintain standards of excellence. CIPE will work directly with chambers tohelp them meet accreditation standards, such as financing or membership recruitment and retention.
• A Small Grants Program totalling up to $200,000. Approximately 20 to 40 grants ranging from $1,000 to $10,000 will be made to support pilot programs that local and regional chambers propose. These programs will reinforce the training.
CIPE has an office in Moscow.

Center for Public Representation
121 S. Pinckney
Madison, WI 53703
Tel: (608) 251-4008
Contact: Michael Pritchard, Project Director

CPR received a grant together with the Russian organization Public Advocates to assist in its development with the goal of developing a model for public advocacy that is self-sustaining.

Center for Development and Population Activities (CEDPA)
1717 Massachusetts Avenue NW
Suite 200
Washington, DC 20036
Tel: (202) 667-1142
Fax: (202) 332-4496
E-mail: adrienne@cedpa.org
cedpa_aa@cerf.net

Contact: Ms. Adrienne Allison, Vice President

Leadership development, management training, family planning services delivery, policy and advocacy work.

Children of Chornobyl Relief Fund
272 Old Short Hills Road
Short Hills, NJ 07078
Tel: (201) 376-5140
Fax: (201) 376-4988
E-mail: ccrfchornbyl@delphi.com
Contact: Nadia Matkiwsky, Executive Director

The Children of Chornobyl Relief Fund (CCRF) was established in 1989 to provide humanitarian aid to children in Ukraine affected by the 1986 nuclear accident in Chornobyl, Ukraine. Since its founding CCRF, which now has over 30 chapters in the U.S., has organized the shipment of 800 tons of medicine and medical equipment, valued at over $32 million. CCRF has sponsored hospitals in Chernihiv, Donetsk, Kyiv, Lviv, Luhansk, Kharkiv, and Vynnytsia; provided fellowships for Ukrainian health professionals to study in the U.S.; and sent more than 100 American volunteer physicians to Uk-raine to train local doctors in Western medical techniques.
In 1991 officials in Lviv transferred the administration of a former Communist Party hospital to CCRF. With contributions of equipment from corporations and expertise from volunteer health care professionals, CCRF has transformed the hospital into a modern 160-bed facility which specializes in treating children with leukemia, Hodgkins Disease, and other illnesses. CCRF volunteers have also installed a dental clinic at the hospital.

The hospital is governed by a joint Ukrainian-American Board of Directors and has recently become the region's official teaching hospital.

Cincinnati-Kharkiv Sister City Project

3620 Carew Tower
441 Vine Street
Cincinnati, OH 45202
Tel: (513) 241-8833
Fax: (513) 241-8833
E-mail: cinkhars@tso.cin.ix.net
Contact: Marilyn Braun, President; Katrina Morley, Project Administrator

The Cincinnati-Kharkiv Sister City Project lists as its major accomplishments:
• provision of humanitarian aid, including vaccine and medical supplies to fight an outbreak of diphtheria among children and young adults in Kharkiv;
• hosting the 1991 International Sister City Conference for USA and USSR cities;
• providing a model for human services, in cooperation with the Cincinnati Salvation Army, which resulted in the opening, in Kharkiv, of an adult day-care center, 13 soup kitchens, six social service centers, a homeless shelter and a halfway house for ex-prisoners;
• promotion of youth and educational exchange activities which have resulted in highly successful programs involving students and faculty at the University of Cincinnati and various other elementary and secondary schools; and,
• establishment of a landmark Municipal Training Program for Kharkiv area public administrators in cooperation with the International Executive Service Corps (IESC) and the United States Information Agency (USIA).
The group has initiated a woman's issues committee which resulted in the first all-female exchange of delegations from Ukraine and Cincinnati. Over 70 women were involved in planning and conducting this activity, and has participated in the production of "Spring-time of Hope", a video about the rebirth of religion in Kharkiv, with Ecumedia of Greater Cincinnati. This video has been aired on public television and other stations.

The organization has received four consecutive awards for outstanding achievement from Sister City International/Reader's Digest and the prestigious Post Corbett Award for its work in promoting a wide range of cultural cooperation.

Citizens Democracy Corps

1735 Eye Street NW, Suite 720
Washington, DC 20006
Tel: (202) 872-0933;
              (800) 394-1945
Fax: (202) 872-0923
E-mail: info@cdc.org
Contact: Diane Rosenbaum

CDC was established in 1990 with major support from USAID "to mobilize U.S. private sector expertise and resources to assist the countries of Central and Eastern Europe and the Commonwealth of Independent States to build democratic institutions and free market economies." It has offices in Moscow, St. Petersburg, Rostov, Novosibirsk, and Khabarovsk, which provide in-country support to CDC's Enterprise and Economic Development Program. Under this program, American Volunteer Advisors provide on-site assistance to private and privatizing businesses and to public and nonprofit institutions that support business development. More than 400 advisors, from 45 states, assisted over 300 businesses and institutions in the region under the auspices of CDC in its first five years of operation.

The Enterprise and Economic Development Program looks for individuals to serve as Volunteer Advisors who have a minimum of:

- ten years of experience;
- the ability to serve as volunteers for two months; and
- prior experience in a foreign country.

CDC provides international airfare. Host institutions and companies provide housing, local transportation, and translation services.

Citizens Network for Foreign Affairs Inc.

1111 19th Street NW, Suite 900
Washington, DC 20036
Tel: (202) 296-3920
Fax: (202) 296-3948
Contact: John H. Costello, President; Jerry W. Leach, Program Director

The Citizens Network for Foreign Affairs (CNFA) is a nonprofit bipartisan organization working to promote a better understanding of the United States' international relationships and their effects on American global leadership. CNFA works with leaders from a number of fields, including agriculture, banking, business, education, government and labor.

As part of the Save the Children consortium, CNFA began its Civic Initiatives Program (CIP) in June 1995 to help build citizen participation in the political and economic leadership of southern Russia. CIP is establishing technical assistance centers in Krasnodar, Stavropol, and Rostov to help more than 150 Russian grassroots organizations in those regions become more effective. CIP will provide training to improve management, increase membership, strengthen communications,

and create partnerships with U.S. nonprofit organizations. Under CIP, CNFA will also design and manage a $600,000 micro-grant program to foster development of new grassroots organizations in southern Russia.

Civic Education Project

1140 Chapel South, 2nd Floor
New Haven, CT 06520
Tel: (203) 781-0263
Fax: (203) 781-0265
E-mail: cep@minerva.cis.yale.edu
Contact: Kerry McNamara, Executive Director

1000 Potomac Street, Suite 401
Washington, DC 20007
Tel: (202) 337-2189
Fax: (202) 342-0763
E-mail: CEPWash@aol.com
         cepprg@ecn.gn.apc.org
URL:
http://minerva.cis/yale.edu/~cep/cep.html

Founded in late 1990 by American graduate students from Harvard and Yale, the Civic Education Project has established a region-wide network of partnerships with universities and higher education institutions to students in fields of economics, law, political science and other branches of social and policy sciences. CEP's focus on education "stems from a conviction that the classroom is a vital laboratory of democracy." CEP plans to send 130 instructors to roughly 65 universities in 15 countries of the region for the academic year 1995-96.

CEP lecturers receive air transportation, health insurance, a shipping allowance, teaching materials, local language lessons and a modest living stipend. The host university provides housing and a local currency salary.

Lecturers participating in the program are involved in classroom teaching and professional development within their faculties. All courses are taught in English, but not all lecturers are American. In 1994-95, 29% of the CEP lecturers were of other nation-alities–and this percentage is expected to climb in 1995-96. Applicants must either have completed their general examinations or hold a professional degree. Deadline for applications is January 1.

On-line resources: CEP maintains several listservs, including an East European Higher Education list, and others on legal reform, women's issues, economics and job announcements. For more information, send e-mail to: *cep@minerva.cis.yale.edu*

Civitan International

PO Box 130744
Birmingham, AL 35213-0744
Tel: (205) 591-8910
Fax: (205) 592-6307
E-mail: hsde35a@prodigy.com
Contact: Rosemary Franklin, Administrative Manager (ext. 108)

Civitan was founded in 1917 by a group of Birmingham business and professional men committed to improving their community. It is a member service organization active in 20 countries with 55,000 men, women and young adults in 1800 clubs. Its purpose is to provide members opportunities for personal and professional development through community service, particularly to the mentally retarded and developmentally disabled.

CI Foundation, established in 1960, is a nonprofit corporation, supported by donations from Civitan members and the general public. It funds grants and scholarships, as well as the Civitan International Research Center (CIRC), a research and treatment facility for mental retardation and other developmental disabilities.

Since 1991, Civitan clubs have been established in Hungary, Romania, Ukraine, Slovakia and Russia. Civitan literature has been translated for these clubs and Civitan has approved a waiver of international dues for these countries for a period of five years. Modest local dues pay club administrative expenses and support further national expansion. Civitan has a sponsor/mentor program that matches established clubs with developing clubs in order to assist them.

In addition to the establishment of clubs, Civitan has established a partnership with Special Olympics Eurasia, headquartered in Moscow. Civitan members in Russia are involved with local and national Special Olympics, and share in the commitment to helping people with mental retardation and developmental disabilities.

Cooperative Housing Foundation

PO Box 91280
Washington, DC 20090-1280
Tel: (301) 587-4700
Fax: (301) 587-2626
Contact: Barbara Jones

The Cooperative Housing Foundation (CHF) sponsors the formation of cooperatives and community-based groups, aids in the construction of housing and basic community infrastructure, provides training for project administrators, and advises governments on housing policies. It has projects in more than 80 developing countries and has started projects in Eastern Europe and the NIS.

Although CHF does not have a formal volunteer sending program it could be a resource for finding volunteer opportunities for individuals with backgrounds in management, property management and banking, particularly home improvement loan experience.

Council on International Educational Exchange

205 East 42nd Street
New York, NY 10017
Tel: (212) 661-1414, ext. 1139
Fax: (212) 972-3231
E-mail: ivpbrochure@ciee.org

The Council on International Educational Exchange (CIEE), founded in 1947, offers study and work camp experiences in the NIS for high school students and undergraduates. CIEE organizes international voluntary work camps in Armenia, Belarus, Lithuania, Russia and Ukraine. These are typically two to four weeks in duration and bring together 10-20 volunteers from different countries to work on any of a variety of projects. Past projects have included renovation work in the historical center of Kyiv, excavation of ancient burial grounds in the Urals, and renovation of an old cathedral in Siberia. The work camp program is open to anyone over the age of 18 and most participants are between 20 and 25 years old.

CIEE charges a $165 placement fee for each individual. (There is a surcharge for Russian programs, depen-ding on the particular work camp site.) Every April CIEE publishes a direct-ory of the work camp experiences to be offered that summer. This lists CIEE's projects in 25 countries, with their starting and ending dates. Cost is $12. If a person chooses to participate in a CIEE work camp, the cost of the di-rectory is credited to the placement fee.

Besides the CIEE placement fee, work camp participants must pay their own

airfare. In-country room and board are provided.

CIEE also organizes school-to-school partnerships, study abroad programs, and publishes many useful resources. To obtain a free electronic version of the CIEE brochure, send an e-mail request to the address above.

Doctors Without Borders / Médecins Sans Frontières USA

30 Rockefeller Plaza, Suite 5425
New York, NY 10112
Tel: (212) 649-5961
Fax: (212) 246-8577
or
1999 Avenue of the Stars, Suite 500
Los Angeles, CA 90067
Tel: (310) 551-4072
Fax: (310) 553-3928
Contact: Chantal Firino Martell, Executive Director; Julie E. McArthur, Western Director

Founded in 1971, Doctors Without Borders/Médecins Sans Frontières USA (MSF), has achieved global recognition for its assistance to victims of armed conflict or natural disasters, and to residents of refugee camps. MSF observes strict neutrality and demands absolute freedom in performing its mission. The kinds of assistance MSF provides include: medical care (from surgery to vaccinations to nutrition and health education); logistical assistance in setting up shelters and communications; water processing and sanitation; power supplies and transportation; and medical and food supplies.

Thousands of volunteers serve annually, in about 60 countries around the world. In 1993 and 1994 MSF sent volunteers to Tajikistan to respond to civil unrest there and the resultant refugee flows.

MSF has been active in Russia providing health care to the homeless, offering hygiene services, tuberculosis examinations, inoculations against diphtheria, etc. The organization has also been active in advocating for the rights of the homeless. In November 1993 MSF protested against the Moscow government's actions to close the medical and social aid facilities at some Moscow railway stations.

Earth Island Institute: Baikal Watch

300 Broadway, Suite 28
San Francisco, CA 94133
Tel: (415) 788-3666
Fax: (415) 788-7324
E-mail: earthisland@igc.apc.org
Contact: Gary Cook, Director

Earth Island Institute, founded by David Brower, develops projects for the conservation, preservation and restoration of the global environment. Baikal Watch is an example of one of EII's projects. It was started in 1990 to promote the protection of Lake Baikal and the surrounding region.

Baikal Watch seeks to strengthen the national park and nature preserve system. Its projects include the Russian Ecotourism Forum for the development of respon-sible tourism in Siberia and eastern Russia. Baikal Watch conducts training programs for park personnel and leads "ecotours" of the parks to raise revenue for park maintenance.

Baikal Watch has projects which need voluntary consultants in a variety of areas, from park personnel such as rangers and directors, to accountants and support staff. They have also used volunteers with expertise in energy, pollution abatement, and international law. Typically, volunteers work on a specific project with a group of about 30 volunteers for three to four weeks.

Earthwatch

680 Mount Auburn Street
PO Box 403
Watertown, MA 02272
Tel: (617) 926-8200
Fax: (617) 926-8532
E-mail: info@earthwatch.org
URL: http://gaia.earthwatch.org
Contact: Andrew Hudson

Earthwatch supports research on a variety of environmental projects which monitor global change, study the possibilities for the conservation of endangered species and habitats, explore the heritage of humankind, and foster world health and international cooperation.

Earthwatch funds scientific research with volunteers' contributions of time, labor and money. Earthwatch solicits proposals for research projects which can use the help of non-specialist volunteers. Once proposals are chosen to be funded the cost of the project is divided by the number of volunteers needed for the project and that cost is passed on to those volunteers who sign up for the project.

Most projects last between two to three weeks. Scholarships are available for teachers and high school students over age 16. They are awarded on the merit of the applicants, including abilities that they bring to the project and what they plan to do with the knowledge gained from the experience.

On average there are six to eight projects in the NIS annually. Projects in 1995 included creating an accurate river model for Estonian rivers to help gather information for their sustainable management, coordinated by Marina Timofeyeva of the Estonian Institute of

Hydrology and Meteorology; and a large predator study in the Eastern Carpathian Biosphere Reserve between Poland and Ukraine, coordinated by two professors from the Jagiellonian University in Poland. The cost for volunteers of both these programs is approximately $1,400. It includes room and board and the volunteer's contribution to project financing, but does not include travel expenses.

ECOLOGIA

PO Box 171, College Street
La Plume, PA 18440
Tel: (717) 945-7358
Fax: (717) 945-7360
E-mail: ecologia@igc.apc.org
Contact: Randall Kritkausky, President

ECOLOGIA (Ecologists Linked for Organizing Grassroots Initiatives and Action) was founded in 1989 in order to support grassroots groups across the Soviet Union. For the past five years, it has provided information, training, and support for grassroots environmental groups in the former Soviet Union, the Baltic States, and Central and Eastern Europe. ECOLOGIA has offices in Moscow, Minsk and Vilnius.

ECOLOGIA is involved in different projects supporting independent environmental institutions. The major ones are:

• Water Quality Monitoring. ECOLOGIA has established a citizen's water quality monitoring network at 21 sites in 10 countries in CEE, the Baltics, and the NIS. ECOLOGIA provides NGOs portable HACH spectrophotometers and training that enables them to test for water pollution indicators, and to carry out their own independent monitoring projects.

• ECOLOGIA's Environmental Technical Information Project (E-TIP), started in January 1995, is designed to provide integrated information support to the environmental community in Russia and other countries in transition. E-TIP combines the following interrelated elements:

∗ the development of a two-language WWW-site providing links to an annotated collection of specially selected sources of environmental information, accompanied by User Guides developed by ECOLOGIA;

∗ the ECOLINE Moscow Open Environmental Library and walk-in information center where the resources of some of the largest Russian and many international NGOs are collected, catalogued, and made accessible for visitors. A free consultation service for NGOs dealing with a broad range of environmental issues.

• Toxics Monitoring Network (TMN). As a precursor to E-TIP, ECOLOGIA and the Sacred Earth Network joined together to establish a computerized network of NGOs. The TMN serves as an information network in which members in four countries exchange information on chemical and nuclear substances and public health via the Internet.

• Conferences and NGO Training Exchanges. More than 200 people from Eastern Europe, the NIS, Baltics, and U.S. have visited other countries within the framework of ECOLOGIA's exchange programs.

• ECOLOGIA Newsletter. ECOLOGIA publishes a bimonthly newsletter which analyzes issues and presents case studies of relevance to the international environmental community. The newsletter is available in English, Russian, and Lithuanian.

Nine people work in the ECOLOGIA Moscow office, and three work in the Minsk and Vilnius offices each.

Economics America

1140 Avenue of the Americas
New York, NY 10036
Tel: (212) 730-7007
Fax: (212) 730-1793
E-mail: econusa@sovusa.com
Contact: Patricia Elder, Director for Special Projects

Economics America (EA), also known as the National Council on Economic Education, was founded in 1949 as a partnership of leaders from education, business and labor dedicated to improving economic literacy. Through a nationwide network of state councils and 275 university centers, it works with 2,600 affiliated local school districts to train about 120,000 teachers each year in economics education. It is the largest teacher training organization in the United States. Economics America also develops curriculum and produces materials for economics teaching at the primary and secondary school level. Its publication, *A Framework for Teaching Basic Economic Concepts with Scope and Sequence Guidelines, K-12,* is designed to aid in the development and teaching of an economics curriculum for students of all ages.

Since 1992 Economics America has worked with educators in the NIS to help develop economics education there. It has organized seminars for more than 700 teacher trainers, teachers, university professors and school administrators in Azerbaijan, Belarus, Estonia, Russia, and Ukraine. It has helped establish the International Center for Business and Economic Education in Russia, which now has 12 regional branches, and has also supported a growing network of similar centers in Ukraine.

In 1995-96, Economics America administered a unique International Education Exchange Program funded by the U.S. Department of Education. The program featured the following activities:

• To develop a strong core of local teacher trainers, a series of four seminars conducted for a group of 40 trainers from partner countries.

• To expand the supply of high-quality teaching materials in translated form, the translation of selected materials into Ukrainian and Russian.

• Participation by economic education leaders from the region in three professional development conferences, in Dallas, St. Petersburg and Prague.

• Two U.S. study tours, one for trainers and one for teachers from the region, to exchange experiences and ideas with American colleagues, observe classroom teaching and teacher training, and become familiar with U.S. educational and economic institutions.

• Teams of teachers and trainers from Ukraine and U.S. working together to develop a package of instructional materials on the economic histories and recent economic transformations of formerly communist nations. The Council will publish these lesson packages for world history and economics classes in the U.S.

Education for Democracy/ International Project

International Affairs Department
American Federation of Teachers
555 New Jersey Avenue NW, Suite 880
Washington DC 20001-2079
Tel: (202) 879-7484
Fax: (202) 879-4502
Contact: Steve Fleischman,

Coordinator, ED/I Project

The American Federation of Teachers represents 875,000 teachers, school support staff, health care professionals and public employees. AFT established ED/I in 1989 "to provide teacher unions and educators in newly emerging democracies with assistance in the development of curriculum materials and teacher training."

ED/I has three main activities: teacher training and curriculum development; democratic skills and leadership training; and publications on democracy and education.

In 1994 ED/I co-sponsored a National Conference on Civics Education in Russia with *Uchitelskaja Gazeta* ("Teachers' Newspaper"). A result of the conference was the creation of a Russian civic educators' association, the Civic Education Union. ED/I continues to work with *Uchitelskaja Gazeta* on a variety of projects, including the creation of an electronic network for Russian civic educators. Most of ED/I's training programs are undertaken by U.S. volunteers.

ED/I has produced a database of more than 300 organizations and individuals working to improve civics education around the world. The *Education for Democracy/International Database* is available in both print and electronic media. ED/I also sponsors a Classroom-to-Classroom program which links U.S. classrooms with counterparts in developing democracies throughout the world. It established an office in Moscow in 1993.

Environmental Law Alliance Worldwide

1877 Garden Avenue
Eugene, OR 97403
Tel: (503) 687-8485

Contact: Jennifer Gleason, Chris Wold, Project Directors

ELAW together with EcoPravo–Ukraine received a grant to help develop environmental laws for Ukraine. This will be accomplished by training EcoPravo staff, providing support for electronic communications for EcoPravo and other Ukrainian environmental groups, and enhancing EcoPravo's litigation capabilities.

Environmental Law Institute

1616 P Street, NW
Washington, DC 20036
Tel: (212) 939-3800
E-mail: eli@igc.org
elip@laigc.org
Contact: Jay Austin, Project Director

The ELI in cooperation with EcoPravo–Ukraine has received a grant to:
• Train Ukrainian judges, lawyers, and government officials;
• Compile and publish laws and legal analyses for an audience of citizengroups, policymakers, and practicing lawyers;
• Assist the Ukrainian Government with law-drafting and implementation assistance for pending and future legislation; and
• Continue to provide legal consultation to individuals and citizengroups.

A similar project is also being undertaken in Russia with EcoJuris.

Federal Bar Association
Democracy Development Initiative

4601 North Park Avenue, Suite 1702
Chevy Chase, MD 20815-4525
Tel/Fax: (301) 652-3075
Contact: Brian C. Murphy, Esq., Chairperson

The Democracy Development Initiative (DDI) of the Federal Bar Association (FBA) provides assistance to countries reforming their governmental and legal systems by providing advisors and consultants. DDI was formed in 1990 by the Federal Bar Association in order to promote democratic efforts in Central and Eastern Europe and the NIS. Since then, the program has expanded to include programs in Africa and Latin America. The FBA is a voluntary association of over 14,000 public and private sector U.S. lawyers involved in federal legal practice.

Volunteers are taken from a talent bank of legal professionals and are placed with government offices, professional associations and NGO's. DDI currently maintains a talent bank of over 200 members of the FBA who wish to volunteer. Talent bank members prepare letters and memoranda on legal issues, review draft legislation, provide on-site assistance with institution structuring and run training activities. The duration of volunteer projects varies from one week to over one year.

Talent bank members have a variety of professional specializations including: administrative law; civil service; energy; entitlements programs; intellectual property; international claims and arbitration; labor law; media law; taxation; transportation; financial institutions; corporate and commercial law, and constitutional law.

Financial Services Volunteer Corps

425 Lexington Avenue, 12th floor
New York, NY 10017-3909
Tel: (212) 692-1200
Fax: (212) 983-9847,
            (212) 286-3310

Contact: Joanne Heyman, Administrative Director

Financial Services Volunteer Corps (FSVC) was founded in 1990 by former Secretary of State Cyrus R. Vance and former Deputy Secretary John C. Whitehead to channel voluntary, technical assistance from the U.S. financial services community in support of the economic transformation in Eastern Europe and the NIS. As of early 1995, FSVC had completed over 170 projects, in countries as diverse as Belarus, Hungary, Mongolia, Poland, Russia and Slovakia. FSVC's executive director is Herbert S. Okun, former U.S. ambassador to East Germany, and the managing director is J. Andrew Spindler.

FSVC activities focus on, but are not limited to, three primary areas:
- commercial banking
- central banking
- capital markets development

In response to specific requests from host country institutions, FSVC places skilled volunteers in the region for periods ranging from several days to two weeks. Each volunteeer assignment is part of a coordinated program of assistance to key financial institutions in host countries. FSVC draws its volunteers from the entire range of U.S. financial services and regulatory institutions. It covers volunteers' travel and out-of-pocket expenses.

In addition to placing American volunteers abroad, FSVC sponsors U.S.-based training programs and internships for qualified professionals from partner institutions. FSVC has representative offices in Bratislava, Budapest, Moscow, Prague and Warsaw.

First Light Partners
2680 McMillan Street
Eugene, OR 97405

Tel: (503) 341-6447
E-mail: frstltptrs@aol.com
Contact: Ted Hicks, Executive Director

First Light Partners is a nonprofit organization working to bring "modern training and treatment methods for alcoholism to the health care professionals of Ukraine." It has support from both the Ukrainian Ministry of Health and Academy of Sciences, which are providing training and treatment facilities, as well as assistance in choosing the best possible Ukrainian candidates to receive training.

First Light Partners plans to train more than 120 health care professionals in a twelve-step "facilitation therapy" program. Each Ukrainian professional will participate in a full-time six-month course of hands-on study. They in-turn will use the manual-based training and treatment program to train others—resulting eventually in treatment for tens of thousands.

The project is designed to last three years. Between each training program, a one-month period will be used to revise both the training and treatment models to better suit the needs of the people of Ukraine.

The Ford Foundation

International Affairs Program
320 East 43rd Street
New York, NY 10017
Tel: (212) 573-5283
Fax: (212) 856-9330
E-mail: J.Schull@Fordfound.org;
             M.McAuley@Fordfound.org
Contact: Dr. Mary McAuley, Moscow Representative, Moscow; Dr. Joseph Schull, Deputy Director, Russia and East Europe Program, New York

The Ford Foundation is a private, nonprofit philanthropic institution dedicated to international peace and the advancement of human welfare throughout the world. Under the policy guidance of a Board of Trustees, the Foundation grants and lends funds to governmental and nongovernmental institutions for educational, cultural, research, training, developmental, and community-oriented efforts that hold promise of producing significant advan-ces in the fields of its program interests.

Since 1950, the Foundation has sponsored a range of activities involving the Soviet Union and East Europe, particularly in the area of education and cultural exchange. Since 1989, the Foundation has expanded and refocused its work in the region, and has begun making grants in direct support of indigenous institutions. During the period 1989-1995 the Foundation spent over $30 million on projects related to this endeavor. Currently, the Foundation makes grants in Russia, Poland, Hungary, the Czech Republic and Slovakia. The Foundation anticipates spending some $4 million in Russia during 1996.

Three broad goals provide a thematic focus for the Russia program: (1) to promote the economic reform process and to support efforts to address the social policy issues raised by the transition to market-oriented economies; (2) to help consolidate democracy through the reform of political and legal institutions and the integration of international human rights standards in domestic law and practice; and (3) to strengthen institutions of higher education and research in the social sciences, and to enhance Western capacity to understand events in the region. Efforts are directed at addressing both short-term and long-term needs, combining research and policy analysis with training and institution-building programs.

The Foundation has an office in Moscow.

Foundation for International Professional Exchange, Inc.

514 S. Vanderlink Drive
Payson, AZ 85541
Tel: (602) 474-6371
Fax: (602) 472-6332
Contact: W. Jackson Wilson, R.Ed.D., Executive Director

The Foundation for International Professional Exchange (FIPE) was created in 1990 at the kitchen table of a farmhouse near Charlotte, North Carolina, by a small group of Russian and American business and professional people whose motivation was "humanitarian, practical and spiritual." During its first year FIPE facilitated the exchange of more than 100 professionals and students between the NIS and U.S., with a focus on people with medical and paramedical specialties, particularly in Russia and Ukraine.

FIPE also operates a Parish Partnership Project (PPP) which is designed to do in church relationships what the organization does in the medical field. Several FIPE directors are Episcopalians, and they have built on a history of exchanges between leaders of the Episcopal Church and the Russian Orthodox Church to link congregations in the two churches at the local level.

Through FIPE, linkages exist, for example, between Episcopalians on Long Island and members of the St. Nicholas Russian Orthodox Church in Sablino, and between Episcopalians in a Texas parish and members of St. Paul's Cathedral in Gatchina, Russia.

Each partnership established between Russian Orthodox and Episcopal congregations involves a visit to each other's community by clergy and laypersons on both sides. Out of these exchanges projects emerge which are specific to each partnership. Their common purpose, in the words of FIPE director Jack Wilson, is "to establish and strengthen personal ties between people . . . Although some American congregations do make financial gifts to their NIS partners, such support is neither required nor expected. Love is the medium of exchange."

FIPE has identified a number of Russian Orthodox parishes which would welcome a Partner Parish in the U.S. FIPE also offers to arrange visits between "American and Russian schools and educators, journalists, artists, persons of any business or profession who have an interest in establishing a mutual personal and professional relationship or sharing their expertise." FIPE can arrange all the elements of a full exchange, including: arranging the necessary documents, formal invitations, visas, air and ground transportation, housing, meals, "excellent guides and interpreters," plus special events and activities during the visit.

Foundation for RUSSIAN/AMERICAN Economic Cooperation

1932 First Avenue, Suite 803
Seattle, WA 98101
Tel: (206) 443-1935
Fax: (206) 443-0954
E-mail: fraec@u.washington.edu
Contact: Carol Vipperman, President; Chris Davis, Executive Director

The Foundation for RUSSIAN/ AMERICAN Economic Cooperation is a nonprofit membership organization representing more than 130 businesses in the U.S., primarily in the Pacific Northwest. The Foundation's programs seek to assist U.S. organizations working in the Russian business environment and to promote the long term goal of improved economic cooperation between the U.S. and Russia.

The Foundation can assist American businesses in finding potential Russian partners, or in locating investment opportunities in Russia. It maintains an extensive library of information on economic trends in Russia, and provides members access to a database of Russian business opportunities and Northwest firms active in the former Soviet Union (FSU). It is developing an electronic bulletin board for members that will allow them to share with one another the latest information on business opportunities, governmental developments, accommodations, etc.

The Foundation publishes the *Russian Business Journal*, which includes information from 130 newspapers and independent publications in the FSU, and *Foundation News*, the organizational newsletter featuring current information on trade issues, legislation and information on doing business in Russia.

The Foundation regularly sponsors seminars, forums and speakers on topics of interest to those doing business in Russia, especially the Russian Far East.

Freedom House

120 Wall Street
New York, NY 10005
Tel: (212) 514-8040
Fax: (212) 514-8050
Contact: Barbara Futterman

Freedom House (FH) was founded in 1941 by Eleanor Roosevelt and Wendell Wilkie, and is a nonpartisan, nonprofit human rights organization dedicated to promoting political rights and civil liberties internationally. FH monitors human rights around the world, organizes programs to strengthen democratic institutions in the U.S. and abroad, and advocates an engaged American foreign policy.

FH maintains several civil-society-building programs in the NIS. The Free Society Project broadcasts Western documentaries (dubbed into Russian) on politics, economics and history to the NIS, and sponsors follow-up panel discussions featuring prominent political, media and academic figures. FH is assisting in the development of the Sakharov Archives in Moscow. It conducted a voter awareness program prior to the March 1994 parliamentary elections in Ukraine. FH is also carrying on a major study of democracy-building indicators in CEE and the NIS.

Friends of Buryat Religion and Culture (FABRIC)

545 E. 11th, #16
Anchorage, AK 99501
Tel: (907) 274-3144
E-mail: angah1@orion.alaska.edu
Contact: Dharm Hall, President; Tatiana Hall, Vice-President; Denise Halliday, Board Member

Since its founding in 1993 as a nonprofit Alaska corporation, FABRIC has supported the renaissance of indigenous culture in the Lake Baikal region. Buryat authors, potters, choreographers, and other artists continue to develop their various art forms, and FABRIC is an attempt to keep in touch with them and raise funds for them. FABRIC has organized fundraising and educational events to support their work. It is a volunteer organization, and all donations go directly to cultural work in the region.

Friends House Moscow

East-West Relations Committee
1163 Auburn Drive
Davis, CA 95616
Tel: (916) 753-6826
E-mail: theharlow@aol.com
Contact: Julie Harlow

FHM is an initiative of Friends (members of the Religious Society of Friends) worldwide which "seeks to encourage [in Russia] spiritual growth and the development of a civil society based on mutual trust and community cooperation." FHM has hired interim staff and leased an apartment in Moscow which will provide space for the gatherings of people interested in Quakerism and Quaker projects. A long-term goal of FHM is to build a Meeting House for the "Moscow Religious Unit of Quakers," as the group is formally called.

Friendship Force

2706 Foster Ridge Road
Atlanta, GA 30345
Tel: (404) 522-9490
Fax: (404) 688-6148
Contact: Ms. Sandra Mullins

FF promotes Citizen Ambassador exchanges and homestays in the NIS.

Fund for Democracy and Development

1001 15th Street NW, Suite 1004
Washington DC 20005
Tel: (202) 296-5353
Fax: (202) 296-5433
E-mail: 5628502@mcimail.com
          fdd@igc.apc.org

Contact: Lewis Townsend, Executive Director

Founded in 1991 by prominent members of the U.S. public and private sector, FDD works "to aid the economic and political transformation of the NIS ...to democratic market economies." Initially FDD managed a project, funded by the U.S. State Department, which shipped more than 9,000 containers of donated materials to 300 cities in the NIS. It has also distributed food aid in Russia and heating supplies in Armenia and Georgia.

In May 1994 FDD established the New Russian Small Business Investment Fund which extends loans to small and medium-sized businesses on reasonable terms. The initial funds came from the sale of commodities from the U.S. Agriculture Department. FDD also organizes training programs in Moscow and St. Petersburg for bankers who manage portfolios of loans to small businesses.

In 1995 FDD was selected as the Siberian-area coordinator of Save' the Children's Civic Initiatives Program. FDD will provide training, technical assistance and consultation to NGOs in the region. FDD maintains offices in Moscow and Novosibirsk, Yerevan, and Tbilisi.

Global Jewish Assistance and Relief Network

1485 Union Street
Brooklyn, NY 11213
Tel: (718) 774-6497
Fax: (718) 774-6891
666 Fifth Avenue, Suite 246
New York, NY 10103
Tel: (212) 868-3636
Fax: (212) 868-7878

Contact: Rabbi Eliezer Avtzon, Executive Director

Global Jewish Assistance and Relief Network (GJARN) was established in February 1992 as a non-sectarian, humanitarian relief organization. Working with partner organizations such as Chernobyl Union, Red Cross, and Miroslava (a women's group), GJARN has not only provided food and medical relief services, but also instituted training and organizational development programs for NGOs in Belarus, Russia, and Ukraine.

GJARN has offices in St. Petersburg, Russia, Kharkiv and Dnepropetrovsk, Ukraine, and Riga, Latvia. It has trained over 75 local NGOs in areas such as accounting and bookkeeping, databases, networking, lobbying, advocacy, grant writing and proposal preparation, mission defining and institutional programming.

GJARN has founded two associations of regional grassroots organizations in Dnepropetrovsk and Kharkiv, and established an NGO Service Center in the latter city.

A GJARN-sponsored "Meals on Wheels" program in Moscow, funded by Russian businessmen and staffed entirely by volunteers from the com-munity, serves 4000 meals per week. Similar programs in Riga, Vilnius and St. Petersburg serve meals to several hundred elderly and invalid people a week. GJARN has created social centers and soup kitchens for pension-ers in several cities and its Doctor House-Call program in Moscow, Kharkiv, and Dniepropetrovsk has hired Russian and Ukrainian physicians who make up to 200 house calls a month.

GJARN distributes USDA surplus food in Belarus, Moldova and Ukraine, and also provides humanitarian relief in each of the Central Asian republics.

GJARN is also establishing an Emergency Response Program dedicated to responding quickly and effectively to "emergency situations that affect the lives of people throughout the world wherever and whenever the call comes through." It is developing a volunteer database of doctors prepared to be on call in case of emergency.

Golubka–USA

c/o Tides Foundation
1388 Sutter Street
San Francisco, CA 94109
E-mail: gwarner@igc.apc.org

Golubka publishes materials and conducts workshops in the NIS on methods of nonviolence, interethnic dialogue, democratic leadership, and "deep ecology." It has an office in Moscow.

Global Volunteers

375 E. Little Canada Road
St. Paul, MN 55117-1628
Tel: (800) 487-1074
Fax: (612) 482-0915
Contact: Michele Gran

Founded in 1984 with the goal of "building a foundation for peace through mutual international understanding," Global Volunteers sends some 100 teams of North American volunteers each year to work on human and economic development projects in 13 countries. Projects originate from the invitation of a local host organization and volunteers work alongside local people under the direction of local leaders. Volunteers pay all program and travel costs for these one-, two- and three-week programs.

Global Volunteers sponsors an English-teaching program in Ryazan, Russia and Poland, working there with Rural Solidarity. In Russia, Poland and Ukraine, it also sponsors one- and two-week seminars oriented to business managers, entrepreneurs and students in these countries. Program costs, exclusive of air fare, are $1,825 for the English-language program in Poland; $1,995 for the English-language program in Russia; and $2,350 for the business program (in all three countries).

Goodwill Industries International, Inc.

9200 Wisconsin Avenue
Bethesda, Maryland 20814
Tel: (301) 530-6500
Fax: (301) 530-1516
E-mail: internat@goodwill.org
             mjordan@clark.net
Contact: Elizabeth Scott, Director, International Programs Office; Melissa Jordan, Grant Manager

Founded in 1912 by Edgar J. Helms, a Methodist minister in Boston, Goodwill Industries International, Inc. (GII) has evolved into a federation of more than 184 autonomous, community-based organizations in the United States and Canada with a growing network of 52 overseas associate members located in 37 countries outside North America.

Goodwill "strives to achieve full participation in society of people with disabilities and other individuals with special needs by expanding their opportunities and occupational capabilities." To achieve this goal, Goodwill trains people with disabilities and vocational disadvantages, such as illiteracy, a history of criminal behavior, or a lack of work experience to meet labor needs of the community. Goodwill provides four

vocational services: (a) vocational evaluation, (b) vocational adjustment, (c) development of job-seeking skills and placement, and (d) transitional employment for those who cannot be competitive in the labor market in the short term.

Since 1989, private and governmental agencies in Eastern Europe and the NIS have requested direct assistance from GII in creating domestic Goodwill-style programs. Current Goodwill organizations exist in the Czech Republic, Hungary, Poland, Russia and Ukraine, with initiatives underway to establish additional Goodwill programs in Russia, as well as in Kazakstan, Kyrgyzstan, and Uzbekistan.

A key element in GII's international growth is its International Partnership Program, which matches North American Goodwill organizations with counterparts overseas. Partnerships encompass trade and informational exchanges, consultancy visits by North American executives and staff to overseas locations, and internships for overseas Goodwill staffers at American Goodwills. In addition, the corporate headquarters in Bethesda, Maryland host dozens of government officials and other leaders from Central Europe and the NIS, many of whom returned home to plant seeds for training centers based on the Goodwill model.

With a $250,000 grant from USAID through World Learning, Inc., Goodwill provided supplies, equipment, and consultant support to Russian colleagues in Moscow, Rybinsk, and St. Petersburg. The grant was designed around a two-year plan, with the first year dedicated to the establishment of Goodwill retail programs and the second year to building rehabilitation programs. In June 1995, the grant was extended so that GII could continue its efforts to assist Russian PVOs in service delivery to vulnerable populations.

Goodwill is currently examining potential programs in Vladivostok, Vladimir, Novosibirsk, and Irkutsk. An intern, Viktor Kharchenko of the All-Russia Society of the Disabled of Vladivostok, trained at the Portland, Oregon Goodwill in the fall of 1995.

In 1994 GII received a USAID grant for $300,000, administered by the COUNTERPART Foundation, to plan for and establish Goodwill organizations in Tashkent, Bishkek and Almaty. By late 1995, the first Central Asian Goodwill was registered in Tashkent under the guidance of Goodwill SABIT internship graduate, Bakhadir Rasulov, and with the help of Goodwill partner, James McClelland, President of the Indianapolis Goodwill.

GII is a founding member of the U.S. Council in International Rehabilitation and a member of Rehabilitation International.

Hudson Institute–Center for Central European and Eurasian Studies

5395 Emerson Way
Indianapolis, IN 46226
Tel: (317) 549-4159
Fax: (317) 545-9639
E-mail: jclark@hudson.org
Contact: John Clark

Indianapolis-based Hudson Institute's Public Policy Research Institute (PPRI) program started in mid-1993 with a grant from Pew Charitable Trusts to help organize and support "think tanks" in Lithuania, Latvia and Estonia. It now works with more than 30 think tanks and university-based research institutes in the Baltic countries, Poland, Slovakia, the Czech Republic,

Ukraine, Belarus, Russia and Kyrgyzstan. Hudson's partners span a broad ideological spectrum and range of concerns–foreign affairs, environmental issues, etc.–but all aspire to being viable and autonomous centers within their nations of high quality research, analysis, and independent thinking on issues of public policy.

The Hudson program has the following major components:
• Institutional consultation. This can involve not only financial assistance but also, for example, doing an analysis of a partner's research, strategic planning, fundraising, and public outreach programs . . . and proposing improvements.
• "Learning by Doing Together." Hudson has entered into joint research projects with think tanks in each of the three Baltic countries, on the theory that practical experience often best illuminates differences in approach to research design, proposal preparation, project managment and public outreach. Research topics have included how to defuse ethnic tensions in Estonia and tax and social policies in Lithuania.
• Education and Training Programs. These have been among the most successful of Hudson's programs. Senior executive officers as well as middle-level management of public policy research institutes overseas have been brought to the U.S. for two week sessions which offer intensive training at Hudson in the various skills needed to sustain a viable PPRI.
• Focus on Fundraising. Since this is so central to the long-term success and autonomy of a PPRI, Hudson has given special emphasis to this area. Besides organizing various forms of training in fundraising, Hudson has also helped

partners prepare multi-year development plans; devise strategies for tapping the emigre communities abroad; and gain access to the international business community.

Human Rights Society of Uzbekistan

1819 H Street NW, Suite 230
Washington DC 20006
Tel: (202) 775-9776
Fax: (202) 775-9770
E-mail: 4201773@mcimail.com
Contact: Dr. Abdoumannov Poulatov, Chairman

This organization shares offices with the Union of Councils for Soviet Jews, of which it is an affiliate.

Infoshare International

743 Addison Street, Suite A
Berkeley, CA 94710
Tel: (510) 204-9099
Fax: (510) 843-4066
E-mail: Infoshare1@aol.com
Contact: Julie Stachowiak, Executive Director

This organization was formed in October 1993 under the name AIDS Infoshare Russia. They work in conjunction with their Moscow office to provide Russian individuals and organizations with the tools that they need to fight HIV/AIDS and STDs. Current emphasis is on the provision of HIV/AIDS information, human rights and public health, and NGO technical support. Infoshare's work is primarily in Russia where they help to distribute–through Russia AIDS Relief, an HIV support program they developed–food, clothing, and medications to over 250 people affected by HIV/AIDS.

Infoshare International has established a library devoted to HIV/AIDS and STDs, and they develop and publish pamphlets for the public on these issues. They have also established SPIDNET, an electronic mail conference for information in Russian on HIV/AIDS and STDs; created an electronic database, containing information on individuals and institutions working in the fields of HIV/AIDS; conducted three seminars on NGO Management and Development for NGOs working in the field of HIV/AIDS; and conducted several outreach events.

See "AIDS Infoshare Russia" in *Russia: West of the Urals* for more information on the Moscow office.

Institute for Sustainable Communities

56 College Street
Montpelier, VT 05602
Tel: (802) 229-2900
Fax: (802) 229-2919
E-mail: isc@iscvt.org
Contact: George Hamilton, Executive Director

ISC promotes "environmental protection, sustainable economies, and participatory decision-making at the community level" in Central/Eastern Europe and Eurasia through training, technical assistance and demonstration projects. The idea for ISC was born in 1990 in Bulgaria, when Vermont Governor Madeleine Kunin and her policy director, George Hamilton, observed that country's first free elections in more than 40 years. "Glimpsing the Bulgarians' enthusiasm for reform, the importance of their environmental movement in helping to overthrow authoritarian rule, and the enormous problems that their new society would face," Kunin and Hamilton decided to found ISC.

ISC is managing a comprehensive three-year environmental project in partnership with the U.S. Environ-mental Protection Agency and several Russian organizations. More than 4,700 sources of pollution have been identified in Nizhnii Tagil, which a health study of 81 Russian cities recently ranked as first in carcinogenic diseases, third in respiratory diseases, and ninth in skin diseases. In a separate analysis of congenital diseases among children, Nizhnii Tagil ranked first for 27 of 60 disease indicators.

ISC's work focuses on three major tasks:
• Setting Priorities for Action. This involves among other things, the formation of a city-wide committee appointed by the mayor, to identify Nizhnii Tagil's most urgent problems.
• Spreading Environmental Education. This has involved intensive work with the city Teachers' Training College.
• Strengthening Institutions and Replicating Results. This has included forming a Center for Environmental Training and Information in nearby Ekaterinburg and promoting a sister city relationship between Chattanooga, TN, and Nizhnii Tagil. (Chattanooga, once a heavily polluted iron and steel town, succeeded in overcoming many of its environmental problems.)

In 1995 ISC created the Eurasia Pro-gram to combine its efforts in this city with new projects in Volgograd and in Ukraine. In Volgograd, ISC is working with EPA on its Russian Air Manage-ment Project or RAMP. ISC is assist-ing with the establishment of a locally-managed Center for Environmental Training that will present both Ameri-can and Russian enviromental man-agement courses to regional environ-mental professionals. Also in Vol-gograd, ISC is coordinating a public participation project to increase public involvement with RAMP component activities. With ISC assistance, the city has established a diverse Public Partici-pation Taskforce which will award small-grant funding to organizations to initiate participatory public activities.

In Ukraine, ISC is managing a USEPA sponsored environmental pub-lic awareness project called the Eco-logical Television and Public Aware-ness Project of Ukraine. This project supports the creation of an Ecological Television Centre, and will also provide small grant funding for environmental public awareness activities in in three regional/topic areas: Donbass region, Dnipro River and biodiversity.

The organization has produced and translated more than 30 documents, including resource guides, training materials and technical reports. ISC has an office in Moscow and a repre-sentative in Volgograd.

International Center for Community Journalism
815 Fifth Avenue
PO Box 226
Grinnell, IA 50112
Tel: (515) 236-3072
Fax: (515) 236-0019
E-mail: iccj@ac.grin.edu
Contact: Robert Anderson, President

Since 1993, the ICCJ has brought more than 30 Ukrainian journalists to America under grants from the United States Information Agency. Working with the University of Iowa's School of Journalism and Mass Communications, as well as newspapers and broadcast organizations in the Midwest, ICCJ has arranged programs of homestays and internships that provide the Ukrain-ian visitors with insights into American journalism, particularly as it is practiced in rural areas.

As President Bob Anderson points out, visiting journalists learn from their internships how newspapers both operate as profitable business ventures in rural American communities and remain accountable to those communities–rather than to special interests, political or other.

Besides bringing Ukrainian professionals to the U.S., ICCJ organizes workshops in Ukraine led by American journalists together with some of the Ukrainian veterans of exchanges. These workshops have been held in Kyiv, Odessa, Lviv and Cherkassy. In the last two cities, ICCJ also hopes to establish independent journalism centers in order to cement permanent relationships.

Much of ICCJ's work has focused on Ukraine, but exchanges have also been carried out with Bulgarians, Georgians, Mongolians, Chinese and Thais.

International Center for Not-for-Profit Law

1511 K Street NW, Suite 723
Washington, DC 20005
Tel: (202) 624-0766
Fax: (202) 624-0767
E-mail: dcinl@aol.com
Contact: Karla W. Simon, Executive Director

The International Center for Not-for-Profit Law (ICNL) was registered in the summer of 1993. Its purpose is to "assist the creation and improvement of laws and regulatory systems that permit, encourage and regulate the voluntary, independent, not-for-profit sector in countries around the world." Together with other local and international organizations, ICNL provides technical assistance for writing laws and regulations that will enable the growth of

a "vital, yet accountable and sensibly regulated, independent sector."

Technical assistance projects coordinated by ICNL are staffed by lawyers and other experts who volunteer their time. ICNL provides preparatory materials, in-country support and follow-through. Airfare and out-of-pocket expenses are reimbursed when a project requires travel, and modest stipends may be available in some circumstances.

ICNL enjoys strong in-country relationships with governmental authorities, parliamentarians, NGOs, lawyers and academics. Working from this base of contacts, ICNL conducts training on issues related to the regulation of the not-for-profit sector; sponsors and conducts research; and organizes conferences and workshops in different regions of the world.

A major research effort of ICNL is the Blueprints Project, which seeks to define the kinds of problems that arise in drafting laws for the not-for-profit sector and to develop options for addressing these problems. This project provides support for legal drafting in many countries in addition to serving as the focus of a series of regional con-ferences for legal experts, government officials and NGO leaders whose principal concerns deal with the development of the regulatory environment in which civil society exists. "Regulating Civil Society," a report to emerge from one such regional conference held in Sinaia, Romania, in 1994, is available from ICNL.

With a regional office in Warsaw, ICNL is active in Central and Eastern Europe as well as the NIS. Among the latter countries, it has projects in all the Baltic states, Georgia, Ukraine, Russia, Kazakstan and Kyrgyzstan.

International Executive Service Corps

PO Box 10005
Stamford, CT 06904-2005
Tel: (203) 967-6000
Fax: (203) 359-3233
Telex: 413874
E-mail: nisiesc@well.sf.ca.us
Contact: Fred Hudson, Vice President, New Independent States

Since its founding in 1964, the International Executive Service Corps (IESC) has helped place volunteer American business executives on technical assistance projects in over 90 countries around the world. IESC maintains a database of 14,000 retired executives who can be matched with requests for assistance from overseas client companies, governments and organizations. In 1994, for example, more than 1,200 volunteer technical and managerial assistance projects were completed worldwide.

In the NIS, IESC Volunteer Executives (VE's) are used in technical assistance projects, business planning workshops, industry restructuring projects and public administration seminars. VE's develop and implement training programs with government officials, work with former defense industry enterprises making the transition to market economies and assist companies to develop viable business plans to attract U.S. partners and/or sources of financing. Since the NIS program's inception in 1992, IESC has sent over 480 VE's to the NIS, providing volunteer service to more than 1,000 enterprises. In addition to its overseas personnel, IESC maintains a full-time U.S. staff to provide support and follow-up services for NIS client companies and organizations. As an example of its impact, IESC, with funding from the Department of Defense and USAID, assisted a Kazakstani scientist/entrepreneur in creating a joint venture firm. The new company, which was awarded $5 million in Nunn-Lugar funds, converted a missile tracking site into an international teleport.

The average length of stay for a technical assistance volunteer in the NIS is two months. IESC covers travel and living expenses as well as spouse accompaniment for projects over 28 days. IESC currently has 18 offices in nine locations throughout the NIS.

International Foreign Policy Association

The Presidio
PO Box 29434
San Francisco, CA 94129
Tel: (415) 771-4567
Contact: Amy Vossbrinck, Project Director

The IFPA with Moscow State University and Tbilisi Business School and the Georgian Management Training Program Alumni Association received a grant to support a program to develop training materials and a training program in Alternative Dispute Resolution. The focus will be on the issues involving labor-management relations and commercial and contracting disputes and will encourage interaction between government officials and small business entrepreneurs between the two republics.

International Foundation for Electoral Systems

1101 15th Street NW, 3rd floor
Washington DC 20005
Tel: (202) 828-8507
Fax: (202) 452-0804
Contact: Richard Soudriette, Director

IFES was established in 1987 to "support electoral and other democratic institutions in emerging, evolving, and experienced democracies." It has worked in more than 80 countries providing pre-election technical assessments, on-site technical support, training of election workers, voter and civic education, and election observation. In 1989 IFES began work in Eastern Europe and the NIS, where it played a key role in the establishment of the Association of Central/Eastern European Election Officials.

In 1989 IFES established a relationship with the Central Election Commission of the Soviet Union. It has produced a training manual for pollworkers in Russia and has developed a curriculum for first-time voters that will be introduced into the Russian secondary school system. In Ukraine, IFES has provided technical assistance to the Central Election Commission and Ukraine's parliament. IFES also has on-going projects in Moldova, Kazakstan and Kyrgyzstan to provide support to legislators as they shape electoral laws and prepare information about democracy, voting procedures, and a pluralist society.

IFES has offices in Moscow, Kyiv Chisinau, and Almaty, where it has established a Democracy and Education Training Center.

International League for Human Rights

432 Park Avenue South
New York, NY 10016
or
325 Pennsylvania Avenue, SE
Washington, DC 20003
Tel: (202) 544-2699
Fax: (202) 546-6589
E-mail: lightman@cais.com

Contact: Ms. Marjorie Lightman, Special Consultant for Women's Projects

ILHR is a member of the NIS-US Women's Consortium. The organization prefers not to receive faxes; please communicate by mail or e-mail.

International Network for Women in Enterprise and Trade (INET)

Adeena Corporation
1111 Jefferson Davis Hwy, Suite 704
Arlington, VA 22202-4306
Tel: (703) 413-4111
Fax (703) 413-4117
E-mail: gayla_salinas@adeena.com
Contact: Ms. Gayla Salinas
or
400 W. 119th Street, apt. 14U
New York, NY 10027-7108
Tel: (212) 799-6628
Contact: Ms. Ann-Marie Karl, International Attorney

INET promotes the establishment of libraries and resource centers for women in enterprise, trade and business, NGO development, coalition development, and networking.

International Republican Institute

1212 New York Avenue NW, Suite 900
Washington, DC 20005
Tel: (202) 408-9450
Fax: (202) 408-9462
Telex: 5106000161 (IRI)
E-mail: iri@iri.org
Contact: Judy Van Rast, Director of CIS Programs

IRI began its efforts in 1984, following Congressional authorization of the National Endowment for Democracy, the umbrella organization for the IRI (as well as the National Democratic

Institute for International Affairs, the Free Trade Union Institute and the Center for International Private Enterprise). It has 11 field offices around the world, eight of which are in Central and Eastern Europe (CEE) and the NIS. In 1995, almost one-third of IRI's annual budget was targeted for programs in the NIS, with CEE receiving the second largest share of funding.

Two-thirds of IRI's programs involve training political parties abroad, based on the conviction that political parties are "an essential outlet for non-violent political expression in a society." IRI trains political parties in campaign and organizational techniques, and works to increase the participation of disenfranchised groups–women, youth and indigenous peoples–in the political process. Other activities include civic education, election administration assistance, institution building, rule of law programs, and economic programs.

In the NIS, IRI's focus is on Russia and Ukraine. In Russia, IRI has a four-part program designed to improve the ability of national and local legislators to govern, strengthen democratic political parties and improve their campaign skills, and ensure the integration of women and young adults into the demo-cratic process. Its political education efforts are conducted in just six regions across Russia in order to concentrate its efforts more effectively.

IRI brings volunteer political experts to Russia for intensive training sessions on basic political skills, and teaches a core group of Russian activists to conduct their own training activities. It has also provided material assistance in the form of typewriters, computers, fax machines and other supplies. Since 1993, IRI has conducted conferences

geared toward involving women in the political process.

In Ukraine, IRI is working to improve the governance skills of democratic legislators and the campaign skills of democratic political parties. It opened its Kyiv office in April 1993 and has been active since in conducting training seminars, civic education, and election monitoring activities. For the March 1994 parliamentary elections, IRI printed and disseminated 10,000 copies of its Poll Watcher Training Manuals throughout the country, and held poll watcher training seminars in Kyiv, Kharkiv, Donetsk, Dnipropetrovsk, Odessa, Lviv, Zhytomyr and Vinnytsia.

International Science Foundation

1054 31st Street NW, Suite 110
Washington, DC 20007
Tel: (202) 342-2760
Fax: (202) 342-2765
E-mail: info@isf.org
URL: http://www.soros.org/isf.html
Contact: Dr. Gerson S. Sher, Chief Operating Officer
or
455 First Avenue, Room 1202
New York, NY 10016
Tel: (212) 576-8450
E-mail: info@phri.nyu.edu
Contact: Alex Goldfarb, Special Advisor

A member of the Soros Foundations family, the International Science Foundation was founded in December 1992 to enable scientists in the former USSR to continue working during the economic crisis in the region. ISF has provided emergency grants to more than 20,000 scientists and has supported more than 3,500 long-term research projects.

A major priority of ISF is to provide scientists in the NIS with access to their colleagues in the West. It gives grants for scientists to attend conferences abroad and sponsors delivery of Western scientific journals to more than 350 academic libraries. ISF also provides researchers with access to the Internet and has underwritten major Internet infrastructure projects in Moscow, Novosibirsk, Yaroslavl, and Kyiv.

International Soros Science Education Program

George Mason University
Department of Biology, MS 3EI
Fairfax, VA 22030
Tel: (703) 993-4362
Fax: (703) 993-4093
Contact: Dr. Valery Soyfer, Executive Director

Internews

PO Box 4448
Arcata, CA 95518
Tel: (707) 826-2030
Fax: (707) 826-2136
Contact: Kim Spencer, Project Director

Internews was founded in 1982 to "support the independent broadcast media in the former Soviet Union and other parts of the world through training programs and equipment grants." The organization has offices in New York, Washington, DC, San Francisco, Moscow and Kyiv. Internews is managing a $10 million, 3-year grants program for USAID known as RAMP (Russian-American Media Partnerships). Grants ranging from $20K to $300K are being awarded to partnerships that strengthen nongovernmental Russian media, print and broadcast. For more information on Internews's work in Russia, see their entry under

Moscow in the section *Russia: West of the Urals.*

IRIS
Institutional Reform and the Informal Sector

2105 Morrill Hall
University of Maryland
College Park, MD 20742
Tel: (301) 405-0117
Fax: (301) 405-3020
E-mail: adam@iris.econ. umd.edu
Contact: Mancur Olson, Principal Investigator; Adam Korengold, Project Coordinator

IRIS was launched in 1990 with funding from USAID not only "to examine specific practical problems of institutional reform . . . but also [to] attempt to provide a better theory of institutions, so that institutional reforms can be guided by a sound general understanding of how institutions affect economic performance." IRIS works with the Moscow Institute for the Economy in Transition to promote research by young Russian economists. It has also worked with drafters of the Russian Federation's new civil code in the development of this important legislation.

IRIS publishes a quarterly newsletter, *Update.* It has representatives in Moscow, Kyiv and Yerevan.

Junior Achievement International

2780 Janitell Road
Colorado Springs, CO 80906
Tel: (719) 540-0200 or 540-2254
Fax: (719) 540-8770
E-mail: 74511.1535@compuserve.com
Contact: Sam Taylor, Chief Operating Officer; David Loose, Director of Operations

Founded in 1919 in the U.S., JA claims to be "the world's oldest, largest and fastest-growing nonprofit economic education organization." Each year, more than 2.3 million primary, secondary and university students in 85 countries take part in Junior Achievement programs. Junior Achievement International (JAI) is responsible for developing and serving Junior Achievement programs outside the U.S.

In 1991, Junior Achievement established its first program in the former Soviet Union with the launching of Junior Achievement of Russia. With the support of organizations such as USAID and multinational corporations, Junior Achievement of Russia has established regional centers throughout the country. In 1995, 180,000 Russian high school students will take part in Junior Achievement programs.

Junior Achievement programs have also been established in the Baltic states, Belarus, Kazakstan, and Moldova–with pilot projects under way in most of the remaining nations of the NIS.

Lawyers Alliance for World Security

1601 Connecticut Avenue NW Suite 600
Washington, DC 20009-1035
Tel: (202) 745-2450
Fax: (202) 667-0444
E-mail: 41263.401@compuserve.com
Contact: John Parachini, Executive Director

The Lawyers Alliance for World Security (LAWS) organizes seminars and ex-changes of lawyers, former government officials and legal professionals relating to issues of non-proliferation and rule of law in the NIS. U.S. participants meet with executive branch and legal officials, members of the defense industry and related NGOs to discuss ways to reduce the threat of nuclear war and military confrontation through the development of effective legislation and policy.

In cooperation with former U.S. senior officials and legal experts, LAWS conducts the Lawmaking for Security Project to promote arms trade regulations and export controls in the NIS. Through workshops, publications and exchanges, the project provides legal training for NIS executive and legislative officials, the business community and NGOs.

LAWS encourages those with considerable experience in the field of national security, the defense industry or export regulation law to participate in their workshops and seminars.

League of Women Voters

1730 M Street NW
Washington, DC 20036
Tel: (202) 429-1965
Fax: (202) 429-0854
E-mail: 75352.2612@compuserve.com (Tamches);
76735.277@compuserve.com (Davis);
73041.3624@compuserve.com
Contact: Ms. Orna Tamches, Ms. Kendra Davis, Project Manager for NIS

LWV recently received a grant to work with the Moscow Center for Gender-Studies and the Ukrainian Center for Women's Studies to bring Russian and Ukrainian women to the United States in order to gain firsthand experience with the role of citizens in local governance and democratic action. Another grant will have the League focus on women's NGOs in the legal reform process in Russia.

Legacy International

128 N. Fayette Street
Alexandria, VA 22314-2902
Tel: (703) 549-3630
Fax: (703) 549-0262
E-mail: legacy@igc.apc.org
Contact: Dr. Ira Kaufman, Executive
Director

Founded in 1979 and affiliated with the
United Nations Department of Public
Information as a Non-Governmental
Organization, Legacy promotes
"sustainable development"; peaceful
resolutions to ethnic, social, and
religious conflicts; and experiential
leadership training.

Currently Legacy is working to
develop "sustainable tourism" in
Central Asia. Legacy also has a
program in the U.S. designed to teach
business and tourism industry skills to
Central Asian students.

Magee Womancare International

c/o Magee-Womens Hospital
300 Halket Street, PO Box 144
Pittsburgh, PA 15213-3180
Tel: (412) 641-4010/4971
Fax: (412) 641-4949
E-mail:
admtmk%msmail{magee/admin/admtm
k}@mhs.magee.edu
Contact: Irma Goertzen, President and
CEO; Tanya M. Kotys, Director

Magee is the obstetrics and gynecology
teaching hospital of the University of
Pittsburgh School of Medicine and a
national leader in both research and the
delivery of "family-centered maternity
care." Since March 1992, Savior's
Hospital for Peace and Charity,
formerly Moscow Municipal Hospital
#70, has been partnered with Magee-
Womens Hospital in a project

supported by USAID in collaboration
with the American International Health
Alliance (AIHA), the Moscow
Municipal Health Administration, as
well as private individual and corporate
donors. (Magee-Womens Hospital is
one of 24 American hospitals
participating in the AIHA program in
the NIS.)

Over the past three years the Magee-
Savior's partnership has:
• opened a Woman and Family Center
(July 1993), presently seeing an average
of 400 Russian women a week from
Moscow and two outlying rural areas;
the Center also teaches more than 1,000
students each month in cooperation
with the Moscow school system;
• started a Woman and Family Planning Clinic (June 1994), "the first low-
cost, high-quality family planning clinic
in the eastern region of Moscow," with
the goal of seeing 5,000 individuals a
year;
• produced and distributed a variety of
educational materials: brochures on
family planning; conception; women's
health; a pregnancy guide and calendar;
breast self-exam cards; and two videos,
titled "Puberty" and "You and Your
New Baby;"
• legally registered the Woman and
Family Foundation, the first nongov-
ernment fundraising arm associated
with a Russian hospital;
• organized numerous collaborations–
professional exchanges, clinical training, conferences, etc.–involving hundreds of Russian health care professionals, to share new technologies and
approaches to different models for education and administration.

Magee-Savior's Birth House, a
jointly administered and staffed prenatal maternity center and teaching clinic,
opened in 1995 after undergoing reno-

vation. Its goal: 3,000 births and 350 Russian obstetricians trained annually.

Also in the implementation phase: the Rural Outreach to Russia Project–a two-year program which will result in a network of 24 independent women's health education centers throughout Russia. 12 have been established thus far.

MiraMed Institute
3255 10th Avenue West
Seattle, WA 98109
Tel: (206) 632-5444
(206) 282-2131
Fax: (206) 285-8216
Contact: Dr. Juliette Engel, MD

MiraMed focuses on health care of women and infants, technology transfer, and medical training programs.

Monterey Institute of International Studies
425 Van Buren Street
Monterey, CA 93940
Tel: (408) 647-3511
Fax: (408) 647-3519
E-mail: wpotter@miis.edu
Contact: Dr. William C. Potter

The Monitoring CIS Environmental Developments (MCISED) Project at the Monterey Institute of International Studies (MIIS) functions as a clearinghouse for information relating to environmental and nuclear safety concerns in the former Soviet Union (FSU).

MCISED publishes the *CIS Environmental Watch* which abstracts Russian-, Ukrainian- and English-language articles and documents. The MCISED Project in conjuction with the MIIS Center for Nonproliferation Studies, maintains the CIS Nuclear Database which is the most compre-

hensive open-source collection of information on nuclear proliferation and nuclear safety in the NIS.

MIIS is currently focusing on nuclear proliferation, nuclear safety, radioactive pollution containment, and export control. It is also developing future projects on water management and pollution issues in Central Asia.

NAFSA: Association of International Educators
Russian & Eurasian Awards Program
1875 Connecticut Avenue NW, Suite 1000
Washington, DC   20009-5728
Tel: (202) 462-4811
Fax: (202) 667-3419
E-mail: REAP@NAFSA.org
Contact: Chris Powers, Program Officer

With funding from USIA, NAFSA administers the Russian & Eurasian Awards Program (REAP), providing supplementary grants of up to $10,000 per student to U.S. institutions on behalf of qualified students from Armenia, Azerbaijan, Belarus, Georgia, Kazakstan, Kyrgyzstan, Moldova, Russia, Tajikistan, Turkmenistan, Ukraine and Uzbekistan. Cost-sharing by the U.S. institution is expected, generally in the form of a tuition waiver. Students must be undergraduate juniors or seniors or graduate students, admitted to an accredited U.S. institution.

Currently about 330 students from the NIS with REAP grants are studying in the U.S. A staff of three at NAFSA administers all aspects of the grant.

Eligible fields of study are: public administration, public policy, political science, urban planning, economics, business, marketing, law, education, journalism, social sciences, humanities (excluding the fine arts), library science, English teaching and computer science.

National Academy of Sciences Office for Central Europe and Eurasia

2101 Constitution Avenue NW
Washington DC 20418
Tel: (202) 334-3680
Fax: (202) 334-2614

The NAS administers three programs in the NIS.

The Radioactive Waste Management Program is funded by the U.S. Department of Energy, and supports American specialists who wish to host colleagues from the NIS to conduct rsearch on radioactive waste management. Grants are awarded in several areas.

The Collaboration in Basic Science and Engineering(COBASE) program was established with the assistance of the National Science Foundation to support the preparation of short collaborative research proposals for submission to the NSF or other funding organizations, and to support longer visits for research projects.

The Cooperation in Applied Science and Technology (CAST) program established with USAID supports American specialists who wish to host NIS scientists and engineers involved in defense-related research, and help them apply their skills to civilian activities.

National Association of Social Workers

750 First Street NE, Suite 700
Washington, DC 20002-4241
Tel: (202) 336-8234
Fax: (202) 336-8311
E-mail: ekelly@capcom.net

Contact: Eileen McGowan Kelly

The National Association of Social Workers (NASW) has programs to enhance the effectivness of NGOs working in the social service sector in the NIS. This includes developing a stronger, more effective professional organization of social workers in Russia, improving institutional and managerial capabilities, and improving communication and information sharing. The communities targeted include Tuva, Yakutia, Mary El, Taymyr, Komi and Stavropol.

National Council for Research on Women

530 Broadway, 10th Floor
New York, NY 10012-3920
Tel: (212) 274-0730
Fax: (212) 274-0821
Contact: Ms. Mariam Chamberlain

NCRW conducts research on women's rights and the status of women. It is a member of the NIS-U.S. Women's Consortium.

National Democratic Institute for International Affairs (NDI)

1717 Massachusetts Avenue NW
Fifth Floor
Washington, DC 20036
Tel: (202) 328-3136
Fax: (202) 939-3166
Telex: 5106015068NDIIA
E-mail: 5979039@mcimail.com
Contact: Ambassador Nelson Ledsky, Senior Associate and Regional Director, Former Soviet Union Program; Karen Clark, Deputy Regional Director, Former Soviet Union Program

NDI was founded in 1983, and is affiliated with the National Democratic

Party. Like its counterpart, the International Republican Institute, it receives the majority of its funding from the National Endowment for Democracy and USAID. NDI runs seminars and workshops for political parties and civic organizers to help strengthen democratic institutions in the NIS. Programs are geared towards political leaders, civic activists, parliamentarians, officials from all levels of government, journalists, professionals, academics and students. Trainers are usually professional political or parliamentary trainers and civic organizers (special interest group and NGO professionals).

NDI's program activities include: political party training (techniques for organizing, communication with constituencies, etc.); technical assistance for election monitoring; civic education programs; legislative training (staffing, research, committee structuring); city management; civil-military relations; and voter education.

NDI trainers work out of one of NDI's regional offices abroad for anywhere from ten days to over a year. Trainers work with indigenous staff to develop presentations and educational materials for workshops. NDI translates these educational packets into the various NIS languages and makes them available to workshop participants around the NIS.

In addition, NDI arranges programs in the U.S. for civic organizers, political party activists and Parliamentarians. These programs provide on-site ex-perience for activists, elected officials and others in the democratic process as practiced in the U.S. NDI has hosted participants from Russia, Ukraine, Georgia, Azerbaijan and Central Asia.

For NDI program offices in the NIS, please see the individual country listings.

National Forum Foundation

511 C Street NE
Washington, DC 20002
Tel: (202) 543-3515
Fax: (202) 547-4101
E-mail: nff1@aol.com
Contact: Therese Lyons

The National Forum Foundation (NFF) is a nonpartisan, nonprofit organization which, since 1988, has been supporting the political and economic transformation of the emerging democracies of Europe and Asia. The NFF's training programs are characterized by a practical, hands-on and on-site approach. They focus on three areas:
• democratic governance and civil society–the legislative process, rule of law, NGO development, political and campaign organization, coalition building, budgeting, city planning and administration, and public, constituency and media relations;
• journalism and media management– domestic and international economic and business news reporting, media organization, sales and advertising, distribution, budgeting, financial systems and controls; and
• economic development and reform– privatization, banking and finance, securities and anti-monopoly regulation, business management, public-private sector development initiatives, and trade finance.

NFF conducts the Central and Eastern European Internship program, which has provided professional internship training in the U.S. for almost 300 leaders from the former "East Bloc." Participants have worked in the offices of hundreds of federal, state and local elected officials; in political campaigns; for NGOs; at newspapers and television stations; in banks, stock and commodities exchanges; in law firms, regulatory agencies and trade and business associations.

The American Volunteers for International Development (AVID) program, chaired by President Vaclav Havel, sends qualified American managers and experts in government, NGO and public administration, journalism, and finance to requesting host institutions in the region. AVID volunteers serve with minimum financial support for 3-12 months. Since 1993, about 70 participants have provided some 480 months of on-site service. NFF maintains a Volunteer Talent Bank of about 400 registered applicants from which volunteers are drawn.

NFF also conducts several shorter term projects in the region which promote democratic, media and economic reform.

National Institute for Citizen Education in the Law

711 G Street SE
Washington, DC 20003
Tel: (202) 546-6644
Fax: (202) 546-6649
Contact: Richard Ody, Program Coordinator, Edward O'Brien, Co-Director

NICEL works with lawyers, judges, professors and secondary school teachers abroad to develop programs and curricula dealing with citizens' rights under the law, human rights, rule of law and democratic principles. NICEL uses professionals and educators to train secondary school teachers how to incorporate these issues into their curricula.

In most cases, NICEL field offices are run out of local universities. Training sessions are held in the language of the country and the curricula produced from these seminars are translated into several languages and distributed to teachers across the country.

NICEL is currently active in Kazakstan and Hungary, and it is looking to expand programs into other countries of Eastern Europe and the NIS. In Kazakstan, NICEL has been working with law students and faculty of an Almaty law school to develop curricular material for use in secondary schools.

New England Water Environment Association

255 Ballardvale Street
Wilmington, MA 01887
Tel: (508) 658-4048
Fax: (508) 658-5509
Contact: Elizabeth A. Haffner, Executive Director

The New England Water Environment Association (NEWEA) is a member association of the national organization, the Water Environment Federation. While initially the NEWEA focused on water pollution control, its responsibilities today encompass a broad spectrum of water related issues: nonpoint source pollution; wetlands protection; groundwater management; pollution prevention and overall watershed and resource protection; hazardous waste; and international and industrial waste.

NEWEA recently established an International Affairs Committee to encourage the exchange of environmental information and the development of an exchange program for training and assistance. It publishes its own newsletter, *International Activities*. This Committee will develop exchange agreements with universities or environmental organizations in developing countries and countries in transition. The program is currently in development.

NEWEA's activities in the NIS resulted from the participation of the International Affairs Committee Chair Alfred E. Peloquin's participation in the 1991 International Conference on Pollution Abatement in the Volga River Basin. NEWEA has maintained contact with the host organization, *Zelonyi Mir* ("Green World," see *Ukraine* section), and plans future collaborative efforts. NEWEA will provide free technical materials to individuals and/or organizations involved in environmental projects outside of the U.S.

NIS/US Women's Consortium
Winrock International
Global Women's Leadership
Program
1611 N. Kent
Arlington, VA 22209
E-mail: gwlp@msmail.winrock.org
srw@dcmail.winrock.org
Contact: Sheila Scott; Stephanie Weishaar

The NIS/US Women's Consortium was formed by Winrock (see below) with a grant from USAID. The Consortium was formed to encourage and facilitate interaction, cooperation and democratic society in the NIS. Consortium members include 19 Russian women's NGOs, 3 Ukrainian NGOs and 14 U.S. NGOs, with four expert advisers. The consortium is working to strengthen women's voices internationally to overcome unemployment, political disenfrachisement and discrimination through: seed grants to NGO programs; cooperative projects and training in

leadership skills; electronic communications; and policy advocacy.

North American Association for Environmental Educators
1255 23rd Street, NW Suite 400
Washington, DC 20037-1199
Tel: (202) 884-8913
Fax: (202) 884-8701
E-mail: jhaley@igc.apc.org
Contact: Joan Haley

The North American Association for Environmental Education (NAAEE) promotes environmental education and supports the work of environmental educators by organizing conferences, seminars, and courses; publishing research and producing materials to help teach about environmental issues; and undertaking special activities to address gaps in the field. Members include professionals working at univer-sities, NGOs, government agencies, nature centers, zoos, parks, elementary and secondary schools, businesses and other institutions.

Since 1992, with support from EPA, NAAEE has worked with the Environmental Education and Information Center (EEIC) in Kyiv, Ukraine. The Center, located at the National University of Kyiv Mohyla Academy, specializes in providing technical support for environmental information dissemination and exchange through electronic communications. It also supports a resource library and a variety of networking activities.

NYU Center for War, Peace and the News Media
New York University
10 Washington Pl. 4th Floor
New York, NY 10003
Tel: (212) 998-7960

Fax: (212) 995-4143
Contact: Robert Manoff, Project
Director; Julie Raskin, Assistant
Director

The center manages a number of
projects to support the development of
a free and independent press in Russia.
In conjunction with the Russian
Academy of Sciences' Institute for the
Study of the USA and Canada, the
center administers the Russian-
American Press and Information Center
in Moscow, which provides a wide
range of training and technical
assistance programs for Russian
journalists. With the Glasnost Defense
Foundation, the center received a grant
to establish a Standing Commission on
Freedom of Information to monitor
adherence to existing legislation and
educate people about their rights and
duties under the law. The center also
administers the Russian-American
Media Partnership program, funded by
USAID, which supports partnerships
between U.S. and Russian organizations in print, television, and radio.

Open Society Institute–DC

1828 Eye Street NW, Suite 400
Washington DC 20006
Tel: (202) 296-5380
Fax: (202) 296-5381
E-mail: pp001965@interramp.com
Contact: John Fox, Director

See profile of Open Society Institute--
New York in section on *Clearinghouse
Organizations*.

Pacific Environment and Resource Center

1055 Fort Cronkhite
Sausalito, CA 94965
Tel: (415) 332-8200
Fax: (415) 332-8167

E-mail: perc@igc.apc.org
Contact: Armin Rosencranz, President

PERC is a nonprofit policy research,
public education, and advocacy
organization seeking to promote
"sustainable development" around the
world, particularly in Pacific Rim and
neighboring countries. Currently,
PERC is engaged in several collaborative projects with environmental
groups in the NIS. PERC directs the
Siberian Forest Protection Project,
which provides Russian forest
protection advocates with direct
funding and information on responsible
forestry practices and conservation
strategies. The program works with
activists in Vladivostok, the Bikin, the
Altai, and Kamchatka, as well as with
Ecojuris, a public interest
environmental law firm in Moscow.

Pacific Rim Connection

750 State Street, Suite 204
San Diego, CA 92101
Tel: (619) 238-0088
Fax: (619) 238-7371
Contact: Patricia Rickon

Pacific Rim Connection (PRC) is
working with women's groups in the
NIS to help at-risk women and children
in their communities. In Vladivostok,
women are trained and employed in
upscale restaurants and a fast-food
service is being developed. In another
project, women supplement their income at home by sewing and repairing
items to be sold at a "thrift shop" run
by the group. The profits enable the
organization to train women in business
skills useful for the emerging trades
and factories that are under
development. In addition, PRC holds
periodic confer-ences to bring women
leaders in Russia together with their

American counter-parts; from such conferences new projects are developed.

In several cities successful businesswomen are assisting in the development of projects that involve medical clinics concerned with reproduction, prenatal care, obstetrics and pediatric care. PRC is providing medicines, supplies and contacts on a regular basis. PRC is also developing a bank of volunteers who will go to the NIS to establish new clinics and offer training in special procedures.

Focusing on developing more women in leadership positions in business, PRC is providing assistance in training for the travel and tourism industry. It is also expanding a nonprofit travel service for American and European groups traveling to the NIS.

Partners for Democratic Change

823 Ulloa Street
San Francisco, CA 94127
Tel: (415) 665-0652
Fax: (415) 665-2732
E-mail: pdc@igc.apc.org
Contact: Raymond Shonholtz, President

Ina recent issue of its newsletter, *Partners International Quarterly*, PDC described itself as an organization evolving "into an integrated, regional organization capable of providing East-to-East ethnic, environmental and educational programs, training and consulting services." In 1995 PDC opened a regional training center in Bratislava, Slovakia which manages its East-to-East Training Initiative. The central purpose of this initiative is "to build teams of culturally-sensitive, indigenous trainers able to meet the need for transnational conflict resolution training."

Besides the five national centers it has in Central European countries, PDC opened a Center in Russia in 1990 and one in Lithuania in 1993. These Centers provide in-country conflict resolution training using indigenous directors, trainers and managers. Since its inception, Partners claims that its Centers have trained 90 local trainers who in turn have trained over 10,000 people.

National Director of Partners–Russia is Nina Belyaeva, founder of Interlegal (with which she continues her association). Programs in Russia have included training sessions directed at NGOs, teachers, government officials, and environmental organizations. These programs have occurred in Moscow as well as the two Russian regional Centers of PDC, in Archangelsk and Krasnodar.

Partners for Democratic Change--New York

222 Mamaroneck Avenue
White Plains NY 10605
Tel: (914) 948-8802
Fax: (914) 948-3925
E-mail: pdc@igc.apc.org
Contact: Jim Isenberg, Vice President of Programs

Peace Links

729 8th Street, SE Suite 300
Washington, DC 20003
Tel: (202) 544-0805
Fax: (202) 544-0809
E-mail: peacelinks@igc.apc.org
Contact: Ms. Carol Williams

PL pursues "sustainable world peace" and community development, works with women environmentalists, and promotes exchanges that involve training for women.

Project on Economic Reform in Ukraine

Kennedy School of Government
Harvard University
79 John F. Kennedy Street
Cambridge, MA 02138
Tel: (617) 496-8816
Fax: (617) 495-1635
E-mail: peru@ksgbbs.harvard.edu
Contact: William Hogan, Director

PERU was created in 1990 in response to a request for assistance by Ukrainian policymakers to help with efforts to reform the Ukrainian economy. Since that time, PERU has maintained offices in Kyiv and at Harvard University's Kennedy School of Government.

PERU's activities have included:
• establishment of the PERU Economic Reform Information Service, which provides articles, books, laws, other documents, and analyses to Ukrainian policymakers working on reform issues;
• monthly publication of the *Ukrainian Legal and Economic Bulletin*, which circulates among business people, Western Government officials, and international organization representatives who are interested in Ukraine;
• monthly publication of *Privatization in Ukraine*, in Ukrainian and English, for Ukrainians and Westerners interested in the privatization process;
• policy-oriented research on topics related to corporatization, housing privatization, the foreign business climate, banking, governmental structures, stock markets, creating a good business environment, etc;
• an annual graduate student summer internship program that has sent more than 50 law, public policy, and business

graduate student interns to Kyiv for a program in which students assist in governmental and nongovernmental organizations and learn about Ukraine; and
• dissemination of information about Ukraine to Westerners.

Project Harmony

6 Irasville Common
Waitsfield, VT 05673
Tel: (802) 496-4545
Fax: (802) 496-4548
E-mail: pharmony@igc.apc.org
Contact: Charles D. Hosford, Co-Director, Special Programs; Todd Kingsbury, Program Coordinator, Business for Russia

Founded in 1985, Project Harmony organizes a wide range of U.S.-NIS exchange projects:
• In the fall and winter of 1995-96, the USIA-funded School Linkages Program featured 13 exchanges between high schools in the U.S. and Russia, two between the U.S. and Ukraine, and one with Belarus.
• The Business for Russia program, designed to introduce Russian business managers to the workings of a market economy and to basic principles of a free market, will bring 50 Russian entrepreneurs to the United States in 1995-96 to participate in five-week internships and practical training programs with American businesses in Vermont, New Hampshire, and Maine. Project Harmony is one of 29 organizations throughout the U.S. picked to administer this program, which U.S. Ambassador to Russia Thomas Pickering has called one of the "brightest and most successful" of all American technical assistance programs.
• The Law Enforcement Exchange Program, in its second year, brought law

enforcement officials from Odessa to the U.S. in late 1995 for programs in New England and Washington, DC.

• Petrozavodsk and Karelia are the locus of several Project Harmony programs. Members of Vermont's Parent to Parent organization have traveled to this region--once a part of Finland--to present workshops for the Karelian Disabled Children's Program. The Fire Prevention Exchange Program has also brought a group of Petrozavodsk firefighters to New England, returning a visit to their city by firefighters from Massachusetts, Vermont and New Hampshire.

For Americans wishing to travel to the former Soviet Union, PH organizes teaching opportunities and living arrangements, which typically are homestays, dormitories, or shared apartments. Applicants must demonstrate an interest in teaching and be able to deal with a wide range of age groups. Participants in Russia must have a good knowledge of Russian. Participants in the Baltic states are not required to know the local language. In addition to teaching, participants may also be asked to help organize various Project Harmony programs and exchanges. Participants pay a program fee, which covers international airfare and visa fees.

Finally, PH offers a 15-day "Russian Wilderness Summer Adventure in the Ostakhov lakes region, near the headwaters of the Volga. Its partner is an experienced hiking and adventure club in western Russia with 12 years' experience in organizing such trips.

Project HOPE

Health Sciences Education Center
Millwood, VA 22646
Tel: (703) 837-2100 **or**
(800) 544-4673
Fax: (703) 837-1813

Project HOPE is a nonprofit health organization, established in 1958 to bring improved medical care to developing areas of the world. Perhaps best known for its hospital ship S.S. HOPE which sailed around the world from 1960 to 1974, Project HOPE is "based upon the premise that we in America do not have the obligation to take care of the world but rather, because of our blessings, to help the world take care of itself. The essence is teaching; the basis is partnership."

Project HOPE's educational programs in the NIS are centered in Moscow. There Project HOPE has a 5-year project to establish a modern burn clinic at Children's Hospital #9. The program involves developing a training program for health professionals in modern burn therapies, bringing selected physicians and nurses to the U.S. to study; and providing fellowships for American specialists to travel to the NIS to teach.

A brochure of current and projected volunteer positions is updated quarterly and is available by writing to the International Recruitment Section of Project HOPE. Qualified short-term volunteers, six months or less, have their transportation and expenses covered. Long-term volunteers also receive a salary.

Project Kesher

1134 Judson Avenue
Evanston, IL 60202
Tel: (708) 332-1994
Fax: (708) 332-2134
E-mail: 74771.42@compuserve.com
Contact: Ms. Karyn Gershon

PK makes grants to U.S. and NIS NGOs for training, networking, and legal development.

REAP International

1427 4th Street, SW
Cedar Rapids, IA 52404
Tel: (319) 368-4230
Fax: (319) 366-2209
E-mail: 0006513571@mcimail.com
Contact: William Mueller, Director

The Rural Enterprise Adaptation Program International (REAP) grew out of an August 1991 program to aid private farmers in Latvia. In March 1992 REAP was officially established with a delegation in Latvia opening the Rural Innovation Center (RIC) at Ogre.

REAP's primary objective is to bring efficient, economical and sustainable farming techniques and technology to private farmers in the former Soviet Union. Some of the means they employ include the establishment of local training and service centers with local staff; introduction of low-tech sustainable methods of farming; diversification of products; small-scale food processing or other infrastructure needs; and farmer-to-farmer training and exchange programs.

In its first year, REAP established five RICs, in Ogre, Dmitrov, Taurage, Ulan-Ude and Irkutsk, staffed by local people who receive training in the U.S. These centers provide the services listed above to private farmers in the area, including administering demonstration projects and model farming techniques. REAP provides financial support and technical assistance where it can, but it tries to utilize local expertise and staff as much as possible.

REAP's activities in 1993-95 included development of a model farm, educational programs, school exchanges, technical assistance and training in the U.S. REAP also funded an agricultural language training program and a documentary/vocational film center.

Since 1992, REAP has brought 100 U.S. technical specialists and another 100 students to its centers in the FSU, and has hosted 30 Russian specialists and about 100 students in the U.S.

Relief International

328 Wilshire Blvd.
Santa Monica, CA 90401
Tel: (310) 395-7745
Fax: (310) 395-0995
Contact: Farshad Rastegar

RI began working in Azerbaijan in the summer of 1992. Its primary focus is the distribution of medicine for refugee populations and it is supported by corporate and individual donations. It operates a mobile medical unit in Barda and has expanded its work to include schools and immunization programs for children.

Russian Ministry Network

PO Box 2806
Murfreesboro, TN 37133-2806
Tel: (615) 849-1354
Fax: (615) 848-9143
E-mail: RichardKew@aol.com
RichardKew@XC.org
Contact: Rev. Richard Kew, Coordinator

The Russian Ministry Network is "committed to providing fellowship and support as Christianity renews itself in Russia, enabling the development of person-to-person and congregation-to-congregation relationships." Its goals are:

• To enable effective communication between Russians Christians and those in other parts of the world;
• To provide an environment in which a broad array of organizations can work cooperatively;

• To seek opportunities to expand the Church's ministry in partnership with the Russian Church.

The network acts as a clearinghouse for individuals or groups seeking involvement in ministry with Russia, or who are planning to expand currently existing ministries. It publicizes and "markets" the variety of opportunities open to churches through a newsletter, *Russian Ministry Network News*, listings on the Internet, etc. RMN also maintains databases of information about the variety of ministries being undertaken in cooperation with Russians. The database includes not only work being done, but also donors, and Christian businesspeople in Russian and the U.S., who might be able to be of assistance. Board Chair for RMN is the Rt. Rev. Roger White, Episcopal Bishop of Milwaukee. Also on the Board is the Very Rev. Leonid Kishkovsky, Ecumenical Officer, Orthodox Church in America.

Sabre Foundation

872 Massachusetts Avenue, Suite 2-1
Cambridge, MA 02139
Tel: (617) 868-3510
Fax: (617) 868-7916
E-mail: sabre@sabre.org
              sabre@igc.org
Contact: Tania Vitvitsky, Director, Scientific Assistance Project

Taking advantage of a provision of the U.S. tax code which enables publishers to take a deduction for donations of current inventory to serve the needy, Sabre Foundation has procured and distributed more than two million books since it launched its Book Donation Program in 1986. The books are primarily new college- and professional level titles in such fields as business and economics, English language and education, the environment, law, medicine, science, and the social sciences. Sabre's partners in the NIS and CEE are responsible for selecting the titles and distributing them within their region.

Sabre's other programs include making academic journals available for reduced rates to CEE and NIS academic institutions and translating and publishing business and economics books into Polish, Ukrainian and other languages.

In 1994 Sabre expanded the concept of book donation by providing delivery of information to the NIS via e-mail and the Internet. Upon request from its in-country partners, Sabre's full-time reference librarian researches and compiles electronic texts related to specific topics and sends them via e-mail or diskette to the requesting organization. Some of these compilations are also made available at Sabre's World Wide Web site.

Sabre recently received a grant in conjunction with the Sabre-Svitlo Foundation and the Ukrainian Legal Foundation to assist in the development of the National Legal Library of Ukraine by helping them develop a system of cataloguing and computer network links.

Sabre's partners in the NIS include the International Humanitarian Foundation, Minsk; Kazakstan Association for the Advancement of International Scholarly Projects and Exchanges, Almaty; the Alexander Men Foundation, Moscow; and Sabre-Svitlo, Lviv.

The Sacred Earth Network

267 East Street
Petersham, MA 01366
Tel: (508) 724-3443
Fax: (508) 724-3436
E-mail: sacredearth@igc.apc.org

Contact: Bill Pfeiffer, Executive Director

The head of SEN, Bill Pfeiffer, founded The Sacred Earth Network (SEN) in 1985 to help people he had met in the then-USSR working against difficult odds on various environmental issues. Fund-raising through the Network, Pfeiffer began supplying activists with computers and modems. Since then, SEN has played a major role in the creation of a computer network of environmentalists spanning over 100 cities in 14 of the 15 former Soviet republics.

Through its Environmental Tele-communications Project (ETP), SEN has provided equipment and training that have directly enabled more than 150 Eurasian environmental groups to communicate via electronic mail.

Once the e-mail connection is in place, SEN also provides information and professional exchanges to strengthen organizations' contacts with similar groups operating regionally, nationally, and internationally.

Environmental projects that have been aided by SEN's e-mail network include the Toxic Monitoring Network started by the U.S. environmental organization ECOLOGIA. ECOLOGIA has been able to coordinate its activities and create a database of toxics in Eurasia via the e-mail network put in place by the ETP.

SEN publishes *The Sacred Earth Network Russian/English Newsletter* twice a year. In addition it published in July 1995 the third edition of its e-mail directory titled, *Eurasian Environmental Electronic Users: A Comprehensive Directory*. The *Directory* profiles scores of ecological groups and lists over 300 e-mail users and their addresses.

SEN's "cutting edge" currently is the regionalization of the ETP. Focusing on regions such as the Trans-Caucasus, it has expanded its activities beyond the technical to include work on network building, organizational development and "deep ecology."

E. F. Schumacher Society

PO Box 76
140 Jug End Road
Great Barrington, MA 01230
Tel: (413) 528-1737
Fax: (413) 528-4472
E-mail: EFSSOCIETY@AOL.COM
Contact: Susan Witt, ExecutiveDirector

Representatives of the Schumacher Society have helped the Olkhon Center for Sustainable Agriculture (see *Russia East of the Urals* section) develop a program of small loans for local businesses. The Center is seeking to market-traditional hand-knit woolen products, and is investigating the possibility of building a wool processing facility in the region. The Schumacher Society will send a Russian-American land planning team to the Olkhon region in 1996 to work with the village of Tolovka to "establish a Community Land Trust for sustainable land use." (Land is held in common, but buildings and equipment can be owned privately. For further information, request the Society's booklet, *Land: the Challenge and the Opportunity*.)

Serendipity: Russian Consulting and Development

1403 Kingsridge Drive
Normal, IL 61761
Tel: (309) 454-2364
Fax: (309) 452-6332
E-mail: 73123.3543@compuserve.com
Contact: Dr. Ronald Pope, President

With a team of Russian and American volunteers, Ronald Pope, a professor of political science at Illinois State University (ISU) in Bloomington-Normal, constructed a ranch-style American home in the center of Vladimir during the summer of 1992. In July 1993, on the first anniversary of the inauguration of *Amerikanskii Dom,* a local newspaper, *Molva,* paid tribute to the project in an editorial titled, "The American Home Has Stood for a Year and Not Collapsed." *Molva* called special attention to the Serendipity attitude:

to complete in Russia small but concrete projects. The professor's motto: It isn't necessary to wait until everything here is in order–we need to work now.

Today, Serendipity operates an American English Program with more than 200 students per term, the program's capacity–and the waiting list currently exceeds 100. The program uses full-time American instructors recruited from around the U.S., with new teachers coming each August. They live with Russian families who are paid room and board by Serendipity. Besides their classes, the teachers do outreach work with local Russian English teachers and participate in the activities of the English Speakers Club which meets Saturday mornings at the American House.

Internships arranged by Serendipity for U.S. college students have yielded products such as a *Foreign Visitors Guide to Vladimir,* a tool for promoting tourism, trade and investment.

Business training is another area in which Serendipity is involved. It has brought specialists from the U.S. to give short workshops in marketing and management. ISU students working together with Russian peers have made an inventory of the region's retail outlets, surveying customers, store owners and others. This data was later used in retail trade workshops offered by Serendipity.

Police training programs involving members of the ISU Police and Criminal Justice Departments and militia (police) officers from Vladimir were among the first exchanges that Serendipity carried out at its inception in 1990. Twenty-five American law enforcement specialists in 1993 and 1994 made "Law and Justice" trips to Vladimir. Two officers from Vladimir's Special Militia School in turn completed 14 weeks of training and observation in police procedures at the University of Illinois Police Training Institute, followed by "hands-on" experience with the police departments of Bloomington, Normal, Rockford and Chicago.

A successful remodeling business has also sprung from Serendipity in Vladimir, and may eventually turn into a full-scale construction firm.

Sister Schools International, Inc.

1201 NE 191 Street, G117
North Miami Beach, FL 33179
Tel: (305) 944-0519
Fax: (305) 944-0644
E-mail: WINFREF@mail.firn.edu
Contact: Dr. Fran Winfrey, President

SSI originally linked schools in Florida with those in the NIS, but has now expanded its operations to include other states. It has paired more than 100 schools to date, some of them through e-mail. SSI is able to help US schools establish e-mail partnerships in the NIS.

Social Science Research Council

605 Third Avenue
New York, NY 10158
Tel: (212) 661-0280
Contact: Susan Bronson, Project
Director

The Social Science Research Council
and the Russian Science Foundation
have received a grant to support
workshops in Russia and Ukraine to
develop scholarship in the field of
political science.

Special Olympics International

1350 New York Avenue NW Suite 500
Washington, DC 20005
Tel: (202) 628-5431
Fax: (202) 628-0068
Telex: 6502841739MCI
Contact: Gregory S. Rehkopf, Direc-
tor, Eastern European and Eurasian
Programs

Special Olympics International (SOI)
was founded in 1968 by Eunice
Kennedy Shriver to support the creation
and expansion of sports programs for
individuals with mental retardation by
providing year-round training and
competition opportunities. The organization estimates that 156 million
people, or 3% of the world's
population, have mental retardation,
and that about 87% of this number are
affected with mild retardation.
    Soviet Special Olympics was estab-
lished in 1989 and during its first two
years trained more than 400 coaches
from throughout the Soviet Union.
Costs for the training seminars were
covered entirely by proceeds from the
sale of "A Very Special Christmas," a
record created through donated services
of singers, musicians, and producers.
In July 1992 Special Olympics-Eurasia

was legally recognized by 12 former
Soviet republics. Later that year 125
athletes participated in the first Eurasian Winter Special Olympic Games in
Petrozavodsk, Russia. In 1993 SO-
Eurasia involved more than 60,000
children and adults with mental retardation in its programs and sent a 156-
member delegation to the Special
Olympics World Winter Games in
Austria. In 1993 and 1994 SO-Eurasia
together with SOI hosted four international seminars for over 400 participants on topics such as "Medical, Diagnostic and Psychological Aspects of
Mental Retardation" and "Special
Olympics Programs for Families and
Volunteers."
    SOI has offices in all of the new in-
dependent states.

TASIC–Teacher And Student International Communication

609 A Street
Davis, CA 95616
E-mail: mbraunlich@glas.apc.org
Contact: Mark Braunlich

The objective of TASIC (Teacher and
Student International Communication)
is to enable U.S. teachers and students,
ages 6-18, to find and communicate directly with their peers around the
world, focusing on Europe and the NIS.
TASIC helps distribute modems and
train teachers in Russia on the uses of
electronic mail to make communication
with their peers abroad faster and more
reliable. It is creating an online database of teachers in the former Soviet
Union and hoped to have added 500
NIS secondary schools to the online
international community by the end of
1995.

Technical Assistance for the Republic of Armenia, Inc.

1 West Walnut Street
Alexandria, VA 22301
Tel/Fax: (703) 683-6638
Contact: Nancy Najarian, Director

TARA is a grantee of CIPE and operates The Entrepreneurial Center in Yerevan. It is a nonprofit, non-partisan organization which combines Western experts with indigenous Armenians–including staff members trained in American-style MBA programs and a Voluntary Advisory Board that helps build local support. To date, there are no organizations comparable to TARA's Entrepreneurial Center in Yerevan, and it has won the endorsement of a host of local business organizations.

Tolstoy Foundation, Inc.

200 Park Avenue South
New York, NY 10003
Tel: (212) 677-7770
Fax: (212) 674-0519
E-mail: THFQ@aol.com
Contact: Xenia Woyevodsky, Assistant Executive Director

The Tolstoy Foundation (TF) was founded and incorporated in New York in 1939 by Alexandra Tolstoy, daughter of the famous author and humanitarian Leo Tolstoy. The Foundation's original purpose was to assist Russian refugees fleeing from Communism to resettle in North and South America and Europe.

Since 1939 it has assisted in resettling over 100,000 refugees, including Afghans, Armenians, Bulgarians, Cambodians, Circassians, Czechs, Ethiopians, Hungarians, Iranians, Iraqis, Laotians, Poles, Rumanians, Tibetans and Ugandans.

TF has overseas offices in Paris, Brussels, Moscow, St. Petersburg, Pskov, Buenos Aires, Sao Paulo, Santiago and Montevideo. TF extended its operations into Russia and the NIS in 1992. It has provided financial and social assistance to two vulnerable groups in Russia: the elderly and intellectuals and scholars who cannot take on a second or third job in order to make ends meet.

TF provides a variety of services to people in need: emergency financial assistance, immigration counseling, housing and social security assistance, legal and financial advice, and simple companionship. The foundation is particularly active in assisting the elderly and the dispossessed.

TF is laying the groundwork for a major capital renovation of its Center in Valley Cottage, New York, in order to create a venue for dialogue, exchange programs and seminars with Russia and the republics of the former Soviet Union.

Tri Valley Growers

101 California Street
San Francisco, CA 94111-5804
Tel: (415) 837-4000
Fax: (415) 837-3900
Telex: 27-9046
E-mail: derekb@well.com
Contact: Derek Brown, Program Manager; Jean Bouch, Volunteer Coordinator

Tri Valley Growers (TVG) is a California farmer-owned cooperative with processing and warehousing facilities throughout the U.S. Started in the Great Depression, TVG has evolved into a major fruit, tomato and vegetable processor over the last fifty years. In October 1992 TVG launched its Farmer-to-Farmer program to send more than

120 American volunteers to Russia to provide short and long-term technical assistance throughout the food production system. Funded by USAID, the program is run in conjunction with the University of California's Division of Agricultural and Natural Resources. Farmer-to-Farmer is slated to continue until late 1996.

TVG maintains offices in Voronezh, Vladivostok and Tblisi, Georgia. Farmer-to-Farmer Project Managers in each office solicit technical assistance requests from private and privatizing agribusinesses. TVG Project Managers review the requests and the San Francisco staff select volunteers for the approved proposals. Since the program began, TVG has fielded over 100 volunteers to agribusinesses in Russia and Georgia. Past projects have included re-designing ventilation and temperature control systems for fruit and vegetable storage facilities, helping an integrated farming operation obtain $300,000 in dollar financing to purchase processing equipment, and preparing an engineering assessment for the feasibility of a tomato paste remanu-facturing operation.

TVG's program in Russia focuses on post-harvest preservation, processing, packaging, and distribution of fruits and vegetables, but it places volunteers in all areas of agriculture and the food system.

Volunteer assignments range from 3 weeks to one year. In exchange for the technical assistance provided by volunteers, host organizations usually contribute in-country lodging, meals, transportation and interpreter services.

Trickle Up Program, Inc.
54 Riverside
New York, NY 10024
Tel: (212) 362-7958

Fax: (212) 877-7464
E-mail: 73444.557@compuserve.com
Contact: Mrs. Mildred Robbins Leet, President and Co-Founder; Ms. Suzan Habachy, Executive Director; Ms. Valerie Stern, Program Officer for Central & Eastern Europe

Trickle Up promotes micro-enterprise development and training in business planning. It is a member of the NIS-U.S. Women's Consortium.

Ukrainian American Bar Association
318 W Roosevelt
Phoenix, AZ 85003
Tel: (602) 254-3872
Fax: (602) 254-1918
Contact: Orest A. Jejna, President

Founded in 1977 the Ukrainian American Bar Association (UABA) is composed of 400 American lawyers of Ukrainian heritage. In the past the UABA focused on human rights issues in Ukraine. More recently it has worked to support the development of the rule of law in Ukraine, especially in the areas of economics and business. With its many contacts in Ukraine, UABA is a good resource for American attorneys interested in volunteering their services in Ukraine.

The UABA has provided technical assistance to the Verchovna Rada, the Parliament of Ukraine, on matters of legal reform, and two UABA members have served as in-residence advisors to the Rada. Many UABA members have participated in a wide range of conferences and projects on legal issues in Ukraine. UABA is a founding member of the World Congress of Ukrainian Jurists and in 1991 established a scholarship program with Southern Methodist

University Law School to host Ukrainian graduate students.

Ukrainian-American Educational Exchange Association

PO Box 116
Castle Creek, NY 13744
Tel/Fax: (607) 648-2224
E-mail: ny000536@mail.nyser.net
Contact: Ronald Czebiniak, President

The Ukrainian-American Educational Exchange Association (UAEEA) was established in February 1992, shortly after Ukraine gained its independence from the Soviet Union. The UAEEA works to foster educational exchange between the U.S. and Ukraine by promoting contacts in academia, government, and between private foundations and individuals.

UAEEA's Teachers for Ukraine program places U.S. faculty, post graduate, graduate and undergraduate students in teaching positions in many of Ukraine's higher education facilities. Subjects taught include English, economics, business and marketing, and civics. Guest professors, teachers and teaching aides are provided room, board and a normal faculty salary of the host institution, but are responsible for their own airfare.

The HostAmerica program places Ukrainian high school students with American volunteer families, usually for a full academic year. Students are covered by major medical health insurance, and are required to bring spending money. Food costs and other living expenses are the responsibility of the host family.

UAEEA also facilitates academic and government cooperative projects and exchanges, and provides logistical support for U.S. academics in Ukraine. It coordinates donations of technical equipment (computers, faxes, etc.) and English-language teaching materials (textbooks and reference materials) to institutions in Ukraine.

Ukrainian and American Women's Action Project

PO Box 7268
Santa Rosa, CA 95407-0268
Tel: (707) 823-0410
E-mail: 74671.2067@compuserve.com
Contact: Ellen Masland Salyer, President

UAWAP works with the Ya Zhinka group in Cherkasy, Santa Rosa's sister city in Ukraine.

Ukrainian Congress Committee

203 Second Avenue
New York, NY 10003
Tel: (212) 228-6840
Contact: Askold Lozynskyj, Project Director

The UCC with the Ukrainian Legal Reform Task Force received a grant to create and implement laws which will support economic reform in Ukraine.

Ukrainian National Association

Attn: Teaching English in Ukraine
30 Montgomery Street
Jersey City, NJ 07302
Tel: (201) 451-2200
Fax: (201) 451-2093
Contact: Prof. Zirka Voronka, Director

For more than 100 years the Ukrainian National Association (UNA) has served the needs of Ukrainian-Americans in the U.S. Its newspapers, *Svoboda*, the longest running Ukrainian daily in the world, and *The Ukrainian Weekly*, contain news of activities in the Ukrainian-American community, and are among the best sources of information in

English on the current situation in Ukraine.

In the summer of 1992 the UNA, under the direction of Professor Zirka Voronka, launched its Teaching English in Ukraine program. Over the next four years more than 300 volunteer teachers from the United States, Canada, Europe and Africa taught over 4,000 students in over 80 cities throughout all of the provinces of Ukraine. The UNA supplies the textbooks and teaching materials. UNA encourages volunteers with teaching experience or a very high aptitude for teaching. Experience in teaching English as second language is preferred. Volunteers should expect difficult living conditions and be in good physical health. Some knowledge of Ukrainian is helpful, but not required.

Ukrainian National Information Service
214 Masschusetts Avenue NE
Washington, DC 20002
Tel: (202) 547-0018
Contact: Michael Sawkiw, Director;
Marta Kunasz, Associate Director

Supported in large part by the Ukrainian Congress Committee of America, UNIS lobbies on behalf of the 1.5 million-strong community of Ukrainian-Americans.

Ukrainian Student Association in the USA (USA/USA)
PO Box 3874
Albany, NY 12203
Tel: (518) 471-4249
Fax: (518) 452-0236
Contact: Michael Heretz, President

The Ukrainian Student Association in the USA (USA/USA) is associated with the project Americans for Democracy in Ukraine, based in Albany, NY.

Established in late 1994, USA/USA recently announced that it had received office space at the University of Kyiv-Mohyla Academy and will be represent-ed there on a full-time basis by Olena Kramar. The organization also intends to register in Ukraine as an official educational organization called UKRAMEREZHA.

Goals of UKRAMEREZHA will include:

• developing an e-mail network of Ukrainian students and scholars studying abroad;
• programs to network alumni of English-language universities in Ukraine;
• holding an annual "academic workshop" in Kyiv; and,
• developing a database of English-language secondary schools in Ukraine.

U.S.–Azerbaijan Council
1030 Fifteenth Street NW, Suite 444
Washington, DC 20005
Tel: (202) 371-2288
Fax: (202) 371-2299

The Council publishes a regular newsletter, available upon request. It can also furnish information about 9-10 other Azerbaijan-related organizations in the U.S.

U.S. Civilian Research and Development Foundation for the Independent States of the former Soviet Union
1800 North Kent Street, Suite 1106
Arlington, Virginia 22209
Tel: (703) 526-9720
Fax: (703) 526-9721
E-mail: information@crdf.org
URL:
http://www.internext.com/crdf
Contact: David H. Lindeman, Program Manager

The CRDF is a private, nonprofit foundation created in August 1995 as an American response to the dramatic decline of resources for science and engineering research in the former Soviet Union. It fosters opportunities for collaborative projects between NIS and U.S. researchers by encouraging productive civilian employment opportunities for former Soviet defense scientists, and by providing opportunities to pursue these goals in a framework of mutual benefit which promotes the values of democratization and market economies. The CRDF's initial endowment of $10 million derives from a $5 million contribution from the U.S. Department of Defense's "Nunn-Lugar" program to promote demilitarization in the FSU, and from a $5 million gift from philanthropist George Soros to the U.S. National Science Foundation.

In November 1995 the CRDF announced a call for proposals for its first initiative, the Cooperative Grants Program. This program will allow joint teams of former Soviet and U.S. scientists and engineers to apply jointly for support of cooperative projects in any area of civilian research and development. Teams may apply for $10,000 to $80,000 of funds for a two-year period.

U.S.-Georgia Foundation
1110 Vermont Avenue NW, Suite 600
Washington, DC 20005
Tel: (202) 429-0108
Fax: (202) 293-3419
Contact: Mr. Eduard Gudava, President

U.S.-Ukraine Foundation
1511 K Street NW, Suite 1100
Washington, DC 20005
Tel: (202) 347-4264
Fax: (202) 347-4267
E-mail: ukraine@access.digex.net
Contact: Nadia McConnell, President

USUF's goal is to foster democratic and free-market economic reforms in Ukraine. The foundation works closely with the Pylyp Orlyk Institute for Democracy in Kyiv and the two organizations recently received a grant to help develop participation by Ukrainian citizens' organizations in the public policy process.

University of Tulsa, Russian American Management Program
600 South College Avenue
Tulsa, OK 74104-3189
Tel: (918) 631-2281
Fax: (918) 631-2950
E-mail: imc_ss@centum.utulsa.edu
Contact: Saeed Samiee, Ph.D., Director and Professor, International Management Center

The Russian American Management Program (RAMP) in the International Management Center of the University of Tulsa's College of Business Administration provides an intensive business leadership program for mid-level Russian managers. The course consists of on-the-job training for three months in Tulsa area businesses, and a series of concurrent management development seminars covering key management principles and issues in a market economy.

The program provides hands-on experience in American business practices for Russian interns, and potentially valuable contacts in Russia for participating Tulsa businesses. Interns have access to all aspects of company operations, working closely with sponsoring supervisors. They are subject to performance reviews on the job, and are required to attend all evening and weekend development seminars. Upon successful completion of RAMP, the participant receives a certificate of participation from the University.

Costs are shared by sponsoring American firms and the University of Tulsa. Participating Russian organizations are required to provide round-trip transportation from Russia. English proficiency (a minimum score of 550 on the TOEFL) is required of all participants. Potential candidates submit an application and essay, and the University and business sponsors are responsible for selecting participants.

Urban Institute

2100 M Street NW
Washington, DC 20037
Tel: (202) 857-8775
Fax: (202) 466-3982
Contact: Ms. Vida R. Megahed, International Activities Center

Assisting Russia in developing a comprehensive set of laws on housing and in other aspects of reforming this critical economic sector is the Urban Institute, a nonprofit policy research and educational organization established in Washington, DC, in 1968. With funding from USAID, the Urban Institute began work in Moscow in mid-1992, assembling a project team in which, today, Russian professionals outnumber Americans.

The principal activities of the program are:
• advising the Russian government on housing reform legislation, e.g., the Law on Fundamentals of Housing Policy, a Moscow regulation on condominiums, and a forthcoming Law on Mortgage;

• carrying out a series of demonstration projects, e.g., placing thousands of municipal rental units in Moscow and Nizhni Novgorod oblast under the management of several independent, private maintenance firms, and evaluating the experience;
• development of detailed procedures and supporting materials for implementing simultaneously broad-scale rent increases and programs of housing allowances (subsidies);
• training and advising personnel in eight cities, mostly in Central Russia, in the development of condominiums;
• working initially with Mosbusinessbank and more recently with ten additional Russian commercial banks to provide training and assist staff in strengthening all phases of long-term mortgage lending: documentation, loan servicing, risk management, etc.

The materials developed under the last program are being made available to other banks through the production of a Mortgage Handbook series, published by the Center for Mortgage Business in Moscow. The Urban Institute offers a list of "Papers on Housing in Russia," the great majority of which exist in Russian translation.

Volunteers for Peace

43 Tiffany Road
Belmont, VT 05730
Tel: (802) 259-2759
Fax: (802) 259-2922
Contact: Peter Coldwell, Executive Director

Volunteers for Peace (VFP) offers organized travel experiences, language study, and workcamps in the NIS. It was founded in 1981 and is part of an international network of groups organizing workcamps under the aegis of UNESCO. Workcamps originated in

Europe over 70 years ago. Generally 10-20 people from four or more countries arrive on a given day in a host community. Living arrangements are generally cooperative and the work is unskilled and casual. VFP's 1995 International Workcamp Directory lists 800 programs in more than 50 countries.

In the summer of 1995 VFP offered eight four-week workcamps for young people over 18 in Ukraine, Belarus, and the following cities in Russia: Yekaterinburg, Volgograd, Astrakhan, Petrozavodsk, Perm and Irkutsk. The work activities included: cleaning a natural park and planting trees, working in a children's hospital, and renovating churches and a kremlin. Costs range from $650-$750.

Volunteers in Overseas Cooperative Assistance

50 F Street NW, Suite 1075
Washington, DC 20001
Tel: (202) 383-4961
Fax: (202) 783-7204

Since 1970 Volunteers in Overseas Cooperative Assistance (VOCA) has sent skilled volunteers to provide technical assistance to agricultural, business, and environmental organizations around the world. It has offices in 30 countries around the world.

Since 1992 VOCA has sent volunteers to Russia, Ukraine, Belarus, Armenia and Kazakstan. They have helped with marketing of agricultural products and the development of agricultural policy. Work in Armenia has focused on strengthening that nation's self-sufficiency in food production. Some VOCA assignments have resulted in new American business linkages or joint ventures in the region.

VOCA develops "long-term relationships in a context of multiple short-term assignments." Its volunteers come from a wide variety of backgrounds: business management, cooperative development, marketing, finance, food processing, conservation, forestry, vegetable and fruit production, agricultural extension and farming, veterinary medicine, beekeeping, meat processing, and dairy farming. The typical volunteer has 10 to 15 years of experience and the typical assignment lasts two weeks to three months.

VOCA has regional recruiting offices in Sacramento, CA; Madison, WI; and Columbus, OH. It also has offices in Moscow, Kyiv and Saratov.

Wheeled Mobility Center

1930 Parker Street
Berkeley, CA 94704
Tel: (510) 548-3652
Fax: (510) 548-3652
E-mail: krizack@sfsu.edu
Contact: Marc L. Krizack, Russia Project Manager

The Wheeled Mobility Center at San Francisco State University works for social integration of people with disabilities and has over 15 years' experience in developing countries. WMC's involvement with Russia began in 1990 and its work since then includes setting up two private, competing factories in Novosibirsk and providing both with marketing and technological assistance.

Demand for wheelchairs depends largely upon how many facilities are accessible to wheelchair users, and Russia's buildings and transportation system are notoriously inaccessible. Through its "architectural barrier removal program," WMC's Russian partner, a disabled persons' sports club, has restructured part of the sport complex

"Spartak" where the group meets. Additionally, the Regional Department of Social Protection completed an accessibility survey of downtown Novosibirsk in early 1994. Developing a wheelchair-accessible infrastructure in Novosibirsk will both improve the quality of life for disabled people and ensure a market for the wheelchairs produced.

An important part of the WMC project involves training Novosibirsk's disabled community in organizational development and activism. WMC is working with the Novosibirsk Regional Disabled Sports Club, "FINIST," to establish a wheelchair repair shop and an independent living center. According to WMC, FINIST has incorporated democratic principles into its constitution and learned how to manage its social and economic programs more efficiently.

WMC also developed the Disabled Women's Project within FINIST in December 1993. Women belong to every type of disabled group in Russia; however, they often do not hold leadership positions. During 1994 two Russian women involved in the DWP, Larisa Tokareva and Lyuba Ievinsh, visited the U.S. on International Disabilities Exchanges and Studies grants to learn about organizational development, health care and independent living.

In 1995 WMC's plans included designing English/Russian brochures to promote the newly designed wheelchairs; buying equipment for the wheelchair repair shop; and holding an Independent Living Center Training for ten Russians in Helsinki. WMC also continued to develop the Disabled Women's Project and planned to launch a Disabled Community Health Clinic. In addition to a formal partnership with Planned Parenthood of Northern New England, WMC has cooperated with World Institute on Disability and Access Exchange International. WMC invites volunteers in the areas of wheelchair design and repair, organizational development, small business, and health to become involved in the Novosibirsk program.

Winrock International Institute for Agricultural Development

Petit Jean Mountain
Route 3, PO Box 376
Morrilton, AR 72110-9537
Tel: (501) 727-5435, Ext. 258
Fax: (501) 727-5417
Telex: 910-720-6616 WI HQ UD
E-mail: patm@ollie.winrock.org
Contact: Dr. Andy Martinez, Program Director.

The Winrock International Institute for Agricultural Development came into being in 1985 with the merger of three organizations rooted in the philanthropic tradition of the Rockefeller family. Through its research and technical assistance programs, Winrock International works to reduce poverty and hunger in the world by promoting sustainable agriculture, rural development and civil society building.

Winrock International–Women's Leadership Program

1611 North Kent Street, Suite 600
Arlington, VA 22209
Tel: (703) 525-9430
Fax: (703) 525-1744
E-mail: srw@msmail.winrock.org
Contact: Ms. Elise Fiber Smith, Program Director; Ms. Stephanie Rubin Weishaar, U.S. Consortium Coordinator

WI–WLP's work in the NIS includes leadership training, human resource development, rural development, agriculture, environment, and advocacy/policy work.

Women, Law and Development International

1350 Connecticut Avenue NW
Suite 407
Washington, DC 20036-1701
Tel: (202) 463-7477
Fax: (202) 463-7480
E-mail: iwld@access.digex.net
Contact: Ms. Marge Schuler

WADI combats violence against women and enages in research, public education, advocacy of women's rights, and the development of "legal literacy." It is a member of the NIS-U.S. Women's Consortium.

Women of the World, Inc.

5602 SW Fairlawn
Topeka, KS 66610
Tel: (913) 862-6000
Fax: (913) 862-0537
E-mail: wownow@databank.com
Contact: Ms. Lynn Hinkle

WOW is also a member of the NIS-U.S. Women's Consortium. It conducts workshops in leadership training, campaign management, and fundraising.

World Vision Relief and Development Inc.

220 Eye Street NW
Washington, DC 20002
Tel: (202) 547-3743
Contact: Serge Duss, Associate Director, Government Relations
or
PO Box 1131
Pasadena, CA 91131

Tel: (800) 488-6437
E-mail: jos@vanhee.msk.su
URL:
http://solar.rtd.utk.edu/friends/wvision/index.html

World Vision is a Christian relief and development organization. In Russia it has helped to develop the elements of a federation-wide Nurses' Association and conducted training programs aimed at improving the professional skills of nurses. It has also worked with Dr. Alexander Zaichenko's Center for Business Promotion in Moscow, offering workshops in management training. In Belarus it has operated a Children of Chernobyl project, providing medicines, training and counseling for victims of the Chernobyl explosion.

NIS-Based Organizations

Armenia

Country Code: 374

Yerevan (2)

All Armenian Women's Union
Yerevan
Tel: 58-39-64, 58-60-73
56-56-80, 56-76-86
Contact: First Lady Lucia Ter-Petrossian, Honorary Chair; Gulnara Shahinian, Chair & Coordinator

Created in January 1994, the union has worked as a coordinating, information and referral service for 22 women's organizations. Their future plans include expansion of the union to rural areas of the country by creating links and joint programs. The Women's Union has ties with 22 local women's organizations as well as with international organizations such as the Women's Association of Great Britain, the American Institute for Women's Studies, and Women's Group of Germany.

Aragast Youth Club
Children's Uro-Nephrological and Surgical Center CUNSC
30 Furmanov Street
Yerevan
Tel: 24-79-92, 64-82-59
Tel/Fax: 23-80-39
Contact: Gayaneh Kroyan,
Artur Der-Toomassian

Established in October 1993, the club has worked to create a place for the youth of Yerevan to gather, spend free time, discuss and inform themselves about current topics and meet young people from other countries.
Projects include:
• Free time activities. Organization of extracurricular activities for young people, like a video club, discussions, parties, theater, and sports;
• Social action. Social and cultural activities with and for people living in difficult conditions, e.g. refugees, impoverished people, handicapped people, etc.
Future plans include organization of social and cultural activities together with young people from abroad; training of 2-3 Armenians in the field of youth leadership in England or Switzerland; and invitation of professional youth workers from England or Switzerland to organize workshops and training sessions in Armenia.

Araratian Patriarchal Diocese Charity Office
ul. Israelian 21
Yerevan
Tel: 58-73-68, 58-75-05
Fax: 15-10-40
Contact: Alvard K. Tzulikian, Director

Created in 1992, the office provides aid to orphans living in the diocese, to workers in the areas of culture and science, and to needy individuals through programs such as cafeterias for the elderly and handicapped.
The charity office is currently working on a project distributing foreign aid from Armenian churches in the U.S.

Armenian Assembly of America NGO Training and Resource Center
Moskovian 24, #2
375002 Yerevan
Tel: 56-10-64 /Training
58-15-77 /Resources

52-86-54 /Seminars
E-mail:
postmast@aaango.aremania.su
Contact: Arpi Vartanian, Director;
Wim Aspeslagh, Technical Assistance
Advisor

The purpose of the center is to support
the growth of NGOs in Armenia. It
does this in four ways:
• offering a meeting place for local
NGOs to discuss common concerns,
pool resources, and plan their future;
• conducting training and technical
assistance seminars and workshops,
such as a ten-week Management and
Leadership Training Course offered in
the summer of 1995;
• providing access to e-mail communications, databases, printed materials
and other resources;
• maintaining an extensive database
and serving as a clearinghouse for those
seeking information about specific Armenian NGOs.

Subcommittees on Health, Human
Rights and Education–part of an NGO
Club–meet regularly at the center. The
center publishes *The NGO Newsletter.*
It plans to open a regional office in
northern Armenia in the near future.

Armenian Assembly of America
Yerevan Office
Independent Media Center
2 Republic Square
375010 Yerevan
Tel: 52-95-13, 56-06-74
Tel/Fax: 52-58-76
Contact: Edith Khachatourian, Office
Director

The Armenian Assembly of America
opened its Yerevan office in 1989 with
two people. Today it has a full-time
staff of 9, supporting projects such as:
the Armenia Tree Project; a housing

materials factory in Gyumri; the Spring
Wheat Seed program; the Winter
Warmth 1994 humanitarian aid
program; and more. The Media Center
was opened in mid-1994 with
assistance from USIA and offers both
local and international journalists high
quality telecommunications lines,
computer services, modem and satellite
capability, and facilities for press
conferences. See a recent *Annual
Report of the Armenian Assembly of
America, Inc.* for a full description of
these programs.

"Armenian Bureau" Information Agency
Yugo zapadny massiv
B-2 quart. 21, kv. 23
Yerevan
Tel: 74-33-22
             73-33-22 (home)
E-mail: hsargsian@glas.apc.org
Contact: Grant Sargsian, Member of
Council of the Socio-Ecological Union.

Armenian Foresters' Association
Yerevan
Tel: 56-63-35, 58-36-55
Contact: Karen Ter-Ghazarian

This association was first created in
1991 for the purpose of teaching
refugees about timber production and
cultivation, including creating
greenhouses and woodworking.
Current projects include sustainable
forest development in Armenia with
special reference to refugee problems.

Armenian Goldsmiths' *Regoul* Association
26A Tigran Medz
Yerevan
Tel: 56-22-64

Contact: Mr. Margarian, President

Created in 1994 for the purpose of lobbying Parliament on issues of interest to goldsmiths.

Armenian International Women's Artist Association
ul. Plekhanova 3
Khachatourian Museum
Yerevan
Tel: 27-47-64, 58-94-18
Contact: Alice Adamian

The association holds charity concerts and art exhibitions with proceeds going to dead and wounded soldiers' families.

Future plans include: establishing ties with both Armenian and non-Armenian women's organization in the U.S. and throughout the world; creating an information center on Armenian artists; and organizing international exhibitions and concerts for charity.

Armenian Little Singers
ul. Kievian 26, kv. 39
Yerevan
Tel: 27-31-09, 56-36-16
Contact: Tigran Hekekian, Chairman; Varduhi Baghdassarian, Director

The organization attempts to unite musically gifted Armenian children from all over the world for the purpose of performance in competitions. Past projects include participation in a 1992 concert tour in France, and competing in the international music competition "IDETEDFOD" in 1993 and 1994.

Armenian National Chamber of Commerce and Industry
39 Republic Street
375010 Yerevan
Tel: 56-54-38

Fax: 56-45-98
Contact: Mr. Ashot Sarkisian, President

Armenian Progress Fund, Defense of Human Rights and Charity
ul. Nalbandiana 5
375010 Yerevan
Tel: 56-15-60, 56-33-32, 56-15-05
Fax: 15-17-87
Contact: Levon Nersesian; Agasi Arshakian, Vice-President

Armenian Real Estate Association (AREA)
Yerevan
Tel: 25-47-92, 25-27-89
Tel/Fax: 15-13-50
E-mail: icma@sovam.com
Contact: Gagik Poghossian, President; Artem Pribilisky, Vice-President

AREA strives to: support the private real estate brokerage, management and maintenance industries; assist the development of the real estate market in Armenia; and advocate members' interests in the community and in various government institutions. This is accom-plished through the use of integrated information systems, organized training programs and market research.

Armenian Society for Cultural Relations and Cooperation with Foreign Countries
ul. Abovian 3
Yerevan
Tel: 56-45-14, 58-12-41
Contact: Henrik Igitian, Co-Chair; Lavrenti Barseghian, Co-Chair

This organization was created in 1992 to: promote the development of "people's diplomacy;" encourage the involvement of citizens in international relations; demonstrate Armenian culture in other countries; and promote mutual understanding between peoples.

Projects include the organization of cultural festivals, both internationally and within Armenia.

Armenian Union of Culture

ul. Toumanian 5
Yerevan
Tel: 52-53-48, 52-39-41,
             56-52-92
Contact: Gevork Minassian, Chairman; Gevork Gamaghelian, Vice Chairman

Created in 1990 with the goal of: promoting the development of national art; presenting Armenian art abroad; and assisting artists in Armenia. Projects include the organization of an international folk dance festival; organization of exhibitions of national art in Armenia and abroad; and establishing an International Center for National Art in Armenia.

Armenian Women's Alliance

13 Grigor Lusavorich
375015 Yerevan
Tel: 58-76-86, 58-39-64
Fax: 56-56-80
Contact: Natalia Martirosian, Coordinator; Liudmilla Petrosian, Representative

Armenian Young Painters' Center

ul. Toumanian 21
or
ul. Barbusse 63, kv. 27
Yerevan
Tel: 22-57-96, 22-94-44

39-98-27
Contact: Khachik Abrahamian, Chairman; Vahram Haroutiunian; Gagik Badalian

Created in 1990 to organize exhibitions in Armenia and abroad and assist needy groups and individuals.

Proceeds from the sale of paintings given to various charities. Future plans include a simultaneous exhibit under the motto "Art against AIDS" in several countries.

Arpi Benevolent Fund

ul. Hakhtanaki 44, kv. 30
Gyumri
Tel: 27-73-61
Contact: Tigran Pashabeghian, President; Haroutiun Petrossian, Vice-President

Created in 1993, Arpi helps reconstruct valuable historical-architectural monuments and assists needy students and schoolchildren. It provides annual scholarships for three students and 10 orphans and financial support for two artists to organize personal exhibitions.

Assistance to Farms Union

ul. Abovian 26B, kv. 6
Yerevan
Tel: 58-96-61
Contact: Edvard Dadashian, Chairman; Armen Mkertichian,Vice Chairman

Created in 1995, the union's projects include international marketing of Armenian fruits and vegetables, and creating a model farm which will provide other farms with animals and seeds and process potatoes into sugar and gasohol.

Association to Assist the Sovereignty of Armenia

1 Nar-Dos, #20
375018 Yerevan
Tel: 56-75-39
Contact: Edward Harutuinian, Chairman

Created in 1995 with the goal of creating a stable, anti-blockade economy, and assistance to the socially needy. Projects have included support to the army and charity projects after the earthquake. Future plans include the ecology of Sevan, rice growing, and development of solar energy.

Back to Hyak

ul. Nalbandian 48
Yerevan
Tel: 52-58-93, 52-73-81
Contact: Robert Melik-Pashayev, President; Rafael Seiranian, Member

Created in 1990 to protect the rights of refugees. The organization assists refugees and seeks to increase awareness of refugee rights under international law.

Bars Media

ul. Plekhanov 56/1
375009 Yerevan
Tel: 56-18-67
Tel/Fax: 115-1677
E-mail: bars@arminco.com
Contact: Vardan Hovhannisyan, President

Bars Media is an independent non-profit documentary film production studio.

Blind Persons' Union

ul. Issahakian 18
Yerevan
Tel: 56-05-21, 56-05-72

58-25-92
Fax: 58-22-66
Contact: Abel Hakobian, Chairman; Tovmas Movsissian, Deputy Chair

Founded in 1930, the union works to create favorable conditions and jobs for blind people through subsidiary enterprises.

Children's Security League

ul. Nzhdeh 29, kv. 34
Yerevan
Tel: 44-05-67, 26-81-44 (home)
         28-70-00 (work)
Contact: Gilda Gharibian

Created in 1989, the league assists orphans. Projects include creating a complete databank of children orphaned by the earthquake; organizing conferences devoted to educational activities and healthcare at school; and creating an educational research center.

Committee of Soldiers' Mothers

ul. Khandzhiana 5
375010 Yerevan
Tel: 52-99-31, 53-01-57
         24-79-96
Contact: Greta Mirzoian

Consumers Association of Armenia

Yerevan
Tel: 22-41-31
Contact: Ashot Ohanian, Chairman; Nora Avakian

The Consumer's Association was created in 1994. The organization's three main goals are to check fraudulent market practices, set up an independent laboratory to check food and non-food items for safety and quality, and establish border checks to stop unsafe materials from entering the country.

Deaf Persons' Works #1
ul. Yeznik Koghbatsi 73
Yerevan
Tel: 53-73-92, 53-33-53
Contact: Hrach Khachatrian, Director;
Armineh Mesropian, Chief Accountant

Founded in 1991 to create work places
for the deaf and ensure their
educational and spiritual development.
Projects include finding ways to put
existing footwear and textile
manufacturing units into operation; and
providing assistance to families of
handicapped and dead soldiers.

Defense of Civil Rights "Dostoinstvo"
Yerevan
Tel: 56-64-17, 46-02-00
Contact: Gaer Margarian

Dignity Civil Rights Society
ul. Abovian 8
Yerevan
Tel: 56-10-67, 52-62-49
Contact: Vardan Haroutiunian, Presi-
dent; Hrair Markarian, Vice-President

The society's goal is: to help Armenia's
development as a democratic nation
through the promotion of human rights;
protect religious minorities through the
mass media; struggle against current
army recruiting methods; and defend
the case of Dashnaktsutiun.

The Eurasia Foundation
Caucasus Regional Office
22 Isahakian Street, Suite 9
375009   Yerevan
Tel/Fax: 15-18-24
E-mail:
armenia@eurasia.arminco.com

See profile for the Eurasia Foundation
under *Clearinghouse Organizations*.

Euroclub UNIPAX Youth Organization (Union for Peace and Fundamental Human Rights)
ul. Manoukian 5A, kom. 402
Yerevan
Tel: 55-15-15, 52-29-56
26-81-44 (home)
Contact: Nairi Petrossian, President;
Shushanik Papanian, Secretary; Karen
Danielian

The organization raises human rights
issues; promotes a solution to the
problem of Karabakh through "youth
diplomacy;" and carries out various
educational projects. These include
international competitions, participation
in an Armenian television series, and
holding anti-war meetings with
members of other youth organizations.

Film Producers Association of Armenia
Ministry of Culture
Toumanian 5
Yerevan
Tel: 59-73-28
Contact: Arsen Asatrian, Co-Chairman;
Naira Mkrtchian, Co-Chairman

Established in July 1995, the association works to create a film industry in
Armenia; to develop co-production
through similar foreign associations;
and to market Armenian films

Fund Against Arbitrary Rule
ul. Moskovian 11
375001   Yerevan
Tel: 52-45-71, 65-59-25
Fax: 24-44-04
Contact: Larisa Asaturovna Alaverdian

The Ghevond Alishan Cultural-Educational Association
Nalbandian 25/27, kv. 7

375001   Yerevan
Tel: 58-56-77
Fax: 56-71-64
Contact: Svetlana A. Aslanian, President

The association was established in 1991 to promote Armenian culture through information exchange, and to assist in the repatriation of refugees from war in the Caucasian states. It provides language instruction and support to refugees resettled in Armenia, and to Armenians throughout the former Soviet Union.

Green Union Of Armenia
Yerevan
Contact: Akop Sanasaryan
E-mail: armgreen@arminco.com
YERANOS@armgreen.arminco.com

Deals with nuclear issues.

Group for the Defense of Human Rights in Armenia
15 Grigor Lusarovich
375015   Yerevan
Tel: 56-32-55, 56-21-82
Fax: 56-34-52
Contact: Vardan Astsatrian; Mark Grigorian

Gushamatian ("Memorial")
ul. Tumanian 17
Yerevan
Tel: 52-14-81, 56-46-15
Fax: 58-49-93
Contact: Aaron Adibergian; Sergei Akopovich Amirian

Hayouhi Women's Association
ul. Babayan 36, kv. 23
Yerevan
Tel: 25-68-23
Contact: Susanna Vardanian, Chairwoman; Ivetta Yakubova, Deputy Chair

The association works within the guidelines of the UN Charter of Human Rights to protect women's rights; to enhance women's role in public, social, cultural and political life; and to expand ties with women's organizations abroad.

Helsinki Citizen's Assembly
ul. Derian 57, kv. 22
375009   Yerevan
Tel: 58-34-17
Fax: 52-15-81
Contact: 58-34-17

Human Rights League
Yerevan
Tel: 56-58-96
Contact: Arshaluis Papazian

ISAR
Yerevan
Contact: Anakhit Alakhverdian
E-mail: nakhit@avninco.com

See ISAR profile in section *Clearinghouse Organizations.*

Issahakian Writer's Association
ul. Hakovian, 3-rd Lane
School #130
Yerevan
Tel: 22-23-00
Contact: Hakob Arzumanian, President; Henry Aghajanian, Vice-President; Gevorg Ohanian, Secretary

Established in 1994 to support young writers, and help publish their works. Projects include organizing a meeting devoted to the 80th anniversary of the renowned Armenian poet Hovhannes Shiraz, and developing a partnership between the Writers' Union of Karabakh and IWA.

Jewish Community

ul. Brusov 2, kv. 35
Yerevan
Tel: 23-06-52, 23-65-33 (home)
         52-58-82 (home)
Contact: Rimma Varzhapetian, Acting
President; Sofia Bagyan, Director of
Repatriation Center; Igor Zaslavsky,
Member of Coordinating Council.

Established in 1991, the organization
works to promote Jewish traditions and
culture. Projects include a school for
children and adults; establishing a
cultural center; lectures, commemora-
tions of religious holidays, and distribution of humanitarian assistance.

Lawyers' Youth Union

ul. Terian 65, kv. 18
Yerevan
Tel: 72-38-97
Contact: Karen Zadoyan, President;
Gevorg Minassian,Vice-President

Established in 1995 to disseminate
legal knowledge among students and
young people, and to help develop the
rule of law in Armenia.

Loris Benevolent Union of Families with Many Children

ul. Haghtanaki 26/8
Yerevan
Tel: 73-23-00, 72-75-25
Contact: Zhirair Karapetian, Chairper-
son; Gegham Khachatrian, Assistant

The organization attempts to assist
families with many children through
the creation of a soup kitchen and
discount shops for those families.

Movses Khorenatsi Union of Young Historians

ul. Dekabristi 23, kv. 47
Zeitun

Tel: 58-20-46
Contact: Artavazd Melkonian, Presi-
dent; Mher Mkhitarian, Vice-President;
Emma Martirosian, Secretary

The union helps to preserve and
rehabilitate historical monuments in
Armenian-populated areas. It organizes
tours to historical places in Artsakh to
collect data on historical monuments
and folk traditions for later incorpora-
tion of the findings in brochures, booklets and printed materials.

National Democratic Institute– Armenia

Yerevan
Tel/Fax: 58-13-75
E-mail: ndi@public.arminco.com
See profile of NDI in section *Special
Focus Organizations.*

National Scouts' Movement of Armenia

ul. M. Khorenatsi 72, kv. 3
Yerevan
Tel: 53-67-30
Contact: Harut Harutiunian, President;
Hratchia Shmavonian, Member; Lilit
Berberian, Member of Administration

Associated with the International
League of Scouts, the NSMA works to
develop the youth of Armenia both
physically and morally.

Npast Benevolent Fund

ul. Furmanov (Mamikoniants) 27
Yerevan
Tel: 23-32-65
Contact: Marzpetouni Avakian; Levon
Ghoukassian

The fund assists vulnerable families
and their unemployed members. Projects include a sausage production
enterprise, pharmaceutical production

from Armenian herbs, keeping bee-hives, and breeding foxes.

Oukhtatun (Pilgrim House) Museum–Institute of the Great Armenian Massacre and the Fight for Liberation

ul. Abovian 15, etazh 1, kom. 9
Yerevan
Tel: 56-79-96, 58-92-21,
              22-04-52
Contact: Sasoun Grikorian, Director

Created in 1993 for the purpose of collecting documents on the Armenian Genocide, currently spread throughout the world. The institute first studies and evaluates the documents scientifically, then publishes and exhibits them internationally.

Pyunik (Phoenix) Handicapped Sports Organization

Old Trade Union Bldg
Republic Square
Yerevan
Tel: 56-19-86, 56-14-80
Contact: Hakob Abrahamian, Karen Assatrian

The organization was created in 1988, although not registered until 1990, with the goal of physical, psychological and social rehabilitation of disabled children.

Scouts of Armenia National Union

ul. Toumanian 23
Yerevan
Tel: 56-48-34
Contact: Levon Mkhitarian, Chairman; Siranoush Petrossian; Arkadi Ter-Tadevossian

The union has 30 sections throughout the country. See also National Scouts' Movement of Armenia.

Special Olympics Armenia

ul. Kuznetsov 12
375078   Yerevan
Tel: 55-24-95
Fax: 52-70-22
Contact: Mr. Gavrush Mnatsakanyan, Chairman

Technical Assistance for the Republic of Armenia (TARA)
The Entrepreneurial Center

ul. Nalbandian 5, etazh 3
Yerevan
Tel: 58-47-15
Fax: 15-14-14

The Entrepreneurial Center is a project of Center for International Private Enterprise in Washington, DC. It assists Armenian entrepreneurs and leading reform-minded organizations through business consultations. It aims to:

• help build civil society by strengthening independent business, trade, women's and other associations;
• mobilize and train advocacy groups to propose policy reforms to improve the business climate and remove key obstacles to private sector development and entrepreneurship;
• provide management and technical training for new small business owners; and
• train a corps of business consultants who can expand this assistance to smaller cities in Armenia.

Union of Merchants of Armenia

ul. Vardanants 13, etazh 2
Yerevan
Tel: 57-07-72, 57-03-21

Contact: Makich Demirian, President; Hovsep Poghosian, Vice-President; Milleta Hakopyan, Vice-President

The union's goals include the defense of the legal and economic interests of merchants and consumers (especially women consumers) in Armenia and creation of a respected legal environment for this purpose. Projects include the publication of a specialized newspaper *Zarkerak*, and the NUNE enterprise.

Union of Nationalities

ul. Tigran Metsi 8, kv. 16
Yerevan
Tel: 52-55-94, 58-24-95
56-51-51, 64-84-47 (home)
Contact: Vladimir Chatoyev, President; Pavel Tamrazov, Member

The organization helps national minorities in Armenia to preserve their culture, religion, and language. This is accomplished by assisting the socially vulnerable groups, promoting friendship and understanding between nationalities, and creating employment opportunities for members of national minorities.

Union of the Deaf

Vahram Papazian 23
Yerevan
Tel: 26-27-20, 22-04-50
Contact: Zhora Varagyan, President, Varazdat Boretsian, Head of Rehabilitation Center; Zoubetta Melikian, Translator

The union works to unite the hearing-impaired into one organization to improve their living standards, and to help their social integration. Current projects include two specialized schools in Yerevan, and the development of a cultural center.

Vernatoun Cultural Club

ul. Kochari 4
Tel: 22-03-23 (work)
22-71-59 (home)
Contact: Sergei Galstian, Chairperson; Nora Danielian, Vice-Chairperson

The club encourages talented young people to participate in exhibitions, concerts and theatrical shows, and to publish their works. It gives scholarships to creative children. Projects include organizing exhibitions of Armenian painters' works; publishing books; publishing translations of children's stories; and arranging cultural events and exchanges.

Voluntary Service of Armenia
National Headquarters of
Student Brigades

ul. Koriun 19A
Yerevan
Tel: 52-27-01, 52-27-72
52-27-88
Contact: Stepan Stepanian, Chairman; Eduard Balyan, Vice-Chairman; Gegham Sarkissian, International Projects

Created in 1970, the service creates international student work teams under the auspices of UNESCO; provides for participation by Armenian volunteers in different international projects; assists lonely elderly people and handicapped children; offers care and help to sick children; and assists war refugees.

Women's Council of Armenia

Moskovyan 35
Yerevan
Tel: 55-85-91, 53-45-06
Contact: Nora Hakopian

Yerevan Press Club

#39/12 Mesrop Mashtots pr.
Yerevan

Tel: 52-92-06, 52-29-26
Contact: Boris Navasardian, President; Elina Poghosbekian, Member of Administration; Michael Diloyan, Executive Director

The club promotes the development of a free press in Armenia through a publications program, yearly assessments of the mass media in Armenia, creation of a database for journalists, and occasional seminars on topics such as press coverage of parliamentary elections.

Young Architects' Union
ul. Toumanian 31, kv. 67
Yerevan
Tel: 58-20-46, 53-31-72
Contact: Zarouhi Toumanian, Chairperson; Madelaine Igitkhanian, Vice-Chairperson

The organization's goal is to enhance the professional skills of young architects, and to promote the protection and study of architectural monuments. This is accomplished by organizing student exhibits, establishing ties with architectural students in other countries, and organizing trips to Armenian architectural monuments.

Youth for Armenia
Aigedzor 38
Yerevan
Tel: 22-59-47
Contact: Ara Vardanian

Youth for Armenia was formed in 1995 by a group of students who had participated in the Freedom Support Youth Exchange program in the U.S. It has 18 active members and intends to serve in part as an "alumni association" for the FSYE program in the Caucasus region. One of Youth for Armenia's first events brought together FSYE program alumni from Azerbaijan, Georgia and Armenia in a workshop to discuss the concerns of young people in these countries.

Youth Center for Gender Research
1 Alex Manoogian Street
Yerevan
Tel: 55-03-85, 25-51-51
27-39-73
Contact: Armineh Mkhitarian, Scientific Board Chair; Anoush Abrahamian, Scientific Board Member

Created in 1995 for the purpose of investigating the place of the Armenian woman in the family and in political life; and to monitor the implementation of UN resolutions in Armenia. Projects include organizing seminars on women's issues, studies on women's participation in elections, and participation in the TACIS (European Community) Democracy program.

Zinvori Mair (Soldiers' Mothers)
ul. Khandjian 5
Yerevan
Tel: 52-99-31
Contact: Greta Mirzoian

Established in 1991, the organization advocates the human rights of soldiers fighting in the war at Artsakh. It also provides legal, economic and social services to soldiers and their families. It works with young people who have not yet been called to service, organizing volunteers to assist in caring for wounded soldiers, and works to improve support services for mothers who lost their sons in war. Future plans include providing employment for handicapped soldiers and the mothers and widows of dead soldiers.

Azerbaijan

Country Code: 994

Baku (12)

ACCELS Baku
ul. Aliayarbekova 9
370005 Baku
Tel: 93-19-56
E-mail: akselsaz@sovam.com

See the profile for ACTR/ACCELS in
Special Focus Organizations.

**Adventist Development
Relief Agency**
ul. F. Amirov 1, kv. 53
Baku
Tel: 93-73-88
Fax: 98-68-96
Contact: Peter Howell, Country
Director

**"Analar Faryadi" Society
"Shout of Mothers" Society**
ul. A. Alekperova 565, kv. 5
376500 Baku
Tel: 38-51-52 (home)
Contact: Dilyara Kerim kyzy Orudjeva,
Chairwoman

**Azerbaijan Branch of the
Association of Victims of Illegal
Repression**
ul. May 28, 3-11
Baku
Tel: 39-13-61
Contact: A. F. Mekhtiev

Azerbaijan Civil Defense Center
ul. May 28, 3-11
Baku

Tel: 64-03-30
Tel/Fax: 98-75-55
E-mail: eldar@hrcenter.baku.az
Contact: El'dar Zeinalov

**Azerbaijan Committee for the
Defense of Peace**
ul. P. Beibutov 8-58
Baku
Tel: 93-41-33, 92-54-07
Fax: 98-60-41
Contact: Anar Mamedkhanov

**Azerbaijan Committee of Social
and Legal Defense**
Baku
Tel: 38-12-51, 95-63-84
Contact: L. Nuraliev

**Azerbaijan Gadin Huguglary
Mudafiasy
Association for the Defense of
Rights of Azerbaijan Women**
ul. Injasanat 1
370004 Baku
Tel: 92-14-83, 92-74-56 (office)
          32-27-93 (home)
Fax: 98-31-65
Contact: Novella Dj. Djafarova,
Executive Chairwoman

**Azerbaijan Gadinlary
Azerbaijan Women's Association**
ul. Boyuk Gala 6
370004 Baku
Tel: 92-74-87 (office)
          93-65-00 (home)
Contact: Zenfira Nadirovna Verdieva,
Chairwoman, associate member of
Azerbaijan Academy of Sciences

**Azerbaijan Gadinlary Baki
Assosiasiyasi
Baku Association of Azerbaijan
Women**
18 Bul-Bul pr.

370000 Baku
Tel: 93-19-02 (office)
        94-80-33 (home)
Fax: 98-32-96
Contact: Zarifa T. Salakhova,
Chairwoman

Azerbaijan Intelligent Women's Unity "Ziyali Gadinlar"

ul. K. Shikhlinsky 59
370000 Baku
Tel: 66-88-06 (office)
Contact: Sevil A. Mammedly,
Chairwoman

Azerbaijan League for the Defense of the Rights of Children

ul. Mirzagi Alieva 130, kv. 33
Baku
Tel: 94-81-42, 98-20-26
Contact: Iusif Berikov

Azerbaijan Madeniyetinin Dostlari
Azerbaijan Friends of Culture

Baku Arts Center
Baku
Fax: 98-37-55 (Kauzlarich);
        98-71-89 (Badalbeyli)
E-mail:
72103.3340@compuserve.com
Contact: Anne Kauzlarich, Mehriban
Aliyeva, Co-chairs.

Anne Kauzlarich, creator of the
foundation, is wife of the American
ambassador to Azerbaijan and highly
regarded for her fluency in Azerbaijani.
She was moved to create this
foundation when she learned that the
National Ballet did not have $5,000
needed for its corps of dancers in the
next season. With the support of major
figures in Azerbaijan's arts and
business circles, Kauzlarich and

Aliyeva formed AzMD. It has sent
singers and pianists from Baku to the
U.S., brought artists from Azerbaijan
who work abroad back to Baku for
performances, and plans a competition
for scholarships for aspiring young
artists throughout Azerbaijan.

Azerbaijan National Committee

ul. May 28, 3-11
Baku
Tel: 98-33-78, 93-33-72
Fax: 98-75-55
E-mail: hca@ipca.baku.az
Contact: Arzu Abdulaeva,
Coordinator; Tamilla Zeinalov, Deputy
Coordinator

Azerbaijan Neftchy Gadinlar Society
Society of Women in the Oil Industry of Azerbaijan

pr. Neftchilar 73
370004 Baku
Tel: 92-06-85 (office)
        92-55-34 (home)
Fax: 92-32-04
Contact: Solmaz A. Gadjieva,
Chairwoman

Azerbaijan Peoples Accord Commission for Solidarity

pr. Metbuat, d. 36, block 5
Baku
Tel: 32-37-23, 96-09-97
        31-79-82
Contact: Viktor Romanovich Zotov

Azerbaijan People's Front Human Rights Commission

Baku
E-mail: nva@azad.azerbaijan.su
Contact: Ali Mustafaev, Deputy
President

Azerbaijan Society of Lawyers
ul. Khagani 14
Baku
Tel: 98-51-71, 38-05-50
Contact: I. Ragimov

Bakin Civil Defense Group
ul. May 28, 3-11
Baku
Tel: 93-81-48, 62-29-84 (home)
Contact: Tamilla Zeinalova

Baku and Village Association
ul. Uzeir Gadzhibekov 30, kv. 308
Baku
Tel: 93-13-80

CARE–USA
ul. U. Hajibayov 19, kv. 78/29
Baku
Tel: 98-20-81, 98-91-05
Fax: 98-03-71
E-mail: root@care.baku.az
Contact: Golam Azam, Unit
Administrator

Center "Shehyd Analary"
Mothers of the Sacrifices of War
ul. Ataturk 2-A
370039   Baku
Tel: 93-96-21 (office)
          64-81-69 (home)
Contact: Rafiga A. Askerova,
chairwoman

Chernobyl-Azerbaijan Alliance
Baku
Tel: 96-11-33

Committee for Rule of Law and Human Rights in Azerbaijan
Office of Musavat Party
ul. P. Beibutov 3
Baku
Tel: 94-93-37, 64-93-26

Fax: 98-35-71
Contact: Khagani Dzhafarov; Hargiz
Akhmed Pashaeva

Defense Committee of Law and Human Rights in Azerbaijan
Pr. Azerbaijan 37
Baku
Tel: 98-31-50
Contact: Adalet Rahimly

The Committee gathers information about human rights abuses in Azerbaijan and publishes an English-language bulletin.

Echo
ul. Khagani 26/32, kv. 79
Baku
Tel: 98-42-12
Fax: 154-6515
Contact: Gunter Bousher,
Humanitarian Aid Coordinator

Feed the Children
ul. Khagani 54, kv. 42
Baku
Tel: 93-93-64
Fax: 93-93-64
Contact: Leramy Craft, Director

Gadin Ve Inkishaf Center
Women and Development Center
ul. S. Rustamova 3/6, kv. 65
370001   Baku
Tel: 67-21-39 (office)
          92-79-20 (home)
Fax: 92-56-99
E-mail: paolo@un.azerbaijan.su
(Subject: for Elmira Souleimanova)
Contact: Elmira T. Souleimanova,
chairwoman and doctor of chemistry.

German-Azerbaijan Association
ul. H. Sultanov 7/9
Baku

Tel: 39-73-44, 39-44-29
Fax: 39-92-80
Contact: Kamran Rustamov, Director

Global Care
ul. Rafibeyli 3/5, kv.26
Baku
Tel: 92-53-94
Fax: 93-47-22
E-mail: hfa@globalcare.ganja.az
Contact: Gordon Coure, Project
Leader/Administrator

Group for the Defense of Peace in Azerbaijan
Baku
Tel: 93-33-78, 66-94-93
Fax: 62-9850
Contact: Liudmilla Grigorievna; Kostin
Aleksandr, Coordinator

GTZ
ul. Injasanat 9
Baku
Tel: 92-74-90
Contact: Dr. Hosrof Saidi, Director

Hajibeyov Museum
Ketskhoveli 67
Baku
Tel: 92-45-64, 92-43-52

This museum is housed in the original
residence of the composer Uzeyir
Hajibeyov–renowned for his synthesis
of Eastern and Western traditions in
music–and includes a small theater
where one may see early films relating
to Hajibeyov's operas, such as "Archin
Mal Alan," composed in 1945.

Hajibeyov is also remembered for
having founded Azerbaijan's Music
Academy, a school for professional
musicians.

Hayat
ul. Mendeleyev 11/13
Baku
Tel: 95-75-39, 95-80-23, 95-69-21
Fax: 95-80-80
Contact: Vusal Rajabli, President

Helsinki Group of Azerbaijan
Baku
Tel: 39-86-08, 96-34-15
Contact: Nadir Mekhtiev

Human Rights Commission of the Azerbaijan Democratic Party of Independence
Baku
Tel: 92-10-32
Contact: Maksim Abramov

Independent Association of Azerbaijan History Researchers
ul. Gogol 6, kom. 3
370000 Baku
Tel: 98-45-04
Fax: 98-81-13, 98-45-04
Contact: Dr. Rafig Radjabov,
Chairman

With Azerbaijan's Academy of Science
and Unocal Khazar, IAAHR sponsored
a symposium in late 1995 on
"Azerbaijan in a World of Multilateral
International Intercommunications."

Independent Committee for Defense of Human Rights in Apsherone
Baku
Tel: 61-02-31, 38-18-18, 38-12-61
Contact: Azer Abdulaev; Adaliat
Memedov, Coordinator

Insar Khuguglary Gazet
(Azerbaijani Party for the Defense of Human Rights)
Baku

Tel: 39-04-43, 39-37-92
Contact: Guseinaga Ganiev

International Human Rights Society–Azerbaijani Group

Baku
Tel: 21-3163, 92-31-63, 69-53-88
Contact: Kamal Abdulaev, Director; Mekhdi Mamedov, First Deputy

International Committee of the Red Cross

Sankt-Peterburg pr. 98a
Republic Stadium
Baku
Tel: 64-00-43, 64-41-80, 62-05-07
Tel/Fax: 64-00-43
Contact: Bernhard Julier, Director

International Federation of Red Cross and Red Crescent Societies (IFRC)

ul. Niazi 11
37000   Baku
Tel: 92-57-92, 92-74-30, 92-07-43
Fax: 93-18-89
Contact: Patrick Howard, Director

IFRC, which is based in Switzerland, began work in Azerbaijan in 1993, offering technical assistance and advice. Actual distribution of relief aid is done by the national Red Crescent society.

International Rescue Committee

ul. Vidadi 107, kv. 11
Baku
Tel: 94-46-85
E-mail: office@irchg.baku.az
Contact: Maha Muna, Emergency Coordinator

Interparty Commission for Defense of Rule of Law and Human Rights

ul. R. Bubutov 3 ("Musavat" Party Office)
Baku
Tel: 94-93-37, 94-33-76
Fax: 94-93-69
Contact: Khagani Dzhafarov; Leyla Yunusova, Coordinator

Ishguzar Gadinlar
Business Women's Association

ul. Pervomaiskaya 215
370014   Baku
Tel: 92-30-22 (home)
Contact: Svetlana Chingizovna Kasumova, Chairwoman

Jewish Women's Society of Azerbaijan

ul. Sh. Badalbeily 39
370072   Baku
Tel: 95-54-29 (office)
Tel/Fax: 66-17-58 (home)
Contact: Isabella Abramovna Bairamova (Kleiner), President

Karitas

ul. Iskra 6
Baku
Tel: 94-95-25
Contact: Leyla Yunusova

Legal Investigation Center of the Azerbaijan Fund for Democratic Development

ul. Khagani 33
Baku
Tel: 39-86-06, 96-34-15

Médecins Sans Frontières– Belgium

ul. Sheikh Shamil 4, kv. 8
Baku
Tel: 92-66-18, 92-66-21
Fax: 92-66-95
Contact: Philip Rijckaert, Arnold Govaert

Merlin
84 Azadlig Prospekti, kv. 40
Baku
Tel: 96-10-49
Contact: Natalie Man, Administrator

"Musavat" Party Human Rights Commission
ul. Beibutov 3
or
37 Azerbaijan Prospekti
Baku
Tel: 98-31-50, 98-31-65
Fax: 98-31-65
E-mail: root@musavat.baku.az
Contact: Eiyubov Burgun

National Azerbaijan Independence Party Human Rights Commission
Baku
Tel: 61-17-28, 61-52-56
Contact: Sevil' Dzhakhani

Oxfam International (UK)
Adil Iskanderov 4
Baku
Tel: 92-17-52
Fax: 98-72-57

"Peace" Women's Society "Sulh"
ul. Sabael 54, kv. 25
370003 Baku
Tel: 39-56-51 (office),
91-56-05 (home)
Contact: Rurriya Gambar kyzy,
Chairwoman

Red Crescent Society of Azerbaijan
Azerbaijan Prospekti 19
Baku
Tel: 93-19-12
Contact: Adulgalim Akhmedzade,
Chairman of the Executive Committee

Red Cross International
St. Petersburg Prospekti 98-A
Baku
Tel: 62-05-07, 64-41-80
Fax: 64-01-98

Refugee Society
pr. Karl Marx 48/54
Baku
Tel: 39-49-50, 32-15-65
Contact: Niftali Godzhaev

Relief International
ul. F. Amirov 2, kv. 49
or
pr. Bul Bul 11, kv. 12
Baku
Tel: 98-42-76, 98-05-67
Tel: 98-90-01, 98-90-04
(78922) 93-13-77
Fax: 98-05-67
E-mail: root@relief.baku.az
Contact: Mike Kendellen, Director

In 1993 this organization, based in Santa Monica, CA, helped distribute 36 tons of medical supplies and equipment to hospitals in Baku and to their refugee distribution centers in Yevlakh and Agdjebedi in central Azerbaijan. It worked with the construction company Brown & Root, Project Hope, and U.S.-chartered aircraft from Andrews Air Force Base to accomplish this humanitarian initiative.

Relief Organization of Azerbaijan "Sensiz" ("Without You")
ul. Gara Garaev 114, kv. 37
370119 Baku
Tel: 74-43-13 (home)
Contact: Zenfira Abdulla kyzy
Ragimova, Chairwoman

Republican Union of Soldier–Internationalists "Adaliat"
Baku
Tel: 92-91-68
Contact: F. Mamedov

Save the Children
ul. Kaverochkin 13t,kv.8 & 9
Baku
Tel: 98-06-29, 98-41-51
Fax: 98-92-93
E-mail: kabir@savebaku.az
Contact: Lutful Kabir, Director

Society for Georgian Azerbaijanians "Garachep"
pr. Azerbaijan 40
Baku
Tel: 93-82-71, 93-83-01

This is a headquarters for the repatriation of Azerbaijani refugees from Georgia.

Society of Azerbaijan Mothers "Hope" ("Umid")
ul. Nizami 58
370005 Baku
Tel: 93-96-11 (office)
            93-02-75, 92-73-14 (home)
Fax: 62-29-84
Contact: Mokhabbat L. Gousseinova, Chairwoman; Timilla Zeinalov, Coordinator

Special Olympics Azerbaijan
ul. Chjoban-zade, kv. 1
370060 Baku
Tel: 221-62-34
Contact: Mr. Shahin Aliev, Chairman

Turan Independent Association of Trade Unions
ul. Kadyrbekov 38, DK 3-da
Sattarkhana
Baku

Tel: 67-71-74, 66-75-24, 67-70-54
Contact: Neimat Panakhov

Women's Charitable Society "Fate"
Government House, kv. 930
370000 Baku
Tel: 93-02-08 (office)
Contact: Chimnaz Allahyar kyzy Mamedova, Chairwoman

Women's Council of Azerbaijan
ul. Krepostnaia 6
Icherishekher
Baku
Tel: 92-74-87, 92-75-83
Contact: Zemfira Verdieva

World Learning
Baku
Tel: 93-43-35
E-mail: Lepisto@wrlding.baku.az
Contact: Eric Lepisto, Field Staff

See profile in section *Clearinghouse Organizations*.

World Vision International
ul. Sh. Badalbayli 100, kv. 5
Baku
Tel: 98-83-10
Fax: 98-96-73
E-mail: wvi@wviaz.baku.az
Contact: Keith Buck, Relief Program Director

See World Vision profile in section *Special Focus Organizations*.

Berde (210)

International Committee of the Red Cross
ul. Sabir 35
Berde

Tel: 2-20-31
Contact: Jean-Paul Corboz

Médecins Sans Frontières–Belgium
ul. Gusy Gadjievic 68
Berde
Tel: 2-34-73

Oxfam International (UK)
ul. Nushaba 25
Berde
Tel: 2-34-34
Contact: Stanly Mukkath, Program Coordinator

Oxfam International (UK)
ul. Sharg 37
Imishli
Berde region
Tel: 5-36-39, 5-23-21

Relief International
ul. Bursa 10
Imishli
Berde region
Tel: 57-00

See Relief International in Baku.

Gyandja

Society of Muslim Women "Famita-Zahra"
ul. Tebriza 41
374747 Gyandja
Tel: 2-05-56 (office)
4-30-55 (home)
Contact: Zenfira Isfendiyar Kyzy Isayeva, Chairwoman

Mingecevir (274)

IFRC: International Federation of Red Cross and Red Crescent Societies
Building of Executive Committee
Mingecevir
Tel: 4-66-93
Telex: 142 421 TUFAN
Contact: Daniel Valle, Relief Delegate

Stepanakert (8852)

Helsinki Initiative--92 Nagorno-Karabakh Committee
ul. Sakharov 3
Stepanakert/Khankedi
Tel: 4-33-76, 28-09-28
4-39-46
Fax: 28-18-97
E-mail: karandge@arminko.com
Contact: Karen Ogandzhanian; Tevan Pogosian, Member of Delegation

Belarus

Country Code: 375

Minsk (0172)

ACCELS Minsk
pr. Skaryny 35, kom. 21
220005   Minsk
Tel: 36-68-83
E-mail: fsa.minsk@sovcust.sprint.com

See the profile for ACTR/ACCELS in
Special Focus Organizations.

Alarm: an Independent Socio-Ecological Newspaper
ul. Myasnikova 39
220048   Minsk
Tel: 20-39-04
Fax: 71-58-19
E-mail: sasha@by.glas.apc.org

Alarm is an independent newspaper
emphasizing environmental issues in
Belarus.

Alcoholics Anonymous
Minsk
Tel: 60-89-11
Contact: Stanislav

ATM (Belarusan International Youth Labor Association)
a/ya 64
220119   Minsk
Tel: 27-81-83, 27-33-95
Fax: 76-86-62
Contact: Sergei V. Stepanov

Areas of interest include environmental
education of teens and children,
alterna-tive energy, ecotourism and
networking.

Asana Association
a/ya 43
220015   Minsk
Tel: 56-82-72
Fax: 76-86-62
Contact: Aleksei I. Mikulich

Areas of interest include environmental
education, nature conservation, biodiversity and nature reserves.

Belarus Ecological Union
Green Parties of Belarus
ul. Osipenko 19, kv. 51
220068   Minsk
Tel: 20-11-16, 37-35-81
Contact: Mikhail Y. Fridland
E-mail: minsk@gluk.apc.org

Belarus Socio-Ecological Union "Chernobyl"
pr. Izvestiya 17, kv. 172
220000   Minsk
Tel: 20-39-04, 71-58-19 (home)
E-mail: sasha@by.glas.apc.org
Contact: Vasily Yakovenko, Member
of the Council of Socio-Ecological
Union

Belarus Science and Industry Association
ul. Lenina 19
220030   Minsk
Fax: 27-15-29
Contact: Vladimir Sobolev, Director of
Overseas Economic Relations

Belarusan-American Educational Project on Radiation Monitoring
pr. Gazety "Pravda" 58/2, kv. 40
220116   Minsk
Tel: 36-35-81
E-mail: root@pchela@by.glas.apc.org
Contact: Olga V. Klimanovich

Active in environmental education and NGO development work.

Belarusan Association of Journalists

pr. Pravda 22, kv. 672
(temporary address)
220016 Minsk
Tel: 68-28-22, 68-29-23
Fax: 36-95-73
E-mail: mmc@glas.apc.org
Contact: Ales' S. Mikalaichenka, Representative

BAJ is a newly formed public organization. Its objective is to strengthen the social, economic, and professional position of journalists as well as to give them legal assistance. The association cooperates with the Legal Service of the Mass Media Center.

Recently, according to BAJ, the deputy chief of staff of the president of Belarus ordered state printing houses not to print, distribute, or deliver editions of *Narodnaya Volya, Belaruskaya Delovaya Gazeta,* and *Imya* (all independent newspapers). The association protested this action as repressive and dicriminatory, inasmuch as no such actions were taken against newspapers favorable to the administration.

BAJ seeks ties to international associations of journalists in order to exchange information and obtain support for its activities.

Belarusan Association for the Victims of Political Repression

ul. F. Skorina 1, kv. 308
220072 Minsk
Tel: 39-58-89, 55-47-21
Contact: Valentina Vergei, Coordinator

Belarusan Children's Fund

pr. F. Skorina 31
220029 Minsk
Tel: 36-63-67, 36-66-74
Fax: 36-63-67
Contact: Vladimir Lipsky, President

The fund has been working with the Christian Children's Fund to enhance treatment and health care delivery systems in Belarus, particulary for children and survivors of Chernobyl. Many of its efforts are focused in rural areas where health care facilities are difficult to access or unavailable.

Belarusan Climate

ul. Gaya 14, kv. 31
220068 Minsk
Tel: 37-91-38
Contact: Igor Pavlovich Korzun

Active in environmental education, "eco-philosophy."

Belarusan Ecological Alliance

ul. Lenina 15a
220030 Minsk
Tel/Fax: 27-87-96
Contact: B.P. Savitskii, President; L.G. Tarasenko

Belarusan Entomological Society

ul. Skarny 27
220072 Minsk
Tel: 39-51-92
Fax: 39-31-63
E-mail: zoobel@bas30.basnet.belpak.by
Contact: Eleonora Ivanovna Khotko

Belarusan Helsinki Group

Tel: 63-31-58 (home)
Tel/Fax: 36-95-73
Contact: Karlos G. Sherman

Belarusan Humanitarian Center for Education and Culture

ul. Kirav 21
220050   Minsk
Tel: 26-10-73
Fax: 29-31-06
Contact: Vladimir Kolas, Director

Belarusan League of Human Rights

pr. F. Skorina 4
220010   Minsk
Tel: 26-58-97, 68-68-94
Fax: 24-80-61
Contact: Evgenii Novikov

Belarusan Soros Foundation

pr. F. Skorina 65, korp. 11 A
220027   Minsk
Tel: 39-93-46, 32-70-64
Fax: 32-80-92
E-mail:
smedley%sfebl.minsk.by@relay.ussr.eu
.net
Contact: Peter G. Byrne, Executive
Director

"Belaya Rus" Environmental Youth Movement

ul. Karla Marksa 40
220030   Minsk
Minsk
Tel: 39-91-29
Fax: 31-30-49
E-mail: dmitry@wri.belpak.minsk.by
    or,
ecology_zone8%infra.belpak.minsk.by
@demos.su
Contact: Dmitri G. Sherbakov, Sergei
V. Dorozhko

Active in environmental education for
youth, networking among NGOs,
nature conservation, and independent
environmental consulting.

BellR (Belarusan Intellectual Resource)

a/ya 535
22019   Minsk
Tel: 36-32-46, 39-31-14
Contact: Stanislav Romanov

BellR is involved in solid waste
disposal issues and promotion of
recycling.

Chamber of Commerce and Industry of the Republic of Belarus

pr. Masherova 14
220600   Minsk
Tel/Fax: 26-99-36
Contact: Vladimir Lesun

Chernobyl Children Belarusan Committee

ul. Pritytskogo 60/2
220600   Minsk
Tel: 51-43-11
Fax: 52-15-89
Contact: Irina Kh. Martynova

The Chernobyl Children committee is
interested primarily in environmental
education of youth.

Cinema School

ul. V. Khorunzhei 10/2, kv. 164
220123   Minsk
Tel: 68-67-01
Contact: Yuriy A. Stayunivchev

The Cinema School is interested in
NGO development, and environmental
education through the mass media. It is
connected with Socio-Ecological
Union.

COUNTERPART

ul. Karalya 16, kom. 201
220004   Minsk
Tel/Fax: 20-55-55

E-mail: cpminsk@attmail.com
Contact: Nina Efimova, Acting
Country Representative

See profile in section *Clearinghouse
Organizations*.

"Discussion" Women's Club
ul. Karbysheva 11-48
a/ya 5
220119 Minsk
Tel: 63-77-36
Fax: 30-80-54, 31-04-72
E-mail: beluwi@minsk.sovam.com
pkp.2@pkp2.belpak.minsk.by
Contact: Anna Sergeeva, President

Discussion is an independent NGO
founded in 1993. Its purpose is (a) to
strengthen women's influence in
national life by means of partnerships,
training activity, and informational
exchanges, and (b) to develop contacts
with women's organizations in Belarus
and throughout the world.

The club has organized workshops
and round table discussions on
problems of nonprofit women's
organizations and the status of women
in Belarus. It has also developed
psychology and language courses for
women. It collects information about
women's NGO activity in Belarus and
abroad, plus statistical and other
materials related to different aspects of
women's life.

DWC has participated in international conferences and seminars in
Germany, Holland, Russia and the U.S.
It plans to set up an Informational
Women's Center and to organize a
series of training workshops for women
on the problems of leadership,
democracy, partnerships in the family,
etc. The workshop project will end with
an international conference on the
theme: " Women under the Circum-

stances of Socio-Economic Crises: the
Experience of Eastern Europe."

Staff consists of 30 volunteers.

Ecohome "Edoma"
pr. F. Skorina 76-18
220012 Minsk
Tel: 32-45-44
Fax/tel: 21-81-79
E-mail: mike@by.glas.apc.org
nextlife@glas.apc.org
Contact: Mihail Lipay

Activities of Ecohome include
construc-tion of a model "ecodom" in
northwest Belarus; summer
international "eco-camps" for youth
and children; a perm-anent ecological
education program for children in
Minsk; seminars and confer-ences on
current environmental prob-lems; and
environmental consulting.

ECOLOGIA
Belarus Office
a/ya 170
ul. Olega Koshevogo 24
220113 Minsk
Tel/Fax: 30-27-78
E-mail: ecobel@glas.apc.org
Contact: Oleg Cherp, NIS Program
Director

See ECOLOGIA profile in section
Special Focus Organizations.

European Humanities University
pr. Masherova 1-2-5
220004 Minsk
Fax: 39-31-63
Contact: Prof. Dr. Anatoli Mikhailov

This is an independent university,
started by a professor of philosophy.

For the Children of Chernobyl
ul. Starovilenskaya 14

220029 Minsk
Tel: 34-12-15, 34-21-53
Fax: 34-34-58
Contact: Gennady Grushevoy, Ph.D.,
Chairman of the Board

For the Children of Chernobyl was
founded in 1989 and legally registered in
1990. Dr. Grushevoy has been a
professor of philosophy at Belarusan
State University since 1973 and, since
1990, a member of the Belarus parliament. The organization claims to be one
of the largest self-supported social
organizations in Belarus. It has support
teams in over 20 cities or regions of the
country and over 40 long-term programs
of charitable, medical and humanitarian
outreach.

Among other accomplishments, it has:
arranged for nearly 400 sick children to
receive medical treatment abroad;
provided direct material aid to thousands
of evacuee families, Cherno-byl invalids,
and rescue workers; con-structed a
facility for producing organi-cally grown
food on a collective farm in the Brest
district; created specialized nursery
school programs for handi-capped
children; and facilitated direct relations
between foreign partners of the Fund and
hospitals, schools, orphan-ages and other
public organizations in 32 areas of
Belarus.

Independent Institute of Socio-Economic and Political Studies, Ltd.

a/ya 329
220101   Minsk
Tel/Fax: 25-10-54
E-mail: iiseps%iiseps.minsk.by
@sequent.kiae.su
Contact: Prof. Oleg Manaev, Chairman;
Alexander Dobrovolsky, Executive

Director; Dr. Igor Pelipas, Deputy
Director

IISEPS, Ltd. is a nongovernmental,
nonprofit organization offering "an
alternative to official state-sponsored
social science." It was founded in Minsk
in April 1992 by a group of private
entrepreneurs, new politicians,
journalists and academics, and is based
on the values and principles of liberal
democracy. It receives support from the
Center for International Private
Enterprise.

IISEPS is involved in surveying public
attitudes towards democratic and market
principles in Belarus. The main aim of
the project is to promote the principles
of a free market economy through the
activities of leading political and
economic figures in Belarus. The
project conducts research and advocacy,
including consulting, publishing and
educational activities. Policy papers,
newspaper articles, seminars and other
activities deliver the Institute's
recommendations to policymakers, the
private business sector, the media and
the general public. The Chairman of
IISEPS is a member of the International
Associa-tion for Mass Communication
Media.

Independent Union

a/ya 368
220050   Minsk
Tel: 24-80-17
Contact: Mikhail Doroshevich

Independent Union is active in
education on environmental issues.

International Academy of Ecology, Belarusan Branch

ul. V. Khorunzhei 31-A, kv. 421
220002   Minsk
Tel: 34-75-27, 34-70-65

Fax: 34-75-27
Contact: Yevgeniy Ivanovich Shirokov

The Academy of Ecology is interested in environmentally sound but efficient energy alternatives, as well as eco-tourism and environmental education.

International Institute of Radioecology

Minsk
E-mail: root@iscr.minsk.by

KAYA International NGO

ul. Oboinaya 10, kv. 3
220004 Minsk
Tel: 23-38-57
Contact: Irina E. Zaslavskaya-Alers

KAYA has developed a Children's Village Project, and is involved in developing ecologically sound architecture. Through educational programs in architecture, it teaches children about environmental issues.

Labor Confederation of Belarus

ul. Kakhovskaia 64, kv. 62
220068 Minsk
Tel: 37-41-49
Contact: Mikhail Sobol, Representative

Martyrology of Belarus

ul. Skorina 1
22072 Minsk
Contact: Mikhail Sobol, Executive Secretary

Mass Media Center

ul. Skariny 15-a
220072 Minsk
Tel/Fax: 39-40-86, 39-45-36
E-mail: mmc@glas.apc.org
Contact: Mikhail V. Doroshevich

The Mass Media Center was founded by a group of Belarusan journalists who wanted to improve the standards of journalism in their country. With the support of the Soros Foundation and Internews the center organizes training programs for journalists and others working in the mass media. It provides them with access to Western news sources and produces news programs which can be broadcast by TV stations in Belarus. The focus of MMC is on helping non-state, independent media outlets.

Minsk Gender Center

Minsk
E-mail: titarenk@servax.fiu.edu
Odessa94@aol.com (home)
Contact: Larissa Titarenko, Director

Professor Titarenko taught a course on "Women and Labour" at Florida International University in 1995. She has written on this theme and on the topic of young women and AIDS in Belarus.

National Brokers Guild of the Republic of Belarus

ul. Karla Marksa 40
220030 Minsk
Tel: 27-40-75
Fax: 27-89-95
Contact: Alexander Yelovik, President

Nature Protection Society, Minsk Branch

ul. Krasnozvesdnaya 8
220034 Minsk
Tel: 33-18-63, 33-13-79
Contact: Anatoliy Tarasovich Fedoruk

The Nature Protection Society is active in the western states of the NIS. It focuses on habitat conservation and biodiversity issues, as well as public education on environmental issues.

Nerush-Press Green Information Agency
ul. Ivanovskaya 38, kv. 16
220088   Minsk
Tel: 33-20-53, 36-50-76
Contact: Valeriy A. Dranchuk

This organization is involved in issues of health and the environment; developing networks of NGOs active in the ecological community; public education on the environment; and development of alternative energy sources.

Next Stop–New Life
ul. Mayakovskogo 172-A, kv. 44
220028   Minsk
Tel: 21-81-79, 21-27-22, 21-16-61
Fax: 24-07-90, 21-81-79
E-mail: nextlife@glas.apc.org
Contact: Irina Sukhii, Svetlana Koroleva

Interested in the development of alternative energy sources, permaculture and environmental education.

Professional Ecologists' Association of Belarus
Oboiniy per., d. 4
220004   Minsk
Tel: 26-71-06
Fax: 26-71-06
Contact: Vladimir N. Bakhirev

Areas of interest include monitoring air pollution and environmental education.

Public Relations Association
a/ya 88
ul. Kranoarmeiskaya 24
220030   Minsk
Tel: 27-83-75, 43-56-43
Fax: 27-83-75
Contact: Andrei V. Laptenok

This association is interested in public education, development of NGOs, and the role of mass media and publishers in environmentalism.

Small Rivers International Association
ul. Slavinskogo 1/2
220086   Minsk
Tel: 63-59-06, 64-12-01
Fax: 64-27-34, 63-08-43
E-mail: gerar@wri.belpak.minsk.by
Contact: Tamara M. Pushkareva

Small Rivers is interested in environmental education, developing NGO networks for information sharing, nature conservation and sustainable natural resource development.

Special Olympics Belarus
ul. Sovietskaia 9
220626   Minsk
Tel: 20-11-86
Fax: 20-84-83
Contact: Mr. Valentin Shukh, Chairman

Sphere
ul. V. Khorunzhei 31-A
220002 Minsk
Tel: 34-07-25, 34-01-62
E-mail: pekot@be.glas.apc.org
Contact: Svetlana Petrovna Koptel

Sphere is interested in developing information sharing networks among environmental NGOs in Belarus, as well as in environmental hazards monitoring.

Students' National EcoCenter of Belarus
ul. Makaenka 8
220023   Minsk
Tel: 64-50-70
Contact: Zinaida V. Borisova

The Students' EcoCenter is interested in issues of sustainable natural resource management, as well as environmental education.

Students' Nature Protection Team

Belarusan State Technical University
ul. Sverdlova 13-A
220630 Minsk
Tel: 27-82-73
Contact: Andrei Ivanovich Rovkach

This organization is interested in biodiversity, nature conservation, and public education on the environment.

Union of Cooperatives of Belarus

per. Voyskovy 12
220034 Minsk
Tel: N/A
Fax: 39-12-90

Union of Entrepreneurs and Lessees of Belarus

ul. Bersona 16
220079 Minsk
Tel: 20-31-14
Fax: 27-03-42

Union of Entrepreneurs of the Republic of Belarus

ul. Internatsionalnaia 13
220050 Minsk
Tel: 27-14-83
Fax: 27-15-96
Contact: Vladimir Karyagin, President

United Way of Belarus

ul. Uralskaya 3-30
220038 Minsk
Tel: 30-32-76
Tel/fax: 30-80-54
E-mail: beluwi@minsk.sovam.com
cmwilde@minsk.sovam.com

Contacts: Caryn M. Wilde, Executive Director; Anna I. Sergeeva, Program Coordinator

United Way International began its activity in Belarus in 1993 with a research grant from World Learning. Funding from the Eurasia Foundation made it possible to establish United Way Belarus, a national organization. In 1994, United Way Belarus created a Belarusan Center for NGO Development. The Center offers the following services free-of-charge to newly created NGOs: use of computers, a fax, e-mail, tele-phones, a photocopier; a library of NGO development materials; quarterly semi-nars; monthly round tables for both the PVO and NGO community; publication of a monthly newsletter; consultations on how to prepare proposals; legal advice; a database of existing NGOs and PVOs; and temporary office space for visiting PVOs.

Objectives for 1995-1996 include opening three affiliate offices, in Brest, Vitebsk and Gomel; establishing a computer training lab; creating a civilian volunteer initiative; and developing an East-West Linkage program. The office employs 6 people full-time, 3 part-time, and about 30 volunteers.

Young Volunteers' League

ul. Karla Marksa 40, kom. 16
220030 Minsk
Tel: 63-76-30
Fax: 63-75-54
Contact: Inna Leontievna Bylitskaya

The Young Volunteers' League is involved in environmental education.

Youth for the Environment and Service

BGU, Geology Division
pr. F. Skorina 4
220000   Minsk
Tel: 61-90-09
E-mail: sweta@by.glas.apc.org

YES is interested in environmental monitoring. It is associated with the Ecological Information Center School.

Brest (0162)

Environment and I

ul. Mopra 5, kv. 25
224013   Brest
Tel: 25-63-08
Contact: Sergei Leonidovich Sonchik

Involved in supporting and developing the NGO community in Belarus, and advocating for the environment in public policy-making.

Human Rights Committee

b-r Shevshenko 3, kv. 23
224013   Brest
Tel: 25-40-28, 25-84-90
Contact: Evgenii Kotliar,
Representative

IPO "Memorial," "Martyrology"

ul. Kirov 135-64
224013   Brest
Tel: 5-28-98, 1-67-31
Contact: Elena P. Mazko, Coordinator;
Vladimir A. Komolov, Coordinator

Gomel (0232)

"Green Class" Belarusan National Association

ul. Sovetskaya 106, kv. 65

246028   Gomel
Tel: 56-99-17
Fax: 44-23-52
E-mail: gnkaropa@by.glas.apc.org
Contact: Dr. Gennadiy N. Karopa,
Ph.D., President

Green Class, formed in 1993, seeks to develop "modern systems of environmental education in Belarus." It has more than 180 members and 16 regional branches in Belarus and abroad. All members of the association are volunteers.

Special fields of interest include: gathering and distributing information about the environment; publishing; conservation actions; conducting seminars and conferences; and NGO development.

Green Class created a system of environmental education in conditions of nuclear contamination for schools in the Chernobyl region. It has conducted many conservation actions in the Gomel region. The association collaborates with organizations of the US, France, Poland, Moldova, Ukraine, Russia, and Kazakstan. It has received grants from ISAR and Soros Foundation and its activities have received wide publicity in the Belarusan mass media.

Green Class is presently creating an International Center of Environmental Education in Gomel. It says it is "always seeking new information and contacts, and welcomes both in its challenging work in the highly polluted country of Belarus."

School of Tomorrow

ul. Zhukova 12
Gomel
Tel: 4-40-22

Contact: Galina Buoy

The School was established in 1991 with students between the ages of 6 and 10. The School emphasizes English language instruction, and conducts social studies, science and mathematics courses in English.

World Vision

Pushkina 14
a/ya 346
246050   Gomel
Tel: 55-00-17
Fax: 55-06-23
E-mail: david@wvb.gomel.by
Contact: David Stickney

Gorki (02233)

"Memorial" Society–Gorki

ul. Lazo 10
213410   Gorki
Mogilevskaia Region
Tel: 2-16-15
Contact: Anatolii M. Tretiakov, Coordinator

Krichev (02241)

"Memorial" Society–Krichev

ul. Timiriazeva 45a
213500   Krichev
Mogilevskaia Region
Tel: 2-30-12
Contact: Liubov D. Volobueva

Vitebsk (0212)

Daugava, Western Dvinsk Regional Branch of SEU

ul. Gagarina 48-A

210026   Vitebsk
Tel: 37-28-83
Fax: 96-26-81
E-mail: fa@ekog.belpak.vitebsk.by
Contact: Gennadiy N. Koshnerov

Daugava monitors radioactive pollution, promotes organic farming and sustainable urban development, and is the regional office for the Socio-Ecological Union.

Georgia

Country Code: 995

Tbilisi (32)

A Call to Serve Georgia (ACTS–Georgia)
ul. Asatiani 7
380002   Tbilisi
Tel: 96-91-33, 39-37-76
Fax: 95-38-94
E-mail: actsg@actsg.ge
Contact: Gia Tomadze, Executive Director; Gia Tsilosani, President; Eric Johnson, Program Officer.

This organization, formed in August 1993 and affiliated with ACTS International in California, works with the Salvation Army, Georgian Red Cross and other relief organizations. It has provided significant quantities of food, medicine and shelter to refugees from civil conflicts. It works closely with the Georgian Medical Association, the first private professional association in the country. With four regional offices in the country, ACTS claims to have the only nationwide distribution system for medications and medical supplies.

ACCELS Tbilisi
4 Taquaishivili, kom. 15
380079   Tbilisi
Tel: 22-01-53
E-mail: accels@tiblisi.ge

See the profile for ACTR/ACCELS in *Special Focus Organizations.*

Amnesty International
Georgia Office
ul. Shdosha 1 kv. 14
380079   Tbilisi
Tel: 23-38-13
Contact: Leo Asakiia

Association for Atlantic Cooperation
ul. Machabeli 8
Tbilisi
Tel: 99-75-84
E-mail: root@itic.ge
Contact: Irakli Melashvili

The association's main goal is to explore and publicize prospective areas of cooperation between Georgia and NATO member countries. It had 10 members at the end of 1995.

Association of Biomonitoring
G. Khandzteli 10
Tbilisi
Tel: 61-60-19, 39-03-01
E-mail: root@itic.ge
Contact: Maka Chichua

The association was founded in 1995 and is working to bring attention to the health dangers of toxic substances. It has conducted training sessions in western Georgia regarding the danger of utilizing chemical pesticides and herbicides. It has also coordinated a conference for young doctors, lawyers, economists and chemists to establish a common policy to present to government regarding chemical substances. Members numbered 13 in late 1995.

Association Green Wave
Vazha Pshavela pr. 45, etazh 18
Tbilisi
Tel: 99-71-69
E-mail: gwave@itic.ge
Contact: Maka Jakhua

Founded in 1995, Green Wave's main goal is the establishment of an independent nonprofit educational radio station dedicated to strengthening the NGO sector. Programs include economics lessons, "environmentalgrams," legal advice, discussions of ethnic conflicts, exploration of religious issues, presentations by NGO representatives, English lessons, etc. It has 58 members.

Association of Journalists
Leselidze 8
Tbilisi
Tel: 62-37-36
Contact: Tamaz Bibiluri

This association supports the development of independent journalism in Georgia and has 20 members.

Association of Scouts of the Republic of Georgia
Uznadze 52
Tbilisi
Tel: 95-63-95
Contact: Nana Bilashvili

The Scouts have prepared camps for young leaders, international gatherings and ecological explorations. They also have coordinated distribution of food to refugees and senior citizens. There are 480 scouts in this association.

Association of Young Georgian Economists and Business Leaders
26 May Square
ul. Dolidze 2, kom. 708-709
Tbilisi
Tel: 36-32-13
E-mail: aygeb@itic.ge
Contact: Kakha Shaiashmelashvili

The Association formed in 1994 to prepare skilled economists through

seminars for youth and university students. It has 70 active members.

Biological Farming Association "Elkana"
Tarkhinishvili Chikhi 9
Tbilisi
Tel: 29-46-42
E-mail: gior@elkana.ge
anatolz@elkana.ge
Contact: Nana Nemsadze

Elkana was established in 1993 and officially registered in 1994 by a group of farmers and members of the Georgia Green party to promote organic and biological farming in Georgia. Nearly 30 farms across Georgia participate in Elkana. Each farm serves as an organic farming model for its area, and each farmer is required to contribute a percentage of his or her produce to a local charity. For example, one farm provided vegetables for a soup kitchen for pensioners in Tbilisi, and in return, the employees of the soup kitchen assisted the farmer during harvest.

Elkana is establishing an organic farming school and demonstration site near Tbilisi, and provides courses on farming, ecology and mechanics. It intends for the school to serve as an extension service and provide on-site consultation for local farmers. It is translating nearly 200 books and documents on organic farming into Georgian, and, with a grant from ISAR, will publish brochures on a variety of organic farming methods and topics.

Caucasian Institute for Peace, Democracy and Development
Davit Agmashenebeli pr. 89/24, etazh 6
a/ya 4 (158)
380002 Tbilisi
Tel: 95-47-23, 71-61-65

Fax: 95-44-97
E-mail: cipdd@cipdd.ge
             cipdd@iphil.kheta.georgia.su
             giat@iphil.kheta.georgia.su
URL: http://ourworld.compuserve.com/
homepages/armazi/cipdd.htm
Contact: Ghia Nodia, Chairman;
George Tarkhan-Mouravi,Vice-
Chairman; Irakli Mchedlishvili, Executive Director.

CIPDD was founded in August 1992 in Tbilisi. It is a nongovernmental, nonprofit organization involved in research, publishing, and related activities. Its main objective is "to promote democratic and free-market values, publicize the major achievements of Western democratic thought, and encourage non-partisan theoretical analysis of problems related to the post-Communist transition process in Georgia and the Caucasus region."

The Institute has sponsored a survey of public attitudes toward law and legality in Georgia; coordinated a project for the UN Development Program which resulted in publication of a Human Development Report for Georgia; and organized seminars and conferences on topics such as regional problems of the Caucasus and the socio-psychological problems of a post-communist transition.

It is also part of a research project on Ethnic Conflicts in the NIS, financed by the European Community and led by the London School of Economics.

CIPDD has translated and published the Universal Declaration of Human Rights; Montesquieu's *Spirit of the Laws*; early 20th century essays by Russian philosophers on themes of democracy and revolution; M. Mamardashvili's *Classic and Non-Classic*

Ideals of Rationality; Vaclav Havel's *The Power of the Powerless*; and *Reason from Woe*, a collection of original essays on the problems of democratic transition in Georgia.

CIPDD issues a monthly bulletin in English, *The Georgian Chronicle*, available by e-mail or international mail upon request. An informational brochure on political parties in Georgia was published in October 1992 and another is forthcoming soon.

Besides CIPDD's permanent staff, 25-30 persons are associated with the Institute on a contractual basis and loosely organized into four units: Publishing House; Video Studio; Information Unit; and Conference Unit.

Center for the Study and Protection of Small Animals
ul. Toidsa , 6
380002   Tbilisi
Tel: 93-25-55
E-mail: cspsa@itic.ge
Contact: Ramaz Gokhelashvili

The Center for the Study and Protection of Small Animals was established in 1994 to preserve threatened and endangered small animal species in Georgia, particularly amphibians. With funding from ISAR, the center has produced informational and educational literature. It is supporting measures for the preservation of three amphibian species, as well as the captive-breeding and re-population of natural habitats where extinction has already occurred. It has 15 members.

Center for Sustainable Tourism
Griboedovi 14
Tbilisi
Tel: 99-63-04
E-mail: levano@ecopro.ge

Contact: Vano Vashakmadze

The Center for Sustainable Tourism was formed in 1995 out of the activities of the Caucasus Club, one of the first NGOs in Georgia. It is dedicated to developing an ethical code for ecotourism, educating future guides and operators, and exploring ecotourism opportunities in Georgia. The 10 members of the group have organized regular clean-up activities in ecologically sensitive parks near Tbilisi, led volunteer trail repair actions and workshops on ecotourism, and conducted a survey for the UNDP on ecotourism possibilities in the Black Sea Basin.

Child and Environment
ul. L. Asatiani 60
Tbilisi
Tel: 93-14-56
Contact: Nana Iashvili

The center was founded in 1995 and works on the problems of poor and homeless children in Tbilisi. Child and Environment has organized a benefit concert to raise money for homeless children, and has organized numerous art exhibitions for children. It has 60 members.

Curatio International Foundation
144 Tsereteli pr. 123
380000   Tbilisi
Tel/Fax: 99-63-80
E-mail: cif@curatio.ge
Contact: Dato Gzirishvili, President

Founded in 1994 by a group of specialists in the field of emergency medicine, CIF conducts intensive public education campaigns to upgrade the general level of medical know-

ledge in Georgia. It provides information to the media, especially through a special newspaper on medical issues, *New Carabadin*. It conducts CPR courses through seminars and television for police, firemen and other citizens. Recently, recognizing that the current level of utilization of antibiotics by Georgian children is 40 times higher than international standards, CIF has conducted one-on-one discussions with parents about the dangers of overdosing.

Beginning in September 1995, as part of a new system of local social security, implemented with the assistance of the Khashuri city administration, CIF has provided membership cards to single at-risk individuals which give them access to emergency medical assistance. This is one of several social security projects undertaken by CIF in cooperation with the international community and with Georgian local administrations.

With funding from USAID, CIF has helped to restore three enterprises that provide income to the blind community, the Saguramo boarding house, Akhalgori orphanage, and refugees.

The Eurasia Foundation
ul. Ninoshvili 19B
375009   Tbilisi
Tel: 95-45-55
Fax: 93-28-20
E-mail: eftbilis@iberiapac.ge

See the profile for the foundation in *Clearinghouse Organizations*.

Group "EcoPro"
Society "Caucasian Club"
c/o ITIC
a/ya 7
380002   Tbilisi

Tel/Fax: 98-77-97
E-mail: levano@ecopro.ge
Contact: Vano Vashakmadze, Project
Coordinator,

EcoPro is a small working group of the
Society "Caucasian Club" (SCC), one
of the first registered NGOs in Georgia
(1988). Founded by a group of volunteers working on the Transcaucasus
Railway project, the SCC aims to
preserve the nation's cultural and
natural heritage, to advance humanitarian ideals in society, and to promote
small initiative groups. In 1994 SCC
established EcoPro, dedicated to
developing Georgian standards for ecotourism and later that year EcoPro
received a small grant from ISAR to
combine environmental protection
with the development of tourism.

  With the support of the Guides and
Scouts Association of Georgia and the
municipal service of the Mtatsminda
district, EcoPro organized a number of
clean-up activities outside of Tbilisi.
Teenagers pulled trash out of the beautiful Tsavkisi Canyon and participated
in small lectures about transforming
the cleaned paths into "greenways."

  EcoPro aims to popularize the
concepts of eco-tourism in the regions
outside of Tbilisi. It has supported the
establishment of a regional office at the
Kazbegi Museum of Alpinism which
will in the near future include training
classes in different environmental
fields, the renovation of the alpinism
library, volunteer trail programs, and
summer camps.

English Teachers Association of Georgia

Zemo Vedzisi 121
Tbilisi
Tel: 37-08-21
Contact: Rusiko Tkemaladze

The association formed in 1994 in
order to coordinate English teachers
across Georgia and provide
opportunities for them to improve their
skills and techniques. It has 200
members.

Fair Elections Society

89/24 Agmashenebeli pr., etazh 5
Department of City Projects
Tbilisi
Tel: 96-72-89, 95-45-59
Contact: Zaal Kikodze, Chairman of
Coordinating Council; Nugzar
Ivanidze, Executive Director

Forty-six political parties, eight
electoral blocks and six presidential
candidates participated in Georgia's
November 1995 elections. The Fair
Elections Society was formed with the
support of the National Democratic
Institute for International Affairs at the
initiative of a group of Georgian
NGOs. It aims to assist in the creation
of a democratic political process and
the promotion of an active role by
citizens in governmental life. During
the 1995 elections it deployed hundreds
of trained poll watchers and elections
monitors to ensure the integrity of the
democratic process.

Gaia

Agmashenebeli 178
Tbilisi
Tel: 37-36-04, 38-45-41
E-mail: gaia@itic.ge
Contact: Zaal Kikvidze

Gaia was formed in 1995 to implement
new educational methodologies in
Georgian schools, especially through
environmental and human rights
education. Gaia has established a
Teachers Training Institute and opened
the first two "model" grades in a Tbilisi

public school. Gaia had 15 members at the end of 1995.

Georgian Arts and Culture Center

3 Rustaveli pr., etazh 3
Tbilisi
Tel: 93-56-85
Fax: 29-14-02
E-mail: art@georgia.org.ge
Contact: Maka Dvalishvili

Founded in 1995, the GACC's mission is two-fold:
- to increase the economic viability and technological capability of Georgian artists and crafts people, and
- to ensure the continuation and preservation of Georgian art and culture. It has 50 members.

Georgian Center for Transition Economic System and Sustainable Development

Gamsakhurdia pr. 4, kom. 611
Tbilisi
Tel: 36-70-42
E-mail: socecinf@iberiapac.ge
Contact: Dato Adeishvili

This organization was established in 1994 to work out a coordinated concept of sustainable development for Georgia. The group has conducted educational activities for sustainable development for youth and specific analysis of the Mstskheta region. It has 16 members.

Georgian Chamber of Commerce and Industry

ul. I. Chavchavadze 1
380079 Tbilisi
Tel: 12-25-54
Fax: 99-73-13

Georgian Ecological Foundation

ul. Universiteti 2
380086 Tbilisi
Tel: 22-46-36
Contact: Nika Oniani

Established in 1992, the foundation has developed environmental education manuals for teachers and students.

Georgian Society for the Protection of Animals

ul. Galaktioni 20
Tbilisi
Tel: 22-57-91
E-mail: me@chat.kheta.ge
Contact: Mzia Lolishvili

The society formed in 1993 to protect domestic animals and to encourage humane treatment of animals. It has worked with the World Society for the Protection of Animals and the Bridget Bardot Foundation to improve conditions for animals in the Tbilisi Zoo. With a grant from ISAR, the society has also established and implemented a strategy for addressing the problem of stray dogs in Tbilisi. It had a membership of 200 at the end of 1995.

Georgian Women's Congress

ul. Lermontov 8
Tbilisi
Tel: 22-50-40
Contact: Neli Bobokhidze

Founded in 1993, the congress has a membership of 20.

Georgian Young Law Association

ul. Orbeliani 30
Tbilisi
Tel: 93-61-01

E-mail: lawyer@gyla.org.ge
Contact: Dato Usupashvili

Since 1994 the association has supported the establishment of civil society based on law. GYLA has an active legal library, provides free legal advice to NGOs and refugees, conducts educational programs on the importance of law, and has helped in the drafting of nonprofit legislation for Georgia. It has a membership of 200.

Grana
ul. Tskneti, 1
Tbilisi
Tel: 22-52-78
Contact: Liana Gogichaishvili

Grana was established in 1994 to address health issues facing the Georgian population. One of its projects has been creating a monitoring system of aller-genic diseases. It has five members.

Green Earth
Mazniashvili 43
380002 Tbilisi
Tel: 95-52-56
E-mail: temo@coira.kheta.ge
Contact: Nugzar Meladze

Since 1994 Green Earth has been active promoting solar energy in Georgia. It has a small center to exhibit solar technologies and the advantages of solar energy.

Handicapped Persons League
ul. Tsemi 9
Tbilisi
Tel: 34-76-89
Contact: Goga Kokhreidze

The League was established in 1995 to integrate handicapped persons into society, for example, by providing opportunities for handicapped persons to participate in expeditions in the Caucasus mountains. It has 163 members.

Helsinki Citizens' Assembly–Georgia
Tsinamdzgvrishvili 31
Tbilisi
Tel: 96-15-16
Fax: 35-16-74
E-mail:
sasha@mesame.kheta.georgia.su
Contact: Alexander Russettsky

Since 1991 HCA has conducted conferences and seminars which bring together different ethnic groups from around the Caucasus, in an effort to advance peace-building initiatives in the region. HCA participated in the Transcaucasian Dialogue which assisted in the release of many prisoners from the Nagorno-Karabakh conflict. Its membership numbered 97 at the end of 1995.

Human Ecology Center
Irakli Abashidze 116A
Tbilisi
Tel: 22-24-32
E-mail: shery@iberiapac.ge
humeco@itic.ge
Contact: Maia Mgaloblishvili

HUMECO was established in 1994 to work on environmental issues in Georgia. Its membership consists of scientists, health care providers and ecologists.

HUMECO's initial project is to study the effects of the Chernobyl nuclear accident in western Georgia and its current effect on the thyroid gland disease of the affected population. It has brought its research to the attention of government and humanitarian organizations. It has also conducted an investigation of the manganese pollution around a Georgian mine and its effect on the health of the local population. The organization has received support for its projects from the ISAR/USAID Seeds of Democracy program. It had 54 members as of the end of 1995. HUMECO is a member of GREENWAY, an international network of environmental NGOs.

International Center for Conflict and Negotiation
Chavchavadze 16, entry 3
Tbilisi
Tel: 22-36-18
E-mail: iccn@iccn.aod.ge
Contact: George Khutsishvili

The center was established in 1995 and has five members. It monitors conflicts in the country and region and publishes information about them.

International Center for Georgian Reform and Economic Development
26th May Square 2, rooms 415-416
Tbilisi
Tel: 98-47-06, 36-01-77
E-mail: icrdge@itic.ge
postmaster@glas.apc.org
(Sb: for Orvelashvili)
Contact: Niko Orvelashvili

ICRDGE was established in 1994 and has been active in writing investment legislation, establishing Junior Achievement in Georgia, conducting summer camps on the interaction between economics and ecology, and conducting surveys of the population's attitudes towards economic changes. It has 55 members.

International Telecommunications and Information Center
a/ya 7
Agmashenebeli pr. 89/24,
etazh 10, kom. 102
Tbilisi
Tel/Fax: 98-77-97
E-mail: root@itic.ge
Contact: Valeri Nanobashvili

The center was established in 1995 to be a clearinghouse to the developing Georgian NGO community by providing computer and e-mail training, publishing a monthly newsletter on Georgian NGO activities (*New Georgia*), coordinating networking meetings among NGOs, and publishing a monthly database on Georgian NGOs. The organization has 40 members.

ISAR–Caucasus
Agmashenebeli pr. 89/24
Tbilisi
Tel: 96-91-30
Fax: 98-77-97
E-mail: mclayton@isargeo.ge
postmaster@isargeo.ge
Contact: Michael Clayton

See profile of ISAR in section *Clearinghouse Organizations*.

Khomli
Nutsubidze Plato, 3rd mikroraion, 16
Tbilisi
Tel: 31-14-51
E-mail: khomli@itic.ge
Contact: Rezo Shalibashvili

Established in 1993, Khomli is a film production studio which highlights the unique cultural and historical monuments of Georgia with regular television and radio broadcasts. It has 17 members.

Mteni
ul. Vazha-Pshavela 5, korp. 4, kv.12
Tbilisi
Tel: 31-74-46
Contact: Aza Mdinaradze

Established in 1995, Mteni initiated an
anti-smoking campaign, aimed at
Georgian youth. It has 12 members.

Multiple Assistance for Georgia
K. Gamsakhurdia pr., 10
380060 Tbilisi
Tel/Fax: 37-19-18
E-mail: mag@if.ge
Contact: Marina Murvanidze

MAG was established in May 1994 to
provide humanitarian assistance and
support the development of Georgia's
civil society. MAG seeks to bridge the
gap between providing relief assistance
and the actual development of an
indigenous NGO community capable of
responding to societal needs. MAG has
also worked in the health sector,
supporting programs in maternal and
child health, AIDS awareness,
education and prevention, and
development of a local pharmaceutical
industry. MAG works with local NGOs
and community groups, governmental
organizations, UN agencies, and
international NGOs.

National Democratic Institute–Georgia
Tbilisi
Tel/Fax: 93-58-30
E-mail: Tbilisi@ndi.ge

See profile for NDI in *Special Focus
Organizations*.

Noah's Ark Center for the Recovery of Endangered Species

ul. Shanidze 33
Tbilisi
Tel: 22-57-91, 29-00-58
E-mail: jason@nacres.ge
Contact: Dr. Jason Badridze, Director

Established in 1989, NACRES focuses
on the protection and reintroduction of
large mammals, especially those in
danger of extinction. NACRES has
conducted scientific surveys on hyena
and wolf populations in protected areas
in Georgia, has written wildlife legislation for Parliament, and has pushed for
the passage of environmental conven-
tions in Georgia. It is currently the lead
agency for the UNDP\UNEP Biodiversity Country Study. Its members
numbered 20 at the end of 1995.

Open Society–Georgia Foundation
Veriko Anjaparidze 9
380008   Tbilisi
Tel: 29-10-52, 93-89-99
Fax: 22-06-89
E-mail: kartuli@osgf.ge
Contact: Ulana Trylowsky

See profile of Open Society Institute in
section *Clearinghouse Organizations*.

"Peaceful Cultural Bridges" International Association of Youth
ul. Kekelidzc 25
Tbilisi
Tel: 23-23-15
Fax: 93-31-99
Contact: Eka Shanshiashvili

Since 1994, this organization has
worked to provide opportunities for
youth of different nations and beliefs to
interact and share experiences. Cultural
Bridges has established cultural days of
different countries in Tbilisi.

Poseidon Marine Association

E-mail: poseidon@iberiapac.ge
Contact: David Nikoleishvili

The association is interested in the Black Sea, mussel farming, and environmental education.

Society for Memory and Support of Victims of Political Repression in Georgia "Memorial"

pr. Kindzmaraulskii 13-16
380123   Tbilisi
Tel: 37-85-55, 37-02-26
Fax: 93-37-77
Contact: Mindiia Salukvadze

Special Olympics Georgia

Chavchavadze pr. 49a
380071   Tbilisi
Tel: 66-33-49
Contact: Mr. Teimuraz Mikiashvili, Chairman

"Student" International Association of Youth

ul. University 11
Tbilisi
Tel: 37-28-71
Contact: Misha Gelashvili

"Student" was organized in 1995 to help youth in different branches of art, social and charitable activities. The group now has 107 members.

Udabno

Nutsubidze 77
Tbilisi
Tel: 39-54-73
Fax: 99-88-23
E-mail: root@itic.ge
Contact: Lado Miranalasvhili

Founded in 1994, Udabno is working to preserve the David Gareji monastery sights and the sensitive ecological situation on the Georgian-Azerbaijan border. Udabno has 20 members.

Vitacenter of the Georgian Children's Federation

Vazha Pshavela pr., 76
380086   Tbilisi
Tel: 30-22-53
Fax: 98-39-98
E-mail: root@itic.ge
Contact: Shota Makhlakelidze

Vitacenter was established in 1991. It is developing ecological education for children through the creation of an ecological museum (formerly the Soviet Army Museum in Tbilisi). It also sponsors regular expeditions for children. The organization has six members.

World Wide Fund for Nature– Georgia

Academy of Sciences
Rustaveli pr. 52, kom. 203
Tbilisi
Tel: 99-84-64
Fax: 99-86-28
E-mail: isargeo@glas.apc.org

The World Wide Fund for Nature, at the request of the Georgian government, is working to preserve the natural and cultural heritage of the country. Based on data from ecological research and with the objective of nature conservation and sustainable development, WWF has assisted in selecting seven planning regions for a new Protected Area System.

Youth Association of the UN

Vazha Pshavela pr. 45
380077   Tbilisi
Tel: 39-86-33
Contact: Ana Nakashidze

Since 1993 the Youth Association of the UN has been working to involve youth in sessions and activities which advance the goals of the United Nations. As of the end of 1995, it had 137 members.

Dzhvari

Dzhvari
ul. Rustaveli. 3, etazh 3
Dzhvari
Tel: 3-11-36
Contact: Londa Khasaia
Established in 1995 to develop activities for the young children of the small village of Dzhvari, and to involve them more fully in their own education. Dzhvari recently established a full-time eco-school/museum (focusing on local cultural and environmental traditions). It is also active in bringing attention to the environmental and cultural impact of the development of large hydroelectric dams in Georgia.

Khashuri

Eco-Law
ul. April 9-5
Khashuri
Tel: 98-60-39
E-mail: root@itic.ge
Contact: Paliko Abaiadze

Eco-Law was established in 1995 and promotes pro-environmental legislation through the publication of booklets. It has eight members.

Regional Fund for Environmental Protection
Tabidze 2
Khashuri

E-mail: root@itic.ge
Contact: David Tsikarishvili

Founded in 1992 to promote environmental journalism, the fund has published a regular newspaper on local environmental problems and coordinated the creation of an ecological park in the middle of Khashuri.

Rustavi

Energy Efficiency Fund
7 microregion 13/33
383040   Rustavi
Tel: 12-11-81
E-mail: energy@itic.ge
Contact: Vakhtang Zarkua

The fund was established in 1995 to encourage the use of alternative energy possibilities, especially during the current difficult situation with energy in Georgia. Its 35 members have created a model biogas generator in a village in eastern Georgia and installed energy efficient stoves in orphanages in Tbilisi.

Kazakstan

Country Code: 7

Almaty (3272)

ACCELS Almaty
pr. Seifullina 531, kom. 208
480083 Almaty
Tel: 63-20-56, 63-30-06
E-mail:
accels.almaty@sovcust.sprint.com

See the profile for ACTR/ACCELS in section *Special Focus Organizations*.

Almaty City Ecology Center
74-a Ablay-chan
480091 Almaty
Tel: 62-70-03, 63-92-54
Contact: Svetlana Mitrofansky, Director

Almaty City Uigur Cultural Center
ul. Vinogradov 85, kv. 129
Almaty
Tel: 65-46-41

The Center works on the revival and development of the Uigur culture, traditions, and language. It offers classes in ancient history and culture of the Uigur people; children's courses in the Uigur language; and contributes to the improvement of inter-ethnic relations in Kazakstan. The Center would like to establish contacts with Uigurs living in the U.S.

Almaty Helsinki Committee
Mikroraion Koktem 1, d. 26, kv. 43
480070 Almaty

Tel/Fax: 47-70-79
Contact: Ninel' Konstantinovna Fokina

Artists' Union
Almaty
Tel: 63-43-23
Contact: Andrei Vishnayakov, Secretary

BRIF
Social & Marketing Research Agency
ul. Mukanov 227
a/ya 107
Almaty
Tel: 44-19-60
Fax: 53-64-68
E-mail: slava@brif.alma-ata.su
Contact: Alexander Ruzanov, President

BRIF is an independent private research company founded in 1991 to analyze the social, political, and economic processes in Kazakstan, the second largest republic of the former Soviet Union. It has been described by objective observers as "the first private and really independent research group in Kazakstan." The firm was established by sociologists who left RCIOM (the Republic public opinion research institution). They began with public opinion polls, initially conducted in Almaty only, but gradually expanding throughout the republic. They now claim to cover all Central Asia.

Businessman's Congress of Kazakstan
ul. Naurisbai Batir 65/69
480091 Almaty
Tel: 69-20-01
Fax: 53-51-17
Contact: Stanislav V. Urzhumanov, Vice President

Center in Support of Environmental Education

Zhetysu 2-49-6
480063 Almaty
Tel: 22-34-54
Fax: 63-12-07 (specify box 898)
E-mail: network@glasnet.apc.org
Contact: Gulmira Dzhamanova,
Coordinator

The center was organized in 1989 by a group of students and lecturers from Kazak State National University. Its mission is to increase the environmental awareness of citizens of all ages. The center has three main projects:
• Green Education was the center's first project. In 1991, it organized a national competition for young environmental scientists. The competion is now a yearly event sponsored by the Center.
• GLOBE (Global Learning and Observations to Benefit the Environ-ment) is a worldwide science education program that coordinates the work of students, scientists and teachers to study and understand the global environment.
• The CASDIN (Central Asian Sustainable Development Information Network) project was developed in 1994 when the need for an NGO support organization was identified. CASDIN publishes the monthly newsletter "Sustainable Development"; is in the process of developing a database of Central Asian NGOs; provides NGOs with information on local, regional and international funding sources; announces upcoming network-ing events such as conferences and meetings; assists NGOS with proposal writing; and provides access to computer, fax, photocopying and e-mail on a limited basis. CASDIN also organizes, together with international NGOs, seminars and workshops on NGO management, fundraising and community involvement.

Staff includes five paid members, four active volunteers, and one U.S. Peace Corps Volunteer.

Charitable Fund for the Promotion of Business Undertakings by Orphans and the Protection of their Rights

ul. Begalin 87
Almaty
Tel: 23-11-59

The fund works to provide children with professions, bank accounts, and apartments through job-skills training (in sewing, knitting, construction, embroidery, cooking, typing, furniture making, agriculture, etc.). It would like to establish contacts with analogous NGOs in order to receive technical assistance, and to develop further training opportunties for its students.

Chernobyl Union of the Republic of Kazakstan

ul. Vinogradov 85, kv. 415
Almaty
Tel: 63-39-00

The Chernobyl Union assists victims of the accident with rehabilitation and medical services. The Union also provides jobs for disabled individuals. The Chernobyl Union is searching for partners willing to assist in making further contacts with public organiza-tions, and provide technical and material assistance.

Congress of Entrepreneurs

ul. Naurisbai Batir 65/69
480091 Almaty
Tel: 269-2001

Fax: 253-5117
Contact: Bolat B. Dgamishev, Deputy Chairman

COUNTERPART Foundation
Central Asia Headquarters
ul. Vinogradova 49/22
Almaty
Tel: 63-18-40
Tel/Fax: 63-82-68
E-mail: root@cpart.alma-ata.su
Contact: Leonard Klein, Central Asia Regional Director

COUNTERPART heads a consortium of organizations awarded a grant by USAID to "foster the creation of effective, democratic and sustainable indigenous NGOs." The three components of the program are: (a) training; (b) facilitating information exchange among regional NGOs and between them and the international community; and (c) operating a small grants program for qualified Central Asian NGOs. For more information, see *Clearinghouse Organizations.*

Democratic Committee for Human Rights
ul. Vinogradova 85, korp. 405
480070 Almaty
Tel: 34-869
Contact: Oleg Arbaev, Committee Representative

Ecocenter of Almaty
ul. Lenina 74
Almaty
Tel: 62-70-03
Contact: Murat Chembulatov

Ecofund of Kazakstan
Almaty
Tel: 67-74-59
Fax: 53-85-80

E-mail: ecostan@glas.apc.org
Contact: Lev Ivanovich Kurlapov, Victor Zonov, Co-Chairs; Yuri Rubezhanskiy

Ecofund is involved with issues related to the effects of nuclear testing, use of agrochemicals and pesticides, and ecological education.

Ecological Fund of Kazakstan "Initiative"
ul. Toslonko 31
400037 Almaty
Tel: 29-55-59
Fax: 67-21-24
E-mail: ecostan@glas.apc.org
Contact: Victor Zonov

The fund conducts scientific and environmental research, including research in habitat mapping, alternative energy sources, and environmentally related health problems. The Ecological Fund of Kazakstan is interested in an exchange of information with foreign NGOs in a variety of areas, including: publication of environmental children's books; joint arrangements of ESL courses in Almaty; and partnerships to devise and construct sewage and waste treatment facilities.

The Eurasia Foundation
Panfilova 151, kv. 6
480064 Almaty
Tel/Fax: 69-97-29

See the profile for the foundation in the section *Clearinghouse Organizations.*

Flamingo
Aksai 4, 75-27
480127 Almaty
Tel: 24-21-61
Fax: 63-12-07

Flamingo is involved with charitable activities, crafts, and commerce in the arts. This international organization seeks contacts with women's NGOs and organizations that support creative cultural work, and would like to cooperate in an exchange of exhibitions between the U.S. and Kazakstan.

Friendship Society
ul. Kurmongazy 4
Almaty
Tel: 62-99-22
Contact: Zhibek Amirkhanova, Chairman

Fund in Support of Ecological Education
Almaty
Tel: 41-29-91, 29-48-20
Contact: Zharas Takenov, Chair

Green Salvation
Almaty
Tel: 67-89-06, 67-13-52
E-mail: ecoalmati@glas.apc.org
Contact: Sergei Kuratov, Chair

Intergovernmental Association of Uigurs
Aksai 4, 57-50
480127   Almaty
Tel: 24-16-78

The association works to preserve and revive the Uigur culture, its traditions, and language. It holds anniversary celebrations and festivals and provides education for young people in the Uigur tradition. The organization is in search of foreign partners and concentrations of Turkic-speaking peoples.

"Interlegal"–Kazakstan Branch
8 mikroraion, 4a, kom. 301

480035   Almaty
Tel: 39-83-21, 23-07-62
Fax: 68-07-56
E-mail: polex@aebexc.alma-ata.su
            serge@aebexc.alma-ata.su
Contact: Sergei Mikhailovich Zlotnikov, Coordinator; Aleksandr Petrovich Poliakov, Coordinator

This is an affiliate of the Interlegal organization based in Moscow.

International Center of Business Cooperation
ul. K. Marxa 18
480016   Almaty
Tel: 33-29-71, 32-21-46
Fax: 33-29-75
Contact: Gala Medvedskaya

ISAR–Central Asia
Almaty
Tel: 32-57-79
E-mail: isarata@glas.apc.org
Contact: Steve Wolff, John Sturino

See ISAR profile in section *Clearinghouse Organizations.*

Kazakstan-American Bureau on Human Rights
Amangeldy 50, kom. 26
480012   Almaty
Tel: 63-17-32, 63-23-39
            67-03-52, 47-09-66 (home)
Tel/Fax: 67-66-10
E-mail: omaz@aebexc.alma-ata.su
Contact: Evgenii Zhovtis, Executive Director; Zhemiz Turmagombetova, Coordinator

The Bureau is affiliated with the Union of Councils for Soviet Jews, profiled in the section *Clearinghouse Organizations.*

Kazakstan Association of Women Invalids with Children

ul. Baizakov 109/116
Almaty
Tel: 53-61-82
Contact: Bibigul Imangazina, President

Kazakstan Voluntary Society "Adlilet"

ul. Abaia 39
480064 Almaty
Tel: 62-91-42, 30-13-36
Fax: 33-42-97
Contact: Manash K. Kozybaev, Representative; Saule R, Aitambetova, Executive Secretary

Lop Noor Semipalatinsk Ecological Committee

Almaty
Tel: 63-04-64, 63-49-02
Contact: Azat Mirtazovich Akimbek, Chair

Luis Armenian Cultural Center

ul. Geherbakov 2/22-17
Almaty
Tel: 35-88-08
Fax: 32-84-88, 32-62-62

Luis works in cooperation with similar centers in other regions to popularize Armenian history, art, and culture through the mass media. The center teaches the Armenian language and traditions as one way to improve ethnic relations and diversity in Kazakhstan.

Meyirman

Park Panfilova Shakbestoi Pavilion
480018 Almaty
Tel: 33-01-74

Meyirman provides medical assistance and other forms of aid to the single, elderly, poor, disabled, orphans, large families, and disadvantaged people.

Among its activities Meyirman delivers free food to single bedridden patients; provides one-time-only financial aid; supplies indigents with second-hand clothing; arranges and pays for the medical treatment of orphans; and has established a club for pensioners.

Meyirman would like to locate partners for charitable activities and contacts with potential sponsors.

NET Alumni Center

531 Seifullin ul., kom. 209
480083 Almaty
Tel: 69-18-60
Fax: 63-75-49
E-mail: zhalgas@sovam.com
Contact: Serik Abildinov, Director

A resource center and library for alumni of the NET training project managed by the Academy for Educational Development.

National Democratic Institute– Kazakstan

Almaty
Tel/Fax: 233-0888
E-mail: ndicasia@glas.apc.org

See NDI profile in section *Special Focus Organizations*.

Nevada–Semipalatinsk

pr. Lenina 85
480021 Almaty
Fax: 63-12-07
Contact: Alina Nesterova, Coordinator

Nevada-Semipalatinsk was established in 1989 when 5,000 people filled the hall of the Writers' Union in Almaty to hear Kazak poet O. Suleymenov denounce nuclear testing and call for a public meeting the next day. Since then the movement has achieved the suspen-sion of nuclear testing in the area, made links with groups abroad, and launched an investigation into the extent of radiation sickness in the area.

Peace House
Almaty
Tel: 63-19-40
Contact: Erzhan Oralbekov

Pokolenie (Generation) Pensioners Movement
ul. Vinogradov 85, kv. 413
Almaty
Tel: 63-48-00, 47-79-05

Pokolenie advocates for social and legal protection of pensioners, and provides assistance to the elderly. Pokolenie would like information on comparative social security systems, and would like to develop international partnerships for joint activities against discrimination against the elderly through the UNO committee for Human Rights, as well as to establish joint ventures and charitable activities with foreign NGOs.

Red Cross and Red Crescent Societies of Central Asia
ul. Kunaeva 86
480100 Almaty
Tel: 61-80-63, 54-27-42
Fax: 54-15-35
E-mail: ifrckz.ala@glas.apc.org
Contact: David Eby, Development Delegate

Republican Society for the Legal Development of Kazakstan (OPRK)
ul. Tole Bi 12-35
480100 Almaty
Tel: 53-16-18, 69-92-12
Fax: 69-92-12
E-mail: vitaliy@vs.kustanai.su

Contact: Vitalii I. Voronov, Representative; Andrei E. Chebotarev, Executive Secretary

OPRK was created for the purpose of developing legal education in Kazakstan. Projects include an informational-analytical bulletin and the creation of an information network within the framework of OPRK.

Shalom Jewish Cultural Center
ul. Zhibek Zholy 10/20
480002 Almaty
Tel: 30-94-04

Shalom plans and implements programs aimed at the protection and use of the Jewish language as the primary language among Jews. Those programs include study of the history, culture and art of the Jewish people, and revival of the handcraft industries of Kazak Jews. Shalom works to protect Jews' rights, and to withstand anti-Semitism in all forms. The Center seeks cooperation with foreign NGOs in the spheres of education, culture, medicine, religion, and family contacts.

Society of Greeks of the Republic of Kazakstan
ul. Vinogradov 85, kv. 425
Almaty
Tel: 62-10-88

The society organizes Greek language courses and tours of Greece as a part of its revival of the national culture and traditions of ethnic Greeks in Kazakstan. The society seeks contact with Greek Americans.

Socio-Ecological Union

ul. Furmanova 91-97, #21
480098 Almaty
Tel: 33-78-62
E-mail: isarata@glas.apc.org

Soros Foundation–Kazakstan

ul. Furmanova 117, kv. 20
480091 Almaty
Tel: 62-69-73
Fax: 62-87-83
E-mail: bkemple@soros.alma-ata.su
Contact: Brian Kemple, Executive
Director

See Open Society Institute profile in
section *Clearinghouse Organizations.*

Special Olympics Kazakstan

Prospekt Lenina 38, kom. 906
480100 Almaty
Tel: 262-3524
Fax: 263-1207
Contact: Ms. Olga Bakhareva, Director

Tagibat (EcoUnion and Green Party)

Almaty
Tel: 63-17-17, 21-39-93
Contact: Mels Hamsaevich Elusizov

Tatar-Bashkin Social and Cultural Center

ul. Vinogradov 85, kv. 431
490012 Almaty
Tel: 22-07-90

The center works to revive and preserve
the national culture and distinctiveness
of the Tatar-Bashkir population of
Kazakhstan. It maintains business and
cultural ties with similar centers in
other countries and is active in work to
improve inter-ethnic relations in
Kazakhstan.

Turan Azerbaijan Cultural Center

ul. Vinogradov 85, kv. 411
Almaty
Tel: 69-41-69

Turan organizes clubs for children and
provides education in the national traditions and language of Azerbaijan. It
also sponsors activities for adults aimed
at establishing friendly relations
between all Turkic peoples.

Ukrainian Cultural Center

ul. Vinogradov 85, kv. 432
Almaty
Tel: 33-56-97
Fax: 33-84-97

The Ukrainian Cultural Center has
established a Sunday school for adults
to study the Ukrainian language, its
history, and the national liberation
movement in Kazakhstan; organized
amateur talent activities teaching
children and adults Ukrainian folklore;
and provides current information about
Ukraine. The center is looking for
contacts with similar centers in the U.S.

Unity of Families with Many Children of Almaty

ul. Pushkin 33/3
480004 Almaty
Tel: 33-45-05
Contact: Kulbara Pautova, Chairman

Volunteers in Overseas Cooperative Assistance (VOCA)

SAIKES Business Center
ul. Lenina 85-27
480021 Almaty
Tel/Fax: 263-1991
Contact: Mark Leverson, Country
Representative

See VOCA profile in section *Special Focus Organizations.*

Winrock International Institute for Agricultural Development

Kazak State Academy of Management
ul. Saina 81
480084 Almaty
Tel: 26-14-79
Contact: Kenneth A. Clatfelter, Food Scientist

See Winrock profile in section *Special Focus Organizations.*

Zhardem (Help) International Charitable Fund

ul. Furmanov 274/8
480099 Almaty
Tel: 64-74-49

Zhardem's diverse activities span from providing social services to environmental monitoring. The fund works to promote Kazak science and culture, to establish Slavic theater, as well as centers for children and teenagers to learn music, theater, fine arts, medicine.

Dzhambul

Green Movement "Oasis"

Djambul
Tel: 25-24-83
E-mail: alex@zagribelny.jambyl.kz
ecostan@glas.apc.org
(Sb: for Djambul)
Contact: Aleksander Zagribelini, Chair

Dzhezkazgan (310)

"Adilet" City Branch

ul. Sovetskaia 9a, kom. 4
472810 Dzhezkazgan

Contact: Ortsabai Dasaevich Isaev, Coordinator; Valentina Dmitrievna Marycheva, Coordinator

Karaganda (3212)

"Adilet"–Memorial Branch

ul. Dzhambula, 1-16
470061 Karaganda
Tel: 51-76-94, 51-22-17, 57-33-92
Fax: 57-33-92
Contact: Ekaterina Borisovna Kuznetsova

Karaganda Regional Ecological Center

Stepnoy-3 mikroraion, 3, kv. 249
470070 Karaganda
Tel: 75-71-40, 74-41-70 (home)
E-mail: karaganda@glas.apc.org
Contact: Kaisha Atakhanova, Member of the Socio-Ecological Union; Igor Mikhaelevich Budov, Director

The Ecocenter is involved in environmental education, eco-monitoring, biodiversity, zoology and nuclear issues.

Intercollegiate Ecology Council

Karaganda
Tel: 56-59-12, 58-07-94
E-mail: Kruis!bond@mastak.msk.su
Contact: Galina K. E. Aleksander

International Physicians for the Prevention of Nuclear War

Karaganda
Tel: 74-20-88
Contact: Marat Temirhanovich Sagimbaev

Nura

Temirtau
Tel: (3235) 2-34-10

Contact: Amankul Omarovich
Mizanbekov

Semipalatinsk (3222)

Union for Nuclear Test Victims
a/ya 296
490050   Semipalatinsk
Tel: 62-25-91
Fax: 62-34-11
E-mail:
untv@untv.escom.glas.apc.org
Contact: Galina Sumarokova; Gulsum
Kakimzhanova

UNTV seeks to protect the rights and
interests of people who suffered from
nuclear testing in Semipalatinsk.
Officially registered in January 1991,
UNTV conducts medical and
environmental research, provides
medical assistance to radiation victims,
distributes medicines and supplies
donated by foreign governments and
sends children to France and Germany
for medical treatment. In 1995 UNTV
established an Ecological Resource
Center to improve public understanding
of environmental issues and to facilitate
contact between local NGOs and
organizations around the world.

Uralsk

Association of Ecological Enlightenment
Uralsk
Tel: 5-39-65, 2-28-35
E-mail: soceco@glas.apc.org
Contact: Sergei Pavlovich Churlin

Ust-Kamenogorsk

Snow Leopards Lovers Club, Irbis
ul. Likhareva 9-24
492024   Ust-Kamenogorsk
Tel: 65-01-34
E-mail: eko@irbis.east.alma-ata.su

The snow leopard (*irbis*) is one of the
rarest of the world's big cats, and it is
threatened by extinction. The Snow
Leopards Lovers Club was created in
1993 and has members throughout the
NIS. The Club collects and disseminates information about snow leopards
to activists, the public and government
officials. It is encouraging cooperation
between the Russian Federation and
Kazakstan to expand the Russian Ust-
Kokinsky National Park across the
border into Kazakstan in order to
expand the cat's protected habitat. It
has also organized demonstrations
against the snow leopard fur trade.

Kyrgyzstan

Country Code: 7

Bishkek (3312)

Aalam Nury
ul. Paniflova 178-14
720016 Bishkek
Tel: 26-76-62, 42-95-82

Aalam Nury is dedicated to the development of Kyrgyz national culture and cooperation with other countries in the cultural sphere. It organizes international concerts and festivals. It also coordinates citizens' actions against drug abuse and works on AIDS-related issues. The organization would like to conduct joint cultural programs with U.S. NGOs, as well as develop joint educational workshops on drug abuse, AIDS, and environmental protection.

ACCELS Bishkek
ul. Kievskaya 69, kom. 9-11
720000 Bishkek
Tel: 26-42-26
E-mail: rita@accels.bishkek.su

See the profile for ACTR/ACCELS in section *Special Focus Organizations.*

Aesthetic Education Center
ul. Moskovskaja 53
720021 Bishkek
Tel: 46-54-45
Contact: Dinara Z. Chochunbaeva

Almaz Radio Station
ul. Logvinenko 13
720067 Bishkek
Tel: 22-68-63

Fax: 24-74-53

Since 1992, the independent station Almaz has broadcast programs in the Bishkek and Chui valleys in both Kyrgyz and Russian. Almaz cooperates with many NGOs–including the Association of Women of Kyrgyzstan Against Nuclear War and for Ecological Safety, the Meeim Fund, and the Women's Congress of the Kyrgyz Republic–in order to develop public interest programming. Listeners can participate in live broadcasts that deal with topics such as economic conditions in Kyrgyzstan, environmental safety, and women's and children's issues. Branches of Almaz have been opened in Osh and Jalal-Abad, and Almaz plans to expand to television.

Association of Independent Ecologists
a/ya 702
Bishkek
Tel: 41-03-84, 47-16-54
Contact: Pavel Greber

Association of Women Artists and Art Critics
ul. Maldybaeva 20, kv. 65
Bishkek
Tel: 44-55-99
Contact: Orozgan Mambetalieva

Association of Young Historians
Kyrghyz National University, Department of History
ul. Frunzaya 547
720024 Bishkek
Tel: 22-19-53
Fax: 62-05-17
Contact: Tyntchtytbek Choroev

Bishkek Lyceum of Youth Policy

per. Nerynsky 2
Bishkek
Tel: 27-19-52, 25-64-93, 41-96-36
Fax: 29-38-64
Contact: Elmira Toktogulova, Director; Zulfia Kochorbaeva, Coordinator

BLYP was developed in recognition of a need for involvement of young people in the formation of a democratic society and to provide in youth a sense of investment in a developing civil society. BLYP intends to provide a meeting ground for this process.

According to its organizers, BLYP is an intellectual laboratory, a studio for educational and cultural projects, where the organizers and their workers are young people themselves. The main interests of the Lyceum are in conducting research into the problems of young people in Central Asia, developing new teaching technologies and systems, and involving young people in a variety of civil society-building projects.

Bishkek Resource Center

National Library, kom. 92
ul. Sovetskaya 208
720000 Bishkek
Tel/Fax: 26-45-48
E-mail: bjb@adv.bishkek.su
Contact: Lena Batsman, Director; Barbara Babcock, Program Coordinator

Sponsored by the Soros Foundation, the center specializes in educational advising and English language support.

Center for Independent Research

Logvinenko 13
Bishkek
Tel: 22-48-32
Fax: 22-44-14

The Center for Independent Research conducts research in two areas: ethnic relations in the regions of Osh-Fergana and environmental issues. The center would like to establish joint research projects in these areas with other organizations.

Center on Socio-Political Problems and Connections with NGOs

Bishkek City Administration
pr. Chuy 166
Bishkek
Tel: 21-74-43, 21-14-43, 28-14-96
Fax: 22-60-21
Contact: Mrs. Mira Dzhangracheva

The Center works to establish coordination and cooperation with NGOs, women's and youth movements, and national cultural centers. It is interested in organizational experience exchange, private and public cooperation, assistance from governmental structures, movements, cultural centers, and women's social projects in occupational and educational fields.

Chamber of Commerce and Industry

ul. Kievskaya 107
720001 Bishkek
Tel: 21-05-65, 26-49-42
Fax: 21-05-75

Children's Fund

ul. Abdymomunova 276
Bishkek
Tel: 22-02-02, 22-02-12
Contact: Zarimbek Abylaev

Committee for the Defense of Lake Issyk-Kul

Bishkek
Tel: 42-27-49, 22-19-68

Contact: Omor Sultanov, President

Congress of Private Entrepreneurs

ul. Isanov 42
72000   Bishkek
Tel: 47-34-25, 46-49-49, 22-03-47
Fax: 21-36-53
Contact: Omurbek A. Abdyrakhmanov

COUNTERPART Consortium

ul. Pushkina 78
Bishkek
Tel: 22-15-91
Fax: 22-68-66
E-mail: root@world.bishkek.su
Contact: Jay Cooper, COUNTER-PART Director; Thomas Carmody, Citizens Network Director

See profile in section *Clearinghouse Organizations*.

Eco-Resources

Geologichhesky pereulok 4, kv. 53
Bishkek
Tel: 44-52-06
Contact: Oleg Kholodyyazhny

Erkin Kyrgyzstan Democratic Party

ul. Kievskaya 96 B, kv. 706
Bishkek
Tel: 22-05-24
Fax: 22-68-88

The Erkin Kyrgyzstan Democratic Party describes itself as a human rights organization that offers educational and juridical assistance. The party would like to participate in exchanges dealing with democracy training, business training, training in Western educational administration, and rule of law issues.

The Eurasia Foundation

a/ya 1966
Glavpochtampt
720000   Bishkek

See the profile for the foundation in the section *Clearinghouse Organizations*.

Foundation for Humanitarian Initiatives

bul. Erkindik 54
Bishkek
Tel: 22-04-40, 22-04-41
Fax: 22-44-14

The foundation provides assistance to Kyrgyz citizens interested in studying abroad. It organizes cultural and humanitarian exchanges with foreign NGOs. The organization would like to continue its program through student and cultural exchanges, and internships in U.S. companies.

Fund for Multi-Children Families

ul. Pushkina 78
Bishkek
Tel: 26-45-33
Contact: Erke Bayali

Fund for Protection of Maternal and Child Health

ul. T. Moldo 1
720361   Bishkek
Tel: 22-44-09, 29-70-07
Contact: Anatoly A. Ilyin, MD, President

Human Rights Movement

Tel: 22-28-58
Fax: 22-12-72, 28-83-62
Contact: Joldosh Asanov, Chairman

This informal collection of activists went through a difficult period in 1994. It now has new leadership and a "stronger commitment to nonpartisanship in its activities." It was involved together with other organizations in a hunger strike in September 1995 challenging efforts to amend provisions in the Kyrgyzstan constitution calling for periodic elections.

Independent Journalists Association

ul. Belinsky 64-8
Bishkek
Tel: 26-19-34, 28-37-43

The association issues occasional reports analyzing progress toward an independent mass media. It is interested in foreign partnerships in the areas of education, training in modern technologies, the law of mass media, and protection of journalists' rights.

InterBilim

a/ya 2024
Pushkina 78/2
720000 Bishkek
Tel: 22-85-77
Fax: 22-85-77
E-mail: root@cbilim.bishkek.su
root@world.bishkek.su
Contact: Emil Sultanbaev

InterBilim is a registered nonprofit organization that supports the community of NGOs in Kyrgyzstan through information, training and services. It particularly emphasizes those organizations working in areas of poverty alleviation, health, environment, human rights, and education.

InterBilim has a paid staff of four Kyrgyz and a voluntary director/advisor who is American. Its two areas of focus for the immediate future are NGO support and communications.

Currently InterBilim is developing a database of indigenous NGOs. It is also developing a newsletter for the nonprofit sector to inform NGOs of training opportunities and events of interest. This includes articles about NGOs in Kyrgyzstan and other countries, and articles for NGOs to use as reference materials. The newsletter is published in Kyrgyz, Russian and English.

The communications division of InterBilim will provide support for NGOs through access to information and organizations by e-mail, and eventually the Internet. Computer training, including word processing and spreadsheets, will give NGOs the ability to write proposals, develop documents and manage their accounts. Currently the organization has a small lab with four computers that is providing some immediate training and e-mail access capability.

InterBilim also intends to develop English language and computer training for adults.

International Benevolent Foundation for Childhood and Maternity Support

Bokonbaieva 102
720000 Bishkek
Tel: 22-86-66, 29-80-38
Fax: 22-13-91
Contact: Chinara S. Imankulova, Director

International Executive Service Corps

Tel: 50-62-46, 61-50-11
Fax: 50-62-46
Contact: Almazbek Chormonov, Susan Johnson

See IESC profile in section *Special Focus Organizations.*

International Physicians for the Prevention of Nuclear War
Bishkek
Tel: 22-39-37, 28-04-37
Contact: Nurlan N. Brimkulov

ISSA Ltd.
ul. Bokonbaeva 126
Bishkek
Tel: 22-05-90, 22-05-92
Fax: 22-05-80

ISSA Ltd. provides financial aid, moral support, and social rights protection to families with many children. It collects and distributes donations and other humanitarian aid to families with many children. ISSA Ltd. also advocates for support of large families.

Ittypak Association of Uigurs
ul. Pushkin 78
Bishkek
Tel: 26-52-62, 26-10-07

Ittypak is dedicated to restoration of the Uigur language, traditions, and customs, and would like to establish exchanges and internships with similar U.S. NGOs.

Kargylach
ul. Abdumamunov 205
Bishkek
Tel: 22-90-57, 22-46-94

Kargylach works to protect children from physical and sexual abuse, and encourages greater participation of children in Kyrgyz-language television programming. Kargylach also distributes cassettes of children's concerts, and establishes student exchanges. It would like to cooperate with private companies seeking investments, including in agriculture, political parties, and nonprofit NGOs.

Kyrgyz-American Bureau on Human Rights and Rule of Law
ul. Sovetskaya 175
720011 Bishkek
Tel: 26-57-54
Fax: 26-38-65
E-mail: ma@rights.bishkek.su
Contact: Natalia Ablova, Director; Marina Adamovskaya, Program Officer

The Kyrgyz-American Bureau on Human Rights and Rule of Law was created after an international conference titled "Human Rights and the Fate of Nations in Central Asia," held in Bishkek in December 1992. The main task of the Bureau is to monitor human rights violations and appeal on behalf of victims to Kyrgyz authorities or interna-tional human rights organizations.

The Bureau's investigations into specific human rights cases have revealed what they describe as "a complete ignorance by militiamen [police] in all subjects concerning human rights. . .and this is also typical of the *prokuratura* and the courts, especially on the local level." Accordingly, the Bureau has launched a program of human rights education in the secondary schools and universities.

Another major focus of the Bureau is to develop a regular exchange of information between Kyrgyz human rights groups using computer networks. There are local civil rights groups in Osh, Jala-Abad and Naryin, but communication among them at present is very limited.

Kyrgyz Medical Institute
ul. T. Moldo 1
720361 Bishkek
Tel: 22-44-23
Fax: 47-14-71
Contact: Dusne K. Kudajrov, Director

Kyrgyz Peace Research Center
ul. Pravda 108, kv. 2
720000 Bishkek
Tel/Fax: 28-04-23
E-mail: root@kprc.bishkek.su
Contact: Anara Tabyshalieva, Director

The KPRC was established to conduct research and develop materials on topics that support the process of democratization in Central Asia. Founded in November 1994, KPRC's main activity has been to train teachers in new strategies for teaching democratic values at the high school level. Under the auspices of its Education for Democracy program, the KPRC held a training seminar in Kashka-Suu in April 1995.

Kyrgyz Union of Consumer Societies
ul. Pushkin 50
720021 Bishkek
Tel: 22-54-77
Contact: Temirbek Asanalievich Kulov

Kyrgyzstan Democratic Movement
Bishkek
Tel: 22-46-94
Contact: Zhypar Zhekshyiev, Deputy Chair

Kyrgyzstan Legal Aid Movement
ul. T. Abdumamunova 205
720000 Bishkek
Tel: 27-95-28
Tel/Fax: 29-36-62
Contact: Tursunbek Akunov, Representative

Kyrgyzstan Open Development Association
Vostochnaya Promonzona 16, etazh 2
Bishkek
Tel: 43-13-83
Contact: Anatoly Maryshev, Chairman

Lop-Nor Antinuclear Movement of Kyrgyzstan
Physics Institute of the National Academy of Science
Bishkek
E-mail: root@aacadem.bishkek.su
Contact: Ivan Vasiliev

Lop-Nor Semipalatinsk Ecological Committee
Bishkek
Tel: 44-43-97
Contact: Mazhit Hussainov

"Memorial"–Kyrgyz Branch
ul. Dzerzhinskogo 664-14
720000 Bishkek
Tel: 47-44-36, 26-3-65
Fax: 24-05-60
E-mail: na@rights.bishkek.su
Contact: Natalia A. Ablova, Coordinator; Aleksandr A. Kniazev, Coordinator

Memorial–Kyrgyzstan monitors human rights violations and elections, and offers training in advocacy work.

Mercy and Health Fund of Kyrgyzstan
ul. Erkindik 10
Bishkek
Tel: 26-26-70, 26-26-55

The fund provides money, food, clothing, wheelchairs, and "meals-on-wheels" to the disadvantaged.

Movement for the Protection of Rights in Kyrgyzstan
Bishkek
Tel: 22-24-86
Contact: Tursunbek Akunov, Chair

NET Alumni Center

ul. Kievskaya 69, kom. 11
720000 Bishkek
Tel: 26-10-59, 26-35-73
Fax: 62-15-35
E-mail: netkg@sovam.com
Contact: Erkimbek Djamanbaev,
Center Manager

This is a resource center and library for alumni of the NET training project, managed by the Academy for Educational Development.

Nature Protection Movement of Kyrgyzstan–"Aleyne"

Institute of Biology
Bishkek
E-mail: emil@aleyne.bishkek.su
emil%aleyne.bishkek.su@sequent.kiae.su
Contact: Emil Shukurov

Oner Association of Craftswomen

Bishkek
Tel: 22-54-98
Contact: Sagynbubu Botabyeva

Ornithological Society of Kyrgyzstan

Bishkek
E-mail: erkin@cpart.bishkek.su
emil%aleyne.bishkek.su@sequent.kiae.su
Contact: Erkinbek Kaybekov

Republican Society for Nature Protection

ul. Pervomayskaya 54
Bishkek
Tel: 22-68-66
Contact: Temirbek Koshoyev

Rights Protection Movement of Kyrgyzstan

ul. T. Abdumamunova 205
Bishkek
Tel: 22-24-86

The "movement" provides educational and juridical assistance on civil and human rights issues. It would like to cooperate with international NGOs active in human rights issues to exchange lawyers and literature.

Social Democratic Party of Kyrgyzstan

Bishkek
Tel: 22-47-44
Contact: Mark Matus

Social Democrats of Kyrgyzstan

10 Microregion, 9-30
Bishkek
Tel: 42-59-29

The Social Democrats organization works for human rights protection and support of private entrepreneurial activity.

Soros Foundation–Kyrgyzstan

Abdumomunova 205
720301 Bishkek
Tel/Fax: 22-38-29, 22-18-94
E-mail:
humm%sfkyr.bishkek.su@sequent.kiae.su
Contact: Chinara Jakypova, Executive Director

See Open Society Institute profile in section *Clearinghouse Organizations*.

Special Olympics Kyrgyzstan

Krasnooktyabrskaya 258
720088 Bishkek
Tel 22-85-57
Fax: 22-86-04

Contact: Ms. Victoria Gorkina, Director

Tabiyat Ecological Movement
prospekt Chui 265, kom. 406
Bishkek
Tel: 25-53-84, 24-26-19
Contact: Temirbek Choduraev

Women's Congress
bul. Erkindik
720040   Bishkek
Fax: 26-70-40

The Women's Congress coordinates groups involved in the women's movement and the development of women's NGOs in Kyrgyzstan. The Congress seeks cooperation with women's NGOs abroad.

Women's League for Development of Handicrafts and Culture
Bishkek
Tel: 22-54-98
Contact: Zhanyl Tumenbayeva

Osh (33222)

ACTR/ACCELS Osh
Osh University
K. Datka kechesu 331
Main Korpus, kom. 220
714000   Osh
Tel: 22-273

See profile for ACTR/ACCELS in section *Special Focus Organizations.*

Osh Resource Center
Osh Oblast Library
ul. Kamandaktar 271
714000   Osh
Tel/Fax: 2-57-07

Contact: Bumairam Ismailova, Director; Ludmilla Kankova, Program Coordinator

Sponsored by the Soros Foundation, this center specializes in educational advising and English language support.

Moldova

Country Code: 373

Chisinau (2)

21st Century Fund for Ecology, Art and Culture, 21st Century Youth Fund, and Cumpul Ecologic Young Ecologists' Association

a/ya 7478
277008 Chisinau
Tel: 23-71-49, 26-55-32
Fax: 24-55-33
E-mail: iorgu@soros.moldova.su
iorgu@fund.xxi.moldova.su
Contact: Iorgu Apostol, Paul Strutsesku

The Youth Fund promotes environmental education through development of NGOs and an environmentally oriented mass media. The Young Ecologists' Association is promoting eco-tourism and environmental education.

ACCELS Chisinau

ul. Stefan del Mare 163, kom. 605, 606
277004 Chisinau
Tel: 24-80-12, 24-80-37
E-mail:
fsa.chisinau@sovcust.sprint.com

See profile for ACTR/ACCELS in section *Special Focus Organizations*.

Acme National Public Association

ul. Schuseva 63
277012 Chisinau
Tel: 22-16-90

E-mail: andrey@ave.moldova.su
Contact: Sergei Antonovich Kuznetsov

Acme works on environmental health and law issues.

Altair International Ecological Agency

a/ya 91
277012 Chisinau
Tel: 56-88-44
E-mail: altair@glas.apc.org
Contact: Larissa Petrovna Milovanova

Altair carries out public education about the environment and monitors environmental hazards. It distributes electronically a free monthly journal–published in English and titled *Heritage*–of news on environmental themes.

Amnesty International

ul. Kuza-Voda 37-24
277072 Chisinau
Tel: 56-65-59
Fax: 63-48-24
Contact: Viktor G. Suruchanu

Association for Environmental Education and Information "Terra Nostra"

ul. Kolomna 121, kv. 63
277012 Chisinau
Tel: 24-00-43
Fax: 23-73-86
E-mail: nostra@envinet.kiev.ua
Contact: Natalia Kravchuk

Terra Nostra works on environmental education, NGO development, and environmental law.

Ave Natura Environment and Art Society

ul. Khyngesht 64
277028 Chisinau

Tel: 72-10-97
Fax: 72-35-37
Contact: Andre V. Dumbreveanu

Areas of interest for this organization include environmental education and eco-journalism.

Botanical Society of Moldova
Botanical Institute
ul. Peduri 18
277002   Chisinau
Tel: 55-04-43

The society is involved in developing nature reserves to protect biodiversity.

Chamber of Commerce and Industry
ul. Eminescu 28
Chisinau
Tel: 22-15-52
Fax: 23-38-10
Telex: 163118 OMEGA SU
Contact: Vasily Dmitrievich Gandrabura, President

COUNTERPART
ul. Stephen cel Mare 77, #17
277012   Chisinau
Tel: 22-34-71
Fax: 22-76-93
E-mail: inga@counterp.moldova.su
Contact: Inga Koutcherenko, Country Representative

See profile in section *Clearinghouse Organizations.*

Ecological Society BIOTICA
ul. Teilor 4
277043   Chisinau
Tel/Fax: 56-15-40
E-mail: biotica@mdearn.cri.md
       bio@mdearn.cri.md
Contact: Petr Nikolaevich Gorbunenko

Biotica seeks to influence environmental legislation and promotes conservation of biodiversity, environmental impact assessments, and development of the environmental NGO community in Moldova. It authored a draft of Moldova's law on NGOs which was read in Parliament and has prepared a study on "The Legal and Financial Environment for NGOs in Moldova."

Environmental Education Association
ul. Khristo Boteva 11/1, kv. 117
277043   Chisinau
Tel: 56-56-04
Contact: Alla Ilinichna Chumak

Active in environmental education and research on environmentally-sound agricultural practices.

Environmental Movement of Moldova
Chisinau Branch
ul. Eminesku 1
277000   Chisinau
Tel: 22-15-16
Contact: Vladimir Spiridonovich Garaba

Family and Child Protection Center
pr. Dachia 32
Chisinau
Tel: 56-45-44, 23-71-80
Contact: Svetlana Myslitskaya, President

Fauna Independent Research and Public Awareness Promotion Group
ul. Ion Pelivan 2, kv. 63
277000   Chisinau
Tel: 73-97-86, 62-73-47
Contact: Andrei Georgievich Vasiliev

Fundatia De Caritate Sociala Pentru Apararea Copiilor Invalizi Si A Batrinilor

ul. Columna 76
277012 Chisinau
Tel: 22-11-10, 73-58-20
Fax: 73-57-38
Contact: Maricica Gretsu-Livitskaya, President

The Philanthropic-Social Foundation for the Protection of Disabled People and Pensioners also gives special attention to children's needs. In 1995 the Foundation planned to open a modern clinic and it was renovating a house in the center of Chisinau for its headquarters. To provide schooling for children while they are in the clinic, the center also plans to employ a team of teachers.

Ms. Gretsu-Livitskaya is a member of the Moldovan Parliament. She has a doctorate in sociology and a degree in law.

Helsinki Citizens Assembly

ul. Tielor 4, kom. 39
277043 Chisinau
Tel: 56-15-40, 24-12-95
E-mail: biotica@mdearn.cri.md
Contact: Petr Gorbunenko, Executive Director

Helsinki Committee for Human Rights

ul. M. Kostina 16-109
Chisinau
Tel: 63-48-24, 44-87-49
Contact: Shtefan Urytu, Representative

Independent Journalism Center at the Open World House

ul. Armeneasca 20
Chisinau
Tel: 22-25-07, 26-42-25

Fax: 26-05-07, 22-86-91
E-mail: cb.jc@owh.moldova.su
Contact: Corina Cepoi, Director

The center receives support from the Soros Foundation.

International Center for Economic Transformations Research

ul. Miron Costin 7, kv. 711
Chisinau
Tel/Fax: 44-43-55
Contact: A. Caraganciu

The Center's main activities include economic, social and legal research. It is seeking international partners to conduct joint research.

Kishinov Historic Enlightenment Society "Memorial"

pr. Molodexhi 20, kom. 45
Chisinau
Tel: 22-70-10
Fax: 23-28-30
Contact: Aleksei Valentinovich Kheistver, Representative

Kishinov is the Russian name for Chisinau.

Mold-Eco Foundation

ul. Yelishesku 50, kv. 15
277001 Chisinau
Tel: 26-54-50
Fax: 23-38-06
E-mail: root@eco.moldova.su
or
ul. Mihai Eminescu 50, kom. 15
277012 Chisinau
Tel/Fax: 22-19-44
E-mail: moldeco@cni.md
Contact: Valeriu Briceag, President; Liliana Ursu, Executive Secretary

Mold-Eco officially registered in May 1994. Membership dues are the U.S. equivalent of $5 for individuals, $25 for organizations or institutions.

Mold-Eco receives some financing from the Non-Budgetary Ecological Fund of the Republic of Moldova, other grants, and consulting fees. Principal staff is six persons: the president, vice-president, manager, chairman of the Board, secretary, and computer pro-grammer. None of these persons is paid a salary.

Mold-Eco supports itself on the basis of specific projects which are funded by grants. Active members number 39. Members range in age between 16 and 40. They work on translations, project development, programming, organizing wokshops, etc. The organization's associate members number more than 100.

Accomplishments of Mold-Eco in 1995 included coordinating the project "Feasibility Study for Moldova–New Regional Environmental Centres," and organising a forum of NGOs of Moldo-va on the Protection of the Danube River Basin. Mold-Eco has also been carrying out the project "Ecological Clean-up of the City of Chisinau" since September 1995.

Mold-Eco promotes the development of lawyers with ecological specializa-tions. They work with "Eco-Pravo" (Lviv), CEELI, the Association of Lawyers-Ecologists of Moldova, and NGOs in Germany.

The home address of the organiza-tion's director is: Moscova bul. 5, kv. 99, Chisinau 277068, Republic of Moldova. Home telephone: 49-25-95

Moldova-Florida International Center
Renasterii 2

277012   Chisinau
Tel: 22-51-37
Fax: 23-40-51
E-mail: lydia@florida.moldova.su
Contact: Lydia Spataru, Director;
Victor Koltsa, Associate Director

The Moldova-Florida program was established under the auspices of the Eastern Europe Linkage Institute of the State of Florida in March 1994. During its first year of existence, the Moldova-Florida program carried out or initiated the following projects:

• Agribusiness Education and Train-ing. Five students from Florida studied and worked in Moldova during the summer of 1994. Five Moldovan students also studied in the U.S. for the 1994-95 academic year.

• Media Education and Training. 20 Moldovan journalists spent one week in Washington, and seven weeks in Central Florida. They participated in an education and training program designed to help them establish and maintain an independent media center in Moldova.

• High School Student Exchanges. 20 students and 4 teachers from Ion Creanga School in Chisinau visited Washington, DC, and Winter Park High School in Orlando in October 1994. A similar number of Winter Park students and teachers visited Bucharest and Chisinau in March 1994. The two visits were made possible by Junior Achievement's "Project Globe." This project was the model for a larger program which will involve 12 high schools (6 in Moldova, 6 in Central Florida). This project, like the two previous ones above, were funded by USIA.

• Public Administration Education and Training. With funding from the Eurasia Foundation, 12 Moldovan

local and regional officials will study in Florida for a month in the spring of 1996. Later in the year Moldova–Florida plans to establish a Center for Local and Regional Government in Moldova under the auspices of the Academy of Public Administration.
• University exchanges. Agreements have been signed for student and faculty exchanges between the University of Central Florida and the Moldovan State University, the Moldovan Technological University and the University of Humanitarian Studies. Also, under the auspices of the Eastern Europe Linkage Institute's statute, approximately 50 students per year from East/Central Europe can study at any public university or community college in Florida without paying out-of-state tuition.
• Investment Promotion. Through the efforts of the Eastern Europe Linkage office, Moldova–Florida is working with Florida business leaders to stimulate investment opportunities in Moldova. Similarly, it is encouraging business leaders in Moldova to investigate joint ventures and other business opportunities in Florida.
• NGO Training. Moldova–Florida held large workshops throughout Moldova on the preparation of project proposals for nongovernmental organizations. This was part of a competition for nongovernmental, nonprofit organizations funded by The Eurasia Foundation; the program was reportedly very successful.

Moldova–Florida sponsors seminars, disco nights, film festivals and other events designed to acquaint Moldovans with America generally, and Florida specifically. Moldova–Florida also publishes a monthly newsletter for NGOs, students and businesses in

Moldova. The newsletter is distributed free of charge.

Moldova Peace Alliance
ul. Pushkina 24, kv. 7
Chisinau
Tel: 21-23-82, 23-70-86
Fax: 22-75-41
Contact: Eshanu, Representative

National Animal Protection Society of Moldova
ul. Akademicheskaya 1, kv. 431
277028   Chisinau
Tel: 73-98-21
Contact: P.I. Nesterov

The society is working to sustain biodiversity in Moldova.

Nature Newspaper
ul. Sergeya Lazo 13
277004   Chisinau
Tel: 23-71-49, 23-74-23
Fax: 23-71-57
Contact: Ioanna Yevseyevna Bobinye

The Nature Newspaper promotes activism and public education in environmental fields.

Open Society Institute–Moldova
ul. Bulgara 32
277001   Chisinau
Tel: 26-00-31, 26-44-80, 26-53-15
Fax: 26-05-07
E-mail: lbalteanu@soros.moldova.su
Contact: Lorina Balteanu, Executive Director

Rainbow–Moldova
bul. Dachia 20, kv. 12
277043   Chisinau
Tel: 22-82-83
Fax: 53-21-96
E-mail: root@sohnut.moldova.su

Contact: Oleg Mikhailovich Goldenstein

Promotes NGOs and mass media in protecting the environment. Also interested in developing eco-tourism in Moldova.

Silvik Progress Association
ul. Muncheshtskaya 788, kv. 63
277000   Chisinau
Tel: 52-68-83
Fax: 73-78-27
Contact: Aleksei Ivanovich Palanchan

Silvik is interested in networking among Moldovan environmental organizations.

Special Olympics Moldova
ul. Pushkin 26
277012   Chisinau
Tel: 22-26-78
Contact: Nikolai Barbieru, Chairman

Young Ecologist/Chisinau
ul. Schuseva 63
277012   Chisinau
Tel: 22-16-90, 22-24-94

Environmental education.

Beltsy (04231)

MoldAgroEco
ul. Kalya Yeshilor 28
279200   Beltsy
Tel: 3-02-12
Fax: 3-02-21
Contact: Boris Pavlovich Boinchan

MoldAgroEco promotes environmentally sound agricultural practices through seminars and conferences.

Bendery

Bendery Environmental Club
Glavpochtamt, a/ya 8
278100   Bendery
Tel: 2-22-53
Fax: 4-40-70
Contact: Leonid Illarionovich Tkachuk

The club is promoting environmental tourism and working to preserve the Dniester watershed.

Drokiya

Pro Natura
ul. Geriy 86-A
279400   Drokiya
Contact: Roman Vasile Gutsu

Environmental education, ecotourism and preservation of biodiversity.

Russia: West of the Urals

Country Code: 7

Moscow (095)

ACTR/ACCELS Moscow
General Administrative Office
Leninsky Prospekt 2, 5th etazh
117049   Moscow
Tel: 237-91-16
E-mail:
actr.moscow@sovcust.sprint.com

FSA Secondary School Program
Hub Office
Svetnoi bulvar 25, k. 301, 302
Moscow
Tel: 200-5305, 200-2898, 200-6130
E-mail:
fsa.mosinfo@sovcust.sprint.com

Educational Advising Center
Library of Foreign Literature
American Center, 3rd floor
ul. Nikolo-Yamskaya 1
109189   Moscow
Tel: 956-30-22
E-mail:
sac.moscow@sovcust.sprint.com

See profile for ACTR/ACCELS in section *Special Focus Organizations.*

ADL–Women's Information Project
a/ya 414
121019   Moscow
Tel/Fax: 366-9274
E-mail: tatiana@adl.msk.su

feminist@glas.apc.org
Contact: Liza Bozhkova

The project has three components aimed at organizing an effective information network for the women's movement and for gender studies in Russia. The first component of the project is the Women's Archive in Moscow to collect documents relating to women's history. The Women's Information Project Library collects women's fiction and non-fiction, including books on philosophy, history, religion and health. The Data Base WomIN+ contains information on individuals, organizations and events in the women's movement.

Aesop Center
a/ya 27
Rublyevskoye Shosse 87, kom. 2
121552   Moscow
Tel/Fax: 141-8315
E-mail: aesop@glas.apc.org
Contact: Kevin Gardner, Chairman

A major project of Aesop has been to establish and operate SPIDNET, the first HIV/AIDS information network in Russia. This includes an e-mail network, database, library, and periodical bulletin focused on HIV/AIDS issues. Its primary goal is to reach civic groups and individuals, especially those outside of Moscow, with up-to-date information HIV/AIDS and other sexually transmitted diseases.

It has also developed the Russian Sexual Health Coalition to promote education and information on STDs as well as a variety of other reproductive health issues.

Agency of Social Information
M. Gnezdnikovski per. 9, # 3B
103009   Moscow

Tel: 229-0432
Fax: 229-0554
E-mail: asi@glas.apc.org
Contact: Anna Savortyan,
Correspondent

Agudath Israel of Moscow
ul. Pervaya Brestskaya 60
Moscow
Tel: 250-9202
Fax: 250-9216
Contact: Aleksandr Rubinovich,
Chairman

Agudath of Moscow works with Agudath Israel in New York city to promote
microenterprises which can provide
employment and income generation
opportunities.

AIDS Infoshare Russia
a/ya 51
105037 Moscow
Tel: 110-2469
Fax: 383-7553
Contact: Lena Pyroshkina, Program
Director

AIDS Infoshare Russia works in conjunction with their U.S. office to provide Russian individuals and organizations with the tools they need to fight
HIV/AIDS and STDs. The core staff of
AIDS Infoshare Russia is located in
Moscow and consists of two Americans
and four Russians but also relies on donated time through a volunteer/intern
program.
    See also Infoshare International in
Special Focus Organizations.

Alcoholics Anonymous
Moscow
Tel: 113-8207
Contact: Igor

All-Russian Association for the Blind
Protopopovski per. 9
129010 Moscow
Tel: 280-7929 (office)
        282-3048 (home)
Contact: Evgeni Ageev, Editor

This association is over 70 years old. It
operates 178 enterprises for the blind
and sight-impaired and publishes a
monthly, *Nasha Zhizn*, both in Braille
and in print. It would welcome corre-
spondence and exchanges with similar
American organizations.

All-Russian Foundation for Social and Legal Protection of the Disabled
a/ya 8
Dubninskaya I-540
127540 Moscow
Tel: 480-1459, 480-8182
Tel/Fax: 480-5660
Fax: 903-6567
Contact: Vadim Voevodin, President

The foundation works for the social independence of the disabled, provides
legal assistance, creates scientific-
technical (training) centers, and is
helping to develop a database of all the
disabled in Moscow with the cooperation of UNESCO and the UN.

All-Russian Society for the Disabled
Kutuzovskiy pr. 30/32
121165 Moscow
Tel: 241-2286, -1880, -7825
Fax: 241-8180
Contact: Aleskandr Lomakin, Chair

All-Russian Society Hospice
a/ya 650, Meditsinsky Vestnik
119435 Moscow
Tel: 242-9110

Contact: Marina Alexandrovna Byalik, Chairperson

In April 1994, the All-Russian Society Hospice organized its first conference "Hospices: Conceptualizing and Developing Them." The goal of the conference was to bring out various specialists as well as volunteers and nonprofessionals who support and care for people in the final stages of terminal diseases. The conference was organized with the support of the Institute of Philosophy of the Russian Academy of Sciences, The Institute of Man, The Center for Psychological Support, and the Psychology Department of the Moscow State University.

American Institute of Business and Economics

Moscow State University
Main Building A-416
117234   Moscow
Tel: 939-1070
Fax: 932-8894
E-mail: aibec@co.ru
URL: www.knight-hub.com/aibec
Contact: Edwin G. Dolan, President

AIBEc is a not-for-profit American business school in Moscow. It offers a two-year program of courses taught in evenings, in English, by a mostly American faculty. The curriculum resembles an MBA core program; AIBEc does not currently offer a degree. Students are young Russian men and women who want to enter a career in international business. Entry is competitive; students pay no tuition. Most have science and technical backgrounds before coming to AIBEc. Graduates mostly work for American companies in Moscow or for Russian banks and other firms with American clients. Finance and accounting are strong areas.

Amnesty International

G-19, a/ya 212
ul. Gertsena 22/2, kom. 53
121019   Moscow
Tel/Fax: 291-2904
E-mail: amintglasnet@glas.apc.org
Contact: Tatyana Gorbacheva, Coordinator; Eric Klazerstein

Andrei Sakharov Foundation

Zemlyanoi val 48b,kom. 62
107120   Moscow
Tel: 916-2480
Fax: 299-0232
E-mail: yuriy@sakharovfound.msk.su
URL: http://www.wdn.com/asf
Contact: Yuriy V. Samodurov, Executive Director

The foundation maintains the Sakharov Archives, consisting of documents pertaining to his life and activities as well as materials on the human rights and dissident movements in the USSR. The foundation is also overseeing construction in a park across the street of the Peace, Progress and Human Rights Center, which will house a permanent exhibition on Sakharov and the human rights movement.

Association Against Children's Leukemia

Nagatinskaya 10, kv. 37
115533   Moscow
Tel: 118-0187

Association for Innovative Schools

bul. Sirenevy 58a
105484   Moscow
Tel: 461-0623, 461-0632
Fax: 461-0845
Contact: Aleksandr Tubelsky, General Director

The association publishes books and videos and offers a series of seminars for teachers on teaching methods, new curricula, forms of school development, and teacher-student interaction. Tubelsky is headmaster of an independent, privately financed K-12 school in Moscow which has more than 1300 students, and 110 teachers. The school has won an "Innovative School Project" award from the Soros Foundation.

Association for International Education

a/ya 775
ul. Ordzhonikidze 3
117419 Moscow
Tel: 952-0769
Fax: 232-3654
E-mail: grampo@isrir.msk.su
            dime@isrir.msk.su
Contact: Vladimir P. Kashitsin, General Director; Dmitry L. Tararaev, Executive Director; Aleksandr N. Gruntsev, Programs Director

The association, a not-for-profit entity comprising a number of Russian and international organizations, was created in 1993. Its principal goals are to:
• identify priorities and focus the initiatives of Russian educational institutions in view of decreased state support and increased autonomy;
• establish ties with international organizations, universities and donor organizations to expand opportunities for international educational services in Russia;
• assist participating institutions in granting joint international degrees; and
• support the development of innovative educational methods, such as distance learning and computer and telecommunication technologies.
   A variety of institutions participate in AIE including, the Russian Federation State Committee for Higher Education; Information Systems Research Institute of Russia; Moscow State Institute of Electronics and Mathematics; Moscow State University of Forestry; Moscow Municipal Experimental Center of Computer Learning; and the International Distance Learning Center "LINKOM."
   A primary goal of AIE is the development of distance education in Russia, using telecommunications and computer resources that tend to be concentrated in Moscow and St. Petersburg. To that end, AIE has been working with several U.S. higher education institutes to provide coursework from these institutions to Russian students. AIE is also conducting preliminary studies in the distance training component of the World Bank project "Market Oriented Training in Russia".

Association of Disabled Youth Organizations–"AMIO"

Louchnikov per. 2, kv. 8
Moscow
Tel: 187-9694, 206-8313
            490-5085 (Lebedeva home)
Fax: 206-8313
Contact: Yuri N. Bausov, President; Galya Lebedeva

Established in 1992, this association assists disabled youths in their education, and supports social rehabilitation for the disabled.

Association of Indigenous Minorities of the North, Siberia and Far East of the Russian Federation

ul. Stroitelej 8/2, suite 707
117086 Moscow
Tel: 930-7078
Contact: Yeremy Aipin, President

Association of Parents of Disabled Children
17 Filiovsky bul., kv. 168
121601   Moscow
Tel: 142-7730, 142-1196
Contact: Lev Abramzov, Director;
Svetlana Dukhovnaya, Director

Established in 1985, the association works with 107 children in educational programs, summer vacation programs and special events.

Association of Parents Disabled from Childhood
Zelenograd 11-31-1
Moscow
Tel: 530-5196
Fax: 532-0866
Contact: Yelena Yegorkina

Established in 1990, this organization conducts education seminars for parents, cultural activities, family sports clubs, sports competitions and self-help.

Association for the Protection of the Disabled
Louchnikov per. 4, kom. 2
103982   Moscow
Tel: 206-8023, 197-4095
Fax: 206-8853
Contact: Yurii Ivanovich Kiselev

This organization was founded in 1992 by Yuri Kiselev, a long-time advocate for the disabled in the Russia.

Association Russian Political Encyclopedia
ul. V. Pik 4/1
129256   Moscow
Tel/Fax: 181-0013
Contact: Professor V. Shelokaev, President; Dr. Andrei Sorokin, Acting Chair

The association was formed in 1991 by a group of distinguished Russian scholars. Its activities include research and analysis of current problems in political and social affairs; sponsorship of lectures and seminars on Russian political history; special investigation in Russian archives; distribution of books and journals through its affiliated publishing house, Rosspen; and assistance to foreign scholars needing contacts, reasonable hotel accomodations, etc.

Association of Social Pedagogues and Social Workers
ul. Podgorskaya 8
119906   Moscow
Tel: 248-5496, 247-1598
Fax: 202-6804
Contact: Dr. Valentina Bocharova, President

Association of Women Entrepreneurs of Russia
3-ya Frunzinskaya, kv. 1-a
Moscow
Tel: 291-2408
Fax: 292-8610
Contact: Tatiana Malutina

This association supports small business development and training and education programs. It also advocates for more effective government action to benefit women entrepreneurs.

Association of Women Journalists
14 Bumazhny proyezd
Moscow
Tel/Fax: 238-3641, 943-0070
Contact: Irina Jurna, Nadezhda Azhgikhina

AWJ advocates for women in politics, sponsors roundtable discussions concerning women and the press, promotes research on women in the press, and generally supports women journalists.

Association of Women for Knowledge and Harmony
ul. Kosinskaya 26-2-196
111538   Moscow
Tel/Fax: 375-7537
Contact: Natalya Leibovshaya

Association of Young Invalids of Russia
ul. Ostriakova 3
125057   Moscow
Tel: 157-7327
                230-0506 (home)
Tel/Fax: 157-7652
Contact: Galina Karpova, Executive Director

Established in 1991, this association works for the rehabilitation of youths and to coordinate the activities of voluntary organizations of disabled youth.

Association of Young Leaders
ul. 60-goda Oktyabr 9
Moscow
Tel/Fax: 135-4247
Contact: Anton Lopukhin

Established in 1992 to provide youth leadership training.

"Atlantida"
Povarskaya 52
Moscow
Tel: 299-2429
Fax: 291-4524, 463-6887
Contact: Larissa Vasilyeva, Galina Semenova

Publishes a women's magazine *Atlantida* and is trying to create a women's radio and television station.

Biodiversity Conservation Center
G-270, a/ya 602
119270   Moscow
Tel/Fax: 114-1980, 151-5226
E-mail: biodivers@glas.apc.org

The Socio-Ecological Union (see below) has developed the SEU Biodiversity Conservation Center to promote the preservation of biological diversity, and to provide information and assistance to nature preserves and national parks throughout the NIS.

In conjunction with ECOLOGIA, the Stockholm Environment Institute-Tallin, the Sacred Earth Network and other international NGOs, the SEU BCC is working to resolve the environmental problems of the Peipsi-Chudosky Lakes region on the Estonian-Russian border.

BCC is working with the The Nature Conservancy in a program intended to result in more habitat preservation and the establishment of nature preserves in Russia. TNC is assisting BCC with the creation of national conservation programs, and the eventual establishment of a national conservation association like TNC.

Blagovest
Center for Prenatal Education
ul. Vesnina 24
Moscow
Tel: 265-2232, 241-7141
Fax: 162-2013
Contact: Nina Tchicherina

The Center for Prenatal Education Blagovest, founded in January 1992, now has 10 professionals, many of whom are well-known in the fields of prenatal education and psychology. Center activists provide educational help to older teenage girls and college students. A consulting room in a Moscow maternity hospital is under preparation.

The center provides assistance to patients of a maternity house, consulting with medical personnel on modern delivery techniques. It has also begun an educational program in prenatal and perinatal psychology.

The center plans to launch a new project: "Development of Prenatal Care, Psychological Research and Psychophysical Training of Expectant Mothers and Couples for Active Parenthood." The aim of the project is to train personnel of the maternity hospitals and mothers' centers to improve the existing system of birth attendance.

Businesswomen's Association
2/3 Khlebny per.
121814   Moscow
Tel: 290-6326
Fax: 200-1207
Contact: Ludmilla Kornarva

Carnegie Moscow Center
Mosenka Plaza
Sadovo-Samotechnaya 24/27
103051   Moscow
Tel: 258-5025
Fax: 258-5020
E-mail: carnegie@glas.apc.org

This is the Moscow office of the Carnegie Endowment for International Peace. The activities of the center include seminars, publications and working groups which analyze problems of the post-communist world.

CEC International Partners
Moscow
Tel: 241-3462, 241-4729
Contact: Todd Weinberg

This is the Moscow office of the organization based in New York. See *U.S.-based Organizations.*

Center for Curative Pedagogics
ul. Stroiteley 17-B
117311   Moscow
Tel: 131-0683
E-mail: irkaz@glas.apc.org
Contact: Roman Dimenstein, Director; Irina Kazakova

The center operates a computer communications network among NGOs which work in children's health care and disabilities rehabilitation throughout Russia. Its U.S. partner is IREX.

Center for Democracy
Gorokhovsky per. 14
103064   Moscow
Tel/Fax: 265-3980
Contact: Aleksandr Smirnov

Center for Democracy–Russia
ul. Volkovaya 4
123376   Moscow
Tel/Fax: 255-1922
Contact: Aleksandr Kravstov, Moscow Representative

This is the Moscow office of the Center for Democracy profiled in *Special Focus Organizations.*

Center for Ecological Policy of Russia
Moscow
Tel: 952-2423
Fax: 952-3007
E-mail: anzuz@biotest.uucp.free.net
Contact: Andrei A. Ziouzine, Executive Director

The Center for Ecological Policy of Russia, established in 1993, publishes reports and analyses on environmental problems and distributes them among public organizations, NGOs, federal agencies, and other governmental representatives. The Center also conducts media briefings and provides information to international environmental organizations.

To date the Center has prepared and published two reports on chemical pollution and health and on chemical weapons in Russia.

The Center is currently managing three projects: examining the environmental and other impacts of plutonium production, including analysis of new, previously classified data; a project on whaling; and work on public interest and environmental law issues.

Center for Independent Ecological Programs

Bestuzhevykh 21-13-35
Moscow
Tel:　404-0385
E-mail:　cnep@glas.apc.org
Contact:　Igor Bradis

The center and the Institute for World Affairs are conducting a joint project examining the issue of children's health entitled "Disabled Children in the Regions of Ecological Disasters." With funding from ISAR/USAID's Seeds of Democracy Program, the center conducted the first annual conference of the project in October 1994. The confer-ence brought together 150 experts from 30 regions of the NIS.

Center for International Private Enterprise

ul. Ilinka 5/2, kom. 337
Moscow
Tel:　929-0125 (Frank)
　　　　929-0184 (Wini)
Fax:　929-0059

E-mail:　cipemosc@glas.apc.org
Contact:　Frank Dressler, Sr., In-Country Coordinator; Wini Dressler, Office Manager

This is the Moscow office of CIPE, profiled in *Special Focus Organizations.* The office is in the Russian Federation Chamber of Commerce and Industry. Mail to CIPE–Moscow should be sent to: CPE 396, 208 E. 51st St., Suite 295, New York, NY 10022.

Center for Love and Support

Balaklavsky pr. 36-1-85
113303　Moscow
Tel:　318-2855
E-mail:　cab@glas.apc.org

The center assists terminally ill patients and their families, and organizes home hospices for seriously ill adults and children. It organizes conferences on bioethical problems associated with serious illnesses, death and dying. The Center would like to cooperate with professionals and volunteers working with the terminally ill.

Center for Political Technologies

ul. 2-ya Frunzenskaya 8, C
119146　Moscow
Tel/Fax:　248-2862
E-mail:　Boris@makarenko.msk.su

CPT is a grantee of the Center for International Private Enterprise.

Center for Social Protection "Anti-suicidal Tendencies" Nadezhda Club

ul. Krylatskaya 29/2
121614　Moscow
Tel:　415-7945
Contact:　Irina Saiko, Director

Center for Volunteers
ul. Slavianskaya 4-1
Moscow
Tel: 220-0086, 220-0082
Contact: Yuri Permakov, President;
Antonina Koleshova, Assistant to the
President

Center for Women, Family and Gender Studies of the Institute of Youth
ul. Unosti 5/1
111442 Moscow
Tel: 954-8886, 374-7512
374-7878
Fax: 177-7331
Contact: Tatiana Zabelina, Evgeniya
Israelyan

The center is active in issues of violence against women and disability issues of women.

Center of Working Models for the Social Defense of Children in Microdistricts
ul. Medvedeva 11-6-1
103006 Moscow
Tel: 152-4658, 200-3955
Contact: Svetlana Solomovna Levitina,
President; Galina Sergeevna Potapova,
Vice-President

Charitable Foundation of Technical Assistance to Children with Hearing Difficulties
shosse Khoroshovskoye 48, kv. 116
Moscow
Tel: 309-0482; 941-5377
Fax: 230-2368
Contact: Irina Birkina

Established in 1994, the foundation
provides hearing aids for children in
kindergartens and primary schools.

Charities Aid Foundation
ul. Elizarovoi 10
103064 Moscow
Tel: 928-0557, 917-2514
917-0971
Tel/Fax: 298-5694
E-mail: lenay@glas.apc.org
caftacis@glas.apc.org
Contact: Lena Yang, Executive Director; Rebecca Cronin, Program Coordinator

CAF is a UK-based organization, registered in Russia since 1993, with an active program of publications, seminars and media programming in support of third sector growth in Russia. It describes its mission as being to:
• promote the long-term financial stability and independence of the Russian NGO sector;
• research, document and publicize social conditions in Russia and the work of Russian NGOs;
• provide training and technical help to develop the charity management capacities of the NGO sector in Russia;
• facilitate unity and practical collaboration among Russian and foreign NGOs.

Charitable Society "Charity"
Popov proyezd 2
107014 Moscow
Tel: 269-0392, 268-8037
268-7878
Fax: 269-0392
Contact: Aleksandr Ogorodnikov,
President

This is a crisis center, and a center for homeless support. Ogorodnikov is a lay activist in the Orthodox Church who was imprisoned for his religious convictions in the pre-Gorbachev period.

The Chernobyl Union of the Russian Federation

per. Serpov 3/5
119121   Moscow
Tel: 248-5614, 248-6307
Contact: Vyacheslav L.Grishin, President

Established in 1989 to address Chernobyl and other radiation catastrophes, the union's mission is to defend the rights and interests of citizens and victims of radiation accidents; monitor the fulfillment of legal decisions; and assist the government in preventing another catastrophe.

The Chernobyl Union of the RF is affiliated with the Chernobyl Union of Ukraine.

Child Abuse Protection Fund

Leninsky pr. 88-1-49
117313   Moscow
Fax: 434-9620
E-mail: chapf@#cl.itep.msk.su
Contact: Tamara Safonova, President

The fund was established in 1993 by a diverse group of psychologists, pediatri-cians and attorneys to provide advocacy and treatment to abused and neglected children. CAPF was the first Russian NGO organized specifically for abused children. Its primary programs are maintaining a shelter for abused and homeless children in Moscow, and public education programs for parents, educators and social workers.

Christian Solidarity International

Leninsky pr. 99-524
117421   Moscow
Tel: 133-7591
Contact: Maria Ternovskaya

CSI has been working in Russia to develop support mechanisms for graduates of orphanages in Moscow and St. Petersburg who have developmental disabilities, and to develop programs to assist in their social rehabilitation. In addition, CSI attempts to locate homes for orphans.

Citizens Democracy Corps

ul. Spiridonovka 22/2, kv. 36
103001   Moscow
Tel: 290-6948
Fax: 913-7154

See CDC profile in section *Special Focus Organizations.*

Citizens Network for Foreign Affairs

ul. Pudovkina 4
119285   Moscow
Tel: 143-0925, 143-0308
           143-0928, 143-1378
Fax: 143-0998
E-mail:
moscow@cnfarus.mhs.compuserve.com

See CNFA profile in section *Special Focus Organizations.*

Civic Initiatives Program
Moscow Coordinating Center

ul. Ordzhonikidze 13/2, 15th etazh
117071   Moscow
Tel: 958-2172, 958-2215
           958-2306, 958-2406
Fax: 958-5130
E-mail: scrussia@glas.apc.org
Contact: Lisa Krift, Co-Director of Programs

See profile of Save the Children in the section *Clearinghouse Organizations* for a desription of this ambitious program which it is leading. Staff of other components of the Civic Initiatives

Program are located here, including Galina Negrustueva and Janet McCollum, Co-Directors of COUNTERPART–Moscow (mcounterpart@glas.apc.org); and Sergei Deytsev, representing Center for Democracy (cfd@netcom.com). CIP has developed a well-stocked NGO Resource Center, where more than 200 pieces of literature and reference materials, plus a database of Russian NGOs, are available to anybody who visits the Center. Elena Belova is the Resource Center manager, and Konstantin Gurtovoy is the database information system manager.

Civil Assistance Committee
Kostyanskii per. 13
Moscow
Tel: 208-8802, 917-8961
Contact: Lidiya Ivanovna Grafova, Svetlana Alekseevna Gannushkina

The committee provides aid for refugees and forced migrants.

Civil Center for Assistance in Reform of Criminal Justice
Bolshoi Zlatoustovskii per. 8-7-68
101000 Moscow
Tel: 206-8497, 206-8684
Fax: 241-0369
Contact: Valerii Fedorovich Abramkin

Committee of Soldiers' Mothers
Louchnikov per. 4, kom. 6
103982 Moscow
Tel: 206-0581
Fax: 206-8853
Chechnya hotline: 928-2506
E-mail: hrcenter@glas.apc.org
Contact: Maria I. Kirbasova, Chairwoman; Veronika A. Marchenko; Valentina Melnikova, Press Secretary

Founded in 1989, the committee has worked to expose human rights violations within the Russian military, including the high number of deaths from hazing or severe punishment. It gives legal help and material assistance to the families of dead servicemen; consults on legislation affecting military service; publishes research related to service-related deaths in the military; and publishes *The Memory Book*. This book gives the names, photos and personal stories of soldiers who died in peacetime military service. Appendices include information about the work of various human rights groups dealing with related issues.

The committee advocates for improved living conditions in the military and a true alternative service option for conscientious objectors. It also operates a barracks in Moscow for fugitive soldiers.

The committee received the 1995 Sean MacBride Peace Prize, awarded by the International Peace Bureau for its work in opposing the war in Chechnya, as well as for its previous campaigns to end human-rights abuses within the Russian military.

Committee on Women's Rights
Union of Lawyers
Berseievkaya nab. 20/2
109072 Moscow
Tel: 137-7573, 958-0914
Fax: 238-3530
Contact: Svetlana Polenina, Ludmilla Korbut

The committee does advocacy on legal rights of women, human rights work, research, and legal training.

Compassion Charitable Fund
Komsomolskiy pr. 9, kv. 45
Moscow

Tel/Fax: 245-2209
Fax: 923-4778, 973-2094
Contact: Aleksey Korotaev, Executive Director; Marina Verikovskaya

The center works with the International Rescue Committee in New York to provide medical services to former prisoners of conscience in the Moscow region.

CONTACT Center
Institute of Teaching Materials and Technical Aids of Russian Academy of Education
ul. Pogoniakaya 8
Moscow
Tel: 245-3010, 246-8317
E-mail: zdcontact@glas.apc.org
mbuhar@glas.apc.org
marina@glas.apc.org
Contact: Marina Moiseyeva, Marina Buharkina

The center consists of a group of teachers who serve as coordinators of a telecommunications-based educational program "Telecommunication To Schools," supported by the Russian Academy of Education. Since 1988 the center has been developing relationships with teachers throughout the former USSR involved in new information technologies. CONTACT has developed a course and educational software kit for teachers who are novices in the world of telecommunications. The course covers all basic technical questions and includes recommendations on classroom applications.

CONTACT has worked with Mark Braunlich's TASIC (Teacher And Student International Communication) project and welcomes contacts with American educators who have experience in developing telecommunications training courses for teachers.

CONTACT has developed a distance education course using e-mail, titled "Telecommunications in Education," for its regional coordinators. They are also planning to develop a distance learning course for children and adults interested in learning English on their own, using the Internet.

Conversion For the Environment International Foundation
Zviozdny bul. 4-13
129515 Moscow
Fax: 286-3587
E-mail: cfe@glas.apc.org

CFE is a nonprofit, international organization registered in the Netherlands with an international administrative board and main offices in Russia and the Netherlands. It addresses environmental and defense industry conversion issues. It organizes international conferences devoted to the environmental security of marine and coastal areas around the world and focuses on the problem of chemical munitions dumped in the world's oceans.

Conversion and Women
ul. Vikorenko 7
125319 Moscow
Tel: 157-9880
Fax: 157-7531
Contact: Eleonora Ivanova

Conversion and Women works on issues of protection and development of women's scientific skills, business training, and international disarmament issues.

Creativity Association
ul. Novoalekseievskaya 1, kv. 99
Moscow
Tel: 300-0564, 287-6083

Fax: 200-1207
E-mail: lena@aarw.msk.su
Contact: Elena Alyoshina, Program Director

Creativity works with the Russian Association of Women Business Owners and the Alliance of American and Russian Women to support artisans, mainly women, in developing their business and marketing skills.

Crisis Center

ul. Krasikova 27
117218   Moscow
Tel: 124-6185, 129-1001
Fax: 129-0801
Contact: Marina Pisklakova

The center was founded in 1994 and provides consultations for battered women, either personally or through a hot line. The Center organizes psychotherapy and self-help groups. It is a member of the Association of Crisis Centers for Women.

"Diakhol"–Diabetic Invalid Association of the Frunzensk District

ul. Begovaya 9-4-330
125284   Moscow
Tel: 945-5807
Contact: Olga Moskvitina; Irina Kunina

Established in 1991, the association organizes vacations and medical assistance for children with diabetes.

Doctors Without Borders/ Médecins Sans Frontières

Moscow
Tel: 207-4593, 207-4619

Dubna Educational Center

ul. Sovetskaya 14
141980   Dubna
Moscow oblast
Tel: 926-2215
Fax: 936-2316
Contact: Yulia Muravianskaya

In cooperation with local government and medical institutions, the center has developed a model for rural alcoholism treatment, including counselor training, expanding the availability of AA, Alanon, Alateen and other programs, and in-patient treatment facilities.

Ecojuris-WLED

ul. Usacheva 24, kom. 434
119048   Moscow
Tel: 246-2903, 131-2049
Fax: 246-2903
E-mail: ecojuris@glas.apc.org
         dado@glas.apc.org
Contact: Vera Mishenko, President; Olga Davydova; Natalya Zhavoronkova

Ecojuris, founded in 1991, claims to be Russia's first public-interest environmental law firm. With a staff of eight attorneys, Ecojuris: analyzes and prepares recommendations on environmental laws and regulations; maintains a database of environmental legislation; consults with businesses and foreign investors on potential violations of environmental and land use laws; and conducts litigation. It has brought a number of cases against the Ministry of Defense on behalf of soldiers' who have suffered from military experiments with nuclear and chemical weapons. In cooperation with the U.S.-based Natural Resources Defense Council, Ecojuris published a Russian-language Citizens' Guide, entitled *Environmental Protection: Towards Legal Actions by Russian Citizens*. In 1994 the organization changed its name to Ecojuris-Wled (Women Lawyers for Environment and Development).

Ecoline Library
Bogoyavlensky proyezd 3/3
Moscow
Tel: 926-5081
Contact: Olga Zhdanovich, Director

This library, opened in 1995 in space shared with the Socio-Ecological Union, offers a growing collection of documents, periodicals, and computer databases for researchers interested in environmental issues. It is centrally located, about 100 yards from Red Square, but it's best to call ahead and make an appointment if planning to visit.

ECOLOGIA
Russia Office
ul. 2-ya Tverskaya-Yamskaya 38-13
Tel/Fax: 251-7617, 221-3381
E-mail: ecologia@glas.apc.org
URL: http://ecologia.nier.org/
Contact: Oleg Cherp, NIS Program Director

This organization deals with environmental science, nuclear issues and pollution control. It also has an office in Minsk.

Ecological Foundation
ul. Krasnodonskaya 24
Moscow
Tel: 137-8893
Contact: Rimma Petrovna Vedeneeva

Education Resources and Technology
Kedrova 8
117804 Moscow
Fax: 958-5130
E-mail: irana@glas.apc.org

Contact: Irana Mozheiko, Project Coordinator

Empathy
ul. Novoslobodskaya 62/19, kv. 294
103055 Moscow
Tel: 972-1798, 972-1806

Empathy, in cooperation with the Moscow House of Charity, publishes the monthly journal *Vestnik Blagotvoritel'nosti* ("Herald of Charity"). It includes overviews of experiences of Russian and foreign philanthropy; analytical articles and interviews on various aspects of charitable work; a calendar of events; commentaries; and information about sponsors.

The Eurasia Foundation
Central Russia and Siberia Regional Office
ul. Volkhonka 14, 4th etazh, kom. 403
119842 Moscow
Tel: 956-1235
Fax: 956-1239
E-mail: efmoscow@eurasia.msk.ru
Contact: Melanie Peyser, Regional Director

See profile for the foundation in section *Clearinghouse Organizations*.

Europe and Asia Association of Security Products and Services (EVRAAS)
ul. Profsoyuznaya 78
117420 Moscow
Tel: 335-67-55
Fax: 128-76-41
Contact: Dmitry Petrovich Maslennikov, President

EVRAAS is the largest organization involved in the security products market in Russia. The association incorporates Russia's leading developers and vendors of safety and security items.

European-Atlantic Cooperation Association

ul. Prechistenka 3
119034　Moscow
Tel:　　203-6271, 291-0776
Fax:　　230-2229
Contact: Boris Nikolaevich Topornin, President; Evgenii Konstantinovich Silin, Director-Coordinator

Founded in 1992, EACA has conducted international conferences on Russia and NATO, and a seminar in Poland on questions of European security.

Express-Khronika

a/ya 5
ul. V. Krasnosel'skaya
111399　Moscow
Tel:　　264-4830
Fax:　　264-5742
Tel/Fax: 264-9791
E-mail:　podrabinek@glas.apc.org
　　　　　　chronicle@glas.apc.org
Contact: Aleksander Podrabinek, Editor-in-Chief; Vitali Bogdanov

Express Khronika is a weekly newspaper that reports on human rights issues and democratic movements. It started in 1987 after being circulated for years as samizdat. Its editor-in-chief is a well-known human rights activist who served more than eight years in prison for work that included the 1978 publication of *Punitive Medicine*, a book which documented Soviet psychiatric abuses.

　Express Khronika utilizes a network of correspondents throughout Russia and the NIS. In addition to its weekly newspaper, it also publishes a daily wire service, which is available via fax or e-mail, and periodic special reports,

including a year-end summary of the human rights situation in Russia.

F-1 Club

Kolpatchny per. 9-a
101831　Moscow
Tel:　　921-4723, 371-8287
Contact: Svetlana Aivazova

The club provides scholarship support, does publishing and research on women's issues, and sponsors roundtable discussions on Russian feminism.

Falta, Feminist Alternative Center

Leninsky pr. 123-1-706
117513　Moscow
Tel:　　399-7341
Tel/Fax: 438-6115
Contact: Natalia Abubikirova, Marina Regentova

Founded in 1990, Falta organizes leadership seminars and workshops for women. More than 500 have been trained to date. It also publishes a journal, *Feminf.*

"Family and Health" International Association

ul. Vesnina 24/3
121002　Moscow
Tel:　　241-0306, 148-4774
Fax:　　241-0421
Contact: I.A. Manuilova, Director

Family Fund

ul. Krasnikova 27
Moscow
Tel:　　124-6185, 129-0400
Fax:　　129-0801
E-mail:　isepp@glas.apc.org
Contact: Marina Petrovna Pisklakova, Vice-President

The Family Fund provided the first hotline in Russia for battered women, and provides free telephone and in-person counseling, including legal consultations. The Family Fund is developing a shelter for battered women in Moscow and a women's center for community education on domestic violence.

Feminist Cultural Laboratory for Creative Research "Idioma"
ul. Marii Ulyanovoi 14, kv. 81
Moscow
Tel: 133-4149
Contact: Natalia Ursvna Kamenetskaya

Feminist Orientation Center
Moscow
Tel/Fax: 395-5864, 338-3982
E-mail: feminist@glas.apc.org
Contact: Marina Libarakina, Tatiana Konisheva, Maria Chertok

The center has been active since 1991. It works on projects such as training and education for women in management, fundraising and development for NGOs, and research on discrimination against women. A recent project of the Center is Arts Against Violence, which has brought artists and activists together in a campaign against violence in society.

Fora–Charity Foundation for Youth Economic Education
a/ya N 14 "FORA"
12 Glagoleva
123448   Moscow
Tel: 148-7198
Tel/Fax: 947-5105
Contact: Vera Pozdniakova

Fora has published a textbook on the Russian stock market as well as a number of games which teach children about economics and entrepreneurship. Fora is interested in finding American organizations with which it can work to organize youth exchanges.

Foundation for Agrarian Development Research
Leninsky pr. 85
117261   Moscow
Tel: 134-3364, 932-1182
Fax: 318-8352
E-mail: fadr.ina/ya@parti.inforum.org
             yakushev@fadr.msk.ru
Contact: Evgeniy V. Yakushev

In cooperation with the Rodale Institute, FADR has developed a Networking Support Project intended to improve the ability of NGOs to exchange information and form partnerships to address development issues.

Foundation for the Defense of Children with Epilepsy
Savelyovsky per. 9-a
119034   Moscow
Tel: 202-7642

The foundation provides literature regarding epilepsy for parents and families of children with the disorder, as well as for epilepsy specialists. The materials are generally translated from English and other foreign languages, and adapted to the Russian situation.

Freedom House–Russia
ul. Novi Arbat 19, kv. 819
103025   Moscow
Tel/Fax: 203-6424
E-mail: jbern@sovam.com
Contact: Jonas Bernstein

The Moscow office of Freedom House, profiled in section *Special Focus Organizations*.

"Friends and Partners" Project

c/o Institute of Biochemistry and
Physiology of Microorganisms RAS
142292   Pushchino
Tel/Fax: 923-3602
E-mail: natasha@ibpm.serpukhov.su
Contact: Natasha Bulashova

See "Friends and Partners" in section
NIS-Related Internet Sites.

Gaia International Women's Center

Khlebny per. 2/3
121817   Moscow
Tel:　　　135-3207
Fax:　　 200-1207
E-mail: gaia@glas.apc.org
Contact: Elena Ershova, Nadezhda
Shvedova

Gaia is involved in women's rights,
policy and advocacy, leadership training, small business development, legal
counseling, social work, and health issues.

Gazeta Nekommercheskikh Organizatsi

3-d Frunzenskaia 1-73
119270   Moscow
Tel:　　　268-4035
E-mail: raduga@glas.apc.org
Contact: Lubov Olenicheva, Editor

The *Newspaper of Nonprofit Organizations* shares offices with Raduga
Education Union.

Glasnost Defense Foundation

Zubovsky bul. 4, kom. 432
119021   Moscow
Tel:　　　201-4420
Tel/Fax: 201-4947
E-mail: simonov@fond91.msk.ru
　　　　　 aleks@sovamsu.sovusa.com
Contact: Aleksei Kirillovich Simonov

GDF was organized in February 1991
for "the defense of journalism and the
defense of journalists." Its major activities include:

- giving legal and financial aid to journalists in conflict with local, regional
  or Federal authorities;
- disseminating information on mass
  media legislation within Russia and
  abroad; and
- organizing an independent media
  network in Russia.

GDF organizes conferences and
events and publishes its research. For
example, in 1994 GDF published the
results of a survey comparing attitudes
of Russian journalists working in eight
regions of the Federation with those of
journalists based in Moscow.

"Goluba"–Help Service For Girls

Izmailovskoi shosse 55, kom. 67
105187   Moscow
Tel:　　　369-0346
Contact: Marianna Vronskaya

Goluba was founded in 1994 to provide
medical, psychological and educational
services and support for women under
18 and their children. It delivers lectures for teenagers in schools about
contraception and publishes booklets
for young mothers.

Golubka
Russian-American Humanitarian Initiative

a/ya 3775
ul. Garibaldi 11-76
117313   Moscow
Tel:　　　134-0295
Fax:　　 292-6511
E-mail: golubka@glas.apc.org
Contact: Igor Ouchinnikov, Ivan
Timofeev

Golubka, meaning "dove," facilitates workshops and conferences and publishes materials on themes of nonviolence, conflict resolution, communication skills, group process, and "deep ecology and global thinking." Among the volumes it has translated into Russian are a *Nonviolence Anthology, Getting to Yes* by Roger Fisher, and *Ecocide in the USSR* by Murray Feshbach. It is associated with Golubka–USA in San Francisco.

Goodwill Industries of Russia
Sredny Karetny per. 6/9, kv. 36
103051   Moscow
Tel: 299-0917
Contact: Vera Karpenkova

"Grazhdanin" (Citizen)
ul. Dovatora 5/9
117312   Moscow
Tel: 144-6862
Contact: Yakov Sokolov, Director

Grazhdanin is a Russian civic education network claiming to have more than 20,000 members throughout the country. Members deliver in-service training workshops on teaching democracy during the year and at annual summer institutes. The organization has also developed a series of civic education textbooks for middle school children.

Greenpeace
Moscow
E-mail: gpmoscow@glas.apc.org
Contact: Ivan Blokov, Sergei Tseplenkov

Affiliate of the international Greenpeace organization.

Health and Environment Foundation
Association of Physicians of the Don
CECHE c/o Health & Environment
Pokrovka 22/1
121069   Moscow
Tel: 246-4502, 203-7566
Fax: 206-0941
E-mail: ceche@glas.apc.org
Contact: Irina Demina, Vice President

These two organizations have teamed with the Central European Center for Health and Environment and U.S. organizations to develop a network of Russian NGOs working on public health policy, service delivery, information, and communication.

Helsinki Citizen's Assembly
ul. Ustinova 5-1-464
117418   Moscow
Tel/Fax: 434-3355
E-mail: rtvpress@sovam.com
Contact: Marina Pavlova-Sil'vanskaya

Helsinki Watch
Moscow
Tel: 265-4448
E-mail: jmhancock@glas.apc.org
Contact: Rachel Dember; Alexander Petrov, Coordinator

Helsinki Watch is a human rights organization.

House of Russian Traditions
Moscow
Tel: 965-3434
Contact: Vladimir Teplov, Director

The House was established in Moscow in 1991 to organize folklore expeditions throughout Russia and provide instruction in Russian traditions and folklore for children.

Human Soul (*Dusha Cheloveka*) Charitable Foundation

ul. Martenovskaya 30
111394   Moscow
Tel: 301-7204
Fax: 301-1810
Contact: Igor E. Donenko, President;
Olga Zayarnaya, Program Manager.

Human Soul was founded in 1991 by a group of psychotherapists, mentally ill clients, and their relatives. It assists psychiatric patients and their families in a community setting. The organization consists of volunteers, including doctors and social workers, who run programs for the mentally ill. Their mission is the social readaptation and social integration of the mentally ill, and assistance in protecting their legal rights. Their programs include:
- "Islands of Hope," working to prevent loneliness, suicide and social alienation;
- "Commercial Social Shield," offering survival services such as soup kitchens, help with groceries, medications, and clothing; and
- "Our Own Strength," which assists in integrating the mentally ill into society and provides support for their families.

Fountain House, Inc., in New York City works with Human Soul and this partnership has led to the "Clubhouse" program–a therapeutic environment intended to help patients stay out of hospitals and acquire the skills to live independently. Human Soul intends to extend the Clubhouse model to eight cities across Russia in the near future. It publishes a newsletter in English.

Independent Association of Child Psychologists and Psychiatrists

Moscow
Tel: 169-1812
Contact: Anatoly Severny, Ph.D., President

The association was established in Moscow in 1992. Two years later, in July 1994, representatives attended the annual Congress of the International Association for Child and Adolescent Psychiatry and Allied Professions in San Francisco, at which IACPP was adopted as a permanent member of that body, representing Russia.

Work of the IACPP to date has included: a program for identifying gifted children; development of a group home for mothers who require parenting support and their children; assistance to children in military conflict zones (e.g. Karabakh); and the organization of a charitable foundation for the protection of the mental health of children in Russia.

With assistance from groups in Britain and elsewhere, the IACPP has published two resources that emerged from conferences it organized over the past two years: *Russian Orphans: Problems, Hopes, Future* and *A Special Child and His Surroundings: Medical, Social and Psychological Aspects.* It soon plans to put out a directory of child and adolescent psychology and psychiatry in Russia, and also hopes eventually to publish a periodical on childhood personality problems and pathologies.

Independent Moscow Association of Doctors

Moscow
Tel: 268-1515

Contact: Aleksandr Anatolievich Sviridov

The association works with Doctors without Borders/Médecins Sans Frontières to provide medical and social assistance to the homeless.

Independent Psychiatric Association

Louchnikov per. 4, kom. 19
103982   Moscow
Tel: 456-71-91
Fax: 206-88-53
E-mail: hrcenter@glas.apc.org
            npasav@glas.apc.org
Contact: Lyubov Vinogradova, Board Chair

Established in 1992, IPA focuses on creating a new legal infrastructure for psychiatric care and introducing modern educational and clinical techniques into Russian psychiatry.

In September 1995 in Moscow, IPA, together with the World Psychiatric Association and the World Association for Medical Law and in collaboration with the Russian Ministry of Health and the Moscow Mental Hospital No. 1, co-sponsored a five-day seminar for legal and psychiatric professionals on "Bridging Gaps in Russian Psychiatry: Legal Regulation of Psychiatric Care in Russia and Other Countries."

Each year at IPA's initiative professionals from around Russia gather to discuss the state of psychiatry and the work of the organization, reviewing progress made and setting the upcoming year's agenda.

Another program of the IPA is its Commission for Moral Implications of Psychiatric Care. Since 1989, this body has responded to individuals who requested that their case be looked into by the commission. The commission will review the medical history of a patient, conduct its own exam, and render a decision, which is then provided to both the patient and his or her regular doctor. If the Commission agrees, patients who still have grievances can then pursue legal action using the Commission's report as evidence. The Commission meets with patients two days per week to conduct case research.

Since 1991 IPA has published and distributed across the NIS the *Journal of the Independent Psychiatric Association,* a quarterly scientific/academic journal for professionals in the field.

Independent Women's Forum

Serpukhovskii val. 17/23-91
113191   Moscow
Tel: 954-4429
Tel/Fax: 395-5864
E-mail: tatiana@ttg.msk.su
            feminist@glas.apc.org
Contact: Elizabeth Bozhkova, Marina Liborakina

Established in 1991, the Forum has conducted workshops on women's roles in politics, business, the mass media, etc. It now serves as an umbrella organization for more than 200 women's organizations throughout Russia. The Forum also operates an Information Center. With funding from local resources and a grant from the Ford Foundation, it has developed the Education and Vocational Training for Empowerment project to help women gain professional skills; the Mass Media Against Discrimination project, featuring a quarterly newsletter and development of a network of journalists against discrimination at national and local levels; and the Women and the Arts project, aimed at promoting women's participation in the arts.

Institute for Developing Rule of Law and a Market Economy

Moscow
Tel: 956-6622
Fax: 956-3836
E-mail: shargorodska@lrp.glas.apc.org
Contact: Olga Shargorodska, Head Librarian

Institute of State and Law

ul. Znamenka 10
119841   Moscow
Tel: 291-8743
Fax: 291-8574
Contact: Boris Topornin, Director; Irina Ikonitskaya, Deputy Director

The institute has received funding from the Center for International Private Enterprise to assist in removing barriers to the transition to viable private farming in Russia. To meet this goal, ISL will help create the legal and regulatory infrastructure governing agricultural land and use, assist in the privatization of the agricultural sector, and improve understanding of rights and legal issues related to private farm ownership.

Institute personnel also serve on working groups formed by the parliament and government to help draft various legislation. ISL receives state funding through the Russian Academy of Sciences, of which it is a component. The Institute is not, however, directly attached to a legislative or governmental body.

Institute for Sustainable Communities

Moscow
Tel/Fax: 434-7261
Email: iscmoscow@glas.apc.org
Contact: Elena Milanova, Alexey Tesakov, Project Coordinators

The institute, based in the U.S., is profiled in *Special Focus Organizations*.

Institute of Theoretical Pedagogics and International Research in Education

P. Korchagina 7
129278   Moscow
Tel: 283-8430
Contact: Natalia Voskresenskaya

Institute of Youth

ul. Iunosti 5/1
111442   Moscow
Tel: 374-5441

The institute offers courses and degrees in social work. Its teachers would like to contact leaders of charitable organizations to discuss the possibility of staff training, arranging student internships, and employment referrals for the institute's graduates.

Institute of Social Work of Russia

ul. Losinoostrovskaya 24
Moscow
Tel: 169-7740

This institute is relatively new, offering a four-year educational program in social work for the first time in Russia. The institute would like the assistance of other NGOs in areas of staff training, arranging student internships, and job placement for its graduates.

Interlegal: International Charitable Foundation for Political and Legal Research

ul. Marii Ulyanovoi 16/1
117331   Moscow
Tel: 138-4408
Fax: 138-5686
E-mail: interlegal@glas.apc.org

Contact: Nina Belyaeva, President

Interlegal was founded in 1989 "to foster the development of structures of civil society in Russia and its regions through education, training and legal aid." It operates an information clearinghouse on the emerging nongovernmental sector in Russia; conducts research and publishes directories and newsletters; provides legal and technical assistance to nongovernmental organizations in Russia; and consults with foreign private voluntary organizations with projects in Russia. Interlegal publishes monthly newsletters on women's issues, religious life in Russia and the third sector. It also periodically publishes profiles of public associations in the Russian Federation.

Interlegal has branches in St. Petersburg and Almaty. It also maintains a liaison office in New York.

International Association for the Struggle with Drug Addiction and Narcobusiness

ul. Gilyarovskogo 65
129110 Moscow
Tel: 281-5718
Fax: 971-6835
Contact: Andrei Andreyevich Varfolomeev, Vice President

The association is working on establishing a children's shelter through the Svyato-Nikolaevsky Chernoostrov Convent in Maloyaroslavets, a city in the Kaluga region. It is looking for people who would like to help the shelter with supplies for classrooms and the dormitory. It is also seeking partners and new associate members. The association's plans include building Russia's first rehabilitation center for drug addicts.

International Center for Business and Economics Education

B. Kozlovskii per. 13/17
107078 Moscow
Tel: 928-4632
Fax: 288-9512
Contact: Sergei Ravitchev, Director

International Center for Human Values

ul. Novocheryomushkinskaya 4/54
177418 Moscow
Tel: 120-1347
Fax: 120-1397
E-mail: pauline@sovamsu.sovusa.com
Contact: Dr. Mikhail Matskovsky, Director

The center conducts sociological and market research, including public opinion polls; organizes conferences; publishes books on ethics, cultural interaction, and modern human relationships.

International Peace Foundation Association

Prechistenka 10
119889 Moscow
Tel: 202-4236
Fax: 200-1208

Established in 1992, the association promotes the ideals of democratic citizenship and a clean environment.

The International Press Center and Club Moscow

Radisson Slavjanskaya Hotel and Business Center
Berezhkovskaya nab. 2
121059 Moscow
Tel: 941-8621, 941-8051
Fax: 941-8418
Int'l Tel/Fax: (4481) 913-3219
E-mail: MOSCOWIPC@aol.com

Contact: Aleksandr Shelemekh, President and General Manager; John Dillard, Director of Programs; Eric Blomquist, Operations Director.

The mission of the club, founded in 1992, is to foster excellence in journalism and the expansion of a free and open press in Russia and the NIS. Club members consist primarily of working journalists based in Moscow. At the end of 1995, 817 journalists, diplomats and associates were members.

Programs and accomplishments of the IPCC include:

• A lecture series featuring hundreds of the most influential political, social, and economic figures in Russia and the world.

• Large conferences on topics such as economic and political reform, current legislative issues, and commercial presentations.

• Professional interaction parties featuring high level speakers and guests from the Moscow business community.

• Media training programs bringing together Moscow-based foreign and Russian journalists, regional journalists, publishers, media executives, and information specialists.

• Filing center with wire services, international communications, and a full service library stocked with refernce materials, books, and Russian and international periodicals.

• Professional service departments offering a full array of audiovisual services, simultaneous and consecutive translation, event planning, etc.

Additionally, the club sponsors two journalism awards programs. Freedom of the Press Awards are presented yearly to individuals or organizations which represent the interests of a free and open press. 1995 recipients included journalists of Agence France

Presse (for their Chechnya coverage) and journalists of NTV (Russian independent television).

Awards for Excellence in Reporting on Russia are given yearly by the IPCC and the Foreign Correspondents Association. Applicants in each of ten categories have their work judged by independent juries composed of journalists and media professionals.

International Union of Kurdish Volunteer Organizations

ul. Partizanskaya 25
Moscow
Tel: 149-9844
Fax: 149-9864
Contact: Merab Shamoev, Azhar Kurdasker

International Women's Center "Woman's Future"

ul. 3-ya Yamskogo Polya 14/16, kv. 20
125124   Moscow
Tel/Fax: 257-0436
Alternative address:
ul. Sadovaya Kudrinskaya 18
103001 Moscow
Tel: 257-1694
Fax: 257-0436
Contact: Alexandra Momdjan, President; Natalia Grigoryeva, Deputy Director

The center was founded in 1988. It has received grants from Family Planning International Assistance and the Japanese Organization for International Cooperation in Family Planning, as well as from World Learning in partnership with the Center for Development and Population Activities. The center is developing a model women's reproductive health clinic in Moscow and is training women as managers and providers of health services to other women.

The center has also developed a program for refugees, launched in 1991, when the center provided baby food, clothing, medications and toys to children in conflict areas of Abkhazia and Nagorno Karabakh.

International Federation of Red Cross and Red Crescent Societies

Moscow
Tel: 126-1732
Fax: 230-6622
Contact: Janet E. Silver

International Science Foundation

a/ya 217
121019   Moscow
Tel: 956-2151/2157
            330-6164/7065
Fax: 956-2156
E-mail: info@isf.ru
URL: http://www.isf.ru/
Contact: Dr. Pavel Arseniev

See profile for the ISF in section *Special Focus Organizations.*

International Women Doctor's Association

Baltiskaya 8
125315   Moscow
Tel/Fax: 433-5557
Contact: Larissa Skuratovskaya

Internews

House of Journalists, kom. 30
Suvorovskiy bul. 8a
121019   Moscow
Tel: 973-2144
Fax: 291-2174
E-mail: eric@sovam.com
Contact: Eric Johnson

Internews has an active program in Russia. It produces a national news program in Moscow, called *Vremya Mestnoe* ("Local Time"), made up of news submitted by independent TV stations from around the NIS. It has started a project called Open Skies which involves acquiring quality programming–documentaries, educational programs, many from abroad–dubbing the tapes into Russian, and distributing them free of charge to any independent station that wants them.

Internews works closely with the Independent Broadcast System, a new network of more than 100 independent TV stations in seven countries of the NIS. This network now has the capability of reaching more than 106 million viewers, according to its executive director Andrei Vdovin.

Eric Johnson also started the electronic mailing list, "FSUMedia," described in the section, *Electronic Mailing Lists.*

Inter-Republic Confederation of Consumer Societies (KonfOP)

ul. Varvarka 14
103609   Moscow
Tel: 298-4649
Fax: 298-4718
E-mail: konfop@glas.apc.org
Contact: Aleksandr Auzan, President; Polina Kriuchkova, Project Director

KonfOP works through a network of 86 consumer societies in the NIS to educate consumers and defend their rights. One of its projects seeks to establish a Russian Better Business Bureau. This would:

• promote ethics and transparency in business by devising a code of standards accepted by both businesses and consumers;

• provide a mechanism enabling responsible businesses to distinguish and protect themselves from unethical and unscrupulous competitors; and
• develop a mechanism enabling businesses and consumers to resolve disputes without relying on the state.

KonfOP will coordinate efforts with responsible businesses to do the necessary preparation, and supervise the work of the BBB in the future. It has received funding from the Center for International Private Enterprise.

Interstate Association of Postgraduate Education

2/30 Sadovya-Triumfalnaya
103050   Moscow
Tel/Fax: 299-7636
Contact: Anatoly Demianchenko

Established in 1990 to help promote postgraduate education and training programs. The association works with a union of educational institutions.

IRIS–Russia Project

ul. 1905 Goda 5, kv. 47
123100   Moscow
Tel/Fax: 259-3730
E-mail: blumenfeld@glas.apc.org
Contact: Mr. Lane Blumenfeld, Resident Director

The Moscow office of IRIS (see section *Special Focus Organizations*) has been involved in commercial law reform and drafting of the new Russian civil code.

ISAR–Moscow

ul. Chayanova 4, kv. 13
Moscow
Tel/Fax: 251-7617
E-mail: isarmos@glas.apc.org
Contact: Lyubov Alenicheva; Amy McVey

See ISAR profile in *Clearinghouse Organizations*. To receive the Russian edition of *Surviving Together (Vyzhivem Vmeste)*, send e-mail to *rst@glas.apc.org* or call/fax the Moscow office.

Kosma/Damian Charity Foundation for Orphans and Handicapped Children

Altufyevskoye shosse, 30B
127561   Moscow
Tel: 401-6648, 272-1510
            180-0504
Contact: Victoria Gribovskaya

The foundation was established to combat the increasing problem of children–particularly disabled children–being orphaned because of the inability of their parents to support them.

The foundation has established a regional rehabilitation center in the northeast district of Moscow, which operates as a day care center for families with handicapped children. There are 80 two- to seven-year old children in the center. Moscow local authorities provide for meals, medical care and staff salaries. The Russian Orthodox Church and local businesses donate some training equipment, toys, books, etc.

The foundation has also started a fund-raising program to improve medical treatment for children, purchase medical (especially testing) equipment, and provide training for center employees both in Russia and abroad.

"Krug" Center for Psychological Support

a/ya 17
123371   Moscow
Tel: 324-4278
Fax: 208-5191

E-mail: cab@glas.apc.org
Contact: Tatyana Ighashova, Executive Director

With a grant from World Learning, the "Krug" Center has been working with the Center for Attitudinal Healing in Sausalito, CA to help hospitals and NGOs in the NIS to develop emotional support services for people with chronic and life-threatening illnesses and disabilities, and their families. The project has provided technical and program asistance to the Center of Love and Support to serve as a model for other agencies.

"Let's Help Children to Study" Association
Pogodinskaya 8/2
Moscow
Tel: 328-6904

Library Charitable Foundation
9 Protopopovskii per., kv. 330
129010   Moscow
Tel: 284-2586
Fax: 280-9749
Contact: Galina Zakamskaya

Established in 1991, the foundation specializes in scientific projects, libraries for the disabled, and contests for Russian youth. Publications include "Memory of Russia" and the Russian Library Encyclopedia.

MacArthur Foundation
Khlebnyi Pereulok 8, kom. 2
Moscow
Tel: 290-5088
Fax: 956-6358
E-mail: macarthur@glas.apc.org
Contact: Tatiana D. Zhdanova, Director

The John D. and Catherine T. MacArthur Foundation established a grant-making program in the NIS in 1992 and opened an office in Moscow in 1993. In the NIS the Foundation seeks to:
• "support independent voices to bring new research and creative approaches to pressing societal issues and problems;
• promote the role of the 'scholar-activist' in civil society; and
• enhance the skills and capacities of scholars and practitioners."
The NIS program concentrates on four areas:
• law and society;
• human rights, including the rights of ethnic minorities and women;
• energy and the environment;
• development of an independent mass media.
Grants are made for three types of projects:
• research and writing grants for individuals;
• funding for foreign travel to attend conferences and workshops;
• special project grants.
  In 1993 the Foundation made grants to 102 scholars, journalists, civil activists, community leaders and policy analysts from throughout the NIS totaling more than $1 million. 49 grants were in the area of energy and the environment, 31 in human rights, 17 on legal and economic reform, and 5 in the field of mass media. 62 grantees were men and 40 were women.

Magee Womancare International
Savior's Hospital for Peace and Charity
Federativnii pr. 17
111396   Moscow
Tel: 304-4939, 301-1502

Contact: Aleksandr Goldberg, MD, President

For description of the program, see Magee profile in *Special Focus Organizations.*

"Memorial" Historical, Educational and Charitable Society

Malyi Karetnyi per. 12
103051 Moscow
Tel: 209-7883, 200-6506
      299-1180
Fax: 973-2094
Contact: Elena Zhemkova, International Coordinator

The Memorial organization was founded in 1988 by leading elements of Russia's democratic intelligentsia such as Andrei Sakharov and Yuri Afanasiev. It grew quickly and chapters spread to many cities not only in Russia but other nations of the former Soviet Union. The central aim of Memorial was to recognize the millions of Soviet citizens whose lives passed through (and often ended) in the Gulag, to document their experiences, and to provide support for those still living and their families.

Memorial's projects include:
• research projects dealing with anticommunist resistance during the Lenin and Stalin period and the dissident movement of the post-Stalin period;
• a museum containing more than 1,000 items from the Gulag;
• the Memorial Archives, containing nearly 50,000 documents and more than 5,000 photos;
• a library with more than 8,000 volumes;
• a weekly radio program, *Vybor* ("Choice"), that airs on Radio Russia;
• sponsoring fact-finding missions to conflicted areas, such as Chechnya;

• social and medical assistance to ex-political prisoners and victims of human rights abuses.

Additionally, Memorial is a principal organizer of a national day honoring the victims of totalitarianism, observed annually on October 30.

Memorial Society–Lobnya

ul. Chkalova 17-3-37
141730 Lobnya
Moscow oblast
Tel: 488-6144
Contact: Vitalii Evdokimovich Bolenok

Memorial Society–Noginsk

ul. Trudovaya 8-83
142400 Noginsk
Moscow oblast
Tel: 524-5214

Memorial Society–Pushkino

ul. Galochkina, 4-9
141200 Pushkino
Moscow oblast
Tel: 2-60-44
Contact: Vladimir Sazanovich

Memorial Society–Uzbekistan

Moscow
Tel: 270-2463, 187-3367
Fax: 457-5890
Contact: Iul Takshiev

It is not clear why this organization is based in Moscow, except that it may not be allowed to operate in Tashkent.

Morozov Project
Academy of Management and the Market

Moscow
Tel: 564-8185, 931-9956
      931-9957
Intl Tel: (7502) 222-2185,
      222-2356, 222-2357

Fax: 564-8183
Intl Fax: (7502) 222-2183
E-mail: postmaster@mx.morozov.ru
mcgurn@ccmail.morozov.ru
Contact: George McGurn, General
Manager; Miroslav Nikoruk, First Dep.
General Director

Leaders of five of Russia's most distinguished universities launched the
Morozov Project in 1991 at the former
estate of Savva Morozov, a famous
Russian entrepreneur and philanthropist
who died in 1905. The aim is to provide business training programs on a
large scale throughout Russia, in order
to create in "a short time period a class
of new entrepreneurs with the skills and
resources to manage the firms of Russia's future." The chief vehicle of the
project is a network of 34 Business
Training Centers (BTCs) and 15 additional support centers that teach basic
business skills to aspiring entrepreneurs. Morozov staff claim that the
BTCs and other elements of the Project–e.g., the Morozov Business Development Fund–have led to the creation
of more than 130,000 new jobs over
the four years of its existence. The
project is funded by USAID.

Moscow Association of Parents of Children with Hearing Problems

5th Krasnoselskii per. 2, kom. 36
107140 Moscow
Tel: 445-3719
Contact: Irina Ivanova, President

Established in 1991 in order to raise
money and buy hearing aids, provide
vacations for children and psychological help for parents.

Moscow Center for Energy Efficiency

ul. Novocheremushkinskaya 54, korp. 4
11748 Moscow
Tel: 120-5147
Fax: 883-9563
E-mail: cenef@glas.apc.org
or
ul. Verkhniya 1, Suite 16
127550 Moscow
Tel/Fax: 482-4417
E-mail: cenef@glas.apc.org
Contact: Igor Bashmakov

The center promotes joint ventures and
advises high-level policymakers on
legislation regarding greater energy efficiency in Russian households. It has
set up a FaxBack Business Information
Line for U.S. companies interested in
energy efficiency investment opportunities. The line is accessible by calling
1-800-779-0135.

Moscow Center for Gender Studies

Institute for Socio-Economic Population Problems
Russian Academy of Sciences
ul. Krasikova 27
117218 Moscow
Tel: 440-1904, 126-7792
Tel/Fax: 332-4532, 421-2405
Fax: 129-0801
E-mail: isepp@glas.apc.org
mcgs@glas.apc.org
Contact: Dr. Anastasia Posadskaya,
Director; Lena Kochkina, Moscow
Representative

MCGS describes its mission as:
- providing a gender perspective to the
society and thus incorporating a gender approach into academia and social life;
- playing a coordinating role in the independent women's movement; and

- resisting sexism "in the humanities, mass consciousness and social policy."

The Center is affiliated with the Institute for Socio-Economic Population Problems of the Russian Academy of Sciences. It has a distinguished roster of women scholar associates, and has published numerous articles and books. (An anthology of essays by scholars associated with MCGS has been published in English, titled *Women in Russia*. Contact the Center for a complete list of its publications.) Besides sponsoring research, MCGS organizes conferences, seminars and training programs aimed at "integrating women into political activities and market economies." It is also developing programs in women's studies for introduction into university and high school curricula.

In cooperation with the Network of East-West Women, MCGS is developing an electronic network to link women's NGOs and to address law and public policy issues concerning women.

Moscow Center of Handicrafts
ul. Bolshaya Dekabraskaya 9
123022   Moscow
Tel: 252-1844, 253-8104
Contact: Raisa Emelyanova

The center offers women job referrals and training in business development.

Moscow Charity House
Bolshoy Zlatoustinsky per. 8/7, kom. 32
103982   Moscow
Tel: 206-8331/34/35/38
              292-8475, 452-3092
              (Sviatkina home)
Fax: 200-2265, 206-8335
              241-6368

Contact: Galina Bodrenkova, President; Valeria I. Svyatkina, Program Coordinator; Andrei Verbitsky, Vice-President.

MCH's initial work focused on collecting and delivering food packages to Muscovites during the "crisis" years 1990-91. Today it describes its mission as improving "the quality of life of people with special needs: sick, elderly, disabled, helping to preserve their dignity." As its work has expanded, MCH now divides it into eight program areas. These include:

- "Information and Help." To help coordinate the assignment of various social services to different organizations and individuals in Moscow, and to be a referral point for individuals to the appropriate agency or source of assistance.
- "Kindness Without Limits." To provide humanitarian and financial aid to the poor, elderly, disabled, single parents and families with many children.
- "Accessible Transportation." To create a system of transport from "door to door" for the handicapped and elderly, who cannot use public transportation.
- "Free Meals for the Elderly." For the elderly and poor, free meals in canteens or, if they cannot leave their apartments, "meals on wheels."
- "Centers for the Elderly." Development of community centers to serve the elderly.

MCH claims to have been able to provide "real help to tens of thousands of people" since becoming registered as an independent charity fund in September 1991. It has a paid staff of 15 and about 2,000 volunteers. It also has 40 community agencies throughout the greater Moscow area.

MCH has a project with Access Exchange International to develop a transportation support network for low-income, disabled persons in the Moscow oblast.

Moscow Committee for Democracy and Human Rights

ul. Ivana Babushkina 3, kv. 366
117292   Moscow
Tel/Fax: 124-1677
Contact: Irina Nikolaevna Zorina

Moscow Economic School

Krasnaya Presnya Str. 4a
125922   Moscow
Tel: 250-0450
Fax: 250-0970, 253-4323
Contact: Yuri Shamilov, President

Moscow Ecopresscenter

ul. Rogova 12-46
123479   Moscow
Tel: 947-1909
Fax: 292-6511 (mark fax "a/ya 1695 for EKOPRESSCENTR")
E-mail: larin@glas.apc.org
Contact: Vladislav Larin, Executive Director

The center was created in 1990 by V. Larin as a nongovernmental organization for the collection and dissemination of ecological information. At the time, Larin was associated with a magazine published by the Presidium of the Academy of Sciences of the USSR. Moscow Ecopresscenter assists journalists who have no environmental educational background and no access to sources of objective information. From the other side, it works with specialists who have such information at their disposal, but no interest in making it more available to the public.

The Ecopresscenter does not have permanent staff. It invites skilled specialists to work with it on concrete projects or topics. These have included:

• The environmental problems connected with exploitation of gas fields on the Yamal peninsula.
• The experience of renewable energy use in Denmark.
• Satellite monitoring of the ocean.
• The effects of conducting public environmental impact assessments of large-scale projects, such as hydroelectric power stations and nuclear power stations.
• A study of the public health consequences of the accidents at the "Mayak" enterprise. (Ecopresscenter published a book on this last topic.)

Environmental materials prepared by the Ecopresscenter have been published in different periodicals of Russia and the NIS (*Energiya, Zeleny Mir, Radical, Vratch, Komsomolskaya pravda, Poisk, Chelovek i Priroda, Juny Naturalist, Zhurnalist,* etc.) and in other countries, including the U.S., Germany, Belgium and Denmark.

Presently, the center is working on a large project connected with developing reliable, primary environmental information throughout the NIS—analyzing its sources, evaluating its authenticity, systematizing it, and describing it.

Moscow Organization of Lesbians in Literature and Art (MOLLI)

ul. Chernahovskogo15/4, kv. 34
125319   Moscow
Tel: 152-1657
Fax: 284-3038
Contact: Mila Ugolkova

MOLLI's goal is tolerance towards lesbians and respect for their rights and freedom in personal and public life. Founded in 1990, it organizes artistic exhibitions, concerts, lectures and film shows. It publishes a literary almanac, *Adelfe.* In the spring of 1995 MOLLI together with other women's organizations conducted an international conference on "Woman and Society."

Moscow Religious Unit of Quakers

Moscow
Tel: 940-1379 (Orlova)
915-7438 (Patricia Cockrell)
Contact: Galina Orlova, Clerk of the Meeting

This is the formal name of the Moscow Friends Meeting, started by Friends (or Quakers) from the West. Attenders at the Meeting have assisted the Mothers of Soldiers organization, collected and delivered supplies for refugees from the war in Chechnya, and worked with children on the cystic fibrosis ward of a Moscow hospital.

Moscow Research Center for Human Rights

Louchnikov per. 4, kom. 1-6, 11, 19
103982 Moscow
Tel: 206-0923, 206-8836
Fax: 206-8853
E-mail: hrmoscow@glas.apc.org
Contact: Alexei Smirnov, Executive Director; Vladimir Raskin, Director of Public Relations

The Center helps to coordinate a wide range of human rights organizations and activities in Russia today. It seeks to develop a professional infrastructure for the human rights movement in Russia by enhancing communications networks among groups, providing assistance with regard to funding opportunities, assisting with publishing projects, and serving as a central locus for information regarding human rights work in Russia. The office in Moscow also serves as the working base for more than 15 human rights groups.

On the Center's Advisory Board are some of the most respected names in Russian human rights circles, including Elena Bonner, Sergei Kovalev, Valeri Borshov, Ernst Ametistov and others.

MRCHR publishes a monthly 10-page newsletter (in Russian and in English), as well as a longer (approx. 40 pp.) monthly journal, *Prava Cheloveka v Rossii* ("Human Rights in Russia"). This contains profiles of human rights organizations, practical advice on issues of organizational development, instructions on using telecommunications and Internet resources for human rights work, and commentary on issues facing the human rights community.

An important current program of MRCHR is its Information Network Project, cordinated by Andrei Pribylov with technical assistance from Sergei Smirnov. The INP intends to enhance the infrastructure of the human rights movement in Russia by expanding the telecommunications capacity of regional human rights groups. This involves maintaining contacts with regional groups, making periodic visits to the regions for research purposes, and providing groups with access to the Internet. The Project currently runs training programs for human rights activists on using the Internet for their work. It also provides groups with computers and modems so that they can take part in the Project's network.

Moscow School of Human Rights

Starovatutinskii proyezd 8
129281 Moscow
Tel: 475-9009
Tel/Fax: 444-4542, 475-9492
Contact: Galina Agapova; Irina Kolechinchenko, Coordinator

Moscow School of Political Studies

Kutuzovsky Prospect 4/2, kv. 353
121248 Moscow
Tel: 243-1756
Fax: 940-2806
Contact: Elena Nemirovskaya, Director

Moscow Society to Help Cancer Patients

Moscow
Tel: 319-0571
Contact: Nataliya Stepanovna Kuznestova

The society is a support group established by cancer patients to assist patients and their families. It works with health care providers to develop care programs and conduct weekly informational sessions. The society has established two hospices–one for elderly cancer patients and one for children with cancer.   It publishes a monthly journal, *Bulletin of Hope,* available from its publisher, "Russian Language" at Staropansky per. 1/5, 103012 Moscow, telephone 928-1722.

Movement against Violence

ul. Ozernaya, 27, kv.266
119361 Moscow
Tel: 437-4671, 230-8377
Contact: El'vira Petrovna Bushinskaya, Sergei Egorovich Sorokin

"Names"–Russian Foundation

a/ya 130
113303 Moscow
Tel/Fax: 165-2359
Contact: Nikolai Nedzelsky

Names was founded in 1993 to provide social/psychiatric assistance to AIDS patients, advocacy for patients, and to educate the public on AIDS victims.

New Economics School

ul. Krasikova 32
117418 Moscow
Tel/Fax: 129-3722
E-mail: cfmoscow@glas.apc.org

No to Alcoholism and Drug Addiction (NAN)

ul. Shvernika 10a
117449 Moscow
Tel: 126-3475
Fax: 310-7076
Contact: Oleg Zykov, President

No to Alcoholism and Drug Addiction assists children and teenagers in emergency situations, exchanges medical and social information, and participates in congresses and symposia. NAN has its own publishing house, and a library with literature on drug and alcohol abuse prevention. The fund has also opened a charitable cafeteria and a store.

Novinskoye/Interunity

ul. Tchaikovskogo 20A
121069 Moscow
Tel: 291-4427
Fax: 200-2201
Contact: Aleksandr Akishin

Novinskoye/Interunity was set up in 1989 as a Russian-British-Panamian commercial joint venture. In 1990 it established a charitable program which includes the production of new and repair of second-hand wheelchairs and other equipment for disabled people. The majority of equipment is donated by foreign charitable organizations and individuals, but these deliveries are not regular, and Novinskoye is looking for a reliable and long-term partnership to expand its activities throughout Central Russia.

The wheelchairs are distributed to the disabled free of charge. Novinskoye also fixes, distributes and maintains other equipment and devices for disabled. Since 1990 the organization has produced and distributed 800 wheelchairs (580 of them in 1993 alone).

Novinskoye has also developed a program to provide emergency medical treatment abroad for Russian children. Novinskoye can provide initial expenses, but it wants to find a foreign partner that can assist in promoting the program and pay for the children's medical treatments. Novinskoye will pay transportation costs. The organization has developed a preliminary agreement with a German NGO for this program, and is interested in cooperation with other international organizations.

Obshchina Social Protection Fund

Moscow
Tel: 138-1027
Contact: Larisa Victorovna Trushina

The fund was formed in 1992 to help those traditionally not eligible for aid, such as families in which both parents are unemployed, or big families where some adults are unable to work. Those who are no longer able to work are being helped with food and financial aid. The foundation is developing a program, Nadezhda (Hope), to create a collective farm in the Moscow suburbs on which people will live and work on a temporary or permanent basis.

Omega

Louchnikov per. 4, kom. 4
103982   Moscow
Tel: 206-8819
Fax: 206-8853
Contact: Viktor Alekseevich Popkov

This organization, founded in 1992, is an inter-ethnic, ecumenical charity which addresses ethnic conflicts in Russia and the NIS.

Open Society Institute–Moscow

B. Kozlovski per. 13/17
107078   Moscow
Tel: 921-2065, 928-4632
Fax: 975-2028, 288-9512
E-mail: culini@culini.msk.ru
Contact: Vyacheslav Bakhmin, Executive Director; Anna Muravyova (high school program)

Among the programs of the Moscow office of the Soros-sponsored Open Society Institute (see profile in *Clearinghouse Organizations*) is its Civil Society project, aimed at developing an infrastructure of civil society organizations. It also conducts research on issues of civil and human rights in the region, and disseminates information on the principles and mechanics of creating an open, democratic society.

Order of Charity and Social Defense

ul. B. Nikitskaya 44-B
121069   Moscow
Tel: 202-2403
Tel/Fax: 291-3436
Contact: Evgeniya Yurevna Poplavskaya, Elena Alekseevna Sidorova

Founded in 1991, this organization works with orphans and war refugees.

Pamir Relief and Development Program

ul. Mosfilmovskaya 11, kv. 1
117192 Moscow
Tel: 146-9524
Contact: Iuri Khubonshoyev, Executive Director

PRDP works with the Aga Khan Foundation, USA, to provide training and stimulate economic development through community-based organizations in Tajikistan.

Panorama Publishers

Kalashny per. 10-2
103009 Moscow
Tel: 202-7410, 290-2330
Tel/Fax: 202-5403
E-mail: panorama@glas.apc.org
Contact: Maxim Balutenko

This publishing organization has produced a number of documents dealing with the third sector and social change in Russia and the NIS.

Partners for Democratic Change–Russia

c/o Interlegal Foundation
ul. Marii Ulianovoy 16/1
117331 Moscow
Tel: 321-4597
Fax: 138-5686
E-mail: interlegal@glas.apc.org
Contact: Nina Belyaeva, Director

See profile in section *Special Focus Organizations.*

Peace and Equality

Moscow
Tel: 972-3308
Contact: Natalia Berezhnaya

This NGO promotes "legal literacy," participation in international NGO meetings, and sponsorship of youth orchestras.

Peleng Voluntary Association of the Disabled

14 Admirala Makarova kv.2
125212 Moscow
Tel: 159-7183
Contact: Leonid Kreindlin, President

Established in 1993, the association works on the rehabilitation of the disabled, and supports a computer center for disabled children.

Phystech Management School

Moscow Institute of Physics and Technology
Institutsky per. 9
141700 Dolgoprudny
Moscow oblast
Fax: 417-5255
E-mail: sergei@guriev.niiros.msk.su
Contact: V. Irikov

The school is looking for a long-term American partner for implementation of a joint education project focusing on establishment of management courses.

Politicians and Businesspeople for Children

Moscow
Tel: 188-1017
Fax: 188-8674
Contact: Margarita Abelina

This group supports children's health and engages in social work.

Povarskaya Sloboda Social Initiative Fund

ul. Pisemskogo d. 15, str. 3
131060 Moscow
Tel: 291-4386, 291-4224

Contact: Tamara Anatolievna Byelova, Executive Director

The fund's projects involve free medical care and medicine for the needy, free excursions for children from large or broken families, and daily hot meals for the especially needy.

Preobrazhneniya (Transformation)
Moscow
Tel: 120-1230, 434-6115
Fax: 120-2430, 494-6702
Contact: Liana Mikhailovna

This group publishes a feminist journal and sponsors round table discussions on women's issues.

Profi Nonprofit
ul. Shvernika 10-a
Moscow
Tel: 301-7204

Profi Nonprofit is a club of third sector and charity organization directors that regularly meets to discuss common managerial issues and problems.

Project Harmony–Moscow
2ya Frunzenskaya 7, kv. 9
119021   Moscow
Tel/Fax: 242-4820

See profile of organization in section *Special Focus Organizations.*

"Protecting Children from Violence"–Voluntary Charitable Foundation
Leninsky pr. 88, kv. 49
117313   Moscow
Tel: 279-5659, 138-9010
Fax: 290-4702
Contact: Tamara Safonova, President

This charitable foundation was founded in 1993 as a psychiatric association for sexually abused children. It publishes educational materials.

Raduga Educational Union
3-d Frunzenskaia 1-73
119270   Moscow
Tel: 268-4035
E-mail: raduga@glas.apc.org
Contact: Andrei Vakulenko, President

Raduga publishes books, brochures and newsletters on the work of nongovernmental organizations, charitable and voluntary activity, and educational topics.

RAMP (Russian-American Media Partnerships)
Dom Zhurnalistov
Suvorovski bul. 6-p, 8a
121019   Moscow
Tel: 956-2249
Fax: 291-2174
E-mail: rcoalson@glas.apc.org
Contact: Igor Bobrowsky, Project Director; Robert Coalson, Associate Director for Print.

RAMP is an Internews project funded by USAID and jointly managed with the Center on War, Peace and the News Media at New York University, which also administers the Russian-American Press and Information Center (RAPIC). RAMP funds a variety of projects that based on working partnerships between U.S. and NIS print and broadcast media organizations.

Ray of Hope
Sumskoy proyezd 15-2-123
113208   Moscow
Tel: 311-0501, 312-6887

Ray of Hope was registered in 1994 and works with 15 other children's organizations in Moscow, including orphanages, boarding schools, and children's hospitals, to provide humanitarian aid, social services, and recreational opportunities to these children.

"Right to Life and Human Dignity" Society

Louchnikov per. 4, kom. 19
103982   Moscow
Tel: 206-8589, 276-4183
Fax: 963-9929
Contact: Victor Kogan-Yasni, President; Oleg Konstantinovich Chirikov, Executive Director

This society was established in 1990 to oppose capital punishment in the former USSR. Since then it has expanded its focus to both articles 3 and 5 of the Universal Declaration of Human Rights ("Every person shall have the right to life . . . No one may be subjected to torture, cruel or humiliating treatment or punishment.")
    Principal activities include legal aid to those who cannot afford it; prison reform; organizing help for "socially unprotected categories of people;" and human rights monitoring.
    Activities are primarily in Russia, but include Tajikistan and other Central Asian states–especially with regard to the capital punishment issue.

"Rodnik"(Spring) Charitable Fund

9/1 Avtozavodskaya
109280   Moscow
Tel: 275-1003
Contact: Anna Volzhina, Director General

Established in 1991, the fund focuses on education of mentally ill children and psychological support for families. The fund has developed an education center, in which 16 of their 20 employees work on educational programs for the mentally ill.

Russian-American Bureau on Human Rights

Volgogradskii pr. 26, kom. 609
109316   Moscow
Tel: 270-9343
Fax: 270-0662
Contact: Aleksandr Liberman, Director

The bureau is an affiliate of the Union of Councils for Soviet Jews (see section *Clearinghouse Organizations.*)

Russian-American Press and Information Center (RAPIC)

a/ya 229, Novy Arbat 2
Khlebny per. 2/3
121019   Moscow
Tel: 203-4403, 203-5702
             203-5802
Fax: 203-6831
E-mail: rapic@glas.apc.org
Contact: Vladimir N. Orlov, Peter Khlebnikov, Co-Directors; Yevgenia Voronina, Computer Library (yevgenia@glas.apc.org)

RAPIC is a joint project of New York University's Center on War, Peace, and the News Media and the Russian Academy of Sciences' Institute for the Study of USA and Canada. RAPIC offers a variety of assistance to Russian journalists, including regular press conferences, information services, data services, and educational programs.
    RAPIC has regional centers in Ekaterinburg, Nizhny Novgorod, Novosibirsk and Vladivostok. Each center offers online and CD-ROM databases which journalists can use to access articles from thousands of Western and

Russian newspapers and magazines. RAPIC also sponsors seminars and mid-career workshops for journalists, editors, and media managers.

Russian-American Nongovernmental Group on Human Rights

Novinskii bul. 13, kv. 6
121099   Moscow
Tel: 252-4312
Fax: 245-2209
Contact: Aleksi Korotaev

Russian Association "Family Planning"

Moscow
Tel: 973-1559, 973-1917
Contact: Ludmila Komsuk

Russian Association of the Independent Regional Press

ul. Annenskaya 21
127521   Moscow
Tel: 219-3947
Fax: 219-8244
Contact: I. Dzyaloshinskii, President

The association unites independent press organs from the entire Russian Federation. It is wholly independent of national, regional or local governments, political parties or professional unions, although it does work with them. It has 50 offices throughout the Russian Federation.

The Association's members have agreed upon the following projects as priorities:
• developoing databanks for regional periodicals;
• A center for the study of privatization and market reforms,and regional programs for small business development;
• a communications business incubator, which can provide consultation on

the basics of forming a publishing company–including writing business plans, locating investors, and learning about international standards and business processes, and computer technologies;
• training of qualified personnel, including program exchanges.

Among the items that the association intends to publish are the following:
• A directory, *Who's Who in the Regional Independent Press*;
• resources devoted to individual professions within publishing, i.e. managers, journalists, editors;
• informational material about the regional independent press' publishing activities, including directories and catalogues;
• a digest of the regional press.

Russian Association of Prenatal Medicine Specialists

ul. Barrikadnaya 2
Moscow
Tel: 252-0901
Fax: 254-9805
Contact: V.V. Gavryushov, President

Russian Business Round Table

Center for Complex Social Research and Marketing
Moscow
Tel: 298-4782
Fax: 298-3441
E-mail: centre@ksbr.msk.ru

Conducts research in a variety of areas, including social, economic, political and demographic trends in Russia. In 1996 it will begin publication of the journal *Analytical Overview*, to be issued six times yearly.

Russian Care

ul. Vozdvizhenka 9, kom. 50-51
121019   Moscow
Tel: 290-0761
Fax: 290-0703
E-mail: counterpart@glas.apc.org
Contact: Andrey Stepanov, Director;
Irina Kozyreva, Chairman of the Board;
Rebecca Bryan, COUNTERPART
Country Director

Russian Care (*Rossiskaya Zabota*) is a
program of COUNTERPART Foundation. It works on behalf of demobilized
military servicemen, developing employment opportunities for them and
providing social services for their
families.

Russian Center for Citizenship Education

16 Studiony proyezd, kv. 48
129224   Moscow
Tel/Fax: 479-4556
Fax: 200-1207
E-mail: rcce@glas.apc.org
Contact: Denis V. Makarov, Program
Officer; Igor Nagdasev, Director

The center was established in 1991 as
an outgrowth of the Dartmouth Conference, a longstanding series of exchanges between Russian and American citizens. RCCE is "dedicated to
addressing the needs of civil society
development in Russia through educational, research and publishing programs."

One of its most ambitious projects is
the National Issues Forums program, an
ongoing series of discussions in local
communities, public associations and
educational institutions on issues of
public interest. These are structured
discussion groups that include a pre-
and post-discussion questionnaire
aimed at defining participants' positions on issues. Discussions are moderated and attempt to bring out all
points of view. RCCE has developed
issue books to accompany these discussions. Discussions RCCE have organized include "People and Politics–
Who should govern?" and "Crime–
How to stop the epidemic of violence."

Other programs include training local
activists in community organization and
development of school curricula and
materials in civic education. RCCE
works with more than 30 institutions
nationally, including political parties,
human rights organizations, educational
institutions and private businesses.

Russian Federation Chamber of Commerce and Industry

ul. Ilinka 5/2, kom. 337
103684   Moscow
Tel: 925-1466
Fax: 230-2455, 929-0365
Contact: Aleksandr Udachin, President

Russian Charitable Foundation "Family"

Litovsky bulvar 3/2, kom. 350
117593   Moscow
Tel: 426-0935
Contact: Fanil Satarovich Timerbayev,
President

Russian Civil Fund for Aid for the Persecuted and their Families (The Solzhenitsyn Fund)

Tverskaya 12/8, kv. 169
Moscow
Tel: 229-8862, 229-8659,
          250-2463
Fax: 203-3376
Contact: Natal'ya Dmitrievna Solz-
henitsyna, Elena Nikitichna Sannikova

Russian Fund for Helping Refugees "Fellow-Countrymen"
Basmannyi per. 1-3
Moscow
Fax: 261-1809
Contact: Yuri Vasilevich Roschin

Russian Green Party
Moscow
E-mail: fei@glas.apc.org
Contact: Alexandr Shubin

Russian Orthodox Church
Danilovsky val 13/1
Moscow
Tel: 331-2222, 331-2288
Fax: 952-8059
Tel/Fax: 955-6789
E-mail: ioccmoscow@glas.apc.org

Russian Society for Contraception
ul. Akademika Oparina 4
117815 Moscow
Tel: 438-3044, -6934
Fax: 433-2771

Salus International Health Institute
ul. Dmitriya Ulyanova 37, kom. 3
Moscow
Tel/Fax: 956-9092
E-mail: dyslandsalus@glas.apc.org
　　　　　salus@glas.apc.org
Contact: Olga Petroukhina, Director

Salus has overseen an effort to bring together a variety of drug and alcohol treatment professionals and organizations to develop additional training, resources and information. It has also conducted a substance abuse prevention campaign for teenagers, a media campaign, and disseminated alcoholism statistics and information.

Salvation Army of Russia
Slavyanskaya pl. 4, kom. 338
Moscow
Tel: 220-9676, 151-8785
Fax: 924-9169, 151-8785
Contact: Sandra Foster

Save the Children Federation
Moscow Coordinating Office

See "Civic Initiatives Program" in this section.

School of Self-Determination
Sirenevy bul. 58a
105484 Moscow
Tel: 461-0935
Fax: 461-0845
E-mail: seldet@glas.apc.org

The school provides instruction for children aged three through 17, as well as retraining for teachers in Russia. It places "a premium on freedom, self-perception and uniqueness of individual methods of world exploration."

Seisin Aiki Club
ul. Bakininskaya 58, kom.2
Moscow
Tel: 284-7302

The club is a group of aikido students. Members of the club have participated in developing self-defense courses for Russian women.

Single Mothers' Association
Begovaya per. 5-2-79
125040 Moscow
Tel: 946-1047
Contact: Ludmilla Kuskova, Vice President

The association organizes support groups for single mothers, lobbyies on draft legislation relating to women, conducts advocacy campaigns, and promotes business development for women.

"Sirin" Foundation for Animal Protection

Moscow
E-mail: sirin@glas.apc.org
Contact: Kirill Goryachev

The foundation deals with animal rights and environmental legislation.

Sisters–Moscow Center of Help for Violated Women

Vorontsovskiye Prudy 5, kv. 126
117630   Moscow
Tel: 936-0132
Fax: 141-7226
E-mail: vandenberg@glas.apc.org
Contact: Natalia Gaidarenko

Sisters was founded in 1994 and provides crisis counseling and support to victims of sexual assault. It operates a hot line and is also working on public education and awareness of issues of sexual violence against women. There are 13 women on staff and more than 10 volunteers in the center. Sisters was a founder of the Association of Crisis Centers for Women.

Social Information Agency

5th Donskoi proyezd 21-b, korp. 10
179606   Moscow
Tel: 958-5900/01 ext.140
E-mail: asi@pf.msk.ru

Society for the Defense of Convicted Businessmen and Economic Freedom

Louchnikov per. 4
103982   Moscow
Tel: 354-1321
Tel/Fax: 206-8853
E-mail: sokirko@msk.ru

Contact: Viktor V. Sokirko, Anatolii F. Vladyshevskii

Founded in 1989, this organization-works to appeal the sentences and to help the families of those unreasonably convicted of "economic crimes." They also work to create active models for the supervision of juries, and expand the movement for economic freedom.

Society of Trustees of Penitentiary Institutions

Louchnikov per. 4, kom. 2
103982   Moscow
Tel: 206-8038, 903-1701
Fax: 206-8853
Contact: Andrei Vladimirovich Babushkin

Society to Assist Observance of Human Rights Laws in Central Asia

Volgogradskii pr. 26, kom. 1402
109316   Moscow
Tel: 270-2463, 206-8618
Contact: Madamin Narzikulov, Deputy Representative

The society publishes a monthly bulletin on human rights abuses in Tajikistan, Turkmenistan, and Uzbekistan.

Socio-Ecological Union

a/ya 211
Louchnikov per. 4, kom. 10-11
121019   Moscow
Tel: 921-7161, 928-7608
Fax: 206-9790
E-mail: soceco@glas.apc.org

The Socio-Ecological Union is an international non-profit organization serving as an umbrella group for more than 250 independent non-governmental organizations.

Established in 1988, the SEU is a voluntary association of environmental groups active on the local, city, regional and district level. These member-groups are extremely diverse, including teams of environmental activists, associations of environmentally minded officials, school children, nature clubs, independent research laboratories, societies of victims of radioactive pollution and conservation organizations involved in national park planning, as well as interested individuals.

The SEU's primary aim, as stated in its charter, is to maximize the "cooperative intellectual potential, material and financial means, and organizational capacity of the Union's members" in a variety of environmental and social areas.
SEU links organizations through its Center for Coordination and Information (CCI). In 1993 the CCI established the "LiveNet-Info" information service to distribute information electronically to its members.

The CCI was originally established to support initiatives of SEU members and to provide advice and support to various environmental efforts. As SEU has expanded, many of its member groups have established coordinated efforts in a variety of issue areas and programs:

- Biodiversity Conservation Center (see above) on management of biological resources;
- Center for Nuclear Ecology and Energy Policy;
- EcoSafeGuard, an environmental clean-up task-force;
- Laboratory on Environmental Design, focusing on land-use planning;
- Center for Independent Ecological Programs to conduct environmental

impact assessments and research in environmental medicine;
- Movement for Nuclear Safety;
- Union for Chemical Safety, focusing on chemical weapons; and
- International Association for Environmental Education.

The SEU is governed by a 17-person Council, elected at periodic international conferences. For more information about the organization, including a short history of its significant achievements, see its pamphlet, *We Are the Union* (1995, in English).

"Soglaciya" Women's Society
169 pr. Krasnoy Armiy, kv. 102
Sergeev Posad
141300   Moscow oblast
Tel: (8254) 4-43-34, 4-48-34
Contact: Elena Porus, Larissa Boitkova

Soglaciya provides job training and professional development for women, training for participation in politics and public administration and has organized crisis centers for women and teenagers.

"SpArt" Center
Sireneviy bul. 4
105122   Moscow
Tel: 330-4558 (home)
Tel/Fax: 166-4783
Contact: Vladislav Stoliarov, President

SpArt was established in 1991 as a sports and arts education program for disabled children. It provides games for the disabled, and integrative programs for regular and disabled children. There are branches in 15 regions in Russia.

Special Olympics Eurasia
Luznetskaya nab. 8
119781   Moscow
Tel: 201-1953

Fax: 201-1429
Contact: Ms. Natalia Sladkova, Executive Director

Special Olympics Moscow
ul. Markhlevsky 18
101100 Moscow
Tel: 924-1949
Contact: Mr. Anatolii Grigoriev, Chairman

Soros Center for Contemporary Art
ul. Chernyakhovskovo 4a
125319 Moscow
Tel: 151-8706, -8816
Fax: 151-8816
Contact: Irina G. Alpatova, Director

The Moscow center is one of a network of centers throughout Central and Eastern Europe created to promote and assist national artists. The center hosts conferences, has established a computerized database of regional artists, a slide collection of artwork from the second half of the 20th century, and a library catalogue and periodical reference of contemporary Russian artists.

The center also provides information to artists on the availability of grants and stipends, nationally and internationally, collects information about individual artists' projects, and gallery and museum exhibitions.

In the future, the Center plans to expand its research and instruction activities, and to provide more resources for artists, curators and managers, and students.

"Stimula" Women's Informational and Educational Center
ul. Flerov 10-1
Dubna

141980 Moscow oblast
Tel: (09621) 63-101, 62-214
Fax: (09621) 65-891, 30-301
Contact: Henrietta Savina

Stimula was founded in 1989 and conducts seminars in order to create a new work place for unemployed women based on nontraditional forms of employment. It has a health program, a children's program, and organizes charitable activities.

Transnational Radical Party
Moscow Headquarters
ul. Trubnaya 25-2, kv. 49
Tel/Fax: 923-9127
E-mail: n.khramov@agora.stm.it
Contact: Nikolai Khramov

This group is affiliated with the Transnational Radical Party of Italy. It has worked on issues of conscientious objection to military service in Russia, among other activities.

Tvorchestvo (Creativity) Independent Women's Association
ul. Kosygin 5, kv. 328
117334 Moscow
Tel: 137-4343
Fax: 497-4493
Contact: Vera Glushenkova, Director

Tvorchestvo was founded by the Russian Red Cross to provide assistance to unemployed women in Russia by providing them with skills and training, primarily in arts and crafts.

Tvorets Charitable Association
ul. Gertsena 16, kom. 109
Moscow
Tel: 229-9622

The association coordinates activities and fundraising to support the disabled. One of its programs allows disabled children to learn drawing in the studios of well-known artists. Tvorets organizes other activities that require financial and material support.

"Uchitelskaya Gazeta" (Teachers Newspaper)

Vetoshni per. 13/15
103012 Moscow
Tel: 921-3025, 921-4897
Fax: 928-8253, 924-2927
E-mail: safronov@redline.ru
Contact: Petr Polozhevets, Editor-in-Chief; Sergei Safronov, Director

Uchitelskaya Gazeta is a leader in the educational reform movement in Russia. It is involved in efforts to create a national association of civics education and each of its weekly issues carries materials for teachers on civics.

Ukrainian Library in Moscow

ul. Velozavodskaya 11/1
109280 Moscow
Tel/Fax: 118-9192
E-mail: postmaster@libukr.msk.su
libukr@glas.apc.org
Contact: Natalia Chelovska, Chief Librarian; Yuriy Kononenko, Chief of the Library Council

This library is the descendant of the Central Ukrainian Library founded in Moscow in the 1920s and closed in 1938. It was re-opened in December 1989 with the help of the Moscow Ukrainian Youth Club and a firm called Ukrainian Publicity. The library contains more than 13,000 books and 8,500 periodicals, as well as audio and video recordings and music collections. Besides its collections of books in Ukrainian and Russian, the library also has holdings in Polish, English, German, French and other languages. A computer hook-up to the Internet allows readers to access from Moscow the catalogues of almost any library in the U.S. The library is trying, without success so far, to reclaim the building which housed its collection in the twenties and thirties.

Union of Russian Journalists

a/ya 120
Suvorovskiy bul. 8a, 6-p, 4
127562 Moscow
Tel/Fax: 209-4904
E-mail: root@market.compnrt.ru
Contact: Sergei Kalmikov, Administrator, Regional and International Program

Union of Young Lawyers

a/ya 15
ul. B.Yakimanka 37, kom. 17
125057 Moscow
Tel: 238-8885
Fax: 246-2020
Contact: Vyacheslav Valer'evich Grib; Oleg Vasil'evich Lupaina (Vice President)

The association was established in September 1993 with chapters in St. Petersburg, Rostov-on-Don, and Yaroslavl. It is associated with the journal *Yurist*.

United Way International

ul. Gilyarovskogo 5
129090 Moscow
Tel/Fax: 956-8114; 208-8514
E-mail: uwi@glas.apc.org

See UWI profile in section *Clearinghouse Organizations*.

Urban Institute—Russia

pr. Mira 19, kom. 317-19
129090 Moscow

Tel: 971-1254
Fax: 288-9384
Contact: Raymond Struyk

See the institute's profile in section *Special Focus Organizations*

Vera i Svet
Moscow
Tel: 952-1676, 266-0109
Contact: Olga Gurevich, Natalia Naumova

Vera i Svet works with young people with learning disabilities.

Vesta
ul. Kirovogradskaya 44-1-127
113534 Moscow
Tel: 387-1404

Vesta supports about 130 families with disabled children. Vesta would like to take part in cultural or sporting events for disabled children. The organization would like assistance from national and international NGOs working with disabled children.

Volunteer Organization for Women's Unity
per. Karamzina 9-223
Moscow
Tel/Fax: 958-5455
Contact: Ludmila Kabanova

We and You (*"My i Vy"*) Voluntary Charitable Foundation
a/ya 15, B-120
Moscow
Tel: 227-7868
Contact: Oleg Zobnin, Gennady Rochshupkin

Assists AIDS patients, and publishes about the AIDS problem.

Winrock International Farmer-to-Farmer Program
ul. Verkhnaya 34, NATI, kom. 815
125040 Moscow
Tel: 250-7051, 250-7627
Fax: 945-3192, 257-7990
E-mail: vandenberg@glas.apc.org
Contact: Ms. Martina Vandenberg, NIS Consortium Coordinator

This program provides training, makes seed grants, and promotes networking and communications for Russian and Ukrainian women's NGOs. See Winrock profile in section *Special Focus Organizations*.

Women and Stress
Institute of Pyschology
Russian Academy of Science
Yaroslavskaya 13
129366 Moscow
Tel: 282-1224,404-9924
Fax: 282-9201
E-mail: firm@ipras.msk.su
Contact: Irina Maltseva

Women and Stress was founded by a group of psychologists specializing in stress and women as a result of the vast social, economic and political changes in Russia. The organization's goals include providing public education on mental health, working with women's organizations to further their research, and providing free counseling for women.

Women's Archive
ul. Novogireevskaya 12-2, kom. 32
111123 Moscow
Tel: 305-15-39
E-mail: khot@glas.apc.org
zoya@adl.msk.su
Contact: Zoya Khotkina

This is the first archive in Russia specializing in women. It was founded in 1993 to produce annals about the modern women's movement–in order to create a documentary portrait of Russia's modern woman and to educate about the important role of women in Russian history.

The development of the archives is being accomplished through several collections. The main collections are: Regional Centers of Women's Activities; Stages of the Women's Independent Movement in Russia; Women's rights–Human rights; Women in the Media and Women's Press; Audio archives; Photo archives.

"Women for Children"
Zhigulevskaya 55
Moscow
Tel: 175-2120, 264-0659

Women for Conversion Foundation
2 Vorontsovsky per.
109044   Moscow
Tel: 921-1074
Fax: 274-0090
E-mail: leont@mibit.msk.ru

This foundation was established to assist women employed in high-technology defense industries as the industries convert to civilian production. It assists women with career training and counseling. The foundation is training women for work in community enterprises, social work, ecology, small business development and local government.

Women for Social Democracy
a/ya 35
109044   Moscow
Tel: 322-1443

Tel/Fax: 292-3156
Contact: Irina Doskitch, Galina Venediktova

WSD engages in advocacy and parliamentary lobbying. It also distributes draft legislation of concern to the NGO community.

"Women's Future" Refugee Program
Moscow
Tel/Fax: 257-0436
Contact: Regina Yavchunovskaya, Assistant to the President

The Refugee Program of Women's Future offers humanitarian assistance to women and children who are refugees from areas of conflict around the former Soviet Union. It has worked in Karahak, Abkhazia, Pridnestrovia, North Ossetia, and Ingushetia to provide food, clothing, medicine and toys. The project hopes to create mechanisms for the reintegration of refugees.

Women in Global Security
ul. Kosygina 2
117334   Moscow
Tel: 137-6577, 938-5307
Fax: 938-2030
E-mail: kapitza@magnit.msk.ru
             elvira@glas.apc.org
Contact: Leokadia Drobizheva, President; Nina Astrinskaya

WINGS is interested in issues of conflict resolution (especially ethnic conflict), women in science, and women in social science research.

Women's Innovative Fund
Pokrovski bul. 6-20-2
109028   Moscow
Tel: 298-4704
Fax: 958-1111

E-mail: sokom-russia@mcr1.geo.de
spro@glas.apc.org
Contact: Steffi Engert

Women's Training Network

Chrnishyevskovo 11, kv.5
103030 Moscow
Tel/Fax: 366-9274, 284-3038
E-mail: tatiana@adl.msk.ru
feminist@glas.apc.org
Contact: Tatiana Troinova, T.A. Komissarova

This organization provides job retraining for women and e-mail networking.

Women's Union of Russia

ul. Nemirovich-Danchenko 6
103832 Moscow
Tel: 229-3223
Fax: 200-0274
Contact: Alevtina Fedulova, President

World Learning

Volkov per. 13, kom. 8
123242 Moscow
Tel/Fax: 255-9724, 255-9001
956-5003
E-mail: wldlearn@glas.apc.org

See World Learning profile in section *Clearinghouse Organizations.*

World Vision

ul. Panfilova 18a
125080 Moscow
Tel: 158-7055,192-6260 (home)
Fax: 158-7254
E-mail: david@wvrussia.msk.ru

See profile in section *Special Focus Organizations.*

World Wildlife Fund

Moscow
E-mail: stam@glas.apc.org
wwfrus@glas.apc.org

Contact: Vladimir Krever; Tamara Semyonova

Youth Center for Human Rights and Legal Culture

ul. Molodjoznaya 4-394
117296 Moscow
Tel: 270-3763, 137-3009
Fax: 291-2904, 973-2094
E-mail: yrus@method.ycenter.msk.ru
Contact: Vsevolod Vladimirovich Luchovitskii; Elena Rusakova, Coordinator

Youth Institute

ul. Moldogulova 3-1-46
113538 Moscow
Fax: 374-7878

ZhIF, Women's Innovation Foundation

EDC, Electronic Documentation Center "East-West"
Tel. 952-25-72
Fax: 952-28-23
E-mail: zhif-adm@udn.msk.ru
natali@babich.msk.ru
Contact: Natalia Babich, Irina Filatova

In cooperation with AIDOS, the Italian Association for Women in Development, based in Rome, ZhIF and its "daughter" organization EDC are developing a "Documentation/Information Center on Women's Rights." This project is financed by the Phare and Tacis Democracy Program, a European Union initiative to help promote democratic societies in the countries of central and eastern Europe, and the New Independent States and Mongolia. The Documentation Center is collecting national and international literature on women's basic rights which include human, political, economic and reproductive rights.

This will be available for consultation and research work at EDC's library. Femina from Naberezhnye Chelny will also be a partner in this project, as will one more Russian woman's organization.

The three partners will have basic materials in all three places, but at the same time each will have its special focus. EDC will emphasize women's enterprises and female employment, while Femina will concentrate on the issue of gender and ethnicity. The third partner will specialize in health issues and reproductive rights.

Arkhangelsk (8182)

EcoSevera Ecological Organization
Uricsky pr. 54-2-1
163060   Arkhangelsk
Tel: 43-95-13
Fax: 49-61-34
E-mail: root@yirc.arkhangelsk.su
ecosever@glas.apc.org
Contact: Lyudmila Zhirina,
Sergei Fedorov

Currently working in the areas of industrial pollution, mining, rivers and nuclear issues.

Astrakhan (8510)

Committee for Assistance in Support of Legal Human Rights
ul. Lenina 8, kom. 20
414000   Astrakhan
Tel: 22-13-43, 22-43-67
Contact: Vyacheslav Gladyshev

Green World
Astrakhan
E-mail: ak@green.astrakhan.su
Contact: Alexei Klyushin, A. Pavlov

Current interests are in water pollution, regional industrial development, underground nuclear testing, fisheries, and the Volga river.

"Human Rights"
ul. Boevaya 77, kv. 9
414021   Astrakhan
Tel: 22-45-98, 34-05-09 (home)
Fax: 22-24-45, 24-66-56
E-mail: ddima@sovamsu.sovusa.com
Contact: V.A. Berezkin

This is a fund that does human rights work at the Astrakhan oblast level.

Bolshevo (9497)

Memorial Society
ul. Moskovskaya 4-4-33
141090   Bolshevo
Tel: 284-0025
Contact: Yan Koldunov

Bryansk (8322)

Viola Ecological Organization
ul. Oktyabrskaya 23, kv. 21
241000   Bryansk
Tel: 45-906
E-mail: viola@glas.apc.org

Ivanovo (0932)

Ivan Oblast Society of Human Rights
a/ya 1047
ul. Yevereva 7/2, kv. 1

153000   Ivanovo
Tel: 32-93-67, 32-88-31 (home)
            26-85-66 (home)
Contact: Sergei Valkov

The society supplies legal help for the population, expertise in preparing bills, assistance in the legal process, and support for consumer rights. It also works with penitentiary institutions and with schools focused on human rights.

Kaliningrad (112)

Ecodefense!
Kaliningrad
E-mail: ecodefense@glas.apc.org
Contact: Vladimir Slivyak; Alexandra Kroleva

This organization specializes in eco-journalism, nuclear power and chemical pollution in the Baltic region.

Kaluga (8439)

Association for Environmental Education
a/ya 152
249020   Obninsk-1
Kaluga oblast
Fax: 255-2225 (Moscow)
E-mail: vkalinin@glas.apc.org
Contact: Vadim Kalinin

Kalinin was Chair of the Organizing Committee which sponsored an international conference on children's environmental education in Moscow in April 1995. He is also on the Council of the Socio-Ecological Union.

Darina Cooperation and Development Program
ul. Korolyova 16, kom. 116

249020   Obninsk
Kaluga oblast
Tel: 3-83-55
Fax: 255-2318 (Moscow)
E-mail: obninsk@storm.iasnet.com
Contact: Valery Salazkin

Active since 1989, Darina seeks to promote democratic values and a vibrant civil society in Obninsk and the Kaluga region. Darina conducts courses on the principles of democracy and free market economies for teachers, high school students and the general public. It has organized a training course for teachers of civic education, seminars for leaders of public organizations, and a conference on the experiences of democratization in the Obninsk region. Darina also works with members of the regional mass media and publishes a newsletter on democracy.

IVMA Rehabilitation Center
ul. F. Engels 19, kv. 9
248023   Kaluga
Tel: 7-73-58
Contact: Aleksandr Matveyev, Director

The IMVA Rehabilitation Center is a charitable association of Kaluga families with disabled children. The center helps 507 families with disabled children. Its activities include giving gifts on holidays, distribution of wheelchairs and other aid.

Kazan (8432) and Tatarstan (8439)

"Fantom"
ul. Dekabristov 183
420082   Kazan
Tel: 43-67-32, 42-06-12

Contact: Dmitrii Viktorovich Bokhmenin, Gennadii Alekseevich Gribakov

Fantom is a television cinematographers union.

Femina
ul. 40-let Pobedy 57, kom. 182
Naberezhnye Chelny
423815   Tatarstan
Tel: 59-6838 (home)
Tel/Fax: 56-7020
E-mail: elena@fem.kamaz.kazan.su
Contact: Elena V. Mashkova

Femina was founded in 1993. It conducts sociological research and gives a course, "Gender studies," for students. The organization publishes a supplement to the city's newspaper called "Femina" and produces a TV program for women, "Kamazonka." In November 1995 Femina member Irina Zajceva attended a "Young Women for Democracy" program in Amsterdam. The meeting brought together 35 young women from 16 countries. Activities included seminars and workshops, e-mail training, and public demonstrations against French nuclear testing.

Helsinki–Kazan
ul. P. Zorge 65-7
420110   Kazan
Tel: 35-27-30
Contact: Masgut Mafuzailovich Khafizov

This organization operates as a public legal aid fund.

Kazan State University International Office
ul. Lenina 18
420008   Kazan
Tel: 38-73-90

Kazan Youth Political Club
Kazan
E-mail: petrovd@univex.kazan.su
Contact: Denis Petrov, Vice President

The club describes itself as "a democratic organization intended to give young people a chance to become involved in political activities. This involves studying political topics, meeting with people who are working in political and govermental structures, and exchanging information."

The club would welcome exchanges of information and literature with similarly minded groups or individuals in the U.S.

Traverse
Sibirsky Tract 39, kv. 12
420074   Kazan
Tel: 76-13-89
E-mail: group@infost.kazan.su
Contact: A. Styopochkin

Traverse is a professional sport traveling club.

Krasnodar (8612)

All Russian Society for the Protection of Nature
ul. Krasnaya 19
350063   Krasnodar
Tel: 57-16-16
Fax: 52-47-53
Contact: Rimma Sergeivna Sidanova

The society is a membership organization, registered in 1994, with nearly 650 members. It is attempting to develop a network of organizations and individuals in the territory, and to conduct independent environmental evaluations of problem sites.

"Animal Protection"–Krasnodar Regional Club
Nashi Druz'ya Newsletter
ul. Shaumyana 127
350000   Krasnodar
Tel: 57-35-07
Contact: Giorgii P. Troitskii
(Newsletter), Svetlana I. Danil'chuk
(Animal Protection)

In May 1988 a group of animal lovers
joined to form a club for the prevention
of cruelty to animals. It has developed
several educational programs for
schools and libraries, and hopes to open
an animal shelter with the animal protection newsletter *Nashi Druz'ya.*
Registered in October 1993, *Nashi
Druz'ya* (*"Our Friends"*) has a circulation of 7,000 in the Krasnodar area
and around Russia. It is devoted to
environmental and species preservation
issues, as well as animal protection.

Association for the Protection of Consumer Rights
ul. Pashkovskaya 65
350000   Krasnodar
Tel: 57-64-53, 55-01-60
Contact: Lyubov Ivanovna Bakhme-
tova

Since 1990, the Consumers Rights Association has worked to develop con-
sumer-oriented legislation and for better goods and services to consumers.
They conduct independent evaluations
of products and services, and disseminate this information to the public,
along with consumer education programs. With funding from dues and
private donations, the organization has
30 inspectors and nearly 9,000 members.

Association of Young Journalists
ul. Krasnaya 57, kom. 32
350000   Krasnodar
Tel: 59-34-54
Contact: Stanislav Zhatikov

In 1992 the association began providing
seminars and programs for young people planning to become journalists.
The association sponsors writing competitions, and assists students in preparing applications to attend journalism
programs in institutions of higher
learning.

Center for Kuban National Culture
Society of Russian Culture
ul. Krasnoarmiskaya 53
350000   Krasnodar
Tel: 54-25-68
Tel/Fax: 57-68-34
Contact: Natalya A. Nazarenko
(Society); Sergei A. Kropachev
(Center); Aleksandr Eremin

The Center is working to develop interaction among the various nationalities
in the region. Established in 1992, the
Society provides a meeting place for
artists, poets, writers and musicians of
all nationalities. It organizes cultural
evenings and performances. It has also
developed a theater and studio for artists to use in developing their projects.

Kuban People's Democratic Legal Protection Association "Subjective Rights"
gost. Moskva, kom. 509
Krasnodar
Tel: 31-84-62
Contact: Nikolai A. Alexandrov

The association opened in 1991 to provide low-cost and *pro bono* legal services.

Kuban Union of Veterans of Afghanistan
ul. Krasnaya 57, kom. 30
350000   Krasnodar
Tel: 59-34-35
Contact: Valerii Nikolaevich Kuznetsov

Red Cross, Krasnodar
ul. Gogolya 153
350033   Krasnodar
Tel: 57-34-37, 52-37-63
Contact: Valentina A. Dorokhina

Russian-American International Business Institute
Krasnodar
Tel/Fax: 36-34-27

Women and Families Center
ul. Gimnazicheskaya 93
Krasnodar
Tel: 52-28-18
Contact: Irina B. Kotelevits

The center is associated with the Russian-American Women and Families Center in Moscow.   One of its projects is the opening of a birth clinic on the Western model, where husbands can remain with their wives during delivery. It has also established a learning center for women, with a library and a meeting place for women and girls.

Kursk (0712)

Kursk Regional Center for Defense of Human Rights
pr. Kulakova 5
305018   Kursk

Tel: 57-00-52, 57-15-44, 52-20-19
Contact: Elizaveta Kalinina

Lipetsk (0742)

Lipetsk Regional Department of the Social-Ecological Union
a/ya 917
398046   Lipetsk
Tel: 25-52-50 (Kotov)
Tel/Fax: 77-22-02
E-mail: hrlipetsk@glas.apc.org
         root@green.lipetsk.ru
         contact@green.lipetsk.ru
Contact: Vladimir Kotov, Coordinator;
Elena T. Gygnina

LRDSEU was created in 1991 and is registered as an independent public organization. The purpose of the organization is to carry out public education; develop the public's "ecological consciousness;" and influence public policy.

Its first action involved collecting signatures in a successful effort to block a projected new rolling mill of the Lipetsk Steel and Iron Works. It solicits donations from organizations and private persons to finance specific programs and sustain its information services. Revenues for the organization were about $4,500 in the three-year period 1993-95.

Of the membership list of 25, fifteen people are from Lipetsk and 10 are from Usman, a regional town. All are volunteers. The organization: maintains an "informbureau," called Acid Rain; encourages litigation against enterprises that pollute; operates a "Green Library"; sponsors a children's club, Dinasaurling; participates in the work of public councils on problems of ecology in the region; organizes monthly lectures on environmental protection with the participation of regional specialists; periodically places articles in regional newspapers; and trains others in the use of computer databases and electronic mail.

Murmansk (8152)

Bellona
a/ya 4310
183038   Murmansk
Tel: 57-46-16
          47-789-10414 (international)
Fax: 47-789-10750 (international)
E-mail: igor.kudrk@euronetics.no

Bellona is a Norway-based organization concerned about nuclear and industrial pollution in northwestern Russia. It shares space with Radio Murmansk at Rusanova 7, 3rd etazh.

Committee of Soldiers' Mothers
ul. Volodarskogo 4
183038   Murmansk
Tel: 52-5857, 57-2062
Contact: Tatyana N. Kretova, Irina V. Paikacheva (Legal Consultant)

Lapland Biosphere Reserve
Apatity
Murmansk oblast
E-mail: root@zap.mgus.murmansk.su
Contact: Elena V. Geljazova

This organization works in biodiversity conservation and nature reserves.

Women's Congress of the Kol'sk Peninsula
ul. Polyarnye Zori 60, kom. 205
183038   Murmansk
Tel: 54-6341, 59-1772, 59-1972
Tel/Fax: 57-9551
E-mail: irina@womkongr.murmansk.ru

Contact: Irina A. Fogt, Lyubov V. Sheteleva

The congress is involved in educational programs, support for elderly northern inhabitants, and children's rights work.

Nizhny Novgorod (8312)

ACTR/ACCELS Nizhny Novgorod
ul. Sovetskaya 12
Gostinitsa Tsentralnaya no. 818
603002   Nizhny Novgorod
Tel: 49-04-83
E-mail: fsa.nizhni@sovcust.sprint.com

See the profile for ACTR/ACCELS in section *Special Focus Organizations*.

Association of Families with Many Children
ul. Kominterna 8, kv. 73
603014   Nizhny Novgorod
Tel: 24-47-57, 41-44-65
Contact: Elena Ivanova Mayorova

Since 1990 the Association of Families with Many Children has brought together 700 families. FAMS is now working on a program to raise the status of families with many children and to provide them with material and moral support.

Dront Eco Center
a/ya 34
603163   Nizhny Novgorod
Tel: 34-32-80, 39-11-91
E-mail: dront@glas.apc.org
Contact: Ashkat Kayumov

Kayumov is a member of the Council of the Socio-Ecological Union.

"Family"–Nizhny Novgorod Center of Medical and Social Protection and Adaptation

ul. Krylov 2a-45
603104   Nizhny Novgorod
Tel: 65-55-96
Fax: 35-64-80
Contact: Nadezhda Radina, Sergey Radin

"Family" provides training and support to psychologists and social workers in state orphanages. It also provides training and seminars on issues related to child abuse and neglect, child development, and gifted children.

Nature Conservation

Tel: 39-04-64
E-mail: kam@dop3.kreml.nnov.ru
Contact: Sergei Kaminsky

Nature Conservation was organized in 1994 by scientists, environmental specialists, social workers, and people interested in protection of the Volga River. It sponsored an "Environmental Parliament of the Volga River Watershed and Northern Caspian Sea" in March 1995.

Nizhny Novgorod A. D. Sakharov Apartment-Museum

pr. Iu. A. Gagarina 214
603137   Nizhny Novgorod
Tel: 66-86-23
Contact: Sergei Ponamarev, Director

Nizhny Novgorod Charitable Fund Serafima

Nizhny Novgorod
Tel: 60-30-08, 60-30-05
Fax: 34-05-04
Contact: Larisa Tzezan, Director

In cooperation with Opportunity International, Serafima is working to pro-

vide small business loans, training, and hands-on consultation to pensioners and women to start small enterprises.

Nizhny Novgorod Press and Information Center

603006   Nizhny Novgorod
Tel: 35-62-53
Fax: 35-04-74
E-mail: nnrapic@glas.apc.org
Contact: Natalia Skvortsova and Marina Stepanenko, Coordinators

Affiliated with the Russian-American Press and Information Center in Moscow.

Nizhny Novgorod Society of Human Rights

a/ya 80
Kreml 1, kom. 251
603082   Nizhnii Novgorod
Tel: 39-74-87
Tel/Fax: 39-08-95
E-mail: elena@gpd6.kreml.nnov.su
Contact: Sergei Shimovolos; Oleg Boronkov, Secretary

Founded in 1993, the society acts as a consultation center for the legal rights of the population, produces Legal Aid publications "Pravozaschitnoe izdanie" and "Biblioteka."

Open Society Institute– Nizhny Novgorod

ul. Boslhaya Pecherskaya 29
603155   Nizhny Novgorod
Tel: 36-73-82, 38-43-45
Fax: 36-73-82
E-mail: cinizh@fsoros.sandy.nnov.su
Contact: Alexei Aimnyakov, Executive Director

See OSI profile in section *Clearinghouse Organizations*.

Vozmozhnost
Opportunity International
ul. Bolshaya Pokrovkaya 25, kom. 14
603008   Nizhny Novgorod
Tel/Fax: 33-72-27
E-mail: opportuntiy@glas.apc.org
Contact: Stacie Shraeder

Vozmozhnost operates a training center for indigenous NGOs in the Nizhny Novgorod region.

Perm (3422)

Family Protection Foundation "Badger"
ul. Kutaisskaya 29/2, kom. 12
614084   Perm
Tel: 49-14-57
Contact: Yelena G. Toropova, President

Invaluks
ul. Chaikovskogo 35
614066   Perm
Tel: 27-03-13, 27-45-19
Fax: 27-19-89
Contact: Sergey Putenkov, Director

Invaluks is a four-year old private center providing medical and social rehabilitation for disabled persons. It seeks a U.S. partner to help train its staff in new methods and improve its level of service.

Memorial Society–Perm
Perm Regional Legal Aid Center
ul. Lenina 51, kv. 949
614006   Perm
Tel: 39-49-93, 32-52-30
            48-78-86, 31-43-45
            25-16-18, 39-43-04 (Legal)
Fax: 34-83-74

Contact: Aleksandr M. Kalikh (Memorial); I.V. Averkiev, Andrei B. Suslov (Legal Aid)

Zdravstvui Editorial Publishing Center
Perm
ul. Gazeti "Zvezda" 44, kv. 42
Tel: 48-14-01 (work)
            44-37-21 (home)
Contact: Galina A. Dubnikova, Chief Editor

Zdravstvui publishes periodicals and books for members of the disabled community in Russia. Dubnikova is herself a disabled person. She is associated with the All-Russian Society of Invalids.

Petrozavodsk (81400)

Palace of Youth and Creativity
ul. Krasnaya 8
185000   Petrozavodsk
Karelia
Tel: 74-135, 76-230, 75-649
E-mail: phstp@sovam.com

The organization has worked with Project Harmony, *based* in Vermont, to create a resource and training center to serve the needs of disabled children's organizations throughout the region.

Pskov (8112)

Center for the Social Support of Women
Pskov Training Center
ul. Pecherskaya 7, kv. 119
180094   Pskov
Tel: 22-41-06
Contact: Natalya Vassilyeva, Director

The center provides programs in women's health, job training, self-defense programs and physical fitness. They offer a summer camp for children, as well as programs for orphans and disabled children.

Pskov Free University
Pskov
E-mail: mike@zpp.pskov.su
Contact: Victor Chernyh

Rostov-on-Don (8632)

Alcoholics Anonymous
Rostov-on-Don
Tel: 54-80-05
Contact: Leonid

Center for Citizen Initiatives
Rostov-on-Don
Tel/Fax: 63-13-63
E-mail: root@cci.rnd.su
Contact: Andrei Skorik

See CCI profile in section *Clearinghouse Organizations.*

CEC International Partners
Rostov-on-Don
Tel: 66-50-84
Contact: Mary Shea

See CEC profile in *Special Focus Organizations.*

Regional Organization "Women of Don"
ul. Kalinin 88
Novocherkassk
346427   Rostov-on-Don oblast
Tel: (86352) 31-936
Fax: (86352) 34-107
Contact: Valentina Cherevatenko

"Women of Don" was founded in 1993 and unites the three women's organizations: "Nadezhda" (Kamensk-Shakhtinski); "Sudarushka" (Taganrog); and the Committee on Human Rights (Novocherkassk). It has affiliates in other towns of the region. The three elements of Women of Don's activity are:
- political and public (e.g., civic control over the army);
- work with mass media;
- club activity.

Rostov-on-Don Group for Human Rights
per. Ostrovskogo 105, kv.13
344011   Rostov-on-Don
Tel: 32-24-74
Contact: Yurii Borisovich Bespalov, V. Beletskii

The group focuses on human rights associated with Kazak themes, problems of international relations, and refugees.

Rostov Press and Information Center
Department of Journalism
Rostov-on-Don University
Tel: 65-64-85
E-mail: filfak@rsu.rnd.su
Contact: Vitaly Vinichenko, Professor

Prof. Vinichenko teaches and acts as the RAPIC regional office coordinator.

Ryazan (0912)

Karta Center
a/ya 20
pl. Kostyushko 3
390000   Ryazan
Tel: 75-40-20, 77-51-17
Fax: 55-91-84
E-mail: julia@memorial.ryazan.su

karta@glas.apc.org
Contact: Andrei Blinushov

This is a legal aid and educational center. It is a member of an informal network of democratically-oriented NGOs.

Ryazan Regional Ecological Movement
Ryazan
E-mail: roes@school.ryazan.su
Contact: Vasily Zh. Martinov, Yuri Baranditsa

Rybinsk (085)

Goodwill Industries of Russia
Tel/Fax: 552-4007, 552-3863 (home)
Contact: Vyacheslav Grafenkov

St. Petersburg (812)

ACTR/ACCELS St. Petersburg
General Administrative Office
Student Advising Center
Biblioteka im. Mayakovskogo
Naberezhnaya reki Fontanki 46, 4th floor
191025   St. Petersburg
Tel: 311-4593
E-mail: sac.st.pete@sovcust.sprint.com

See profile for ACTR/ACCELS in section *Special Focus Organizations*.

Alcoholics Anonymous
St. Petersburg
Tel: 534-3388
Contact: Tanya

Amnesty International
St. Petersburg
Tel: 247-4046
Contact: Anatoly Chezlov

Angel of the Neva
ul. Gorokhovaya 3
190000   St. Petersburg
Tel: 312-5892, 315-2033
Fax: 315-1463, 314-3360
            315-1701
Contact: Vladimir Lukianov, Chairman.

This organization provides social assistance, legal and psychological consultations, and training for social workers and NGO managers.

Association for the Defense of the Rights of Servicemen
Admirala Makarova nab. 8
199165   St. Petersburg
Tel: 218-9382
Contact: Sergei Vladimirovich Maslov, Nikolai Leonovich Lebed'ko

This association works to provide housing for servicemen, and gives material assistance.

Committee for Humanitarian Aid "Artsakha"
Vasilevskii ostrov 2-ya 15, kv. 15
199053   St. Petersburg
Tel: 349-9162
Contact: Konstantin Yemmanualovich Voevodskii

"Crosses" Social Charitable Fund to Assist in the Social Rehabilitation of those Imprisoned and Released
Arsenalnaya nab. 7
195009   St. Petersburg
Tel: 534-7298
Contact: Vladimir Korolyov

Crosses works to inform society of prison conditions, provide medical assistance to prisoners, assist those being released to find work, and provide cultural educational events in the prisons.

Gatchina
St. Petersburg
E-mail: school3@lnpi.spb.su
izhora@lnpi.spb.su
Contact: Stella Miroshkina, Chair

Gatchina primarily focuses its work on an environmental project, the School Ecological Initiative. The goals of this project are to increase public participation in environmental issues in the Gatchina region and the creation of an independent regional system of environmental safety. The tasks of the project include: practical help to schools in the organization of ecological education; public dissemination of instructional and informational materials; creation of public consultation and resource centers in schools; development of the so-called APELL system to inform and train local citizens in the cases of industrial and environmental emergencies; and coordination of Russian NGOs and movements with international environmental organizations. The project is carried out by teachers and schoolchildren with help of environmental specialists, organizations, institutions, and industry. The St. Petersburg Institute of Nuclear Physics of the Russian Academy of Sciences oversees the project work.

Goodwill Industries of Russia
St. Petersburg
Tel/Fax: 314-4775
Contact: Elena Chumak

High School for Global Education 631
ul. Shkolnaya 13
197183   St. Petersburg

Tel: 239-8530
Fax: 271-5917
Contact: Tatyana Zorina, Principal

House of Human Rights– St. Petersburg
Chernoretskii per. 4/6
143317   St. Petersburg
and
Komandantski pr. 27-2-8
197371   St. Petersburg
Tel: 274-2641
Tel/Fax: 306-8090
Contact: Vladimir Poresh, Director;
Sergei Levin

This organization works to develop human rights educational programs and projects in institutes and universities.

Humanist Society
pr. Gagarina 38-2, 138
196158   St. Peterburg
Tel/Fax: 126-9013
Contact: Oleg Nikolaevich Azovskii

The society makes trips to investigate isolation wards in prisons in order to expose violations in rules and norms.

Institute for International Entrepreneurship
Tambovskaya 58A
St. Petersburg
Tel/Fax: 166-5766
Contact: Leah Lerner

Women's entrepreneurship and support for small business development.

International Institute of Women and Management
Nevsky pr. 147, kv. 45
St. Petersburg
Tel: 277-1649
Fax: 271-4446
Contact: Elena Kalinina

International Small Business Association

Apraskin per. 3, kv. 75
St. Petersburg
Tel: 310-7941
Fax: 310-7941
Contact: Corey Klaasmeyer

The association maintains contacts between business people in Russia and the West to find collaborative solutions to common problems. It offers services including a reliable mail pickup and delivery link between businesses in Russia and the West, and monthly informational meetings.

Justice (Spravedlivost')

ul. Belinskogo 13, a/ya 713
191028   St. Petersburg
Tel: 272-1551
Contact: Vladimir I. Gomelskii

Memorial–St. Petersburg

a/ya 418
Izmailovsky pr. 8
195220   St. Petersburg
Tel: 259-9145
Fax: 251-1732
E-mail: memorial@glas.apc.org
Contact: Vladimir E. Shnitke, Board Co-Chair

Nevsky Center Society of Families with Many Children

ul. Ivanovskaya 15
193171   St. Petersburg
Tel: 567-7047, 580-3242
Contact: Vasili Ivanovich Shevchenko

The center unites 835 families, 206 of which have four to ten children. Assistance is requested from companies and individuals for especially needy families.

Open Society Institute– St. Petersburg

ul. Tchaikovskovo 29
191194   St. Petersburg
Tel: 273-3383, 272-3678
Fax: 273-1128
E-mail: cisp@ifci.spb.su
Contact: Andrei Skornikov, Executive Director

See OSI profile in section *Clearinghouse Organizations.*

Operation Smile Russia

ul. Belinskogo 13
St. Petersburg
Tel/Fax: 279-8101
E-mail: tom@whitewind.spb.su
Contact: Tom Farrell

Operation Smile has been developing a program to enhance the capacity of Russia's health care system to provide facial reconstructive surgery to children in the Moscow, St. Petersburg and Volga regions.

"Oranzhovoye Derevtsvo" Society for Mothers with Many Children

Omonosov Pobede 22/7, kv. 74
189510   St. Petersburg
Tel: 422-1072
Fax: 528-1830
Contact: Olga Kocharyan, President

Oranzhovoye Derevtsvo (Orange Tree) supports nearly 250 families with many children or single mothers. Its goal is to improve the living conditions of large and single parent families, and to provide them material and social support.

Petersburg Center for Gender Issues

a/ya 83

198097   St. Petersburg
Tel: 528-9293
Fax: 528-1830
E-mail: sisters@sovam.com

This organization is a joint project with a German organization, Frauen Anstiftung e.V., and has been working since April 1993 to educate the public on the elimination of gender discrimination in Russian society. The center conducts research, organizes lectures and seminars, coordinates support and counseling services for women, and distributes information about women's organizations in St. Petersburg and Russia.

Rebyonok Children's Fund

Sovetskii bul. 29
Kolpino
189630   St. Petersburg
Tel: 484-9825
Contact: Natalya Ponomareva

The fund has worked in the Kolpinski region of St. Petersburg since August 1990. It organizes seminars for teachers of gifted children; awards scholarships and stipends; supports children's art groups; and assists sick and disabled children by giving parties, collecting funds for medical treatment, and running a service to locate urgently needed medicines. The fund also has a counseling service for adolescents with problems in family relationships or in school. Support is provided to foster parents who take in children.

Russian Academy of Education Experimental H.S. 157

ul. Proletarskaya Dictatura 1
193124   St. Petersburg
Tel: 271-1329
Fax: 271-1139
E-mail: ehs157@spb.sovam.com

Russian Lawyers Committee for Human Rights

ul. Chaikovskogo 28
191194   St.Petersburg
Tel: 272-4961, 553-8658 (home)
Fax: 119-8454
Contact: Yurii Markovich Shmidt

St. Petersburg Bureau on Human Rights and Rule of Law

Nevsky pr. 139, kv. 1
193024   St. Petersburg
Tel: 277-5161
E-mail:
sovamsu!gopp@pandora.sf.ca.us
Contact: Leonid Lvov, Director

The bureau is affiliated with the Union of Councils for Soviet Jews (see section on *Clearinghouse Organizations*).

St. Petersburg Center of Concerned Teachers

Global Education School 631
Engels prospekt 121-1-209
194356   St. Petersburg
Tel: 293-8530, 598-2062 (home)
Fax: 272-5917
Contact: Irina Koroleva, President

The center promotes experimental approaches to education and the development of new curricula in civic education.

St. Petersburg Human Rights Center

Izmailovskii pr. 8, kom. 18
198005   St. Petersburg
Tel: 251-1971, 550-6104
          550-8668 (Dobacevich home)
Fax: 110-1526
Contact: Vanda M. Dobacevich, Director

St. Petersburg Press and Information Center / Society of Journalists

Nevsky pr. 70
191025   St. Petersburg
Tel: 312-2915, 273-2851
          273-4733
Fax: 272-4672
E-mail: sprapic@glas.apc.org
Contact: Anna Sharogradskaya and Irina Piaro, Coordinators; Chris Hamilton, Information Services

This organization is an affiliate of the Russian-American Press and Information Center in Moscow.

St. Petersburg Psychological Crisis Center for Women

a/ya 604
191002   St. Petersburg
Tel: 275-0330, 528-1830
Fax: 528-1830, 315-9100
Hotline: 166-3955
E-mail: sisters@sovam.com
Contact: Natasha Khodreva, Larisa Korneva

The center was established in October 1991 by volunteers who joined together to organize a hotline and crisis center for rape victims and battered women; and provide individual counseling, assertiveness training, and educational services for their own volunteers and for professionals in the community who work with assault survivors. The center also provides support groups for divorced and unemployed women, single mothers and lesbians.

Soldiers' Mothers Organization of St. Petersburg

Izmailovskii pr. 8, kom. 16-18
198005   St. Petersburg
Tel: 105-7919, 247-2738
Tel/Fax: 259-4968

E-mail: root@osm.spb.su
Contact: Ella M. Polyakova, Director; Vladimir Alekseev, Assistant Director

This organization provides practical assistance to conscripts and their families, including social, legal and medical assistance. Its publications include *Defending the Legal Rights of Conscripts–Examples from our Work* and *Rights of Conscripts and Servicemen in the Russian Army–Material from the Press.*

Sosnovy Bor

St. Petersburg Region
E-mail: bodrov@glas.apc.org
Contact: Oleg Bodrov

Distributes *Nuclear News* in English

"Strategy"–Humanitarian and Political Scientific Center

St. Petersburg
Tel/Fax: 112-6612
Contact: Alexandr Sungurov

Tchaikovsky Fund

Fontanka 4, kom. 311
St. Petersburg
Tel: 311-0937, 217-2527
Contact: Mikhail Ereev, Olga Krause

The fund is active in promoting human rights for gays and lesbians.

Wings

Staropetrovskii pr. 12
St. Petersburg
Tel: 312-3180
Contact: Aleksandr Kikharsky

Wings promotes human rights for gays and lesbians. It is the first registered gay/lesbian organization in Russia.

Samara (8462)

Open Society Institute– Samara Cultural Initiative

ul. Molodogvardeiskaya 151
443001   Samara
Tel: 59-47-30
Tel/Fax: 32-27-85, 39-76-37
E-mail: root@kulini.samara.su
Contact: Nikolai V. Kuznetsov, Executive Director

See profile of OSI in section *Clearinghouse Organizations.*

Socio-Ecological Union– Samara Regional Branch

ul. N. Sadovaya 381, kv. 85
443125   Samara
Tel: 52-05-66 (home)
E-mail: afyodorov@glas.apc.org
Contact: Aleksandr Fyodorov

Fyodorov was elected to the Council of the Socio-Ecological Union in April 1994.

Saratov (8452)

Association Of Women Lawyers

ul. Sovetskaya 44, kom. 53
410600   Saratov
Tel: 24-2834
Tel/Fax: 99-15-78, 24-06-67
Contact: Nadezhda Kuznetsova

The association was founded in 1993. It provides legal consultations for women and organizes educational seminars for lawyers who are engaged in women's problems. It is also assembling a library on legislation concerning women. In May 1995 the association conducted a conference, "Women and Law."

The Eurasia Foundation

Southern Russia Office
a/ya 3321
410601   Saratov
Tel: 24-57-55, 91-01-59
Fax: 24-04-46
E-mail: ef@ef.saratov.su
Contact: Igor Bobrowsky, Regional Director

See profile for the foundation in section *Clearinghouse Organizations.*

"Initiative" Women's League

ul. Chernishevskovo 223/231, kv. 70
410031   Saratov
Tel: 26-06-13, 26-94-46
Contact: Tatyana Katayena

Russian Bird Conservation Union–Saratov Branch

ul. Strelkovoy divizii 53, 6/9, 5th floor
410028   Saratov
E-mail: alex@ef.saratov.su
       voc@voca.saratov.su
       andre@ef.saratov.su
Contact: Andrei Varlamov, member

RBCU–SB was founded in 1994. It has as a major objective the protection of the Great Bustard and Little Bustard. It has 81 members. The Saratov oblast contains the largest population (approximately 7,000 birds) in Russia of the Great Bustard (*Drofa* in Russian). Russia's population of the Great Bustard is the second largest in the world after Spain.

RBCU–SB cooperates with Saratov State University's Faculty of Biology and with zoos in Germany, England and Hungary in protecting important species like the Bustard. It offers a one-week summer ornithological camp and a winter ornithology school for pupils. The latter includes a Christmas registration of birds in cooperation with the Ecological Education Center of the Saratov Oblast. RBCU–SB participated in the World BirdWatch 95 and produced two eductional videos: "Steppes of the Saratov Oblast" and "Summer Ornithological Camp School."

Saratov Exchange Consulting Center

nab. Kosmonavtov, k/t Ekran
410600   Saratov
or
a/ya 3738
410601   Saratov
Tel/Fax: 26-24-52
E-mail: xchange@center.saratov.su
          center@strahov.saratov.su
Contact: Mikhail Strahov, Program Coordinator.

Saratov was a closed city until recently, so there is great interest in participating in exchange programs abroad. But it has been difficult to obtain the necessary information for potential exchange students and to find jobs locally related to the training received abroad for former participants, who have returned to Russia. The Saratov Exchange Consulting Center aims to fill that gap.

The center was registered in 1995 as a joint project of the Association of Economics and Management Students Saratov Local Committee and Saratov Rotary Club. It is a nonprofit, nongovernmental public organization, and was founded with the support of the Eurasia Foundation, city administration and Saratov Rotary Club.

The primarily goals of the center are:
• distributing information about all available exchange programs and foreign traineeships within Saratov;
• providing assistance in obtaining application forms and information

about tests necessary for participating in the exchanges;
• finding employment opportunities for the exchange alumni.

Two paid employees and 17 volunteers currently work at the Saratov Exchange Consulting Center.

Volunteers in Overseas Cooperative Assistance

Saratov
Tel: 25-18-45; 25-02-35
Fax: 24-43-01
E-mail: voc@voca.saratov.su
Contact: Jeff Ferry

This organization participates in the USAID Farmer-to-Farmer Program in Saratov. See profile of VOCA in section *Special Focus Organizations*.

Women's Business Club

nab. Komonavtov 3
Saratov
Tel: 24-04-46
Fax: 24-67-40
Contact: Irina Tsareva, Irina Shkolnikova

Serpukhov

Memorial Society–Serpukhov

Sovetskaya pl., Dom Sovetov, kom. 103
142200   Serpukhov
Contact: Elena Leonova, Viktor Pomazov

Serpukhov Society of Trustees of Penitentiary Institutions

ul. Katoninnaya 14
142201   Serpukhov
Tel: (27) 72-02-92
Contact: Nikolai Rybkin, Irina Kotova

This is a group for the defense of prisoner's rights. It provides qualified legal help in cases of violation of human rights and has published collections of materials.

Sochi (8622)

Children's International Academy of Sochi
ul. Mendeleyeva 10
354341   Sochi
Tel: 44-19-46
Contact: R.I. Kudrina, General Director

The academy is looking for partners to establish a children's international camp on the school's grounds. The teachers of the Art School, which may be set up along with the Academy, can teach languages and art to children at the camp.

Stavropol (7865)

Nadezhda Association of Peasants and Farmers
Krasnogvardeyskoye
Stavropol
Tel: 222-5179, 222-3140
Contact: Nikolai P. Alioshkin, Director

Tula (0872)

Memorial Society
ul. Bundurina 40
300012   Tula
Tel: 21-76-16, 26-64-13, 31-04-19
Contact: Sergei Scheglov, Elena Suvorova

Tula Public Legal Aid Fund
pr. Lenina 28
300012   Tula
Tel: 42-63-39
Contact: Vladimir Sokolov

Founded in 1993, the group supports education for children and teenagers; legal help for the under-represented strata of the population; and work on environmental and health issues.

Tver (0822)

Gaia International Women's Center
ul. Vokazalnaya 2a-58
Zapadnaya Dvina
Tverskaya oblast
Tel: 52-35-46
Contact: Tamara S. Sichevskaya

Mercy Foundation
ul. Fabrichnaya 12
Novozavidovo
171270   Tverskaya oblast
Tel: 2-12-09

The Mercy Foundation of the village of Novozavidovo, in the Tver region, has existed since 1987. Its staff, made up exclusively of pensioners, assists war veterans, the disabled, and families with no means of financial support

Tver InterContact Group
International Institute of Russian Language and Culture
a/ya 0565
Central Post Office
170000   Tver
Tel: 42-54-19, 42-54-39
Fax: (501) 902-17-65
E-mail: richard@ic.redline.ru
            andrei@ic.tunis.tver.su

Contact: Andrei Shkvorov, Director; Richard Smith, International Programs Director

Tver InterContact Group is an independent educational and consulting company which offers both a Summer School and Winter School in Tver, through the International Institute of Russian Language and Culture. Programs range in length from two to eight weeks. Like the Summer School, the Winter School offers an opportunity for intensive study of Russian language and Area Studies in the heart of Central Russia. About 150 Russian students and up to 60 international students from the U.S., Canada, the E.C., Scandinavia, and Japan, attend. They study Russian and enjoy the culture of "Russia's friendliest town."

All programs include weekend tours within Tver to local artists' workshops, area monasteries, churches, and museums, and special excursions to nearby cities such as Moscow and St. Petersburg.

Due to generous financial support from the Tver Regional Board of Education and the City Council of Tver, all tuition and educational materials costs were waived for the Winter School '96.

"Women's Light" Feminist Club
ul. Trekhsvyatskaya 31/11
170000   Tver
Tel: 34-4373
E-mail: val@usp.tunis.tver.su
Contact: Valentina Uspenskaya, Inessa Obratsova

Women's Light is a research and educational center on gender issues, founded in 1991. It delivers courses on gender/feminist studies for university students. The group organized a sale of books, clothing and other used items in the summer of 1995, donating the proceeds to a local children's hospital. In September members held an anti-war and anti-violence action, named White Scarf, in Tver.

Member Inessa Obratsova attended the International Women's Conference in Beijing. In October her account of that event inaugurated a series of "Readings on Women's History," held at Tver public library. Member Antonina Gaidenko, a journalist, has produced a radio program oriented to women.

Ufa (3472)

Association of Women Entrepreneurs–Bashkortarstan
ul. Tukayeva 46, kv. 211
450001   Ufa
Tel: 23-39-81
Contact: E.R. Mahmutova

Mothers of Soldiers Committee
ul. Shafieva 31, kv. 33
450096   Ufa
Tel: 32-90-29
Contact: Valentina Ivanovna Zhukova

Volgograd (8442)

ACTR/ACCELS Volgograd
Prospekt Leinina, 15, kom 61
400066   Volgograd
Tel: 33-56-19
E-mail:
fsa.volgograd@sovcust.sprint.com

See the profile for ACTR/ACCELS in section *Special Focus Organizations*.

American Business Center
Tel: 33-59-46, 36-27-32

Fax: 36-27-32
E-mail: abcv@abc.tsaritsyn.su
Contact: Natasha Kent

Center for Citizen Initiatives
Volgograd
Tel: 93-60-42
Fax: (095) 283-1458 (Moscow)
E-mail: ibimosc@glas.apc.org
Contact: Olga Kriakova

See CCI profile in section *Clearing-house Organizations.*

Volgograd Foundation for Business Development
Tel/Fax: 34-44-09
E-mail: postmaster@rabc.tsaritsyn.su
Contact: Irina Makarenko

Volsk

Union for Chemical Safety
Volsk
E-mail: shikhany@glas.apc.org
Contact: Vladimir Petrenko, Vladimir Uglev

This organization works in the areas of chemical and biological weapons, military and industrial pollution.

Voronezh (0732)

Center for AIDS Prevention
Moscovskii pr., 109
394053   Voronezh
Tel: 73-43-75, 14-09-16, 13-67-42
Contact: Tatyana Alexandrovna Mamchik

The center was established in 1989 to provide AIDS prevention education. It also provides information on hepatitis and other immunodeficiency diseases. It organizes lectures in schools, universities and businesses, as well as publishing materials about AIDS prevention. It also provides anonymous AIDS testing.

"Charity" Philanthropic Society
ul. Nikitinskaya 50
394000   Voronezh
Tel: 52-17-08
Contact: Elizabeta Nikolaevna Bokova

Since 1988 Charity has provided social and material assitance to single elderly people, the disabled and disadvantaged. Originating as a local division of the Moscow-based All Union charitable movement, the organization has become an independent nonprofit. Several social workers provide home health services to shut-in seniors and disabled people in order that they may remain at home rather than be placed in institutions. In 1995, 50 persons were served by this program.

Club "Children and Adult Home"
ul. Kirova, 28 kom. 40
394086   Voronezh
Tel: 36-53-44, 23-36-22
Contact: Boris Giorgievich Svinkin

The club provides social assistance for children and teens who have been discharged from orphanages, as well as single teenage mothers. It was established in 1990, and assists in locating housing and employment. It receives funding in the form of donations as well as some local government support.

"Common Path" Association of Charitable Foundations
pr. Revolutsii, "Dom Knigi," 4th floor
Voronezh

Tel: 55-48-65
Contact: Violetta V. Obtemperanskaya

Common Path was established in 1994 to coordinate the efforts of charitable organizations in the Voronezh area and in 1995 five groups joined. Common Path provides a forum and meeting place for directors of third sector organizations, allowing for collaboration and information exchange. The group also lobbies local authorities on behalf of its members.

"Diabet" Society
ul. Matrosova 6a kv. 73
394052   Voronezh
Tel: 36-77-03
Contact: Lilianna M. Nizhnikova

Since 1990, Diabet has helped more than 17,000 people with diabetes, including 500 children. The organization helps to secure insulin, testers and other supplies for diabetics. It relies entirely upon donations for funding.

Foundation for the Development of Art
ul. Kirova 10, kv. 16
394018   Voronezh
Tel: 36-27-39
Contact: Oleg Alexandrovich Shepel'

The foundation was organized to provide support for young artists, particularly musicians. It provides small grants and stipends to these artists from donated funds.

Foundation for Civil Initiatives
Voronezh
E-mail: kl@kea.voronezh.su
Contact: Konstantin M. Lepiohin

"Hope"–Voronezh Association for Children with Cerebral Palsy

ul. Plekhanovskaya 10a
394000   Voronezh
Tel: 14-28-39
Contact: Valentina B. Manykovskaya

The association was established in 1992 by parents of children with cerebral palsy, and currently has nearly 250 members. Hope's primary objective is to help mainstream disabled children into society. It has organized groups and clubs for disabled children, and, with the assistance of the charitable organization Interlingual, provides English language instruction. Hope receives its funding primarily from donations, and has no paid staff. It is run by a group of 17 parents.

Memorial Society
ul. Nikitinskaya 19, kv. 13
394000   Voronezh
Tel: 55-78-79
Contact: Vyacheslav Ilich Bityutskii

Established in 1988, Memorial researches the history of the purges and repression of the Soviet period and assist individuals who had been persecuted by authorities.   It is active on a regional commission working to restore the rights of the politically persecuted.

"Nye Zhdi" Association of Independent Women's Democratic Initiatives
ul. Nikitinskaya 8, kom. 415
394000   Voronezh
Tel: 52-23-70, 56-54-91,
        36-30-86 (home)
E-mail: forvor@glas.apc.org
or
ul. Volodarskovo 64
Voronezh
Tel: 55-59-26
Contact: Ludmilla Yanovna Tarasova

Founded in 1993, *Nye Zhdi* ("Don't Wait") unites more than 10 public women's organizations and groups working to further women's rights, human rights and the development of civil society. Member organizations–a girls club; the "Galateya" family club; and a workshop on family entrepreneurship, for example–collaborate on projects, share information, and provide consultation to other groups. *Nye Zhdi* is active with groups throughout Russia and abroad. It publishes an annual report about its activities.

Professional Writers Association

a/ya 48, Glavpochtamt
394000   Voronezh
Tel: 36-20-91, 56-67-11
Contact: Aleksandr Sukhrukov

Since 1991 the association has assisted young writers in Voronezh to publish their work. It has organized a literary club as well as a school for beginning writers.

"Renaissance" Club, Voronezh Society for the Protection of Monuments of History and Culture

ul. Engels 5
394000   Voronezh
Tel: 55-08-92
Contact: Lydia V. Kharecheva

This organization is working to revitalize interest in history and culture. It was established by a group of historians in the Voronezh oblast. The group organizes excursions to various historical and cultural sites in the area, and provides a forum and meeting place for poets, writers and other artists. All its funds are provided through excursion fees.

Russian Children's Foundation, Voronezh Division

ul. Lenina 5
394000   Voronezh
Tel: 55-53-30
Contact: Natalya M. Plakhova

Since 1988 the Foundation has helped children in "difficult situations." Its programs include: "Teplyi Dom" (Warm Home) which provides material and social support to orphans; "Zdorovye Detei" (Healthy Children), which provides medical assistance to disabled children; "Skoraya Sotsialnaya Pomosh" (Quick Help) to assist families in crisis situations; and, "Iyunie Talanti" (Gifted Children) to support gifted and talented young people with performance opportunties and small stipends. The program receives donations and some governmental funding.

Socio-Ecological Organization "Endemic"

Voronezh
Tel: 56-63-62
Contact: Valerii Sulin

Established as a *druzhina* (a kind of grassroots environmental organization dating from the Soviet period) in 1988, the organization registered in 1991as "Endemic." Its primary activities are enviromental improvement and creating environmental networks. Endemic also provides environmental education for school-children, conducts scientific and sociological research in environmental issues and lobbies for environmental protection of the region. It has received funding from ISAR.

Tri Valley Growers

Voronezh
Tel: 55-46-44
E-mail: dima@well.com

Contact: Dmitri Kapranchikov, Tanya Ryvkina

This organization participates in the USAID Farmer-to-Farmer program in Voronezh. See profile of Tri Valley Growers in section *Special Focus Organizations.*

Union of Parents of Children Killed in Military Service

ul. Kirova 8, kv. 133
394006   Voronezh
Tel: 36-81-15
Contact: Nina V. Provotorova

This organization was established in 1994 to assist young people undergoing training for military conscription, their families and families of military members killed in peacetime. Organized by parents of deceased servicemembers, the union provides counselling for young people entering military service and their families.

Voronezh Association for the Sight-Disabled

ul. Sakko i Vantsetti 104
39400   Voronezh
Tel: 56-13-68
Contact: Gennadi T. Kashkin

The association was established in 1992 to provide social assistance for members of the association. It has established a medical and health center and assists its members to secure medicine. It is funded entirely through donations.

Voronezh Association of Charitable Organizations

ul. Plekhanovskaya 10
394000   Voronezh
Tel: 55-29-00
Contact: Georgi Orlanov

The association unites nonprofit organizations in Voronezh to establish ties with charitable and business organizations in Russia and the West, and to bring business people into the work of the association. It was founded by six organizations in Voronezh: Interlingua (tel. 55-40-02), Hope (33-68-62), Peace through Culture (49-81-40), Fund for the Development of the Arts (55-29-00), Fund for Public Health (55-29-00), and the Voronezh Municipal Fund for Social Security (55-14-49).

Yaroslavl (0852)

Center for the Formation of Sexual Culture

ul. Pionerskaya 19
150044   Yaroslavl
Tel: 55-66-91
Fax: 25-58-94
E-mail: root@cfsc.yaroslavl.su
Contact: Aleksandr Shmaglit, Director

In cooperation with Planned Parenthood of Northern New England, the center addresses the problems of high abortion rates, teen pregnancy, and the lack of information on sexuality, AIDS, and other sexually transmitted diseases.

Russia: East of the Urals

Country Code: 7

Barnaul (3852)

Barnaul Fund for Humanitarian Aid and Development

a/ya 3950
656099 Barnaul
Tel: 22-23-36
Fax: 24-79-49
E-mail: 74301.3712@compuserve.com

The fund's activities have included distribution of medical aid from U.S. NGO's such as Direct Relief International. They supervised an 18-month program at the Altai Regional Children's Hospital for children with leukemia, during which medicines were provided for the treatment of 30 children.

In addition to ongoing activities distributing medical aid on a monthly basis, the fund is currently working at the request of the regional government to set up an orphanage for 180 children. For the past four summers they have run camps for handicapped children; in the summer of 1995 it ran two eight-day camps with about 50 children in each.

"Katun"–Association of NGOs
Altai State University
Barnaul
E-mail: vup@mezon.altai.su
katun@glas.apc.org
newsserv@koksa.altai.su

Contact: Nikolai Mikhailov, Mikhail Shishin, Irina Fotieva

Chelyabinsk (3512)

Association for Christian Children, Youth and Families

ul. Volodarskogo 52
454080 Chelyabinsk
Tel: 33-57-30
Fax: 33-57-37
Contact: Lev Ivanovich Funtov

The association was founded in 1993 to provide a meeting ground for Christian families, and to work to improve a variety of social and environmental problems in the area.

Association for Hemophiliacs

ul. Tchaikovskogo 185, kv. 43
454016 Chelyabinsk
Tel: 34-15-13
Contact: Vladimir Evstratovich Belopukhov

The association was established in 1991 to help hemophiliacs secure medicine and supplies. It is run by volunteers, and serves about 40 people of all ages. Funding comes solely from private donations.

Association of Independent Musicians

ul. Svobodi 80
Chelyabinsk
Tel: 15-34-15
Fax: 33-14-45
Contact: Anastasia V. Klimenko

The association helps young musicians and musical groups in organizing performances and also provides technical assistance.

Association of Victims of Radiation–"Kishtim 57"

ul. Pushkina 66
454091 Chelyabinsk
Tel: 33-39-21, 33-78-09
Contact: Kirill Alekseevich Shishov

Kishtim 57 works on behalf of victims of nuclear radiation.

Chelyabinsk Charitable Foundation "ANTISPID" (Anti-AIDS)

ul. Griboedova 45
454008 Chelyabinsk
Tel: 77-44-48, 77-13-42
Contact: Natalya Viktorovna Vlasova

Working with national and international groups, ANTISPID provides HIV and AIDS education and prevention materials and provides assistance to HIV-positive individuals and people with AIDS.

Since 1991 the organization has been the primary group in the region working to provide counselling and assistance to HIV-positive and AIDS patients, and training to medical and social workers. It has developed a prevention education program for young people that is used in schools, and works with other NGOs who have HIV-positive and AIDS-infected clients. They have worked with the national government in developing an AIDS policy, and have published several books on AIDS issues for Russia.

Chelyabinsk-Hanford Project

Chelyabinsk
E-mail: VS@chel-hanf.chel.su
Contact: Vyacheslav Sharov

The project addresses health issues and the subject of nuclear waste. Hanford in Washington state is the site of a former nuclear weapons plutonium processing plant.

Chelyabinsk Society "Special Children"

ul. Tretyevo Internatsionala 128
Chelyabinsk
Tel: 66-61-55
Contact: Evgenii A. Yakushov

The society provides social and medical assistance to disabled children and their families.

Diabetes Association, Chelyabinsk Oblast

ul. Pushina 27a, kv. 19
454000 Chelyabinsk
Tel: 36-69-88
Contact: Vladimir Kriukov

The association was founded in 1993 by a group of diabetics and relatives of diabetics.

"FEB" Society for Invalids, Kalinin Region

a/ya 13183
454092 Chelyabinsk
Tel: 36-45-41
Contact: V. Kalishev

The society works both to assist the disabled, and on enviromental projects. For example, it is working to develop a small arboretum and has involved disabled and orphaned children in the project. It has five staff members.

Historical-Ethnographic Museum of the Way of Life of Ural Metallurgical Workers

ul. Zelenaya 20
456970 Nyazepetrovsk
Chelyabinsk oblast
Tel: (256) 2-17-72
Contact: Ivan Votinov, Director

International Union "Ecological Person"

ul. Plekhanova 32
454000 Chelyabinsk
Tel: 34-18-06, 61-16-10
Contact: Uri Mikhailovich Zakharov

This NGO conducts scientific research in areas damaged by nuclear accidents and pollution, and is working on environmentally sound energy sources.

"Lesenka" Club for Exercise Therapy

ul. Kommuni 69, kv. 90
454000 Chelyabinsk
Tel: 33-79-67
Contact: Ludmila Giorgievna Rogova

The "Lesenka" Club provides physical therapy for children with cerebral palsy, trains parents in exercises they can do with their children, organizes social events for the children and supports medical research into children's diseases.

Movement for Nuclear Safety

ul. Vorovskogo 7, kv. 86
Chelyabinsk
Tel: 35-64-59, 36-22-93
Contact: Natalya Mironova

The movement is working for the responsible and safe use of nuclear energy.

Oblast Learning-Education Center

ul. Rossiiskaya 63-A, kv.174
454006 Chelyabinsk
Tel: 72-14-00, 66-73-13
Contact: Maria Sobol, Director

Red Cross, Chelyabinsk Oblast

Chelyabinsk
Tel: 33-89-04

Contact: Ludmila Eduardovna Propst, Mariya Ivanovna Sopova

Russian Foundation for Charity and Health, Chelyabinsk

ul. Vorovskogo 30
454022 Chelyabinsk
Tel: 36-64-50
Contact: Rimma Zaplatina

Scientific-Manufacturing Firm "Nadezhda-Prim"

Komsomolskii pr. 52, kv. 121
454138 Chelyabinsk
Tel: 13-99-96
Contact: Galina A. Teplyakova

The nonprofit arm of Nadezhda-Prim provides charitable assistance to orphaned children, the elderly and disabled. They provide in-kind assistance, help in securing medicine and health care, and provide social functions for a variety of groups, including veterans.

Soldiers' Mothers Association, Chelyabinsk

ul. Zhukova 36, kom. 17
Chelyabinsk
Tel: 24-08-66
Contact: Ludmila Zinchenko

Social Rehabilitation Center

ul. Artilleriiskaya 4
Chelyabinsk
Tel: 73-27-22
Contact: Vladimir K.Novikov

The center provides a shelter and helps homeless people find jobs and permanent housing. It has a staff of 14, and is supported by local government funding and private contributions.

"Union-Chernobyl"–Chelyabinsk Oblast Organization

ul. Kommuni 81
Chelyabinsk
Tel: 33-86-19
Contact: Nikolai N. Slugachev

Union-Chernobyl works to protect the rights of victims of the Chernobyl accident, and people who were forced to move from the area.

Chita (30222)

Baikal Fund

Chita Branch
a/ya 1041
672090 Chita
Tel: 2-19-62
E-mail: chita@glas.apc.org

The Chita branch of the Baikal Fund began work in the late 1980's on the environmental protection of the Arakhley Lakes area in the Chita region of eastern Siberia, part of the Lake Baikal watershed. In conjunction with U.S. land use specialists, and with funding from a number of U.S. foundations and USAID, the Baikal Fund established the Arakhley Lakes Wildlife Refuge. Baikal Fund has secured temporary protected status for the Arakhley Lakes Wildlife Refuge, and is working for its permanent protection and establishment of a larger Chita National Wildlife Refuge.

Chita Nursing Association

Health Administration Directorate
ul. Bogomiakova 23
Chita
Tel: 3-34-46
Contact: Valentina Vishnyakova, Director

Ekaterinburg (3432)

ACTR/ACCELS Ekaterinburg

ul. Mamina-Sibiriaka 193
Biblioteka im. Nekrasova (2nd floor)
620055 Ekaterinburg
Tel: 61-60-34

See the profile for ACTR/ACCELS under *U.S.-Based Organizations.*

"Anima" Hotline and Crisis Service

ul. Engelsa 27
620151 Ekaterinburg
Tel: 55-54-31
or
ul. Sverdlova 34, kv. 55
620027 Ekaterinburg
Tel: 53-76-70
Contact: Natalia Plyukhina

Since 1991 Anima has offered a crisis hotline and educational and support programs for survivors of violence, substance abusers and troubled teens. Anima relies heavily upon volunteers who are trained by psychologists and social workers to work the hotline, lead support groups, provide individual counseling and organize informal social activities. Anima plans to open a shelter for battered women and their children.

Association of Obstetricians and Gynecologists

Regional Children's Hospital No.1
620149 Ekaterinburg
Tel: 44-27-70
E-mail: psieburg@glas.apc.org
Contact: Svetlana Shumkova

The association has been working with Population Services International (see below) to increase the use of contraceptives in the Sverdlovsk region through a public education campaign. It has provided training for health professionals in contraceptive counseling and procedures.

Center for Citizen Initiatives
ul. Bazhova 79, #408
620075   Ekaterinburg
Tel: 55-44-27
Fax: 55-44-25
E-mail: ccieburg@glas.apc.org
Contact: Lena Novomeiskaya, Russian Director; Thomas Broersma, American Director

See profile of organization in section on *Clearinghouse Organizations*.

EcoInfo Group
ul. Marta 8
202 Institute of Ecology
620219   Ekaterinburg
Tel: 22-05-70
E-mail: krin@glas.apc.org
Contact: Sergei Krinitsyn

Krinitsyn is a member of the Socio-Ecological Union's Council.

Ekaterina Charitable Foundation for the Development of Science and Education
ul. Frunze 76, pod. 3
620144   Ekaterinburg
Tel: 22-10-13
Contact: Valentin V. Korona

The foundation supports fundamental scientific research in biology, psychology, and archaeology. It provides support for scholars, innovative teachers, students, and others. A system of grants, individual scholarships, and one-time designated gifts is being developed.

Ekaterinburg Public Nursing Association
Sverdlovsk Oblast Medical College
ul. Akademika Bardina 14
Ekaterinburg
Tel: 51-46-22
Fax: 51-31-91
Contact: Valentina Kharina, Director

Institute for Sustainable Communities
Center for Environmental Training and Information
c/o Society for the Protection of Nature
ul. Pushkina 9, kv. 402
620219   Ekaterinburg
Tel/Fax: 51-61-26
E-mail: iscetiekat@glas.apc.org
Contact: Larisa Strukova

See profile of ISC in section *Special Focus Organizations*.

Memorial Society
Informational Legal Aid Center
a/ya 133
ul. Vainera 16a
620102   Ekaterinburg
Tel: 51-42-27, 51-36-59, 56-80-40
          53-57-11(home)
          23-57-81(home)
Fax: 51-42-27, 28-71-08
E-mail: anna@memory.e-burg.su
Contact: Anna Yakovlevna Pastukhova, Vladimir Ivanovich Popov

This center serves both as the regional branch of the Memorial Society and a source for public educational programs on issues such as problems of the penitentiary system, military reform, etc.

Population Services International
Contraceptive Social Marketing Project

ul. Krylova 2, kom. 225
Ekaterinburg
Tel/Fax: 42-72-82
E-mail: psieburg@glas.apc.org
Contact: Elizabeth Gardiner, PSI
Country Representative

PSI has received a grant from USAID and World Learning Inc. to develop a "social marketing project" to increase the use of contraception among the local population, including those at the lowest socio-economic levels, in order to decrease rates of abortion and maternal mortality and the incidence of sexual transmitted diseases.

The project plans to increase demand for contraceptives in the Sverdlovsk oblast through education and training of medical professionals and the general population through mass media, printed informational materials, and training of 500 doctors, nurses, teachers, and social workers. To meet this demand, the project will distribute approximately three million imported condoms and other means of contraception such as injectable Depo-Provera, with information about contraceptives and instructions for use in Russian. Although focused on the prevention of abortions, the project will also encourage informed discussion of AIDS and other sexually transmitted diseases.

PSI, the world's largest single private, non-commercial provider of family planning products, plans to implement this project with the Association of Obstetricians-Gynecologists and the private firm Harmony. The Association of Obstetricians-Gynecologists is a newly formed non-commercial NGO with members throughout the Sverdlovsk oblast who have extensive knowledge of the regional reproductive health problems. Harmony, a company

with both commercial clinics and a pharmaceutical distribution network in the oblast, is expected to serve as the distributor of the contraceptives for this project.

Russian-American Press and Information Center
Ekaterinburg
Tel: 44-34-39
Fax: 55-74-01, 55-59-64
Contact: Iskhakov Rafail, Coordinator

See profile of RAPIC under Moscow in section *Russia: West of the Urals.*

Social Committee for Shareholders' Rights
per. Tramvainyi 15
620041 Ekaterinburg
Tel/Fax: 41-56-61, 41-56-93
Contact: Galina Dronova, Executive Secretary

The rapid privatization of Russian industry and the formation of thousands of publicly held companies has generated a large movement of shareholder rights associations throughout Russia. This is one of several such organizations.

Sverdlovsk Oblast Charitable Foundation "Healthy Family"
Regional Children's Hospital No. 1
ul. Deriabina 32
620149 Ekaterinburg
Tel: 51-21-57
E-mail: olga@saic.e-burg.su
Contact: Dr. Alexei Kulikov, President; Lily Bouldouian, Outreach Coordinator

The emphasis of the foundation is on outreach to pregnant women and women of childbearing age in the sur-

rounding regions of Ekaterinburg for
early medical care.

Ural Club of New Education
Ekaterinburg
Tel: 24-25-37
Contact: Inna Leonova, Director

Ural Ecological Fund
Ekaterinburg
Tel: 51-75-38
Fax: 55-72-27
E-mail: postmaster@ecofond.intec.ru
Contact: Gennadii Paschupkin, Director

Irkutsk (3952)

"Angara" Union of Women
ul. Lenina 1, kom. 434
664029 Irkutsk
Tel: 34-20-20
Contact: Al'bina Anatol'evna Shirobokova

"Angara" has been active in the Baikal
region since 1992 and was formally
registered in 1995. It is associated with
nearly 30 different organizations, providing consultation and support for
women in a variety of areas. It provides educational programs including
computer courses and leadership skills
training for women. It also provides an
anonymous telephone crisis line for
survivors of physical and sexual assault. The organization's staff is aided
by 30 volunteers. It receives funding
from donations, some governmental
funding and a grant from the Eurasia
Foundation.

Baikal Center for Ecological and Civic Initiatives
ul. Proletarskaya 7-19

664000 Irkutsk
Tel: 33-13-22
E-mail: irkutsk@glas.apc.org
siberia@igc.apc.org
baikalcenter@bce.irkutsk.su
Contact: Irina Dyatlovskaya-Birnbaum

The Baikal Center has worked since
1994 to expand the network of
information and cooperation between
groups, individuals, and govermental
agencies involved in environmental
protection efforts in the Baikal region.
The center also attempts to foster
cooperation among a variety of groups,
interregional and international, that are
working to build civil society in Russia.
The Baikal Center has received funding
from the Eurasia Foundation.

Baikal Ecological Wave
a/ya 1354
664032 Irkutsk
Tel: 46-59-62, 46-77-09
E-mail: sutton@wave.irkutsk.su
Contact: Jenny Sutton

In 1990 a group of "enthusiasts" organized to determine ways that citizens
could act to protect the Lake Baikal region. The core of its activities is the
dissemination of environmental information in order to support concrete actions to protect the area. In 1992 the
group helped to stop deforestation in
the nature preserve "Vityaz" and to
begin reforestation efforts there. In
1993 it prepared a document listing 21
objectives for the stewardship of regional nature preserves. It has also developed environmental education programs for school children.

Baikal Surf Club
a/ya 3441, Primorskii mikroraion 32
664056 Irkutsk
Tel: 46-67-70

Contact: Valeri Nikolaevich Gorshkov

Baikal Surf Club has been active since
1981, organizing surfing competitions
on Lake Baikal.

Cooperative to Assist the Mentally Disabled
ul. Almaznaya 2, kv. 3
664058   Irkutsk
Tel: 36-11-74
Contact: Natalya N. Ragutskaya

In 1995 a group of parents with mentally disabled children established a center
for them, where they might live and
learn trade skills. They also hope to
provide a school for mentally retarded
children, and to provide support
programs for families.

Ecological Tourism School
ul. Proletarskaya 7, kv. 13
Irkutsk
Tel: 33-13-22

The school is attempting to develop the
field of environmental tourism in the
region. It provides outdoor leadership
training and programs in identifying
and protecting the most over-used areas
around Lake Baikal.

Ecologically Sustainable Development, Inc.
Baikal Project
Irkutsk
Fax: 33-13-22
E-mail: irkutsk@glas.apc.org

"EPRA" Ecological Law Foundation
ul. Ulan-Batora 1, kom. 128
Irkutsk
Tel: 46-19-29
E-mail: root@epra.irkutsk.su
Contact: Nelli Romanova, President

EPRA was established in early 1995 to
assist environmental organizations in
questions of law, to promote the
rational use of natural resources, and to
assist in developing the field of
environmental law. The center employs
five people who provide legal consultations for organizations in the area.
EPRA publishes a 25-page periodical
bulletin, "Letters." Staff includes three
lawyers with backgrounds in environmental, land use and procedural law,
and a scientist. EPRA president
Romanova has degrees from Irkutsk
State University in biology and law.

Foundation for the Rehabilitation of the Blind
ul. Rosa Luxemburg 327, kv. 36
Irkutsk
Tel: 24-31-16
Contact: Nikolai L. Shakiro

The foundation was established in 1994
in order to provide social assistance to
the sight-impaired and blind, including
job placement services. Foundation
staff estimate that they have a potential
clientele in the region of 4,000. The
current staff size is five, with 15 volunteers. Funding comes from dues and
donations.

Irkutsk Association of Psychologists and Psychotherapists
ul. Alexander Nevskii 61, kv. 34
664047   Irkutsk
Tel: 34-76-71
Contact: Elena A. Tvorogova

Organized in 1994, this professional association is establishing a three-year
continuing education program for providers in the field.

Irkutsk Children's Foundation

ul. Chekhova 2
664000 Irkutsk
Tel: 33-14-89
Contact: Svetlana V. Kulinich

Since 1988, the foundation has assisted orphans and disabled children to secure medical care and medications. The foundation operates solely on private donations.

Irkutsk Information Center

ul. Stepana Razina 6
Irkutsk
Tel: 33-38-86
Fax: 43-35-36
E-mail: Citzinfo@teleport.com (US)
　Maria@citzinfo.irkutsk.su (Russia)
Contacts: Maria Safonova, Russian Director; Andrea LaFayette-Fisher, U.S. Director

The center was established in 1994 by the Citizens' Information Initiative with funding from The Eurasia Foundation to "establish a center for professional development" in Irkutsk. Currently the center also acts as an East Siberian representative for Interlegal, based in Moscow, and coordinates Russian projects for the New York State-based organization Ecologically Sustainable Development, Inc.

The center provides logistical, communication and networking services for foreign and Russian organizations, for Irkutsk and foreign business people, and for Irkutsk professionals such as scientists, doctors, and journalists. It provides consultation to local organizations in writing grant proposals and business plans. It provides information about organizations and businesses in Irkutsk to potential partners abroad.

The center promotes the use of electronic mail communication. It works in close cooperation with Omniworld Communications, an Irkutsk Relcom node dedicated to the support of local NGOs in the use of computer-mediated communication.

The center also represents the first U.S. government-funded project that promotes professional development through information links in the large and rapidly developing region of East Siberia. The center provides assistance to women and to other less empowered groups in Russia. Half of the board members are women, as are all of the staff.

The organization also works with the Eugene (Oregon)-Irkutsk Sister City Association, East-West Business Association, and Baikal Watch/Center for Citizen Initiatives.

Irkutsk Society for the Deaf

Irkutsk
Tel: 34-90-07
Contact: Leonid S. Magal'nikov

Since 1926 the Society for the Deaf has provided social support to the hearing-impaired as well as the hearing and speech-impaired. The society serves nearly 3,000 people in the Irkutsk region, with a staff of 15 and nearly 175 volunteers. It receives funding from the local government and from private donations.

Olkhon Center for Sustainable Agriculture

ul. Pervomaiskaya 15-1
Olkhon Raion, c. Elantsei
66130　Irkutsk oblast
E-mail: maria@citzinfo.irkutsk.su
　　　(Russian language only)
　　　efssociety@aol.com
　　　(English or Russian)

Contact: Vladimir Markasaev, Director; Anatoli Doksuyev, Agricultural Specialist

The Olkhon region in Siberia is an ecologically and geologically distinct region of 6,500 square miles along the west bank of Lake Baikal. It is home to 9,500 ethnic Buryats, who struggle to provide an adequate livelihood for themselves. The Olkhon Center was formed in 1994 and receives USAID funding. It is partnered with the E. F. Schumacher Society, with the goal of training an Olkhon agricultural cooperative extension team to further "sustainable agriculture practices" in the region. The center has focused on providing support and equipment to local production and processing of vegetables and meats.

Since its formation, the OCSA has brought specialists on sustainable agriculture and land planning into the region, and has distributed seeds, tools, and information on food preservation throughout the region. It has also created a training center in the school to teach young people canning and other food preservation techniques.

Current activities include the collection and distribution of information on food preservation. Additionally, the center is working to market and sell traditional hand knit products, and to investigate the possibility of building a wool processing facility.

The center is preparing for a Russian-American land planning team which will work with the village of Tolovka in the summer of 1996 to establish a Community Land Trust for sustainable land use.

OCSA has four part-time personnel, and benefits as well from the participation of school teachers who run the canning center, and a volunteer board which helps to distribute information.

Prebaikalsky National Park
Bolshoye Goloustnoye
666015   Irkutsk Oblast
Tel: 7-50-63
E-mail: irkutsk@glas.apc.org
Contact: Hank Birmbaum, Park Ranger

The Prebaikalsky National Park is one is six protected areas adjacent to Lake Baikal. Park employees, including American Hank Birmbaum, have worked to upgrade the tourist services of the park. With assistance from the U.S.-based organization, Ecologically Sustainable Development, and a grant from USAID, they are working to improve the park and establish it as the base for the area's economy.

Red Cross, Irkutsk
ul. Chkalova 39/102
664011   Irkutsk
Tel: 33-62-09

The Irkutsk division of the Red Cross has been in operation since 1990. It provides assistance to the disabled, single and frail elderly, refugees and the homeless. It plans to open a medical and crisis clinic in the near future.

Kemerovo (3842)

All-Union Council of Servicemen's Parents
Sovetskii pr. 58, kv. 602
650099   Kemerovo
Tel: 26-58-42
Fax: 23-09-46
Contact: Pyotr Ivanovich Popov

Council of Veterans of War and Work for Democracy
Sovetskii pr. 62, kom. 134
650099　Kemerovo
Tel:　23-41-97
Contact: Anatolii Markovich Makarov

Foundation for Support of Women's Initiatives Nye Zhdi ("Don't Wait")
Sovetskii pr. 62, kom. 134
650099　Kemerovo
Tel:　23-41-97
Contact: Natalya M. Saptsina

Human Rights Defense Union
Sovetskii pr. 62, kom. 134
650099　Kemerovo
Tel:　23-41-97
Contact: Alexandr Rufimovich Efimov

Kemerovskii Committee of the Kuzbass Union for the Defense of Human Rights
Sovetskii pr. 62, kom. 134
650099　Kemerovo
Tel:　23-41-97
Contact: Ada Vasilevna Popova

Khabarovsk (4212) and Amur oblast

American Council for Teachers of Russian (ACTR)
Okeanskii pr. 18, kom. 303
Khabarovsk
Tel:　22-37-98
E-mail:　jerub@actr.marine.su
　　　　allegra@actr.marine.su
Contact: Allegra Harris, Joe Jerub

Amureco Foreign Economic Association
ul. Shabadinaya 19-a
680013　Khabarovsk
Tel:　37-23-68, 37-23-75
Fax:　33-65-57
Contact: Vitaly Kalugin, General Director

Founded in 1989, the association has grown to 59 members and is one of the largest exporters in the Russian Far East. They are currently seeking a U.S. partner for cooperation in timber operations.

Art and Architecture Lyceum
18 Polytecheskaia ul., kv. 111
680049　Khabarovsk
Tel:　72-58-40
Contact: Mira Ivanovna Gornova

The lyceum provides environmental education to children. They conduct expeditions to the national parks and preserves of the Russian Far East and along the Amur River.

Association of Deaf Children (ARIDONS)
85 ul. Zaparina
680000　Khabarovsk
Tel:　33-07-24
Contact: Vera N. Pereverzva, President

Since 1991 ARIDONS has been working to provide hearing aids for hearing impaired children.

Association of Parents with Disabled Children (ARIDI)
ul. Zaparina 85
680000　Khabarovsk
Tel:　33-07-24
Contact: Irina A. Yurievskaia, President

Established in 1989, ARIDI has a staff of 11 and a membership of 5,000 families with children with disabilities. ARIDI provides financial aid to its members and distributes food and clothing donated from abroad. The association organizes parents to help them obtain better education for their children. Future goals include building a children's rehabilitation center in Khabarovsk, sending personnel for training in Hungary, and developing an educational home school, sports center, and special store for children with disabilities.

Cabriolet Association of Disabled Drivers

4 Pogranichny Kvartal, kv. 21
682314   Khabarovsk
Tel: 32-84-28
Contact: Mr. Komissarov, President

Cabriolet promotes independent living for people with disabilities. Its primary purpose is to ensure the mobility of the disabled through repairs to wheelchairs, specially equipped cars, and accessibility in public buildings. Their efforts also include promoting the mainstreaming of disabled children into the regular school system.

Catholic Relief Services

CRS/Khabarovsk
ul. Sheronova 56, kom. 302
680013   Khabarovsk
Tel: 21-22-68, 33-85-66
E-mail: spatz@crs.khabarovsk.su
Contact: Mark Jones, Director

The Catholic Relief Services office in Khabarovsk provides a variety of social services to the disadvantaged, and distributes food in Khabarovskii krai, Amurskaia oblast, Magadanskaia oblast, and Chukotka from a variety of national and international donors, including the U.S. Department of Agriculture and USAID.

Dersu Rehabilitation of Invalids

ul. Frunze 67
680057   Khabarovsk
Tel: 33-52-71, 22-13-39
Contact: Vladimir Bodagov

Dersu is a membership organization involved in the physical and psychological rehabilitation of the disabled.

Far East Regional Foundation for the Protection of Mothers' Health

ul. Amurskaia 63, kv. 9
Khabarovsk
Tel: 35-74-67
Contact: L.V. Savchenko, President

The foundation was established in 1993. It has one full-time employee, 15 volunteers, and nine members. It has implemented a women's health program, and distributes medical supplies donated from international organziations. Future goals of the foundation include creating medical centers for women.

Institute for Water and Ecological Problems

Khabarovsk
E-mail: dmitry@ivep.khabarovsk.su
Contact: Dmitry Kurenshchikov

This organization addresses issues of biodiversity, the Amur River, scientific research, environmental modeling and forestry issues.

International Committee of the Red Cross and Khabarovskii Krai Red Cross Society

ul. Muravev-Amurskay 3
Khabarovsk
Tel: 22-54-18
Contact: Tatiana A. Lebedeva-Kosova, Chair

The ICRC/KKRC program began in 1992 with a $50 million grant from the Japanese government earmarked for the RFE for the distribution of food and medical supplies. ICRC plans to initiate a region-wide training program for the Russian Red Cross as well as a strengthening grant to provide office equipment.

The KKRC has a krai-wide staff of 52 and coordinates medical and material aid to the elderly, families with many children, and refugees. In 1992 and 1993 it distributed 659 metric tons of medical supplies, 5,672 metric tons of food, and 93 metric tons of infant formula.

International Research & Exchanges Board (IREX)
RFE Program
ul. Dalzavodskaia 27, kom. 24
Khabarovsk
Tel: 26-98-60
E-mail: dswal@irex.marine.su

Khabarovsk Chapter of the International Association of Detective and Political Novels
ul. Voikova 6, #242
680025 Khabarovsk
Contact: Aleksandr Ryzhkov

Khabarovsk Council of Women
ul. Karl Marksa 66
Khabarovsk
Tel: 33-47-18
Contact: Zoya Vasilivna Zavgorodniye

Founded five years ago by a group of volunteers, the Khabarovsk Council of Women seeks to help women learn the skills they need to survive in the rapidly changing economy. In recent years, their focus has expanded to include children in orphanages and training in dress-making, massage and hair-dressing skills for young women. Trainees are also taught basic business skills so they can run home businesses.

Khabarovsk Krai Board of the All-Russian Society of Invalids
ul. Frunze 67, kom. 10
680057 Khabarovsk
Tel: 33-52-71
Contact: Evgeny Stoev

The Khabarovsk Krai Board of the All-Russian Society of Invalids works to develop employment training, skills and opportunities for the disabled.

Khabarovsk Regional Productivity Center
ul. Muravjov-Amurskii 4, kv. 532
680000 Khabarovsk
Tel: 39-95-26
Fax: 33-17-02
Contact: Mikhail A. Azarenok, Director, Associate Professor of Economics

The center provides an entrepreneurial training facility patterned after the Small Business Development Centers in the U.S. It employs consultants to support and motivate individuals currently in business. It also facilitates networking among its clients and acts as a conduit for foreign investors in the private sector.

Khabarovsk Women's Council
Khabarovsk Territorial Peace Committee
ul. Zaparina 57

680000   Khabarovsk
Tel: 38-85-60
Fax: 33-17-22
Contact: Galina N. Potapova, Director

Established five years ago as a club comprised of professional women volunteers to help unemployed women, the Khabarovsk Women's Council meets twice a month to discuss job possibilities, training courses, and the basics of entrepreneurship. With the club's support, several women have started small businesses in their homes.

Khabarovskii Krai Society for the Disabled

ul. Frunze 67
680057   Khabarovsk
Tel: 13-42-48
Contact: Georgi Filipovich Podgorniy

Established in 1988, the society now claims to have 20,000 members with disabilities. It provides social support and employment to the disabled.

Khingan Nature Reserve

Dorozhnyi Pereulok
Arkhara
676740   Amur Oblast
Tel: 7-23-02
Contact: Vladimir Andronov, Director

This nature reserve operates a conservation and restoration program for endangered cranes, storks, and other birds. It has worked closely with the International Crane Foundation to protect wetland habitats, and has also worked with the Russian Socio-Ecological Union (SEU) and the Earth Island Institute in the U.S. to promote ecotourism to the region.

Krai Branch of the Children's Fund

ul. Volochaevskaia 164
680000   Khabarovsk
Tel: 33-79-89
Contact: Ludmila K. Ivanova

Likhnis

a/ya 2057
680020   Khabarovsk
Tel: 36-78-74, 35-84-17
Fax: 33-50-88
Contact: Svetlana Murashova, Aleksandr Murashov

Likhnis was established in 1994 and is a member of the Academy of Sciences. It provides social support and employment assistance to the disabled.

Physicians for Nuclear Free Zones

Khabarovsk
E-mail:
kazyonno@ecomed.khabarovsk.su
Contact: Alexandr Metelkin, Vitaliy Kazenov

Priamuria Native Peoples Association

ul. Kalinina 102
682350   Troitskoe
Nanaiski District
Khabarovsk Region
Tel: 4-13-81
Contact: Nikolai Semenovich Aktanko

The association promotes the preservation of the Priamuria people through the development of traditional trades; regulation of sales of furs, fish and other products; access to business and economic training programs; regulation of outside access; and protection of native resources.

Russian Culture Fund–Khabarovskii Krai Chapter

ul. Serychev 60, kom. 713
680038   Khabarovsk
Tel: 33-10-68, 34-58-85
Contact: Svetlana Y. Cherepanova, President

The fund works to preserve Russian culture, develop the talents of gifted children and artists, and develop minority cultures and sciences.

Russian Fund for Charity & Health–Khabarovskii Krai Chapter

ul. Frunze 67, kom. 57
680057   Khabarovsk
Tel: 38-87-69, 22-13-03
Contact: Liudmila I. Kostrykina, Chair

This charity organization provides support to socially unprotected segments of the population, including single, elderly citizens and invalids, children and orphans, and children with cancer. It participated in a program devoted to the international year of the family, and held fundraising seminars for various programs.

Society of Families with Many Children

ul. Zaparina 57
680000   Khabarovsk
Tel: 22-52-38
Contact: Mrs. Kuamenko, Chair

This society was established in early 1991 and has been very active in handling local and foreign donations (including family-to-family parcels through sister city organizations) as well as providing legal assistance to its members. Future plans include building a vegetable storehouse and procuring agricultural implements. The staff includes two full-time people, the chairman and accountant, as well as 10 volunteers. Membership includes approximately 250 families with three or more children.

The Wildlife Foundation of the Russian Far East

a/ya 1769
ul. Lev Tolstoy 15-A
680049   Khabarovsk
Tel: 21-12-98
Fax: 22-04-10
E-mail: wildlife@wf.khabarovsk.su
Contact: Alexander or Valery Kulikov

The foundation preserves biodiversity and has developed a network of new protected territories to combat habitat loss due to logging, mining, and development in the Russian Far East. It works closely with the Hornocker Institute of the University of Idaho to implement programs to protect rare and endangered species such as the Siberian tiger, the Far Eastern leopard, the red wolf, and Japanese and hooded cranes. Membership in the foundation is free.

Krasnoyarsk (3912)

Fund "Defense of the Law"

a/ya 10280
660099   Krasnoyarsk
Tel: 21-94-17, 21-31-92
Fax: 21-60-70
Contact: Alexandr S. Gorelik, Executive Director; Nikolai A. Klepachev, Board Chair

Friends of the Siberian Forest

ul. Acrovokzalnaya 8, kv. 48
660022   Krasnoyarsk
Tel: 45-94-54
E-mail: andrei@fsf.krasnoyarsk.su

kostya@fsf.krasnoyarsk.su
Contact: Andrei Laletin, Kostya Yakovlev

This organization deals with issues regarding the Siberian forest as well as with nuclear issues.

Human Rights Movement "Soldiers' Mothers and Soldiers of Russia"
pr. Mira 110
Dom Sovetov, kom. 120
660009　Krasnoyarsk
Tel:　　22-22-84
Contact: Olga F. Lonshakova, President

Krasnoyarsk Socio-Ecological Organization–"Green World"
Berezovka Village
Krasnoyarsk region
E-mail:　kras@glas.apc.org
Contact: Vladimir Mikheev

This organization deals with nuclear issues, industrial pollution, ecological information exchange, and publishes the *Ecological Bulletin*.

Memorial–Krasnoyarsk
pl. Mira 1
660097　Krasnoyarsk
Tel:　　23-75-63
Contact: Vladimir Georgievich Sirominin, President

Magadan (41322)

Alcoholics Anonymous
Magadan
Tel:　　2-89-04
Contact: Volodya

Caritas Magadan

25 Proletarskaia ul., kv. 1
685000　Magadan
Tel:　　2-46-84, 2-08-54, 2-66-36
E-mail:　austin@apm.magadan.su
Contact: Rev. Austin Morbaecher, Liubov Bolshakova, Tatiana F. Kononova

Caritas Magadan was established in 1991, and has operated through the parish of the Catholic church. It organizes volunteers to provide food and financial assistance to the elderly and disadvantaged.

Foundation of Mercy Fate
ul. Novo-Nagaevskaia 45, kv. 1
685014　Magadan
Tel:　　4-13-47
Contact: Oleg A. Fetkulov, Chair

The foundation was established in 1991 to raise funds from local organizations and banks for food distribution.

Foundation for the Protection of Childhood
Iakutskaia 71
Magadan
Tel:　　5-28-87, 2-63-17
Contact: Oleg A. Fetkulov
or
ul. Lenina 9, kv. 11
Iagodnoe Settlement
Magadan
Tel:　　2-26-46
Contact: Valentina I. Korostelova

Registered in mid-1992, the foundation provides treatment and social services for children with disabilities.

Friends of the Sea of Okhotsk
c/o Institute for Biological Problems
ul. Karl Marx 24
685010　Magadan
Tel:　　5-30-82
E-mail:　ibpn@ibpn.magadan.su

Contact: Aleksandr Andreyev,
Natasha Proskurina

This organization works in environmental education, biodiversity
conservation and marine biology. The
institute is active in environmental
research, and has developed impact
assessments and other biological
surveys of the natural resources and
wildlife habitat of the Russian
northeast.

Iagodinskii Raion Public Fund for the Protection of Children

ul. Leninskaia 9
686230   Iagodnoye
Magadanskaia oblast
Tel: 25-85, 20-49
Contact: Raisa S. Balakhotseva, Chair

Kronotskii Nature Reserve Magadanskii Nature Reserve

ul. Shirokaia 14
685014   Magadan
Tel/Fax: 2-00-71
E-mail: suarc@orca.alaska.edu
Contact: Andrei Kotliar, Director

Both nature reserves are developing
international ecotourism and national
park exchange programs. The
Magadanskii Nature Reserve currently
has an exchange program with the
Chugach National Forest in Alaska.

Lekar Cooperative Medical Society

Magadan
Tel: 4-14-87, 4-27-33
Contact: Viktor I. Bocharov, Chairman

Magadan Council of Women

ul. Gagarin 4-22
685024   Magadan
Tel: 2-00-38

Contact: Svetlana Shishkina

The council provides social and
employment services to women and
families.

Magadan Chapter of the Russian Fund for Charity and Health

Krymskoye Hwy. 4
Magadan
Tel: 4-22-98
Contact: Lydia Vasilievna Popova

The Magadan chapter of the RFCH
provides support to the elderly and
disabled in their homes and collects and
distributes clothing.

Magadan Regional Committee of the Red Cross Society

ul. Karl Marx 8
685017   Magadan
Tel/Fax: 3-08-88
Contact: Liubov M. Zonova, Director

Magadanskaia Oblast Handicapped Society

Skuridina per. 8-b
Magadan
Tel: 2-26-66
Contact: S. N. Karpik, Chairman

The society employs disabled individuals in income-generating activities.

Ola Settlement Executive Committee

Lenina pl. 4
Ola Settlement
686010   Magadan
Tel: 2-55-67
Contact: Aleksandr A. Bulanov, Presi-
dent

Priority areas for the Ola Settlement
include: development of training

programs in management, business and economics for Native associations; preservation of culture and traditions; preservation of nature and its resources; and development of enterprises based upon traditional skills.

Russian Peace Fund Magadan Chapter

ul. Lenin 2
685000   Magadan
Tel: 2-39-63
Contact: Leonid G. Glushenko

Schastlivy Dien (Happy Day) Association of Pupils of Orphanages and Boarding Schools

ul. Gorkogo 1, kom. 89
685000   Magadan
Tel: 2-93-26
Contact: Vladimir K. Novolodskii, Chair

Registered in July 1993, the Magadan Boarding Schools Association is affiliated with the Moscow Association of Pupils of Boarding Schools and Orphanages. The association is staffed by 14 volunteers and has a membership of 74 pupils and former pupils of orphanages. The association distributes money and food to 14 people each month. Future goals are to organize a farm for children and build a boarding home for graduates of orphanages and boarding schools.

Teacher's Development Institute

ul. Transportnaia 5/23
685000   Magadan
Tel: 2-30-10
Fax: 2-30-30
Contact: Liudmila F. Gorbacheva, Director

The institute retrains unemployed professionals with new work skills.

Magnitogorsk (3513)

"Family" Educational Complex

ul. Druzhbi 25
455026   Magnitogorsk
Tel: 37-32-45
Contact: Anatolii Nazarovich Smirnov

The Family complex houses orphans, attempting to create a family environment. Small groups of children of varying ages live and study together as siblings. The complex receives some funding from local government and from private sponsors.

Magnitogorsk Musical Center

ul. Moscovskaya 17
Magnitogorsk
Tel: 32-10-40
Contact: A. Pyatakov

The center is developing a social club for young people, and provides support to talented young musicians attempting to start careers in music. It organizes rock and pop music festivals, and helps musicians find contacts in the music industry.

Magnitogorsk Foundation "ANTISPID" (Anti-AIDS)

pr. Lenina 33
455000   Magnitogorsk
Tel: 32-89-61
Fax: 32-32-99
Contact: Marina Sergeevna Lapshina

"ANTISPID" is working to prevent the further spread of AIDS in Russia, and particularly in the Urals region. It also provides support programs for AIDS and HIV-positive patients. It is affiliated with ANTISPID Chelyabinsk, and receives funding from commercial activities, Russian businesses and from international AIDS research and support groups.

Nizhny Tagil (3435)

Nizhny Tagil Services for Women in Crisis
Center for Psychological Help for Youth/Nizhny Tagil Clubhouse
ul. Tsiolkovsky 7-72
622036   Nizhny Tagil
Tel: 22-47-19
Fax: 22-05-78

The center provides a variety of services and support groups for people in crisis situations, including the mentally ill, at-risk youth, and battered women.

Sverdlovsk Ecological Club– "Ochischenie"
ul. Goroshnikova 64, kv. 75
622034   Nizhny Tagil
Tel: 22-14-30
           25-12-93 (home)
Contact: Vera Baklanova

Novokuznetsk (3843)

Environmental Information Center–InEkA
ul. Tsiolkovskogo 23, kom. 2
654041   Novokuznetsk
Tel: 47-89-51
Fax: 44-55-46
E-mail: elen@mec.kemerovo.su

InEkA was established to provide citizens access to environmental information and to heighten public awareness about the urgency of environmental issues. It has five basic programs:
• production of *Ecological Bulletin*, a monthly newsletter published in cooperation with other Novokuznetsk organizations;
• information services, including an environmental database that contains information on individuals and organizations, information searches on specific questions, and information exchange;
• monthly seminars coordinated with the Siberian Center for Citizen Initiatives and the Environmental Technology Project, both of which are sponsored by USAID;
• consulting services to provide professional assistance in environmental laws and regulations, education and legal issues for third sector organizations; and,
• translation and publication of foreign textbooks and educational materials on issues surrounding environmental protection, natural resource use, environmental economics, and sustainable development.

Kuzbass Center for Invalids' and Veterans' Rehabilitation
ul. Smirnova 8
654032   Novokuznetsk
Tel: 37-98-58
E-mail: ecokuzbas@glas.apc.org

The center was founded in Novokuznetsk in 1994, a region of above average public health problems because of the environmental degradation during the Soviet period. War veterans and pensioners are two of the most vulnerable groups, and comprise about one-third of Novokuznetsk's population.

The Kuzbass Center's activities are aimed at social and medical rehabilitation of people in these groups. It pro-

vides health services including diagnostic, curative and sanitary services.
The Center also plans to assist its clients in professional training and job
placement.

The center is establishing a herb-
processing plant and a computer-
assembly venture in order to provide
long-term employment opportunities
for its clients. It receives financial support from its founders–the firms West
Siberian Steel Corporation and
Kuznetsk-promstroy. It would welcome any contacts with American and
European PVOs which have practical
experience in provision of social services.

Novosibirsk (3832)

ACTR/ACCELS Novosibirsk
Institute of Economics
ul. im. Ak. Lavrenteva 17, kom. 430-A,
271
630090   Novosibirsk
Tel: 35-78-25, 35-79-13
E-mail:
actr.novosibirsk@sovcust.sprint.com

See profile for ACTR/ACCELS in section *Special Focus Organizations.*

Alcoholics Anonymous
Novosibirsk
Tel: 43-08-48
Contact: Alexander

Ariadna
ul. Frunze 15
630091   Novosibirsk
Tel/Fax: 24-38-01
E-mail:
konstantin.kowalev@finist.nsk.su
Contact: Larisa Tokareva

Ariadna is the women's division of the
sports club Finist, which has been
working with the U.S.-based Wheeled
Mobility Center to develop programs
for the disabled. Members of Ariadna
organize and compete in athletic events
and sponsor cultural events. The
group's most recent project is the establishment of a disabled community
health clinic. With support from
USAID, Wheeled Mobility Center and
Planned Parenthood of Northern New
England will train medical professionals in treating the disabled, establish a
peer-counselling program, and develop
a special program to address disabled
women's health issues.

Center for Ecological Initiatives
a/ya 427
630110   Novosibirsk
E-mail: cei@glas.apc.org
            lavria@glas.apc.org
            (Sb: for Novosibirsk)
Contacts: Yulia Gertswolf, Alexei Tin-
gusov

CEI runs an active environmental education center in Novosibirsk. It received a computer from Sacred Earth
Network in early 1995 and distributed
the first edition of the Center's bulletin
two months afterwards. CEI also
maintains a Youth Social Center for
Ecological Initiatives as a place for students to go after school to take part in a
range of environmentally oriented programs. The center has published a local
youth newspaper, run environmental
monitoring expeditions, and put together a small "eco-museum" on the
premises. The first edition of the center's bulletin had an article discussing
environmental conditions in Novosibirsk and "ecological folk tales" written
by children at the Center.

In 1995, CEI published its first edition of an electronic environmental newspaper for children, *Footsteps on the Path*.

EcoClub
ul. Pirogova 20/2
630075   Novosibirsk
Tel: 35-38-55
E-mail: ecoclub@adm.anit.nsk.su

Ecodom
a/ya 443
630090   Novosibirsk
Tel: 35-73-92
Fax: 23-83-44
E-mail: ecodom@glas.apc.org
Contact: Igor Ogorodnikov; Larissa Avrorina, Educational Director

Ecodom has developed a "Natural House" program, creating housing models to provide some solutions for Russia's energy and environment problems. One demonstration house has been built near Novosibirsk, and several others are under construction. The houses are single-family dwellings using renewable energy sources, such as solar and wind, and closed cycles of waste treatment and purification. Ecodom works with Biointensive for Russia in Palo Alto, CA.

Novosibirsk Press and Information Center
Voskhod 15
630200   Novosibirsk
Tel: 46-37-12, 66-17-96
Fax: 46-05-91, 66-75-21
E-mail: azabol@glas.apc.org
Contact: Anatoly Zabolotny, Coordinator; Vladamir Pasenko, Regional Coordinator

This is a branch of the Russian-American Press and Information Center in Moscow.

Novosibirsk Regional Sports Club "Finist"
ul. Frunze 15
630031   Novosibirsk
Tel: 24-03-49, 24-38-01
Fax: 20-07-75
E-mail: finist@glas.apc.org
              wmc@sfsu.nsk.su
Contact: Victor Semenko

See entries for "Wheeled Mobility Center" in *U.S.-Based Organizations*, and "Ariadna" above.

Open Society Institute
Prospekt Lavrentieva 17, kom. 408-410
630090   Novosibirsk
Tel/Fax: 35-39-59
E-mail: cinsk@soros.nsk.su
Contact: Natasha Baranova

See profile of OSI in section *Clearinghouse Organizations*.

Siberian Informational Medical Association
Novosibirsk
E-mail: SIMA@protei.nsk.su
              bandr@protei.nsk.su
Contact: Sergei Vitjasev, MD

For the medical community of Novosibirsk one of the greatest obstacles to providing modern medical care has been the difficulty in receiving up-to-date information through journals and computer networks. SIMA's goal is to monitor and catalogue available online medical information, join online discussion groups and establish contact between various medical research projects in Siberia with interested parties in the West.

SIMA was founded in 1994 by doctors Sergei Vitjasev and Piotr Larionov to take advantage of the vast amount of information currently available on the Internet. SIMA provides free access to the latest medical information to local doctors, hospitals and research institutes. In addition it serves as an outlet for medical researchers in the region to share information concerning medical and technological projects in development in Siberia.

The organizing committee of SIMA consists of eight people working on a volunteer basis. With limited resources they have obtained equipment, a location for the center, and access to electronic mail (through the Protei Company). However, in order for the center to operate effectively and achieve the goals they have established they seek sources of both financial and information support. SIMA would appreciate hearing from any organization with funds or information for its work. In response to any inquiry they will provide a full project proposal.

Siberian Youth Initiative
Novosibirsk State University
ul. Pirogova 2, kom. 225 A
630090   Novosibirsk
Tel: 35-39-41
Fax: 35-26-53
E-mail: root@youth.nsu.nsk.su

SYI held an international forum in May 1995 on trends in world development and global problems, the role of international regulation, and strategies for youth organizations in the areas of environmental development.

Wheeled Mobility Center
Novosibirsk
Tel/Fax: 46-86-76

E-mail: wmc@sfsu.nsk.su
Contact: Elizabeth Schuster, WMC Regional Coordinator in Novosibirsk

See profile of WMC in section *Special Focus Organizations.*

Omsk (3812)

The Human Rights Section of the Omsk Oblast Voters' Club
City Social and Political Center
ul. Krasnii put 9, kom. 430
644099   Omsk
Tel: 23-81-38
Contact: Arkady Frantsevich Lapinus

"Green City of Omsk"
Omsk Union of Consumers
ul. Valikhanova 3
644010   Omsk
E-mail: greenomsk@glas.apc.org
Contact: Natalya B. Agafonova, Galina Lyuboshenko

In 1995, the NGO Green City of Omsk organized an environmental field trip to northern Siberia and provided a catamaran for the field trip, which went from Osmk to the Irtysh and Ob Rivers and the coast of the Arctic Ocean. The project was designed to promote public interest in the Russian North; research into the ecosystems of the tundra and the taiga; and establishment of an environmental monitoring field station.

Petropavlovsk and Kamchatka Peninsula (41522 or 41500)

Fund for the Protection of Kamchatka
Kamchatka

E-mail: fund@defense.kamchatka.su
Contact: Olga Chernyagina

This organization works in environmental law and protected areas.

Kamchatka Association of Greens

Petropavlovsk
E-mail: sol@green.kamchatka.su
kamchatka@glas.apc.org
Contact: Sergey Solovyov

The association deals with environmental education, television and ecojournalism.

Kamchatka Institute of Ecology and Nature Protection

Riabakov prospekt 19-a
Petropavlovsk
683024 Kamchatka
Tel: 2-37-03, 6-24-37
E-mail: pkh@terra.kamchatka.su
burkanov@marmam.kamchatka.su
Contact: Dr. Vladimir Burkanov, Peter Khomentovsky, Robert Moiseev

The Kamchatka Institute of Ecology and Nature Protection works on issues of marine wildlife protection and ecotourism.

Sakha Republic (41136)

Association of Humanitarian Initiatives

ul. Tikhonova 9, kom. 85
Mirnyi
Sakha Republic
Tel: 2-55-13, 4-67-17, 2-10-59
E-mail: formir@glas.apc.org
Contact: Marina Belozerova

Founded in 1991, the association provides educational services for indigenous inhabitants. It cooperates with women's organizations in Russia and abroad. Recent highlights of the organization include the participation of its director in the Fourth World Conference on Women in Beijing. The association publishes materials about women's issues in local newspapers and has its own monthly supplement to the newspaper *Mirninski Worker*, called *Businesswoman Plus*.

Socio-Ecological Center– Sakha (Yakutsk) Republic

Yakutsk
E-mail: ecol@yacc.yakutia.su
Contact: Valentina Dmitrieva

This organization is involved in environmental education, promoting environmentally conscious businesses, and improving air quality.

Tomsk (3822)

Amnesty International–Tomsk Initiative Group

a/ya 3688
634029 Tomsk
Contact: Vladimir Victorovich Lvov

Center for the Valdorf Initiative

ul. Lytkina 22-65
634045 Tomsk
Tel: 24-25-22
E-mail: main@progect.tomsk.su

Ecological Initiative

Tomsk
E-mail: tverd@glas.apc.org

Ecological Initiative was established in the late 1980s in response to the growing problem of radiation contamination of the Tomsk region. It recently assisted the Socio-Ecological Union, the Center for Citizen Initiatives, and the Krasnoyarsk Ecological Movement in organizing a conference in Siberia entitled "After the Cold War: Disarmament, Conversion and Safety."

"Krug"

Elizarovykh 70-A
634048   Tomsk
Tel: 26-63-45, 63-40-45
or
Mokrushina 20, kv. 55
634045   Tomsk
Contact: Larisa Kurbatova

Krug provides services for the mentally ill.

Tomsk Investigative Center for Human Rights (TITsPCh)

ul. Altaiskaia 76-1, kv. 105
634021   Tomsk
Tel: 23-23-62, 76-40-22
Contact: Nikolai V. Kandyba
E-mail: hrc@hrc.trecom.tomsk.su

Provides legal assistance to residents of Tomsk and monitors human rights in Western Siberia (Tomsk oblast).

Tomsk Montessori Association

Nikitina 31-5
634029   Tomsk
Tel: 23-05-49 (home)
Contact: Nadezhda Nadutkina

Tomsk Regional Historic-Educational, Advocacy Society "Memorial"

ul. Nakhimova 15-276
634034   Tomsk
Tel: 22-29-35, 24-22-54
Fax: 76-40-22
Contact: Vilgelm G. Fast, Nikolai V. Kandyba, Co-Chairs

Projects of Memorial include the collection of historic materials about repression, charitable fund advocacy activities, publication of lists of victims of political repression, and transmittal of archives about political repression to the Tomsk oblast government archives.

Tomsk State University Center Supporting Non-commercial Organizations

ul. Vershinina 76
634045   Tomsk
Tel/Fax: 26-97-72, 23-33-44
            23-33-67, 26-97-40
Contact: Ekaterina Syryamkina, Teacher

Tomsk Women's Forum

Komsomolsky prospekt 73, kv. 52
634041   Tomsk-41
Tel: 211-303, 211-372
Tel/Fax: 447-706
Contact: Tatiana Sergeevna Frolova

The Women's Forum was established in 1991 to bring together women's organizations and projects in the Tomsk region. The forum reports that an indication of the success of their efforts is that currently 10 of 18 representatives on the Tomsk City Council are women, and two of four of the Tomsk Regional Council of Representatives are women.

Ulan-Ude (3012)

Baikal Center for Ecological and Civic Initiatives

Ulan-Ude
E-mail: baikaluu@glas.apc.org
            chim@techn.buriatia.su
Contact: Tsypylma Radnaeva, Chimita Garmayeva

See "Baikal Center for Ecological and Civic Initiatives" in Irkutsk section for more information.

Vladivostok and Primorskii District (4232)

ACTR/ACCELS Vladivostok
Biblioteka im. Fadeeva
Okeanskii prospekt 18, kom. 303
690091   Vladivostok
Tel: 22-37-98
E-mail:
fsa.vladivostok@sovcust.sprint.com

See the profile for ACTR/ACCELS in section *Special Focus Organizations.*

Asian-Pacific School
pr. 100-letiya Vladivostoka, 103
Dom Molodezhi kv. 245-6
690039   Vladivostok
Tel: 31-97-42
E-mail: stepan@pub.marine.su
              step@pub.marine.su
Contact: Stepan Galushkin, Director

Association of Far Eastern Nature Reserves
Sikhote-Alin Biospheric National Reserve
692150   Ternei
Primorskii District
Tel: 9-13-59
Tel/Fax: 9-15-59
E-mail: sixote.sen@glas.apc.org
Contact: Anatoli A. Astafiev, Director

Association of Indigenous People of Primorskii Region
ul. Pervaya Morskaia 2, kom. 414
680007   Vladivostok
Tel: 22-99-97
E-mail: amba@stv.sovam.com
              amba@stv.marine.su

udege@glas.apc.org
Contact: Pavel Suliandziga, President

The association is a loosely organized regional grouping of Native people, including Udege, Orochi, and Nanai. The society received funding from the Office of Oceans, Environment and Science, and the U.S. Department of State to assist in planning future development of the Bikin River area.

Association of Spinal Disabled
ul. Alliluiieva 10-2
Vladivostok
Contact: E.S. Muzychenko, General Director

The association was registered in 1992.

Caritas/Vladivostok
a/ya 3185
ul. Svetlanskaia 147
690001   Vladivostok
Tel: 26-17-41
Fax: 26-96-16
E-mail: myron@catholic.marine.su
Contact: Anastasia Potapenko

Caritas is an international European Catholic social service organization which operates through loosely associated indigenous chapters around the world. Caritas Vladivostok was established in 1993. It has mobilized medical and other volunteers and used a small grant from Catholic Relief Services to launch two projects: 1) a clinic providing free medical treatment and psychological counseling for pensioners, children with disabilities, and low income individuals; and 2) monetary assistance to pensioners and families with many children for medicine and food.

Chernobyl-Pb Primorskii Union of Radiation and Ecological Safety

ul. Leninskaia 69
690001   Vladivostok
Tel: 22-23-00, 22-13-85
Fax: 22-88-13
Contact: Vladimir F. Borodkin, Chairman

Children's Burn Foundation

Nahodka pr. 100
Nahodka
Tel: 4-26-41
Fax :   2-36-10
Contact: Liudmila I. Sukhova, President

Children's Foundation Primorskii Branch

a/ya 2294
Vladivostok
Tel: 22-78-83
Contact: Larisa P. Serera, Deputy Chair

Registered in 1988, the Children's Foundation helps orphans and children with disabilities. The foundation has a staff of 5 full-time employees and 50 volunteers. It has provided over five million rubles in financial assistance as well as food and clothing to 20,000 beneficiaries. The foundation also distributed humanitarian aid from New Zealand.

City Council of Women

Okeanskii pr. 20, section 104
Vladivostok
Tel: 22-03-72
Contact: Liudmila P. Dudareva, Director

Together with governmental structures, the City Council of Women develops social protection programs for women and children from large and single-parent families. It also distributes food and clothing donated by foreign organizations to at-risk families.

Dialogue of Nations of the World

ul. Pervaya Morskaia 2, kv. 108
690007   Vladivostok
Tel: 26-59-36, 22-96-20
Fax: 22-95-20
Contact: Nikolai A. Larionov, Chairman

Dialogue of Nations of the World was established in 1991 to provide social assistance to the disadvantaged. Founding organizations include Anna, Vostok, Insat, the Pacific Fleet, the Regional Children's Hospital, the Juridical Center, and the trade union of medical workers. The Dialogue has provided support services to Western organizations that seek to establish a presence in the RFE.

The Eurasia Foundation

Russian Far East Office
Abrekovskaya 8a
690001   Vladivostok
Tel: 30-00-63
Fax: 30-00-64
E-mail: efvlad@sovam.com
Contact: Joy Wagner, Regional Director

See the profile for the foundation under *Clearinghouse Organizations.*

Good Deed Society (Dobroe Delo)

ul. Beliaeva 4-20
Vladivostok
Tel: 23-58-16
Contact: Vasily Fitz

The society provides assistance to the disadvantage.

Museum of Far East Marine Reserve
Institute of Marine Biology
690041   Vladivostok
Tel: 31-09-07
Fax: 31-09-00
E-mail: faribm@visenet.marine.su
Contact: Anna A. Gulbina, Director; Anatoli Lebedev, International Liaison

Part of the Russian Academy of Sciences, this organization was created as an open environmental information center in the region. Future plans include the development of ecotourism in the region. The institute manages a marine nature preserve south of Vladivostok, and is interested in issues of park management and ecotourism.

International Executive Service Corps
Russian Far East and Eastern Siberia
Aleutskaia ul. 45a, kom. 807b
690090   Vladivostok
Tel: 23-12-18
Fax: 23-13-59
Tel/Fax: 7-5049-16-33-59 (Int'l)
Contact: Don and Dina Hansen, Associate Directors

See profile of IESC in section *Special Focus Organizations.*

ISAR–Vladivostok
Vladivostok
Tel: 22-05-15
E-mail: isarfe@glas.apc.org

See profile of ISAR in section *Clearinghouse Organizations.*

Krai Board of the Deaf Society
Rokossovskogo 24, kom. 24
Vladivostok
Tel: 33-89-03
Contact: Evgenii Abramov, Chairman

Mother and Child Health Care Primorskii Fund
ul. Svetlanskaia 22
690000   Vladivostok
or
a/ya 2-58
690002   Vladivostok
Tel: 22-86-76, 25-23-90
Fax: 22-50-10
Contact: A. Akhonin, Director; Dr. Natalia N. Ostapenko, President, Regional Chief Pediatrician; Nikita G. Egorov, Chair

The foundation was established in 1993 to monitor health indicators and provide health services. It is also working to expand maternal and child health and social services in the area, providing assistance to the disabled and deaf, and offering business training. In January 1996 it was actively seeking U.S. organizations with which to work.

Orthodox Union of the Disabled
ul. Pologaia 65
690000   Vladivostok
Contact: Liudmila M. Tokareva, Chair

The Orthodox Union of the Disabled was founded in 1993 and has four full time staff, 10 volunteers, and 76 members consisting of "believers and disabled." Activities of the organization include providing financial and food aid to members. The union would like to create a production/rehabilitation center for people with disabilities in Vladivostok as well as a boarding house for the needy.

Pacific Environment and Resource Center
Krasniy Yar
E-mail: mishaj@glas.apc.org
Contact: Misha Jones

The center deals with forest issues, biodiversity protection, fisheries, and indigenous peoples. See profile of PERC in section *Special Focus Organizations.*

Pervomaiskii Raion Society of the Disabled
ul. Oleg Koshevogo 27
Vladivostok
Tel: 27-66-37
Contact: Viktor Leonidovich Iarchenko

One of the most active societies serving people with disabilities, the Society of the Disabled is active in advocacy and humanitarian aid distribution.

Pervomaiskii Regional Board of the All-Russian Invalid Society of Vladivostok
ul. O. Koshevoi 27
Vladivostok
Tel: 27-66-37
Contact: Viktor L. Kharchenko

Pervorechenskii Region Invalid Society
100 Years Prospect, 36-B, kv. 44
Vladivostok
Tel: 6-15-1
Contact: Lyubov Shakhnazarova

Primorskii Foundation Against Drug Addiction and Drug Business
ul. Russkaia 55-A, kv. 109
690105 Vladivostok
Tel/Fax: 4-62-87

Contact: Viktor Vasilievitch Zubov

The foundation assists government bodies, militia and health service providers in fighting drug-related crime and drug addiction. It assists in providing the technical means to appropriate subdivisions of militia of Primorskii Krai; manages a ward for treating addicts; and runs a bank for keeping valuables.

Primorskii Krai Board of the All-Russian Invalids Society
Lugovay 83B
Vladivostok
Tel: 29-36-16
Contact: Viktor D. Lebedinets

Primorskii Krai Foundation of Mercy
Sukhanova 1-29
Vladivostok
Tel: 26-58-65
Contact: Valerii L. Gonacharov, Chair

The foundation's activities include providing financial assistance to people with disabilities or special needs.

Primorskii Krai Society of the Blind
Okeanski pr. 109-19
Vladivostok
Tel: 5-53-60
Contact: Natalia Viktorovna Shvetsova

Primorskii Krai Society of the Disabled
ul. Lugovaia 83-B
690087 Vladivostok
Tel: 29-36-16
Contact: Olga N. Derevstova, Chair

The society is a decades-old federal organization with state and district level branches. Due to both perestroika and economic constraints, the society has become independent of the government. The society registered in 1988 as a public organization.

The society claims a membership of 20,000, including parents of children with disabilities, and a staff of 10 with an additional 320 volunteers. Its budget in 1992 was 740,000 rubles. Assistance includes everyday help, rent, heat, transportation, medical assistance, etc. The society runs a regional school for the blind. Business endeavors include making lids for bottles and jars, making and repairing electric appliances and telephones.

Primorskii Krai Committee of the Red Cross Society

23 Fokina ul.
690091   Vladivostok
Tel: 26-76-50
Tel/Fax: 22-45-05
Contact: Liudmila M. Reshetnikova, Chair

Primorskii Peace Fund

Okeanskii pr. 90
Vladivostok
Tel: 25-33-46
Fax: 25-55-59
Contact: Larisa Konstantinovna, Director

Primorskii Regional Association of Ex-Prisoners of Fascism

a/ya 48-66
ul. Svetlanskaia 20
Vladivostok
Tel: 22-76-89
Contact: Galina N. Petrovna, Chair

Registered in 1991, the association has one full-time staff member, seven volunteers, and 180 members who are ex-prisoners of concentration camps or former prisoners of war. Its main activities are social and legal assistance to its members and historical research.

Primorskii Regional Organization of Professional Education of Veterans

ul. Pushkinskaia 93
690001   Vladivostok
Contact: Andrei P. Tkalich, Chair

The Primorskii branch of the federal organization has two part-time employees, 70 volunteers, and 850 members who are teachers. Activities include providing financial aid to single elderly people and veterans and locating work places for pensioners.

Primorskii Union of Victims of Chernobyl

a/ya 1559
Okeanskii pr. 20
690001   Vladivostok
Tel: 2-28-00
Tel/Fax: 22-88-13
Contact: Vladimir F. Borodkin, Chair

Registered in 1992, the Primorskii Union has three full-time employees who distribute financial and food aid to 1,235 members who were exposed to radiation at Chernobyl.

Primorye Region Society of Technical Ecology

ul. Chapayeva 14, kv. 107
690022   Vladivostok
Tel: 31-39-24, 22-88-82
E-mail: akub@glas.apc.org
Contact: Andrei Kubanin

Kubanin is on the council of the Socio-Ecological Union.

Russian-American Association of Business Partners
ul. Nerchinskaya10, kom. 213
Vladivostok
Tel: 25-94-22, 25-69-98
Fax: 25-69-98
E-mail: lev@iba.marine.su
Contact: Lev. P. Kurochkin, Executive Director

Russian Disabled Society
Pervomaiskii District Management
ul. Olega Koshevogo 27
Vladivostok
Tel: 27-66-37
Contact: Viktor L. Kharchenko, Chairman

Society of the Blind
10 ul. Magnitogorskaia
690068   Vladivostok
Tel: 31-75-57
Contact: R.G. Bogatiriov, Chair

The society has a paid staff of 27, 180 volunteers, and a membership of 2,760 vision-impaired people. Activities include providing social and financial assistance. The society's budget in 1992 was two million rubles. It has established a regional school for the blind.

Society of the Deaf
ul. Komsomolskaia 27-a, kv. 63
690002   Vladivostok
Tel: 5-07-85
Contact: Alla A. Babanova

Society of Disabled of WWII
Okeanskii pr. 20, kv. 504
Vladivostok
Contact: Larisa A. Zeleina, Chair

The society was registered in 1993, and its staff of six provides services to a membership of 550 disabled World War II veterans. Among the society's activities are selling food at reduced prices and providing holiday gifts to members.

Socio-Ecological Union
c/o Institute for Marine Biology
ul. Palchevskogo 17
Vladivostok
Tel: 31-09-00
Contact: Andre Kubanin, Far East Representative

Souvenir of Dalpribor
ul. Borodinskaia 46/50
Vladivostok
Tel: 46-13-68
Contact: Irina Petrovna Shapovalova

The Souvenir of Dalpribor is a children's dance ensemble. It provides training to children ages seven to 17.

Tiger Ecological Organization
ul. Nekrasovskaia 1, kom. 5
Lazo, Lazovskii District
692890   Primorskii Krai
Tel: 9-11-92
Contact: Dmitri Mezentsev

Tiger Ecological Organization is opening a private Siberian Tiger Reserve to attract ecotourists to the region, with half the profits going to regional government. The group hopes to promote habitat-preservation by showing the economic potential of ecotourism.

Young Russia Children's Association
ul. Kazanskaia 4/6
Vladivostok
Tel: 21-37-67, 22-46-06
Contact: Sergei B. Eliseev, Director

The association plans leisure activities for children and teenagers, and conducts job placement activities on their behalf. At present, there are 1,500 children in the organization. They have hobby groups, and provide social and domestic help to elderly.

Zov Taigi
ul. Radio 7
Vladivostok
Tel: 31-46-22
E-mail: solkin@sovamsu.sovusa.com

The Regional Center for the Defense of Wild Nature Zov Taigi, has been working with the U.S.-based Pacific Environment and Resources Center since 1992 to protect forests and wildlife in the Primorskii region of the Russian Far East (RFE). The organization also publishes a bi-monthly journal, *Zov Taigi*, that educates the public on environmental issues specific to the RFE.

Zlatoust (0236)

Foundation for the Support of Education
ul. Turgeneva 15
Zlatoust
Tel: 3-37-40, 3-36-44
Contact: Olga Kopilova

The foundation supports talented and gifted children, and is working to educate Russia's next generation of leaders. It provides a variety of academic and social programs for children and teens.

Tajikistan

Country Code: 7

Dushanbe (3772)

Academy of Science "Malaya"
ul. Mayakovskogo 28, kv. 18
Dushanbe
Tel: 22-69-91, 21-71-41
35-53-47 (home)
Contact: Svetlana Tikhonovna
Blagoveshenskaya

ACCELS Dushanbe
State Library, 1st floor
Rudaki 36
734025   Dushanbe
Tel: 21-17-95
E-mail: akselstj@sovam.com

See the profile for ACTR/ACCELS
under *U.S.-Based Organizations.*

Adkhamov Fund
ul. Aini 299/1
734063   Dushanbe
Tel: 25-11-08, 25-29-69
25-31-66 (home)
Contact: Akram A. Dzhuraev

Ali Somon Cultural and Intellectual Foundation
ul. Aini 45
734024   Dushanbe
Tel: 22-48-26
Fax: 23-08-88
Contact: Abdulqodir Kholiqzoda,
Ph.D., Director

The Ali Somon Cultural and Intellectual Foundation was founded in Dushanbe in 1994. The name derives from
the period of Somoni rule remembered
as a golden era of high culture, rule of
law, and scientific accomplishment by
Persian-speaking people. According to
its literature, the Foundation "attempts
to build a bridge between yesterday's
epoch and today's life in order to
regenerate the ancient culture, to help
strengthen the liberty and independence
of the Tajik people, and found a
civilized society."

To accomplish this goal, the Ali
Somon Foundation offers scholarships
to aspiring students in foreign
languages, business, law, politics and
medicine. It plans to open a "Free
University" with departments in each of
these fields.

The Foundation currently publishes
books and other literature oriented to
the business sector and operates a small
"Business Center," where instruction is
offered in various aspects of business
and commerce. Novices in business
may apply for a two-year "sponsorship"
from the Ali Somon Business Center.

Association of Medical Students and Young Specialists
pr. Rudaki 139
734003   Dushanbe
Tel: 24-37-85
Contact: Ali Buzurukov

Association of Women with University Degrees
Dushanbe
Tel: 21-17-50, 21-58-08 (home)
Contact: Guldzhakhon Babasadykova

Central Asian Development Agency
Dushanbe
Tel: 21-22-10, 27-13-35
Contact: Shoista Khaidarovna
Shokhimardonova

Chamber of Commerce and Industry
21 Mazaeva Street
734012   Dushanbe
Tel: 27-57-41
Fax: 27-95-19
Contact: Komol Subiev, Director

Children's Coordinating Center for International Development
ul. Bekhzod 20/1, kv. 7
Dushanbe
Tel/Fax: 24-34-43
Fax: 22-83-12
Contact: Zebo Sharifova

Citizen Inititiatives Support Fund
Dushanbe
Tel: 21-50-69, 21-62-66
Contact: Zebo Siddikovna Zaripova

Dushanube Environmental Movement
Dushanbe
E-mail: isarata@glas.apc.org
Contact: Mikhail Tyutin

The organization deals with ecological information, ecotourism, and environmental monitoring.

Ecolog
Dushanbe
E-mail: umeda@glas.apc.org
Contact: Vladimir S. Savvateev

Ecolog works in environmental education.

History Institute, Academy of Science
pr. Kuibisheva, or
ul. Tursun-Zade 38/7, kv. 12
734042   Dushanbe
Tel: 21-23-70
Contact: Lola Dodkhudoeva

Institute of Philosophy and Law
Dushanbe
Tel: 22-73-50
Contact: Muatar Saidmuradovna Khaidarova

Mercy Corps
ul. Bukhoro 40, kv. 32
Dushanbe
Tel: 21-58-69
Contact: Farida Asadova

National Association of Small and Medium Businesses
Dushanbe
Tel: 21-86-21
Contact: Sjavkat Bazarov, President

Net Alumni Center
ul. Rudaki 40, 3rd Floor
734001   Dushanbe
Tel: 21-05-22, 21-05-26
Fax: 21-05-28
E-mail: nettaj@sovam.com
Contact: Fadirum Kamuliddinov, Center Manager

A resource center and library for alumni of the NET training project managed by the Academy for Educational Development.

Physics Society KVANT School Club
ul. Aini 299/1 FTI
734063   Dushanbe
Tel: 25-16-63, 25-34-41 (home)
Contact: Yuri Madzhnunovich Shukrinov

Project BASICS
Dushanbe
Fax: 24-34-43
Contact: Ibod Sharifov, Coordinator

RSYuT Scientific-Pedagogical Society
Dushanbe
Tel: 21-71-41, 21-59-86
Contact: Vladimir Sevastianovich Savateev

Republic Station of Children and Youth Tourism
Dushanbe
Tel: 21-71-42, 21-59-86
Contact: Saodat Yakubovna Azimova

Russian Association of Political Science
Institute of Philosophy and Law
Dushanbe
Tel: 22-73-50, 22-67-21, 33-40-37
Contact: Muatar Saidmuradovna Khaidarova

Scout Association of Tajikistan
Dushanbe
Tel/Fax: 21-05-55
Contact: Rustam Karimov

Socio-Ecological Union
ul. Klara Zetkin 34, kv. 41 (Buzurukov)
or
Shota Rustaveli 11, kv. 40 (Dadabaev)
734000 Dushanbe
Tel: 33-68-80 (Buzurukov)
27-63-04 (Dadabaev)
E-mail: umeda@glas.apc.org
Contact: Anvar Buzurukov, Member of the Council of Socio-Ecological Union; Khurshed Dadabaev

Special Olympics Tajikistan
ul. Chekhov 13a
734055 Dushanbe
Tel: 22-47-48
Contact: Ms. Dilbar Sharipova, Chairman

Tajik Center for Entrepreneurship
Dushanbe
Tel: 26-75-29
Contact: Karim Islamov, President

TajikInterPress
Humanitarian Publicity Support Fund
ul. I. Somoni 8
Dushanbe
Tel: 24-56-56, 35-92-81 (Sattor)
23-45-35, 27-67-83 (Alimov)
Contact: Tursun Sattor, Akmal Alimov

Tajikstan Association of Judges
Dushanbe
Tel: 33-42-97, 35-95-64 (home)
Contact: Vatan Negmatovich Abdurakhmanov

Tajikistan News Independent Agency
ul. Popova 72
Dushanbe
Tel: 23-45-35, 27-25-26 (home)
Contact: Zafar Pachadzhanov

TARL Society of Ham Radio Operators
1 pr. ul. Turcun-Zade
Dushanbe
Tel: 21-88-12
Contact: Masud Mirzoevich Tursunzade

Teachers' Creative Union
ul. Nazym-Khikmet 6
Dushanbe
Tel: 22-50-87, 27-09-52 (home)
Contact: Vladimir Saidovich Mulodzhanov

Umeda Information Center
Dushanbe
Tel: 21-71-41, 21-59-86, 23-30-80 (home)
E-mail: umeda@glas.apc.org
anvar@glas.apc.org
Contact: Anvar Buzurukov, Timur Khasanov

Umeda publishes *Vestnik* electronically, a review of socio-economic and ecologi-cal information from Tajikistan.

Khorog (377910)

Pamir Relief and Development Program
Gorno-Badakhshansky region
736000 Khorog
Tel: 27-19
Contact: Mahmadamin Mahmadaminov, President

PRDP works in association with the Aga Khan Foundation (U.S.) to meet local development needs.

Khudzhand (37922)

Association of Business Women "Dilafruz"
12 Microraion, d. 20, kv. 33
or
Bofanda 6/17 (Tyuraev home)
Khudzhand
Tel: 6-49-41, 2-07-04 (Saidzoda)
4-15-90, 6-05-41 (Tyuraev)
Contact: Dilbar Saidzoda, Faroukh Tyuraev

ECOSAN International Fund
pr. Rakhmona Nabieva 45, kab. 528
Khudzhand
Tel: 6-50-44, 5-57-43
Contact: Maksuda Azizovna Azizova

National Association of Small and Medium Businesses
Khudzhand
Tel: 21-86-21
Contact: Sjavkat Bazarov

Tajikistan Center for Entrepreneurship
Khudzhand
Tel: 26-75-29
Contact: Karim Islamov, President

Umeda Information Center
ul. Ivanitskogo 1, kv. 35
or
ul. K. Khudzhandi 166/4
Khudzhand
Tel: 6-03-41, 6-33-90
6-74-96 (Kamilov)
2-09-80 (Negmatullaev)
Contact: Ikrom Yadgarovich Kamilov, Alisher Negmatullaev

Turkmenistan

Country Code: 7

Ashkabad (3632)

ACCELS Ashgabat
Educational Advising Center
Prospekt Turkmenbashi 32, 1st floor
744014   Ashkabad
Tel: 51-00-46

Administrative Office
104 Maktymguly, room 2
744000   Ashkabad
Tel: 29-71-54
E-mail:
fsa.ashgabad@sovcust.sprint.com

See the profile for ACTR/ACCELS in
section *Special Focus Organizations.*

Ashkhabad Ecology Club
Ashkabad
E-mail: catena@glas.apc.org
Contact: Andrei Aranbaev

The organization focuses on issues of
water pollution, chemistry, air, soil,
environmental education, sustainable
agriculture and environmental impact
assessment.

**Dialogue—Youth Leadership
Center**
Khudaiberdiev 46
Ashkabad
Tel: 41-92-60, 46-62-29
Fax: 46-64-43
Contact: Gaiitnazarov Byashim
Khadjievich

Dialogue publishes materials related to
youth leadership, civic education, and
democracy, and organizes training
programs to teach young people
leadership skills. It was founded in
January 1994 and works with the
International Republican Institute. (See
section, *U.S.-Based Organizations.*)

NET Alumni Center
11 Gogol ul., kv. 12
744000   Ashkabad
Tel: 35-02-23, 35-02-24
Fax: 35-02-23
E-mail: nettur@sovam.com
Contact: Alexander Ipatenko

A resource center and library for
alumni of the NET training project
managed by the Academy for
Educational Development.

**Public Movement for Human
Rights**
ul. Kulieva 56-a
744013   Ashkabad
Tel: 46-83-20, 29-02-08
Contact: Anatolii Petrovich Fomin,
Deputy Director; Amman Kovshutova

**Society for the Preservation of
Nature of Turkmenistan**
ul. Ostrovskogo 26
Ashkabad
Tel: 24-52-68, 29-02-08
Contact: Dr. Chabudula Atamupadov,
Anatolii Fomin

The society, a regional chapter of
World Information Transfer, is
currently involved in a project to
protect a 625 hectare area for the
preservation of rare animal species.

Special Olympics Turkmenistan
ul. Belinskaya 32
744001   Ashkabad
Tel: 25-20-63
Fax: 22-53-79

Contact: Mr. Aman A. Altiev,
Executive Director

Turkmenistan Chamber of Commerce
Ashkhabad
Tel: 25-57-56, 25-30-29
Contact: Ms. Khodjanazarova, Jennet
Khakberdiyevna (English-speaking)

Union of Workers in Enterprise Structures
ul. Ostrovskogo, 26
Ashkabad
Tel: 24-52-68, 29-02-08
Contact: Anatolii Fomin, Deputy
Director

Dashkhovuz (36022)

Dashkhovuz Ecological Club
Microrayon Central 1, 8, kv. 23
746301   Dashkhovuz
Tel: 3-68-17, 3-24-48
E-mail: zatoka@glas.apc.org
Contact: Andrei Zatoka

The club is the first Western style
environmental NGO in Turkmenistan.
It is working with Temurleng Mollaev,
the only doctoral candidate in
agricultural sciences in the oblast, to
develop a training program for local
farmworkers in sustainable agriculture.
With ISAR/USAID Seeds of
Democracy funding, the club and
Mollaev have conducted a series of
seminars in the region on sound
agricultural practices.

DEC has many local projects,
ranging from testing melons on the
local markets for fertilizer chemicals to
starting a model farm using biologically
approved methods. DEC is active in
restoring biodiversity and maintaining
and protecting nature preserves in
northern Turkmenistan as well as
promoting environmental education for
young people.

Krasnovodsk

"Flamingo"
Socio-Ecological Club
Ornithological Zapovednik
E-mail: flam@glas.apc.org
Contact: Alexey Karavaev

These organizations focus on ornithology, ecology, and biodiversity
protection.

Ukraine

Country Code: 380

Kyiv (44)

ACCELS Kyiv
Administrative Office
Kyiv Shevchenko State University
vul. Volodomirska 60, kom. 218-19
252033   Kyiv
Tel: 225-71-82
E-mail: accels.kiev@sovcust.sprint.com

Educational Advising Center
vul. Volodomirska 60, kom. 203
252030   Kyiv
Tel: 225-85-49
E-mail: sac.kiev@sovcust.sprint.com

See profile for ACTR/ACCELS in section *Special Focus Organizations.*

Alcoholics Anonymous
Kyiv
Tel: 483-2954
Contact: Natasha

Afghanistan War Veterans– Kyiv Union
ul. Bankivska 10
252009   Kyiv
Tel: 212-5042, 291-6285
Fax: 212-5130
Contact: Igor Venzitsky, Chairman;
Anatoliy Ivaschenko, Chief manager

This organization is involved in charitable work on behalf of invalids and veterans.

Amnesty International
Kyiv
Tel: 442-7263

Contact: Nikolai Poluschuk

Association of Entrepreneurs "Infobusiness"
vul. Terokhina 80/4, 2nd floor
254080   Kyiv
Tel/Fax: 435-6581, 435-6688,
435-6694
Contact: Bohdan Rybak, President;
Alexander Yozhikov, Vice President

AEI offers aspiring entrepreneurs in Ukraine an independent option for assistance, training and information. The project aims to:
• publish policy recommendations on a sector-by-sector basis addressed to government as well as to businesses, in order to develop a market economy in a democratic state;
• build private institutions that provide entrepreneurs with access to needed information and consulting assistance; and
• provide training aimed at bringing the skills and practices of Ukrainian firms to the level of international standards.

Born in the midst of the RUKH movement, AEI is a nongovernmental, republic-wide association. It was founded in the summer of 1992 to work on economic and business proposals submitted to RUKH from foreign firms and Ukrainian entrepreneurs. It currently includes 14 regional offices. The association's central office works with its regional offices on a contractual basis.

Associations of Protectors of Human Embryo and Newborn
ul. Arsenalna 5
252011   Kyiv
Tel: 294-6462
Fax: 294-7272

Contact: Vasyl Bota, President

Attorneys' Union of Ukraine

Hotel "Ukraina" #748, 749
Bul. Shevchenko 5/7
252025 Kyiv
Tel: 229-0041
Fax: 229-2812
Contact: Volovymyr Medvedchuk,
Director; Tetyana Varfolomeyeva,
Deputy

This is a professional legal association.

BABYN YAR–Public History Educational Center of Ukraine

vul. Chkalova 24, #11
254034 Kyiv
Tel: 446-6072, 225-0834
Fax: 225-0834
Contact: Oleksandr Shlayen, Director

Babyn Yar is the site of a massacre of thousands of Ukrainian Jews in World War II.

Caritas et Misericordia– Public Charitable Organization

vul. Chervonoarmiyska 96
252005 Kyiv
Tel: 261-0195, 261-0184
Tel/Fax: 269-4114
Contact: Yuriy Nagornyy, President

This is a Uniate Catholic charitable organization.

CENOS–All-Ukrainian Ecological Club for the Study and Protection of Natural Communities

Schmalhausen Zoological Institute
vul. Bogdan Khmelnytsky 15, kom. 180
254601 Kyiv
Tel: 440-5409 (home)
224-4562
224-9333 (Institute)
E-mail: alex@cenos.freenet.kiev.ua
Contact: Alexei V. Gumovsky,
Chairman

CENOS was formed in 1992 by students of Kyiv State University and their friends from other regions of Ukraine. Its main aim is to undertake "ecological actions and complex research (studying of natural communities as a whole)," and to publicize the results of such research among administrative circles and the general public in order to obtain "necessary legislative enactments."

In the summer of 1994 CENOS, in collaboration with the Ukrainian Academy of Agrarian Sciences, put on an exhibition of insects used in biological control of pests. This project led to the approval by the Ministry of Nature Conservation for the creation of a national Park "Lesniki," near Kyiv.

In the spring of 1995 CENOS prepared an illustrated catalogue, *Reservation to farmer*, which stresses the economical importance of protecting a variety of insects. The catalogue introduces farmers to beneficial insects in environmental agriculture as well as in nature conservation . Both of these projects received support from ISAR.

The current emphasis of CENOS is "the rationalization of environmental activity." Its main activities involve ecomonitoring (patroling of territories of reservations, help to administrations of protected lands), done under the guidance of specialists in nature conservation. Additionally, CENOS plans to publish an annual review of works of young ecologists.

CENOS has no paid staff members. All members of the organization, scientific advisors and consultants work on projects in their spare time. CENOS has five branches in other parts of Ukraine and members in other countries.

CHARITY–Jewish Society

vul. Nemanska 7
252103   Kyiv
Tel: 220-8472
Contact: Volodymyr Vynokur, Head

Children after Chernobyl

ul. Khreschatyk 50
Kyiv
Tel: 221-2323
Fax: 417-8646
Contact: Elena Goncharova

Children after Chernobyl was organized to assist victims of the Chernobyl disaster. The organization would like to develop partnerships with other international NGOs.

Children of Chernobyl– Ukrainian Society

Druzhby Narodiv bul. 8A
252000   Kyiv
Tel: 519-7716 (home)
              433-0988 (home)
Tel/Fax: 268-6458
Contact: Lyubov Subbotina, Director; Natalya Shenshova, Deputy

Chernobyl Children was founded in 1989 in Ukraine to provide medical and social assistance to children who were victims of the Chernobyl accident. It is an independent, voluntary organization registered at the Ministry of Justice of Ukraine, representing 500,000 children who have suffered from the catastrophe at the Chernobyl Nuclear Power Station. The organization would like to develop partnerships with other international NGOs.

Children's Fund of Ukraine

vul. Khreschatyk 34, #415
252001   Kyiv
Tel: 221-2665
Tel/Fax: 229-8592
Contact: Valentyna Usenko, Director; Lyubov Kyzylova, Deputy

The Children's Fund is a charitable organization benefitting children and orphans.

COMPASS Club–Public Youth Union

vul. Tychyuny 15
Kyiv
Tel: 560-1874 (home)
Fax: 228-7474
Contact: Taras Loginov, Head

This organization is involved with the education of youth and children.

COUNTERPART Service Center

vul. Staronavodnytska 8B, #71
252015   Kyiv
Tel: 294-8954
Fax: 295-8961
E-mail: cpkiev@attmail.com
              cpkiev@cpkiev.freenet.kiev.ua
Contact: Charlotte Watson, WESTNIS Regional Director

The center manages the programs of COUNTERPART Foundation (see *Clearinghouse Organizations* section) to support NGOs in Belarus, Moldova, and Ukraine. It maintains a database of over 1,000 local NGOs and helps to establish linkages between them and foreign organizations.

Echo-Vostok News Agency

a/ya 56
253192   Kyiv
Tel: 544-1780

Fax: 543-5852
E-mail: echo@echo-vostok.kiev.ua
Contact: Andrei Konechenkov,
Director.

NA Echo-Vostok emerged from the newspaper *Echo of Chernobyl*. This publication, started in 1991 as an an attempt "to bring to light the real consequences of this horrible nuclear disaster," convinced Konechenkov and others of the need to establish an independent "eco news" agency. In September 1992 the News Agency Echo-Vostok was registered as a non-govermental ecology, information and publishing center. The founders are the agency staff and the international NGO Chernobyl Union.

Since May 1993 the agency has been issuing a weekly newsletter on nuclear issues in Ukraine and NIS countries. At the request of the Austrian organization "Anti-Atom International," in 1993 NA E-V translated into Russian and published a summary of the book *IAEA– 35 Years of Promotion of Nuclear Energy,* and in 1994, D. Seyfried's book *Gute Argumente–Energie.*

Beginning in late 1994 *Echo-Vostok* started publishing different eco-literature as joint projects with ISAR. In June 1995 the news agency founded, together with the National Technical University of Ukraine, the Library of the Future of Energy.

Promotion of renewable energy sources and energy saving technologies are the current emphases of the agency's activities. The staff consists of five persons.

EcoPravo–Kyiv

a/ ya 750/6
254060   Kyiv

Tel/Fax: 416-4735
E-mail: ecolaw@ecolaw.freenet.kiev.ua
Contact: Boris Vasilkovsky

See *EcoPravo–Lviv* for description of organization.

ESPERO–Fund for Rehabilitation of Deaf Children

vul. Myloslavska 5, #202
253232   Kyiv
Tel: 446-4142
Contact: Taras Kagal, President

The Eurasia Foundation

Western NIS Regional Office
Kreschatik 15, kv. 14
252001   Kyiv
Tel: 229-7521
Fax: 229-4359
E-mail:
eurasia@eurasia.freenet.kiev.ua
Contact: Nicolas Deychakiwsky

See the profile for the foundation under *Clearinghouse Organizations.*

Famine-33

Society "Ukraine"
vul. Zolotovoritska 6
252034   Kyiv
Tel: 277-0116 (home)
Contact: Dmytro Kalenyk, Deputy Director

This is a charitable fund created by the Ukrainian Association of Researchers of the Genocide-Famine in 1932-1933.

Flamenko

vul. K. Marksa 12
252001   Kyiv
Tel: 229-6274
Fax: 432-6648, 228-7272
Contact: Larissa Tsibrukova

Flamenko was founded in 1991 to promote cultural exchanges between Ukraine and countries around the world. It has also worked to assist the victims of the Chernobyl disaster. Its international experience includes: exchange of children's groups with the province of Galicia in Spain; the operation of a children's art gallery in cooperation with the Cultural Society of Berlin; and arranging for diagnostic treatment of Chernobyl children in Tel-Aviv.

Freedom House–Ukraine
vul. Malaxhitomirska 13, kv. 6
252001   Kyiv
Tel/Fax: 228-0914
E-mail: freekiv@sovam.com
Contact: Adrian Hewryk

See profile of Freedom House in section *Special Focus Organizations.*

Fund of Ukraine to Protect Invalids
vul. Nikolsko-Slobodskaya 2A
252097   Kyiv
Tel: 516-8704
Fax: 516-8744
Contact: Valeriy Chbarov, Managing Director

Green Dossier
a/ya 295
252025   Kyiv-25
Tel: 213-2678
Fax: 213-2600
E-mail: dossier@gd.freenet.kiev.ua
Contact: Tamara Malkova, Director

Green Dossier was registered in 1992 as a special center for the compilation and dissemination of environmental information. Current projects include the support of a small Eco-library;

regular publication of an information bulletin "Children Under the Sun" and a Model Organization brochure; as well as conducting training courses and publishing a related newspaper.

Green Dossier is currently producing an environmental television program oriented toward young people in Ukraine.

The organization also works in conjunction with similar organizations in Belarus and Moldova, conducting mobile training courses for NGOs. Paid staff numbers three to five persons depending upon different projects, and 10-15 volunteers.

Greenpeace–Ukraine
vul. Zhitomyrska 27B, #8
Kyiv
Tel/Fax: 212-2943
Contact: Olga Savran, Exeutive Director; Andriy Pleskonos

"Helsinki-90"
Kyiv
Tel: 411-8715, 228-0306
E-mail: jenia@hels90.kiev.ua
Contact: Evgenii Dikii, Vasil Ovsienko

History of Ukrainian Press Research Center
Institute of Journalism, kom. 204-205
vul. Melnykova 36/1
252119   Kyiv
Tel/Fax: 220-6063
E-mail:
osydorenko@iopa.freenet.kiev.ua
Contact: Natalia Sydorenko, Executive Director

The center was founded in 1992 by faculty and students at the Department of Journalism at Kyiv State University, but only officially registered as an independent nonprofit organization in September

1995. A main goal of the center is to investigate how a national journalism developed and was sustained in Ukraine and abroad.

As part of this project, the center has published *Ukrainian Periodicals Abroad* (Winnipeg and Kyiv, 1994). It also held a conference on this theme in early 1996.

The center is working on the creation of a database on Ukrainian journalism from the 19th century to the present. It is also pursuing the expansion of its library's holdings of periodicals and materials on the history of national movements, Ukrainian culture, and national life among immigrants.

The center does not attempt to influence legislation or work for partisan political aims. It does not have any paid staff; all work is done by volunteers, most of whom are associated with the Institute of Journalism. It publishes a periodic newsletter.

HOPE–International Help Fund for Mentally Underdeveloped Children
vul. Sofiyevska 16/17
252001   Kyiv
Tel: 228-5592
Contact: Mykola Nazar, Head

Institute of Statehood and Democracy
bul. Taras Shevchenko 37/122, kom. 304
252032   Kyiv
Tel/Fax: 244-6409
Contact: Ivan Lozowy, Executive Director
E-mail: lozowy@gluk.apc.org

The institute's principal aims are to propagate the ideal of statehood, assist in the dissemination of democratic values, the building of a rule-of-law society and the development of an independent national policy. The institute was registered in June 1995 as a nonprofit civic organization. Its ten founders include five prominent Ukrainian politicians and five private businessmen. The institute's principal task is to establish and run a program of study in politics and governance in Ukraine in order to promote the education and skills of Ukraine's political leaders.

Though the institute was created as an initiative by the Popular Movement of Ukraine "Rukh," Ukraine's "largest national-democratic political organization," it seeks to engage all national-democratic activists from Ukraine's eastern and southern regions.

The institute's first seminars began in November 1995 and have been centered in three areas: skills building, including personnel management skills, computer skills, English language instruction; academic studies including macroeconomics and political science; and political activity skills such as political campaigning, constituent services and organization-building.

A total of 1,000 politicians and activists are expected to participate in the institute's courses per year.

Independent Association of Ukrainian Psychiatrists
Kyiv
Tel: 41-9467
Contact: Semyon Gluzman

International Independent Association for Sobriety
vul. Volodymyrska 54
a/ya 946
252150   Kyiv

Tel: 224-8408
Fax: 224-1579
Contact: Konstantyn Krasovskyy,
Executive Director

International Executive Service Corps

vul. Zankovetskoi 7, #21
252001   Kyiv
Tel: 228-1165
Fax: 229-2995
E-mail: ajh@gemini.kiev.ua
postmaster@iescu.freenet.kiev.ua

See profile of IESC in section *Special Focus Organizations.*

International Management Institute–Kyiv

pr. Peremohy 54/1
252057   Kyiv
Tel: 446-2451
Fax: 446-2447
E-mail:
imikievadm@sovcust.sprint.com
Contact: Andrei Masiuk, Director;
Bohdan Hawrylyshyn, Chairman of the
Board

IMI–Kyiv was established in 1989 as a
joint venture between the Institute of
Economics of the Ukrainian Academy of
Sciences and the International
Management Institute of Geneva (IMI–
Geneva). It was the first such institute in
the Soviet Union to offer a one-year
MBA program based on a Western
European model. By early 1995 IMI–
Kyiv had graduated six classes and more
than 300 MBAs.
    Beginning in 1996 IMI–Kyiv will add
to its program short-term institutes (one
to four weeks) designed for top executives or government officials. It will also
eventually move its classes to a facility
of Kyiv Technical University, which is

presently being remodeled for this purpose.

International Media Center
Information and Press Center

Internews Representative Office
vul. Khreshchatyk 4
252001   Kyiv
Tel: 229-3110, 229-3645
Fax   229-3690
E-mail: ipc@gluk.apc.org or
         imc@sovam.com
Contact: Liubov Pavliukh, Gennadi
Potchtar, Coordinators

IMC is involved in a number of projects, including:
• supporting the development of an
independent broadcasting industry in
Ukraine, by lending studio facilities and
production equipment to fledgling
independent TV stations;
• holding a series of seminars and
workshops for local journalists with
specialists from Ukraine and abroad;
• translating materials for the teaching
of journalism;
• maintaining a reference library and
information center for journalists.
    IMC has an e-mail station, where
lessons in its use are offered.

International Renaissance Foundation

vul. Artema 46
254053   Kyiv
Tel: 216-2596, 216-1324
Fax: 216-7629
E-mail: uarf@vidr.kiev.ua
Contact: Bohdan Budzan

A major initiative of the Soros-funded
International Renaissance Foundation
has been its Retraining of the Military
Program.

RMP aims to aid as many as 60,000 discharged and retired servicemen in "finding a place in the development of Ukraine's civil society." The RMP was established in December 1993 and offers help in three areas: professional psychological consultations; retraining or upgrading of qualifications in a variety of specialties; and job placement. Over 50 educational institutions provide courses in a variety of specialties. RMP pays up to 90% of program participants' costs, estimated at about $79 per serviceman, with the participants paying the remainder. As of early 1995, 10,375 veterans had participated in the program.

RMP, with the help of the French Centre de Formation aux Realités Internationales, is also working to create new jobs for its graduates. Its Officers Enterprises subprogram teaches ex-servicemen how to start businesses, and can offer grants of up to $1,000 for entrepreneurial ventures. The address for RMP is:

Retraining of the Military Program
vul. Turhevnivska 82, kv. 7
254053   Kyiv
Tel: 216-3291
Fax: 216-9163

International Science Foundation
vul. Bogomolets 4
252024   Kyiv
Tel: 293-4877, 293-1661,
             293-4577
Fax: 293-7223
E-mail: sf-ua@pub.isf.kiev.ua

See the profile for ISF in section *Special Focus Organizations.*

ISAR–Kyiv
Kyiv
Tel: 269-2157
E-mail: isar@isar.freenet.kiev.ua
             isarkyyiv@gluk.apc.org
             isar@isar.kiev.ua
Contact: Alyson Ewald

ISAR's Kyiv office serves Belarus and Moldova, too. Environmental networking includes a focus on nuclear power issues represented by Chernobyl and similar plants. (Profile of ISAR is in section *Clearinghouse Organizations.*)

Liga Artis–Organization of Ukrainian Creative Youth
vul. Bogomoltsa 8A, #28
Kyiv
Tel: 559-3243, 244-2341
Fax: 518-1740
Contact: Anna Klimenko

Liga Artis establishes contacts and exchanges with art groups, and takes part in international festivals and contests. The organization would like to receive technical assistance in the following areas: organizational and financial management, leadership training, computer training, and publicity.

Life Time
Kyiv
Fax: 290-6429
Contact: Svetlana Antonyak

Life Time is an association of HIV and AIDS-infected persons. The main activities of Life Time include social and psychological counseling, legal and financial support, organization of non-governmental medical care to the HIV and AIDS-infected persons of Ukraine. Life Time also provides general information and education about HIV and AIDS.

LYBID–Ukrainian International Charity Federation of Businesswomen

vul. B. Hrynchenka 1, #118
252001   Kyiv
Tel: 229-8545, 274-2501
Fax: 228-2893
Contact: Tamara Suplina, President

MAMA 86–Kyiv Children's Environmental Organization

vul. Mikhaylovskaya 22A
252001   Kyiv
Tel: 475-6218 (home)
Tel/Fax: 228-3101
E-mail: mama86@gluk.apc.org
Contact: Ann Syomina

Founded in 1990 by a group of young mothers, this is a charitable organization which focuses on ecology and children's health. The number 86 represents the year of the Chernobyl explosion.

Memorial of Vasyl Stus– Ukrainian Cultural Educational Organization

Lesi Ukrayinsky Sq. 1
252025   Kyiv
Tel: 296-1433
Fax: 296-1360
Contact: Les Tanyuk

This organization focuses on cultural, educational and legal issues. Vasyl Stus is a widely-admired poet of mid-twentieth century Ukraine.

National Ecological Centre of Ukraine

a/ya 89/7
252025   Kyiv

E-mail: kost@necu.freenet.kiev.ua
Contact: Vasiliy A. Kostyushin, Executive Director

The National Ecological Centre of Ukraine (EcoCentre) was registered by the Ministry of Justice of Ukraine as a nongovernmental organization in 1991. Its purpose is to join the efforts of scientists, public figures, environmental groups, and citizen activists in projects to improve the environmental situation in Ukraine.

In 1992 EcoCentre obtained six grants from the Committee for Science and Technology of Ukraine for scientific projects. The most important ones were an evaluation of the state of the Azov water basin for its rehabilitation, and development of plans for aerospace monitoring of vegetation in Ukraine.   Also in 1992 other branches of EcoCentre were established in Kyiv, Berdyansk, Dnipropetrovsk, Kryvyi Ryh, Mariupol, Lviv, Mykolaiv, Sumy, Kherson, Cherkasy, Chernivtsi, Kharkiv, and Donetsk.

Since 1991 EcoCentre has been a partner of Global ReLeaf International, sponsored by American Forests. In cooperation with Global ReLeaf, EcoCentre developed a program, "Green Halo of Ukraine," which included the development of a Heritage Park in Kyiv. On Earth Day members of EcoCentre and of the National Committee in support of European Nature Conservation Year–1995, together with schoolboys and schoolgirls, planted trees at the Heritage Park in Kyiv. Tree planting actions were also conducted in Vinnitsa city and Vinnitska oblast.

EcoCentre has conducted 20 scientific projects, the most important of which were: "The Priorities, Concept and National Strategy of Nature Use in

Ukraine;" "An Investigation of the Impact of the Chernobyl Disaster on Vegetation in the 30-Km Zone;" and "National Report on the Environmental Situation in Ukraine in 1992."

Since 1991 EcoCentre has published an independent bi-monthly scientific and public magazine *Oykumena: Ukrainian Ecological Review*. At the end of 1993 EcoCentre formed the Institute of Ecology to carry on work on scientific problems in areas of ecology and nature protection. In 1994 it founded the Dovkillya (Environment) Publishing Agency.

EcoCentre now has 17 branches throughout Ukraine and more than 300 members, including an active youth division. EcoCentre staff numbers seven people (two full-time). Three of these are members of the magazine *Oykumena*'s editorial staff.

Nova Mova–Mass Media Center for Reform Support
vul. Instytutska 7
Kyiv
Tel: 293-7403, 293-8256
Contact: Oleksandr Tkachenko, Director; Igor Kulyas

Project on Economic Reform in Ukraine
vul. Gorky 23b, kv. 42
252005   Kyiv
Tel: 227-22-04, 220-63-68
Fax: 227-44-56
E-mail: peru@peru.freenet.kiev.ua
Contact: David Snelbecker, Associate Director

See the profile for PERU in the section *Special Focus Organizations*.

Pylyp Orlyk Institute for Democracy
vul. Moskovskaya 40-A
252015   Kyiv
Tel: 290-7756, 290-6563
Fax: 290-6464
Contact: Valentina Telychenko, Deputy Director

The institute is an independent public policy research institute which seeks to promote the principles of democracy, a free market economy, rule of law, and national security reform among policymakers and the general public. POIP prepares analysis of pending legislation for Ukrainian legislators and issues a variety of publications. The institute was founded in 1992 with the assistance of the U.S.-Ukraine Foundation.

"Rakhamim"–Jewish Humanitarian Organization
bul. Lepse 17, #68
252124   Kyiv
Tel: 484-1446
Contact: Faina Neiman

Red Cross–Ukraine
vul. Pushkinska 30
252004   Kyiv
Tel: 225-0157, 225-0334
Fax: 225-1096
Contact: Ivan Usichenko, Director; Nadiya Lapko, Deputy

"Resistance" Information Center
a/ya 279/9
252142   Kyiv
Tel: 444-4395, 446-2142
Fax: 444-3432, 519-8859
E-mail:
office@resistance.freenet.kiev.ua

Contact: Dr. Alexander N. Podlipenets, Managing Director; Dr. Victor V. Lyakh, President

Resistance is a private information exchange center currently attempting to remedy some of the problems faced by the mechanical engineering community in Ukraine. Its mission is to promote free information flow within Ukraine and to assist in the establishment of links between people and organizations involved in mechanical engineering around the world.

In particular, the center has started to pursue these objectives through:
• introducing electronic communications to scientists and engineers in Ukraine;
• assisting in the preparation, publication and dissemination of papers, booklets, short communications, advertisements, etc. (especially for international editions),
• identifying professional partnerships for mechanical engineers in Ukraine and abroad and putting Ukrainian engineers in contact with responsible authorities in other countries;
• assisting in and serving as secretariat for the preparation and translation of international program projects; and,
• realizing projects in the field of mechanics, acoustics, physics and engineering.

Future activities include the following:
• the production of specialised databases, electronic journals, books, teleconferences, etc.,
• organizing consulting, seminars, exhibitions, conferences, and other meetings that pertain to mechanical engineering;
• the distribution of specialised software on a commercial basis.

Rule of Law Consortium
ARD/Checchi
Dom Kino
6 Saksaganskogo
252033 Kyiv
Tel: 227-4617
Fax: 220-8505
E-Mail: mara@ruleoflaw2.kiev.ua
Contact: Mara Moldwin, Grants Manager

See ARD/Checchi profile in section *Special Focus Organizations.*

Small Business Assistance Fund
vul. Gorkogo 47
252005 Kyiv
Tel: 227-0102
Contact: Galyna Iganska, President

SOKIL–Youth Organization of Union of Ukrainian Officers
vul. Grushevskogo 30/1, #330
Kyiv
Tel: 220-0221
Fax: 220-1294
Contact: Olcksiy Milenin, Director; Igor Ponomar, Media

This organization is a labor and professional organization aimed at Ukrainian youth.

Soldier's Mothers Organization of Ukraine
vul. Antonova 4/5
252186 Kyiv
Tel: 277-1104, 245-6194
Contact: Valentyna Artamonova, Director

Soyuz Ukrainok (Ukraine)
bul. Shevchenko 37/122
252032 Kyiv

Tel: 294-8667, 224-9151
Fax: 216-8333
Contact: Atena Pashko, Director

Special Olympics Ukraine
vul. Kuibyshev 42
252023   Kyiv
Tel: 274-7418
Fax: 220-1294
Contact: Ms. Victoria Shelkovnikova,
Executive Director

SUS–Union of Ukrainian Students
vul. Prorizna 27
252034   Kyiv
Tel: 229-2967
Tel/Fax: 229-5834
Contact: Volodymyr Kit, Director;
Yuriy Grabovskyy, Secretariat Chief

St. Andrew's Ukrainian Orthodox Society
vul. Gorkogo 9, #12
252005   Kyiv
Tel/Fax: 227-3269
Contact: Yarina Timoshenko, Social
Service Committee Chairperson

Talented Children of Ukraine Fund
vul. Schorsa 36
252133   Kyiv
Tel: 269-9832, 269-7761
Contact: Victor Mischenko, President

This fund is a charitable cultural
organization for children.

Ukraina Foreign Economic Association
a/ya 475
252023   Kyiv
Tel/Fax: 416-4593

Contact: A. Romanenko, President; V.
Vazach, General Director

Established in 1992, this association
works to develop small business in
Ukraine through increased contacts with
foreign investors.

Ukrainian-American Bureau for the Support of Human Rights
Kyiv
Tel: 410-4160
E-mail: uabphr@sovamsu.sovusa.com
Contact: Semyon Gluzman

Ukrainian Association of Christian Businessmen
vul. Tolstogo 3A
252005   Kyiv
Tel: 545-5472
Tel/Fax: 515-6191
Contact: Oleksandr Shenbuk, President

Ukrainian Association of Political Prisoners and the Repressed
vul. Peremoga 16, #119
252135   Kyiv
Tel: 226-2223, 212-8395,
               291-5591, 274-6131,
               291-5470
Contact: Yevgen Pronyuk, Co-
President; Vasil Gurdzan, Vice Chairman

The association publishes a periodical
Zona and occasional monographs
documenting the witness of political
prisoners and those otherwise re-
pressed.

Ukrainian Association of Women Cinematographers
vul. Saksaganskogo 6/112
252035   Kyiv
Tel: 245-5406

Fax: 227-3130
Contact: Sylvia Sergeichikova, President

Ukrainian Center for Human Rights

vul. Chervonoarmiyska 64
252005 Kyiv
Tel: 227-2124
Tel/Fax: 227-2398
Contact: Valerii Sheludko, V. Evintov

The center was established in November 1993 and is under the Ukrainian Lawyers' Fund. Its overarching objective is to establish the importance of human rights in Ukraine. UCHR assists with the drafting of legislation, develops educational programs for Ukrainian schools, researches human rights issues, and conducts training seminars and workshops for human rights activists. In 1994 the center signed an agreement with the Ministry of Education to develop a human rights curriculum for Ukrainian students in grades 10 and 11. It maintains a database of human rights organizations in Ukraine. In 1995 it established a network of human rights organizations throughout Ukraine.

UCHR issues a number of publications, including: *Herald of the UCHR*, a bulletin of human rights activities in Ukraine; *Ukrainian Journal of Human Rights*, a bi-lingual (Ukrainian and English) quarterly bulletin that includes analysis of human rights legislation in Ukraine and other countries; and the annual *Yearbook of Human Rights in Ukraine*, which is also available in Ukrainian and English.

Ukrainian Center for Independent Political Research

vul. B. Khelmnytsky 78, kom. 25

252030 Kyiv
Tel: 224-9315
Tel/Fax: 224-7742
E-mail: kam@political.kiev.ua
Contact: Ms. Inna Pidluska (Foreign Relations Division); Dmitry Koublitsky, (Post-Soviet Studies Division)

The center was established in early 1991 as a nonprofit, nonpartisan and nongovernmental research institution. A group of young journalists and political analysts established this interdisciplinary, policy-oriented research institution outside the traditional university system and not under state control–albeit with close ties to both the academic and the political worlds. Its purpose is to "enhance the awareness of the Ukrainian people of democracy and to further the analytical research of Ukrainian domestic and international politics and security."

UCIPR has hosted numerous conferences, workshops, seminars and round table discussions, and also produces a number of publications. These include: *Ukrainian News, Military Bulletin, UCIPR's Notes, Ukraine in Documents*, and the UCIPR *Daily News Report.*

The center is working to establish a network of similar offices throughout Ukraine. Through these offices UCIPR plans to create a nationwide database of information on Ukrainian politicians, parties, public movements, enterprises and major events occurring in Ukraine since 1991. There are also plans for a new independent foreign affairs quarterly, *The International Dimension.*

Ukrainian Center for International Security Studies

a/ya 541
252023 Kyiv
Fax/Tel: 410-3507

E-mail: globus@uciss.FreeNet.kiev.ua
Contact: Dr. Leonid Belousov, President; Mr. Alexander Levchenko, M.A., Vice-President, Research and Development

UCISS was formed in 1991 to study and analyze national, regional and global security issues. The center is an independent, commercial research, limited liability company. It brings together specialists working in multiple disciplines in order to carry out research projects. The center is able to attract leading Ukrainian analysts for individual and collective research by offering the studies on a contract basis.

Most of the center's experts are advisors and scientific consultants to government and the Ukrainian Supreme Rada (parliament).

Ukrainian Center for Women's Studies

vul. Konstantinovska 19/15
254071   Kyiv
Tel: 417-5643
Fax: 225-5330
Contact: Dr. Svetlana Kupryashkina, Director

The center has completed an extensive survey assessing the economic, political and social status of Ukrainian women. It is also working with the League of Women Voters in the U.S. under a grant designed to bring Ukrainian and Russian women together in the U.S. in order to observe the workings of democracy and the rule of law first hand.

Ukrainian Committee for Helsinki Citizen's Assembly

Kyiv
Tel/Fax: 224-3208
Contact: Natalya Belitser

Ukrainian Committee for Support of Human Rights

Kyiv
Tel: 229-7910
Contact: Lyudmila Vansovskaya

Ukrainian Consumer's Association

Maidan Nezaleznosti 2
252001   Kyiv
Tel: 216-7249
Fax: 446-7484
Contact: Gennadiy Kuznetsov, General Director

Ukrainian Environmental Education and Information Center

Department of International Relations
Ministry for Environmental Protection of Ukraine
vul. Khreshchatykaya 5
252001   Kyiv
Tel: 412-4509
Fax: 266-9475, 228-7798
E-mail: eeic@gluk.apc.org
              ademydenko@glas.apc.org
              ademydenko@igc.apc.org
Contact: Dr. Andriy Demydenko

In cooperation with the Ukrainian Ministry of Environmental Protection and the U.S. Environmental Protection Agency, the UEEIC will attempt to familiarize the Ukrainian public with U.S. environmental standards, know-how and technology, and create potential business opportunities for U.S. companies.

Ukrainian Federation of Trade Unions

Maidan Nezaleznosti 2
252001   Kyiv
Tel: 228-8788

Fax: 229-0087
Contact: Aleksandr Stoyan, Director

Ukrainian Legal Foundation

Bohdana Khmelnytskoho 10, kv.59
252030 Kyiv
Tel: 224-0197
Fax: 225-5330
E-mail: postmaster@ulf.freenet.kiev.ua
Contact: Halyna Freeland, Director of External Relations

The Ukrainian Legal Foundation was founded in 1992 by members of the executive committee of the Association of Ukrainian Lawyers and lawyers from the Ukrainian diaspora. ULF's projects include: creation of the Ukrainian Center for Human Rights (see description above); an active legal scholarship publication program; establishment of legal library collections; and consultation on the major constitutional /legislative issues in Ukraine.

ULF's directing Board of Supervisors includes: Serhiy Holovaty, Ukraine's Minister of Justice and ULF's President; two attorneys from Canada; Secretary of the Ukrainian-British Law Society and past President of the Ukrainian American Law Society; the President of the High Court of Arbitration of Ukraine; and other prominent Ukrainian government and academic officials. With this collection of important and diverse figures in Ukraine's legal society, ULF has been able to play a key role in the development of Ukrainian constitutional law. In 1994 ULF played a critical role in the drafting and passage of Ukraine's Constitutional Accord and the Law on State Power and Local Self-Government, which helped break the constitutional impasse that was blocking economic and political reform in Ukraine since its independence.

In February 1994 ULF established the National Legal Library of Ukraine, the country's first legal library. In 1995, with assistance from the U.S.-based Sabre Foundation, it began to develop a network of such libraries by establishing a branch in Kharkiv. Future libraries will be established in Lviv and Odessa. ULF's publishing program includes: a quarterly journal, *Ukrainian Law*; books of legal codification; and the publication of drafts of laws. In 1995 ULF, in cooperation with the American Bar Association, initiated a project that will result in the establishment of a professional organization of lawyers in Ukraine.

ULF's 1995 budget exceeded $2 million, of which nearly half came from the Soros/Karl Popper Foundation. The second largest ULF donor was the European Union.

Ukrainian National Committee of Youth Organization

vul. Esplanadna 42, #810
252021 Kyiv
Tel: 220-0221
Fax: 220-1294
Contact: Oleksiy Milenin, Director

Ukrainian Society of the Blind

vul. Percherskyy Uzviz 3
252023 Kyiv
Tel: 224-1127, 224-0592
225-3347
Fax: 225-6227
Contact: Volodymyr Pilchyg, Director

Union Of Afghanistan War Veterans

Kyiv
Fax: 519-7890
Contact: Alexander Zudin

The Union of Afghanistan War Veterans provides social assistance to the disabled, families of war veterans, and orphans. The organization also invests in small plants for the manufacture of consumer goods. The union seeks technical and training assistance in financial and labor management, assistance with charitable help to invalids, educational and practical training of specialists, delivery of equipment to the social rehabilitation centers, and provision of medical care abroad.

Union of Independent Businessmen

vul. Kutuzova 18/7, #617
Kyiv
Tel: 295-2539
Fax: 295-8718
Contact: Anatoliy Khorozov, President

Union of Ukrainian Students– Cinema Producers

vul. Saksaganskogo 6
252035 Kyiv
Tel: 434-4776
Fax: 269-0249, 559-8671
Contact: Katerina Kondratsova

The union supports the process of development of the Ukrainian school of cinema producers. It provides members with material, legal, organizational and other forms of assistance.

Volunteers in Overseas Cooperative Assistance
Ukraine Office
16 Shevchenka bul.
252030 Kyiv
Tel/Fax: 224-3322
E-mail: voca@voca.freenet.kiev.ua
Contact: Ted Gashler, Country Representative

VOCA has been in Ukraine since 1992 and has had 163 projects since opening. Its purpose is to help build up agriculture and agribusiness and the democratic way of life and help Ukraine establish a free market economy. (See VOCA profile in section *Special Focus Organizations*.)

VOCA Ukraine has helped establish many food processing and other value added businesses throughout the country. It has also helped many private farmers get started and improve profitability.

The current emphasis of its activities is on food processing in the private sector and agricultural education in all the agricultural universities and institutes. Paid staff includes one American and three Ukrainians.

Women's Club

pr. Vastionii 11, kv. 57
Kyiv
Tel: 271-5628, 296-2043
Contact: Maria Gashyak-Vlad

Women's Information and Social Adaption Center

vul. Vologimirska 22, kv. 11
or
vul. Saksaganskogo 88, kv. 101
Kyiv
Tel: 220-9750
Contact: Valentina Smirnova

The center is active in research, publishing and education.

Women's Legal Center

vul. Kosiora 10
Kyiv
Tel: 225-3110, 299-7310
Contact: Ludmila Vantsovskaya, Galina Laustova

The center promotes the legal rights of women and job retraining.

Women's Union of Ukraine

vul. Institutska 16/3
252021 Kyiv
Tel: 293-5311, 293-6778
Fax: 293-1532
Contact: Mariya Orlik, Chair; Valentyna Dovzhenko, Secretary

Youth Alternative

vul. V-Vasilevskaya 6, kv. 211
252116 Kyiv
Tel: 422-1270
Fax: 417-2426
Contact: Luba Shara

Zelenyi Khrest/Green Cross

vul. Sevastopolskaya 5
253091 Kyiv
Tel: 562-7810, 530-2449
Contact: Vladimar Lisovyi

Zeleny Khrest works to "support citizens in need of social help, professional training and retraining, and job placement." The association is seeking assistance with medicine and medical equipment for the disabled and veterans.

Zeleny Svit/Green World

vul. Mykhailivska 6, kom. 306
252001 Kyiv
Tel: 228-6425
Fax: 228-1086
E-mail:
 anufr@nikgrpc.freenet.kiev.ua
 fedoryn@grworld.freenet.kiev.ua
Contact: Serghiy Fedorynchyk, Chief, ZS Information Center

Zeleny Svit, a federation of local environmental groups, has in the aggregate nearly 3,000 members but many thousand more supporters across Ukraine. In recent years some representatives of ZS were elected to municipal or regional offices. (The biggest number is in Chernihiv, which has 15 "green" deputies.)

ZS has lobbied for a halt to further construction at the Chernobyl Nuclear Power Plant, for the use of unleaded gasoline, and for assistance to victims of the Chernobyl accident. Zeleny Svit has staged scores of meetings, demonstrations, pickets, tests and examinations, and has worked on public environmental education projects.

Zeleny Svit was founded by a group of Kyiv writers and artists in December 1987 and established as a national organisation at its first Congress in October 1989. The by-laws of ZS were registered with the Ukrainian Ministry of Justice in December 1992. Since 1991 ZS has been an associate member of Friends of the Earth International.

All local ZS organisations–there were more than 70 in 1995–are fully independent as long as they operate in accordance with ZS by-laws. A "Green Council," consisting of representatives of different regions of Ukraine, meets periodically to discuss and coordinate activities.

Local ZS groups carry out different activities, usually organised around local environmental problems. Among these are: tree planting, environmental tourism, protests against pollution, human rights protection issues, providing independent environmental expertise, and so on.

Presently, the main priorities of ZS activities include: environmental education; revision of the Law for the Protection of Nature and public pressure on its violators; and development of

ZS groups as model communities, or examples of civil society: that is, builders of democracy and its institutions from a grassroots level.

Zhinocha Hromada (Women's Community)
vul. Zolotovoritska 6
Kyiv
Tel: 227-2420
Tel/Fax: 227-2401
Contact: Mariya Drach, Director; Ms. Halyna Zhulinska, Deputy Head

This is a women's organization with branches in other cities of Ukraine.

Aleksandria (05235)

Memorial Society
pr. Lenina107
317900 Aleksandria
Tel: 20-311, 36-277
Contact: Vilen Ochakovskii

Cherkasy (472)

Memorial Society
vul. Frunze 1
Cherkasy
Tel: 47-03-05
Contact: Svetlana Sidorchuk

Ya Zhinka Women's Center
vul. Gogol 250, kv. 68
257002 Cherkasy
Tel: 45-20-57
E-mail: yazhinka@gluk.apc.org
Fax: c/o John Masura 45-08-08
Contact: Victoria Kuzmina, Director and Magazine Editor; Katya Koval, Center Director.

Ya Zhinka is a legally registered small enterprise. It is both a women's magazine and a social center. The magazine was first published in 1992, while the women's center began in 1994. The purpose of *Ya Zhinka*, the magazine, is to present and discuss information and issues of importance to Ukrainian women. The magazine and center deal with women's problems at all levels: political, economic, social, and personal. *Ya Zhinka* is now operated primarily by volunteers and with limited outside support.

Cherkasy is the sister city of Santa Rosa, California and since 1985 people from the two cities have been meeting on various levels. Journalists became involved early in reporting on these meetings and it was in this process that several women journalists in Cherkasy began to learn more about the lives of women in America, about women's issues and publications, and decided to launch their own women's magazine in Cherkasy.

The Women's Center developed as an outgrowth of the magazine. Women started gathering with the journalists and discussing various issues. They met also with women visiting from Santa Rosa, especially therapists trained in leading women's groups. A group of about 20 Cherkasy women began to meet weekly and invited local psychologists, gynecologists, alcoholism specialists, and other professionals to meet with them and share information. A Santa Rosa woman who had seen this desire growing purchased a three-room flat in Cherkasy and has offered it rent free as a home for the magazine and women's center.

One recent exchange resulted in a long term plan to build a rehabilitation center in Cherkasy utilizing Santa Rosa equipment and training. To continue these various programs a nonprofit corporation, Ukrainian and American Women's Action Project, has been formed in Santa Rosa, California. The address for the magazine is:

Ya Zhinka
vul. Sumgaetskaya 16, kv. 7
257032   Cherkasy

Chernihiv (4622)

Memorial Society
pr. Okt. Revolyutsii, 102-42
250000   Chernihiv
Tel: 7-56-05
Contact: Vitalii Rostalnoi

Chernivtsi (3722)

National Ecocenter of Ukraine
Chernivsti
E-mail: petro@bukovina.chernovtsy.ua
Contact: Yuri Masikevich, Alexander Rezhko

The center addresses the issues of environmental education, independent river monitoring, preservation and restoration of the Carpathian forests, and environmental tourism.

Zhinocha Hromada
64A Nezalezhnosti pr., #23
274018   Chernivtsi
Tel: 3-35-08, 5-37-79
Fax: 3-35-08
Contact: Halyna Tarasyuk, Director

Dnipropetrovsk (562)

Alcoholics Anonymous
Dnipropetrovsk
Tel: 47-21-08
Contact: Tamara

FYI Information Resources
a/ya 2797
320094   Dnipropetrovsk
Tel/Fax: 41-77-30
Contact: Sergei Dascalu, Project Manager

Global Jewish Assistance Relief Network, Ukrainian Affiliate
vul. Sverdlova 6, kv. 313-315
320101   Dnipropetrovsk
Tel: 78-34-43
E-mail: gjarndniepr@gluk.apc.org

The Ukrainian Affiliate of GJARN provides humanitarian relief to needy people in Ukraine.

International Renaissance Foundation–Dnipropetrovsk
pr. Karla Marksa 35, korp. 4, kom. 40
Dnipropetrovsk
Tel: 44-81-76
Fax: 44-26-31
E-mail: vidrodg@tjs.dneprop.ua
Contact: Ivan Shpitun

Memorial Society
vul. Berezinska 23-107
320125   Dnipropetrovsk
Tel: 65-45-01, 24-16-67
Contact: Yelvira Birtukova, Iosif Dzenish

Pridnieper Ecological Foundation
a/ya 4159
320002   Dnipropetrovsk

Tel: 41-60-38
Fax: 41-65-90
E-mail:
andrey@ecofund.Dnipropetrovsk.ua

In May 1995, PEF organized an international conference on "Industrial and Agricultural Changes for Environmental Improvement in the Dnieper and Black Sea Region."

Union of Ukrainian Women

pr. Karla Marksa 35
Dnipropetrovsk
Tel: 44-81-76
Contact: Elena Nazarenko

Networking, social problems, women in national traditions.

Donetsk (622)

Bakhmat Environmental and Cultural Center of Green Movement of Donbass

vul. Gorbatova 45/20
343400 Artyomovsk
Donetsk region
Tel/Fax: (06274) 3-59-54
E-mail: berezin@bahmat.donetsk.ua
Contact: Vladimir Berezin, director

ECC Bakhmat was formed in 1990 as part of the national ecological organization *Zeleny Svit* (Green World). It registered in 1995 as the Environmental and Cultural Center Bakhmat.

Bakhmat's first initiatives were to restore the historical names of towns, streets and monuments in their region; and to protect the local river Bakhmut from pollution.

Nobody is paid in the organization. Membership consists of 200 volunteers, among which the most active number

50. Among its accomplishments, ECC Bakhmat states that:
• 20% of its members have won electoral campaigns and become deputies in the local parliament;
• it succeeded in creating a weekly eco-program on local TV;
• illegal waste disposals into the river Bakhmut have stopped;
• representatives of ECC Bakhmat have participated in a number of international conferences on problems of the environment such as "Eco-forum '95" in Kyiv.

Among priorities for future activities are the creation of public environmental television in Donbass and Ukraine; developing cultural and environmental NGO partnerships with Western organizations; and locating funding sources. All of the organization's work is done by volunteers from its membership of 200.

Center For Political Studies

vul. Universitetska 24
340055 Donetsk
Tel: 92-40-97
Fax: 92-60-67
E-mail: greg@cps.donetsk.ua
Contact: Dr. Gregory Nemiria, Director

CPS is located in Donetsk University. Founded in 1992, it pursues two primary objectives: education and research. By introducing Western-style education, CPS hopes to promote the development of a democratic culture and open society in Ukraine. Additionally, CPS conducts regional public opinion polls and seeks to organize theoretically grounded and policy-relevant research on both the domestic and foreign politics of Ukraine and Eastern Europe.

CPS director Nemiria was educated at Donetsk and Kyiv Universities. Dr. Nemiria is a specialist in international relations and comparative politics. He is an Adjunct Fellow of the Center for Strategic and International Studies, Washington, DC.

CPS has an agreement with the Civic Education Project, based in New Haven, CT, for Western academics to teach social science courses at Donetsk University. CPS also has an active student exchange program with the Central European University in Prague.

International Renaissance Foundation

bul. Shevchenka 25, kom. 207-209
340017   Donetsk
Tel: 95-47-50
Fax: 92-60-67
E-mail: found@soros.donetsk.ua
Contact: Viacheslav Koval

See IRF profile under Kyiv.

Memorial Society

a/ya 4863
vul. Artema 163a-26
340048   Donetsk
Tel: 55-07-48, 23-07-95
Contact: Aleksandr Bukalov, Boris Parsenyuk

Drogobych (03244)

Amnesty International

vul. Vladimira Velikogo 12, kv. 29
Drogobych
Tel: 3-95-05
Contact: Mioslav Marinovich

Ivano-Frankivsk (3422)

Soyuz Ukrainok (Ivano-Frankivsk)

vul. Pushkina 117-A, #23
284000   Ivano-Frankivsk
Contact: Paraska Rykhtyk, Director

Kharkiv (572)

ACCELS Kharkiv

ul. Sumskaja 13, kom. 9-10
310057   Kharkiv
Tel: 12-78-29
E-mail:
fsa.kharkov@sovcust.sprint.com

See the profile for ACTR/ACCELSin section *Special Focus Organizations*.

BEREGYNYA–Kharkiv Women's Association

vul. Sumskaya 64
310002   Kharkiv
Tel: 43-29-38, 40-52-87
Contact: Lyubov Chub, President

Center for Educational Initiatives

vul. Sumskaya 37
310002   Kharkiv
Tel: 47-16-32, 12-02-61
Fax: 47-16-32
E-mail: vita@cei.kharkov.ua
Contact: Victor Pasisnichenko, CEI Coordinating Board Member

The regional charitable foundation Center for Educational Initiatives was started in the summer of 1992 by a group of Ukrainian scholars and educators. In 1994 it was established as an autonomous charitable foundation dedicated to nongovernmental support and reform of education as a high priority in transitional Ukrainian society. CEI director Pasisnichenko is a Ph.D. Candidate in Philosophy.

CEI has received substantial funding from the Soros Foundation. It has two divisions, a Humanities Center and a School Leaders Center. A Coordinating Board, which consists of the leaders of initiative groups, prominent scholars and representatives of the municipal Board of Education, sets basic strategy for the organization.

CEI's mission is to find and direct resources toward meritorious individual educators, scholars and initiative groups. This support seeks to promote the transformation of humanities, economic and social sciences in Ukraine through a pluralistic approach to learning and thinking.

EcoPravo–Kharkiv

a/ya 2873
310100   Kharkiv
Tel/Fax: 36-87-54, 36-82-54
E-mail: ALEX@eco.kharkov.ua
Contact: Alexei Mikhailovich Shumilo, Sergei Variamov

See EcoPravo–Lviv for description of organization.

Gender Studies Center

vul. Heroev Stalingrada 177-140
310096   Kharkiv
Tel: 47-17-56, 43-31-40
          97-57-21 (home)
Contact: Irina Zherebkina

The center is involved in research, education programs for girls, leadership training, and publishing a history of Ukrainian feminism.

"Humanitarian Initiative" Feminist Association

vul. Sumskaya 56
310002   Kharkiv
Tel: 33-44-42
Fax: 76-38-48
Contact: Katerina Levchenko, Victoria Nodgorhaya

HOPE Large Family Society

pr. Ordzhonokidzaya 6
Kharkiv
Tel: 93-71-32
Contact: Raisa Ryazanova, Chairwoman

International Renaissance Foundation–Kharkiv

vul. Chernyshevskoho 4, kv. 4
310057   Kharkiv
Tel/Fax: 19-94-48
E-mail: ren@sfond.kharkiv.ua

See IRF profile under Kyiv.

Kharkiv Local Women's Fund

bulvar Yureva 2
Kharkiv
Tel: 92-33-62, 43-27-54
Contact: Natalia Kachanova, Lilia Kim

The fund promotes entrepreneurship and women's political advocacy.

Kharkiv Legal Aid Group

a/ya 10430
vul. Artema 3, kv. 23
310002   Kharkiv
Tel: 43-17-97, 97-89-60, 68-90-39
Fax: 57-08-11
E-mail: root@khghr.kharkov.ua
Contact: Viktor Baranov, Evgenii Zakharov

Memorial Society

vul. Derevyanko 4-50
310103   Kharkiv
Tel: 33-82-11, 40-83-19, 43-91-38
Fax: 22-81-18
Contact: Evgenii Zakharov, Nina
Lapchinskaya

Myroslava–Kharkiv City Women's Club

vul. Myposytska 94, #42
310023   Kharkiv
Tel: 47-97-73
Contact: Tetyana Konokenko, President

Women's Council of Alekseyetskyy Region

Pobedy Pr. 48, #221
Kharkiv
Tel: 36-34-92
Contact: T. Dashuk, Deputy

Women's Council of Ordzhonokindze District

Kharkiv
Tel: 94-25-68
Contact: Margarita Cheryomkhina

Kherson (055)

Khersonskii Women's Fund

vul. Nerekopskaya 175, kv. 34
Kherson
Tel: 226-5151
Contact: Olga Gritsenko

Memorial Society

pr. Ushakova Gorispolkom, kom. 101
325000   Kherson
Tel: 002-3131, 004-5731
Contact: Orest Dvornikov

Titan

vul. K. Libknekhta 33
326400   Skadovsk
Kherson Region
Contact: V. Gaguyn, Director

Titan is a small collective enterprise
founded by the Charity and Health
Fund of Ukraine. Titan manufactures
foodstuffs with medicinal herb additives which allegedly help remove
radionucleides from the human body.

Khmelnytsky (03822)

Komitet Ekonomiky

Mydon Nezalezhnosty
Bydinok Rad
280005   Khmelnytsky
Tel/Fax: 6-50-13
Contact: Ludmilla Romanyuk, Economic Committee Director; Mikola
Savyuk, Director of Small Business
Development

Khmelnytsky leads Ukraine's regions in
small-scale privatization. Though
largely agricultural, the regional capital
contains a number of manufacturing
complexes. There are also a number of
defense sector facilities seeking to convert to the production of consumer
goods. The Economic Committee was
created to assist this process.

Krasnoarmeisk (06239)

Memorial Society

m-n Solnechnyi, 1–45
Krasnoarmeisk
Tel: 2-34-97
Contact: Vladimir Burik

Lviv (322)

ACCELS Lviv
Naukovo Technichniy Center
vul. 700-richa Lvova, 57
200058　Lviv
Tel:　　27-11-25
E-mail:　fsa.lviv@sovcust.sprint.com

See the profile for ACTR/ACCELS in the section *Special Focus Organizations.*

CARITAS/Small Enterprise Women Christian Society
vul. Kopernyka 15
290000　Lviv
Tel:　　76-14-79
Contact: Lidiya Nesterenko, Director

Environmental Public Advocacy Center EcoPravo–Lviv
vul. Krushelnitska 2
290000　Lviv
Tel/Fax: 72-27-46
E-mail:　epac@epac.lviv.ua
Contact: Svitlana Kravchenko

The center is a joint project between EcoPravo-Lviv and the American Bar Association's Central and East European Law Initiative (CEELI). A pilot project of CEELI, which hopes to set up a network of EPACs in Eastern Europe, the center's principal goals are:
• Environmental Protection. Empowerment of individuals and groups in their relationship with decision-makers, leading to resolution of environmental issues on a higher level.
• Legal Education. Raising the level of environmental and legal culture of citizens and NGOs.

• Public Interest Professionalism. Training a new generation of environmental lawyers, providing a practical education, with a high level of professionalism
• Promotion of Professional Support. Increased awareness by lawyers and judges of environmental issues and the need for action.
• Networking. Developing a coordinated network of legal professionals and experts throughout Ukraine.
• Civil Service. Protection of citizens' environmental rights, raising the level of responsibilities of government administrators, increasing the transparency of governmental action.

All EPAC services are offered free of charge and include:
• provision of legal and advisory services to environmental NGOs and citizens;
• consultations on legal issues;
• representation of citizens' and NGOs' interests in state and prosecutor bodies as well as in courts;
• clinical program: provision of practical legal education to students of the Law Department of Lviv State University, working on issues arising from actual cases under the supervision of highly qualified lawyers;
• organizing training programs on legal issues, advocacy topics, negotiation and alternative dispute resolution for NGOs, government and professionals such as judges, prosecutors, attorneys and others;
• creating a data base on the environmental legislation of Ukraine and other countries, establishing a small library;
• developing a regional network of legal professionals interested in environmental law and public interest advocacy;

• taking part in drafting of new environmental laws and regulations of Ukraine;
• providing accurate information on environmental and legal issues.

EPAC has other offices in Kyiv and Kharkiv.

"Future Women" Club
a/s 3139
Lviv
Tel: 62-40-35
Fax: 76-38-48
Contact: Victoria Logvinenko

Geneza Political Science Center
a/ya 7485
vul. Richchia Lvova 700
290058 Lviv
Tel: 52-74-97
Tel/Fax: 52-18-81
E-mail: igor@geneza.lviv.ua
Contact: Ihor Markov, Supervisor

Geneza was conceived as an "information and analytical research and educational institution formed in order to study changes in political space in the post-communist world, specifically, in Ukraine." Besides its headquarters in Lviv, it has a branch in Lugansk.

Geneza has 15 professional staff, most of them between 25 and 35 years old, who conduct and publish research on behalf of governmental institutions, political parties and movements, periodicals, businesses, and other institutions. It collaborates with Lviv University, Ukrainian research institutions and the mass media. The center maintains continuous relations with similar institutions in the U.S., Germany, Austria, Poland, Russia and other countries. It is a corresponding member of the Foreign Policy Research Institute in Philadelphia.

International Renaissance Foundation–Lviv
vul. Mateika 4
290000 Lviv
Tel/Fax: 79-70-86
E-mail: sofij@west.lviv.ua
Contact: Olkeander Sofij

See IRF profile under Kyiv.

Lviv Women's Community
vul. Mateyka 4
Lviv
Tel: 74-00-00
Contact: Yulia Makar

Policy and advocacy, leadership.

Memorial Society
pl. Shashkevicha, 1, kom. 21
290000 Lviv
Tel: 74-12-06, 72-47-51
        33-48-26, 67-26-71
Contact: Evgenii Griniv, Inna Feduschak

Prosvita Publishing Union
vul. Drukarska 6
290008 Lviv
Tel: 72-25-71
Fax: 76-51-56
Contact: Ms. Oleksandra Koval

Prosvita organized the Second Annual Forum of Ukrainian Book Publishers, held at the Lviv National Museum in mid-September 1995. The four-day event hosted over 120 Ukrainian state and privately owned publishing houses and 60 book distributers from countries around the world, including Slovakia, Germany, Poland, and the U.S. The event opened with an intensive seminar program which discussed the problems of publishing, distributing, and selling books and other printed products in Ukraine and abroad.

The event also included an awards ceremony, which recognized the most innovative publishers present at the forum.

Soyuz Ukrainok--Lviv
vul. Stefanika, 11, kv. 85
290000 Lviv
Tel: 76-44-21
Contact: Iryna Kravchuk, Director

Svitlo
24 Vynnychenka
290008 Lviv
Tel: 72-07-36, 76-51-56
E-mail: postmaster@sabre.lviv.ua
Contact: Olga Isayevich

This is a publishing house and book distributor associated with Sabre Foundation in Cambridge, MA.

Ukrainian Educational and Cultural Center
Shevchenka pr. 7
290008 Lviv
Tel: 72-67-87, 72-89-76
Fax: 72-93-00

The center offers educational and vocational services training to disadvantaged, abandoned and disabled children living in youth homes in Ukraine.

Western Resource Center
vul. Matskia 4
290000 Lviv
Tel/Fax: 74-00-00
Contact: Yulia Tereshuk

Zhinocha Hromada (Lviv)
ul. Petlyura 18B, #25

Lviv
Tel: 62-23-91, 62-78-48
Contact: Lyuba Pankiv, Director

Mariupol (0629)

Institute of Economic, Social and Cultural Research
10 Michmana Pavlova Square
341001 Mariupol
Tel: 33-04-28, 33-31-10
Contact: A.Vasilyev, Director

The institute is currently seeking a joint venture partner in accounting and joint finance-related research.

Memorial Society
vul. 50-letiya Oktyabrya 32-13
341047 Mariupol
Tel: 25-61-48
Contact: Galina Zakharova

Mikolayiv (0512)

Fund of Ukraine for the Protection of Invalids
vul. Rosa Luxemburg, 46
327001 Mikolayiv
Tel: 35-14-14
E-mail: center@fupi.nikolaev.ua
Contact: Galina Tazaratcheva, Director

The fund has worked to find alternative care situations for disabled children whose disabilities are not severe enough to warrant permanent institutionalization. It works with a Pennsylvania organization named Elwyn, Inc.

Memorial Society
a/ya 140
vul. Parkovaya. 30-39

327018   Mikolayiv
Tel: 23-23-82, 39-27-01, 34-52-82
Contact: Yurii Zaitsev, Vladimir Miko-
layiv

Mykolayiv Regional Ecological Association "Zeleny Svit"

a/ya 158
327001   Mikolayiv
Tel: 36-50-80 (Zolotoukhin office)
          39-82-58 (Zolotoukhin home)
          24-66-84 (Shapovalov office)
          39-94-12 (Shapovalov home)
E-mail: anufr@nikgrpc.freenet.kiev.ua
Contact: Anatoliy Zolotukhin, Chairman; Sergei Shapovalov, Vice-
Chairman; Vladimir Chernitskiy, Foreign Relations Dept

Founded in 1988, this organization
claims to be the first NGO in the Mikolayiv region. It is affiliated with Zeleny
Svit based in Kyiv and the International
Socio-Ecological Union (Moscow). The
association came into being in the
wake of the Chernobyl disaster as a result of people's protest against a
planned expansion of the South-
Ukrainian Nuclear Hydropower Plant
(NHPP) and the destruction of the
southern Bug river. The association
consists of experts, scientists and activists in the Mikolayiv region. Its motto
is "Preserve Nature for Future Genera-
tions."

Public meetings and the collection of
210,000 signatures against the South
Ukrainian NHPP project resulted in a
decision by the Council of Ministers to
reduce the scale of the South Ukrainian
NHPP by 50% and to impose a mora-
torium on the Konstantinovka reservoir
and Hydro-Accumulating Power Station construction. This saved the unique

Migia Canyon, important archaeologi-
cal sites and the southern Bug river basin.

The association continued to organize against dam-building and nuclear
power plant construction in the early
nineties, urging the government to convert to gas turbines for energy production. It also started a program for environmental education in the schools,
published a textbook and opened the
first shop in Mikolayiv selling products
with ecological themes.

Nikopol (5662)

Memorial Society

pr. Lenina 27, kom. 206
322909   Nikopol
Tel: 1-01-70, 4-06-85
Contact: Arvet Grams, Liliya Tretyak

Zeleny Svit of Nikopol

Usov 36, kv. 40
322900   Nikopol
Tel/Fax: 1-42-05
E-mail: ZSNikopol@gluk.apc.org
Contact: Vyacheslav Sandul, Executive
Director

Zeleny Svit of Nikopol was registered in
1989 and re-registered in mid-1995. The
organization was founded by local activists for environmental improvement
because the city of Nikopol is sur-
rounded by "powerful power plants of
all types: nuclear, thermal and hydro."
The organization has organized local
protest meetings, participated in conferences, and engaged in ecological studies
together with members of local government. The organization consists of 12
volunteers.

Odessa (482)

ACCELS Odessa
Odessa Pedogogical Institute
ul. Staroportofrankovskaja, 26, kom. 60
270020   Odessa
Tel: 32-15-16
E-mail: fsa.odessa@sovcust.sprint.com
smchale@accels.odessa.ua

See profile for ACTR/ACCELS in section *Special Focus Organizations.*

Adult Children's Home at the Odessa Union of Youth Clubs
vul. Pushkinskaya 34
270001   Odessa
Tel: 25-09-45
Fax: 21-82-38
Contact: Tikhon Ivanovich Yemelyanov

The home was founded in 1992. It brings together adults of all ages who at one time or another have lived in orphanages or other children's institutions. The Union of Youth Clubs collects clothing, toys, and books for children's homes and institutions, and arranges recreational evenings and concerts. In addition, it helps those leaving institutions to find work and provides legal consultation for the protection of orphans' rights.

Alcoholics Anonymous
Odessa
Tel: 23-28-52
Contact: Sergei

International Renaissance Foundation–Odessa
vul. Kirova 48, kv. 1
270014   Odessa
Tel/Fax: 24-63-37
E-mail: office@vidr.odessa.ua

Contact: Hanna Morozova

See IRF profile under Kyiv.

International Society for Human Rights, Ukrainian Section
Abonementny yashik 100
270069   Odessa
Tel: 25-00-37
Contact: Valentin Denda, Director

ISHR was founded in Germany in 1972, and serves as an independent NGO supporting the principles of the Declaration of Human Rights adopted by the United Nations in 1948. The organization publishes collections of legal documents, UN materials on human rights issues, information on particular cases of persecution, and other documentation related to specific legal topics. Currently ISHR focuses on the problems of social and legal protection of military conscripts, former political prisoners, orphans, and ethnic minorities.

Memorial Society
per. Chaikovskogo, 10
270001   Odessa
Tel: 21-87-76, 21-41-88, 24-68-85
Contact: Nikolai Danilov, Georgii Razumov

Odessa Socio-Ecological Union
vul. Podbelskogo 38a, kv. 1
270021   Odessa
Tel: 26-82-75
E-mail: odessaeco@glas.apc.org
Contact: Alla Shevchuk, Member of the Socio-Ecological Union

The Odessa SEU has existed as an ecological club since 1977 and was officially established under its current name in 1989. Between 1978 and 1984 club members created a arboretum that has been awarded the status of "park monument." The club also has helped to improve the care of animals in the Odessa zoo. In 1990, it acted to restore 92 hectares of the Tiligulsky estuary. Other projects included halting the erosion of the banks of the Baraboy River and conducting a public investigation of water quality. Additionally, OSEU published over 500 works on conservation, and the scholarly research of Union members has been gathered and published in *Ecological Tales*.

Prof. I. E. Pusanov Natural Heritage Fund

Odessa
E-mail: ivan.rusev@envinet.kiev.ua
Contact: Ivan Rusev

The fund is involved in environmental education, eco-monitoring protected areas and actions to preserve nature.

Poltava (05322)

Memorial Society

vul. B. Khmelnitskogo, 28-23
314037   Poltava
Tel: 3-14-25
Contact: Vladimir Idzinskii

Rivne (3622)

Committee of Soldier's Mothers

vul. Petlyura 1
266000   Rivne
Tel: 26-46-59, 24-74-42
Contact: Alla Chesnokova, Co-Director

Soyuz Ukrainok--Rivne

vul. Petlyura 1
Rivne
Tel: 26-14-69
Contact: Lyuba Gavryllyuk, Director

Ukrainian Union of Women

Prosvity Sq. 2/1
Rivne
Tel: 2-34-26, 3-33-88
Contact: Mariya Rozhko, Director

Symferopil (0652)

Association of Russian, Ukrainian and Belorussian Writers

ul. Gorkogo 7
333000   Symferopil
Tel: 27-52-62, 27-87-42
Contact: Anatoly Dombrovsky, President; Vladimir Savenko, Secretary

The association publishes a journal, *Briga Tavridy*, six times per year.

Businesswomen's Club

vul. G. Stalingrada 7a
Symferopil
Tel: 48-59-91
Fax: 48-59-46
Contact: Tatiana Yevstafeva

Crimean Initiative–Ecological Information Center

a/ya 35
333022   Symferopil
Tel/Fax: 27-79-39
E-mail: root@crin.wildwind.com
Contact: Tatyana Lysak

Crimean Initiative engages in a variety of programs to promote public education about environmental issues. It maintains a library of environmental resources and provides environmental information to the local media. CI also works to support the development of a range of NGOs by: helping other groups with organizational development issues; maintaining an information exchange service; and helping organizations establish e-mail capabilities. CI is interested in working with Western organizations and would welcome donations of educational materials for its library.

Crimean Regional Human Rights Office

Kirova 24, kv. 13
333000   Symferopil
Tel/Fax: 27-16-05
Contact: Leonid Pilunski

Established as part of the Human Rights Informational Network initiated by the Ukrainian Legal Foundation and the International Renaissance Foundation. Its main objective is to monitor the human rights situation in the Crimea and to conduct public education using the local print and broadcast media.

Eco-Political University

ul. Sevastopolskaia 54
333025   Symferopil
Tel: 27-21-47 (office)
        22-59-35 (home)
Contact: Iurii B. Asmanov, Dean, International Publications

Prof. Asmanov is an authority on the national movement of Crimean Tatars in Symferopil and editor of *The White Book* (1991), a collection of documents on their history.

International Renaissance Foundation–Crimea

vul. Heroiv Stalinhradu 7-a
333047   Symferopil

Tel: 49-58-97
Fax: 48-59-46
E-mail: irf-sim@soros.crimea.ua
Contact: Olena Sokolova

See IRF profile under Kyiv.

Memorial Society

vul. Krylova 9-2
333011   Symferopil
Tel: 25-40-18, 23-20-45
Contact: Vladimir Gurkovich

Sumy (0542)

Memorial Society

vul. Frunze 14/2
244000   Sumy
Tel: 22-27-63, 25-30-28
Contact: Alla Kryganova

Soyuz Ukrainok

vul. Polyova 14, Sad
245301   Sumy
Tel: 24-30-85
Contact: Olga Horobets, Director

Ternopil (3522)

Memorial Society

vul. Ostrovskogo 45
282019   Ternopil
Tel: 2-11-21, 5-28-35
Contact: Ilya Oberishin

Associated with the magazine, *Dzvin*.

Uzhhorod (3122)

Soyuz Ukrainok (Zakarpatya)

39/37 Svobody Pr.
294018   Uzhhorod

Tel: 2-99-96
Contact: Anna Bozhyk, Director

Vinnitsa (4322)

Memorial Society
vul. Lenina, 19
287100 Vinnitsa
Tel: 32-26-71, 46-49-65, 32-64-17
Contact: Lyudmila Karoeva, Larisa Yerlikh

Yalta (654)

Memorial Society
vul. Moskovskaya 35-35
224112 Yalta
Tel: 34-34-67
Contact: Oleg Zavadskii

Zaporizhia (612)

Azov Regional Institute of Management
vul. Uritskogo 3
332440 Berdyansk
Zaporizhia oblast
Tel: 3-54-64, 3-24-47
Fax: 3-23-06
Contact: Galina Kazachkovskaya

The main activities of the Azov Regional Institute of Management (ARMI) include training of specialists in economics, management and law for the northern Azov region, and economic and legal education of the region's general public. The institute is seeking a foreign partner to establish training centers in mass media, and to help create information and educational programs on economics. It would like to receive technical assistance and training in organizational and financial management, plus training of a creative group of specialists for the TV channel of ARMI.

Memorial Society
vul. Respublikansaya 67-30
Zaporizhia
Tel: 35-13-27
Contact: Boris Dubitskii

Young Ecologist Club
vul. Kremlevskaya 61-45
Zaporizhia
E-mail: root@ecoclub.zaporizhzhe.ua
Contact: Anatoliy Ljovin

The club publishes a weekly bulletin, *Ecoclub,* containing material of interest to environmentalists in both Ukraine and the NIS.

Uzbekistan

Country Code: 7

Tashkent (3712)

ACCELS Tashkent
Administrative Offices
ul. Lahuty 16A., 7th floor
700015 Tashkent
Tel: 55-12-71, 56-55-47,55-88-60
Fax: 55-88-60
E-mail:
aksels.tashk@sovcust.sprint.com

Educational Advising Center
ul. Uzbekistan 80, kom. 117
700027 Tashkent
Tel: 45-49-54, 45-42-71

See the profile for ACTR/ACCELS
under *U.S.-Based Organizations.*

American-Uzbek Business Club
Prospekt Uzbekistanski 49, 7th floor
Tashkent
Tel: 45-43-97
Fax: 45-22-61

Business and Education Center
Joint Venture
Alleya Paradov 2
700029 Tashkent
Tel: 39-48-86
Fax: 39-49-15, 39-48-13
Tlx: 116165 INPRO SU

Business Women's Association
of Uzbekistan
Tashkent
Tel: 56-65-78, 57-24-51
Contact: Dildor Alimbekova

Central Asian Free Exchange
pr. Navoii 48
700021 Tashkent
Tel: 93-39-23
Fax: 42-28-82
E-mail:
mala@malstead.silk.glas.apc.org
Contact: Mala Malstead

CAFE focuses on assisting orphans and
children with mental and physical
disabilities. It is also involved in a
variety of environmental projects,
including an investigation of water
quality and its impact on public health.

COUNTERPART Consortium
ul. Abdullah Kodiry 11
Tashkent
Tel: 41-28-78
Fax: 41-21-49
E-mail: lorel@silk.glas.org
Contact: Lorel Donaghey,
COUNTERPART Director; Karla
Hostetler, Aid to Artisans; Bakhadir
Rasulov, Goodwill Representative

For a description of the Consortium's
work in Uzbekistan, see COUNTER-
PART Central Asia Headquarters
profile in *Kazakstan* section.

"Ekolog Unity"–SEU
11A-10 Gaydar Pr.
700105 Tashkent
Tel: 91-39-35
E-mail: tashkent@glas.apc.org
vadims@silk.glas.apc.org
snake@silk.igc.apc.org
Contact: Eugene Chernogaev, Elena
Melnikova, Akhtam Shaymardanov,
Oleg Tsaruk, Co-Chairs

EU was established at the end of 1987
as an environmental organization, and
is affiliated with the Social-Ecological
Union and the Law and Environment
Eurasia Partnership, headquartered in

Weston, MA. It was formed to work on protection of the Aral Sea and to address the loss of biodiversity in Central Asia.

EU has organized several environmental camps for students and two environmental schools, in Tashkent and Chirchik. It has helped organize several regional and international environmental meetings. These include the 8th International Snow Leopard Symposium at Islamabad, Pakistan in November 1995 (together with International Snow Leopard Trust of Seattle) and a regional biodiversity conference, "Cheeta-95," in the same month in Dashkhowuz, Turkmenistan.

The group has no paid staff, a core group of 8-12 people who carry out most of its activities and about 50 other members. Most of its members are natural scientists. Mr. Tsaruk is especially well-informed about both domestic and foreign NGOs working on Central Asian problems.

The Eurasia Foundation
Central Asia Regional Office
a/ya 5808
700000   Tashkent
Tel: 79-44-92
Fax: 79-44-91
E-mail: eurasia@ef.silk.glas.apc.org
Contact: Fred Smith, Regional Director

See profile for the foundation in the section *Clearinghouse Organizations*.

Goodwill Trading International
83 Gorky Pr.
Myrzo Ulugbek District
700029   Tashkent
Tel: 62-42-53, 62-47-35
Fax: 62-63-93
E-mail: root@zap.tashkent.su

International Cultural Center
ul. Rashidova 4a
700017   Tashkent
Tel: 41-05-21, 41-11-15, 41-88-36
Contact: Karim Rasulov, Director

International Institute of Central Asia Biodiversity
11A-10 Gaydar Pr.
700105   Tashkent
Tel: 91-39-35
E-mail: tashkent@glas.apc.org
            zatoka@glas.apc.org
Contact: Andrey Zatoka, Director. See list below of IICAB Coordinators.

The IICAB was established in 1995 at the regional biodiversity conference "Cheeta-95" by over 50 specialists on biodiversity protection from NGOs, state agencies, and academic institutions in Kazakhstan, Russia, Tajikistan, Turkmenistan, the U.S., and Uzbekistan. The organization intends to focus it efforts in Central Asia and adjacent countries, but will work in any biodiversity protection activities throughout the NIS.

One of the primary goals of the institute is to provide a network of specialists with interests in the area. According to its founders, the problems of biodiversity conservation in the newly independent countries of Central Asia and adjacent countries are increasing while the region is losing specialists because of the economic and political situation. The institute hopes to lessen this problem through creation of this network of specialists.

Currently the institute is preparing an investment packet for the international donor community; establishing regional and international cooperation in studies and conservation of biodiversity in Central Asia; promoting information exchange; and preparing databases regarding different aspects of biodiversity protection. On the Board of Coordinators are:

- Andrey Aranbaev, Ashgabat Environmental Club, Turkmenistan <catena@glas.apc.org>
- Andrey Zatoka, Dashkhowuz Environmental Club, Turkmenistan <zatoka@glas.apc.org>
- Svetlana Blagoveshchenskaya, Youth Academy of Sciences, Dushanbe, Tajikistan <pamir@glas.apc.org>
- Tatiana Bragina, Naurzumsky zapovednik, Kazakhstan (no e-mail for now)
- Madjid Buketov, Karaganda Ecocenter, Kazakhstan <karaganda@glas.apc.org>
- Sean Schmidt, International Snow Leopard Trust, Seattle, WA
- Emil Shukurov, Kyrgyzstan Environmental Movement "Aleyne," Bishkek, Kyrgyzstan <emil%aleyne.bishkek.su@sequent.k iae.su>
- Oleg Tsaruk, Ecolog Unity, Uzbekistan, Executive Director

NET Alumni Center

ul. Avolny 20a, kom. 54/55
700100   Tashkent
Tel: 55-69-16, 53-79-55
Fax: 55-77-29
E-mail: nettash@sovam.com
Contact: Eleonora Faisulaeva, Center Coordinator

A resource center and library for alumni of the NET training project managed by the Academy for Educational Development.

Project on Economic Reform and Development in Central Asia (PERDCA)

ul. Furkat 1, kom. 522

700027   Tashkent
Tel/ Fax: 45-54-97
E-mail:
   PERDCA@silk.glas.apc.org
Contact: Rex McDonald, Director

PERDCA was founded in 1992 to facilitate and support technical assistance efforts by foreign development organizations in Central Asia. It has sponsored a variety of conferences and workshops and generally acts as a central clearinghouse for news of "who is doing what" in Central Asia.

One of PERDCA's major initiatives has been the promotion of e-mail and the Internet in Central Asia. In 1993 it established SilkNet, an e-mail network for NGOs in the region. In 1994-95 it established 17 public access e-mail sites in Uzbekistan. In 1995-96 PERDCA expects to play a key role in the development of a network of Information Resource Centers in the region, which will offer access to a variety of electronic information, including business opportunities, technical training, English-language teaching materials, and distance education.

Spiritual Leadership of Musul'man Movaraunakhra

ul. Zarkainor 103
700002   Tashkent
Tel: 40-08-31
Contact: Mufti Mukhtarzhan Abdullaev

Navruz Endowment Fund

ul. Amir Temur 24
700000   Tashkent
Tel: 34-76-19
Contact: Kalam Shadievich Shadiev, First Deputy Chairman of the Fund

Established in 1992, the fund is involved in charitable activities, various kinds of production and trading, marketing, publishing, organization of lotteries, etc.

Public Education Center
Tashkent
Tel: 63-08-44, 72-84-52
Fax: 54-77-66, 68-11-50
E-mail: stella@silk.glas.apc.org

PEC was established in 1995 to develop civic education programs and a curriculum on democracy for high schools in Uzbekistan. It grew out of a 1992 project of the International Republican Institute (U.S.) which sought to introduce leadership skills and democratic practices among Uzbek students. PEC plans to organize training workshops for teachers, psychologists and community activists which will focus on interethnic dialogue, non-violent conflict resolution, and group decision-making. It also hopes to conduct research and development of non-traditional teaching methods.

Soviet of the Federation of Trade Unions
ul. Pravdy Vostoka 24
700000 Tashkent
Tel: 56-83-15
Contact: Khulkar Boksadyrovich Dzhalalov, President

Special Olympics–Uzbekistan
Massiv Chilanzar, B14-2-1
700173 Tashkent
Tel: 20-12-53
Fax: 20-12-94
Contact: Mr. Sergei Kiryushkin, Executive Director

Women's Committee of Uzbekistan
Tashkent
Tel: 45-15-59, 45-90-66
Contact: Dilowar Kubaev

Writer's Union
ul. Dzh. Neru 1
700000 Tashkent
Tel: 33-63-74, 36-26-47, 33-57-61
Contact: Dzhmal Kamal, President; Mirzo Tura, Secretary

Karakalpakstan (36122)

ACCELS Nukus
ul. Karakalpakstan 3, 2nd floor
Nukus, Karapalkistan
Tel: 2-60-06

See the profile for ACTR/ACCELS under *Special Focus Organizations.*

Aral Sea and Amu Darya Protection Union
ul. Gogola, Tupik Lineyni 1
742000 Nukus
Karakalpakstan
Tel: 7-04-67
Fax: 7-72-29
E-mail: nukus@glas.apc.org
Contact: Yusup Kamalov, Chairman and Member of Council of the Socio-Ecological Union; Timur Razackberdiev, Office Manager

UDASA conducts environmental education of high school students, and seeks to restore the rivers, the Aral Sea and the health of the people living in the tri-republic disaster zone near the Aral Sea.

Perzent
a/ya 27
742012   Nukus
Karakalpakstan
Tel: 23-22-37

Perzent conducts independent scientific research on environmental factors on reproduction and maternal and child health. It offers educational programs for women and children on health and environmental issues.

Namangan (36922)

ACCELS Namangan
ul. Ibrat 46
716000   Namangan, Ferghana Valley
Tel: 3-99-57
E-mail:
micheled@disney.silk.glas.apc.org

See the profile for ACTR/ACCELS under *U.S.-Based Organizations*.

Samarkand (3662)

ACCELS Samarkand
15 University Boulevard
Department of Quantum Physics
703000   Samarkand
Tel: 35-67-80
E-mail:
norma@samarkand.silk.glas.apc.org

See the profile for ACTR/ACCELS in *Special Focus Organizations*.

Information Consulting Center
Samarkand University
Samarkand
Tel: 35-14-98, 33-53-40 (home)
E-mail:
ravshan@samarkand.silk.glas.apc.org
Contact: Ravshan Sabirov

Internet Resources

Internet Access in the NIS

Internet access is growing rapidly in Russia and other states in the region. From the outset the NGO community has been at the forefront of this development, both using and promoting the Internet as the optimal means of communication, given the vast distances separating populations in the NIS and the unreliability of alternative forms of communication.

This section provides contact information for some e-mail and Internet service providers in the NIS. It also includes a description of projects which provide NGOs with e-mail access for free or for substantially reduced rates.

IREX has published a good introductory guide to e-mail and the Internet in the NIS and Baltics which is available free of change to people in the NIS or for a nominal fee to people in the U.S. The guide is also available on-line at:

http://www.irex.org/FAQ.htm

There are two basic levels of access available in the NIS. The most common is a simple e-mail account–sometimes referred to as a UUCP account. With this account one can send and receive e-mail messages and subscribe to electronic mailing lists, but nothing else. The second type of account is a full Internet access account–sometimes referred to as a "live" or "interactive" account. Internet accounts are more expensive but include access to popular Internet services such as FTP, Gopher, and the World Wide Web. An Internet account requires a good telephone connection, and so may not be available at any price in certain areas of the NIS.

We divide the presentation of Internet Service Providers below into two sections: commercial service providers and organizations and projects which offer e-mail and Internet access to nongovernmental organizations for reduced charges or for free.

I. Commercial Internet Service Providers

Among others, America Online, AT&T, Compuserve, MCI, and Sprint all offer some form of e-mail service between the U.S. and the NIS. Information about these services is easily obtainable in the U.S. from representatives of these companies. The services described below include a number that will be less familiar to some readers, since they are based in the NIS. These companies will gladly answer andy questions, including providing a list of cities which they serve. Much of this information can also be found at their World Wide Web sites.

In addition to national and multinational Internet service providers, increasingly companies are being formed which offer Internet service in just one or two cities. A simple way to begin learning about the range of Internet service providers for a particular city in the NIS is to check the ads in any local paper–whether published in English for the "expat" community or not. Other ways to find e-mail providers in specific cities include:

• Subscribers to Electronic Mailing Lists. These are one of the best sources of information about Internet service providers in the NIS. Find a list that focuses on the geographic area you are interested in and you are sure to find people who have experience with e-mail providers in that part of the NIS.

• WWW Sites in the NIS. Many WWW sites in the NIS are created, in part, by local companies to advertise their Internet services. When you visit their site you will find contact information and the services they offer.

Immediately below are six sites–some more comprehensive and up-to-date than others. Together they offer leads to a large number of Internet service providers in the NIS. Further below we give contact information on some of the better known Internet service providers in the NIS. New service providers are entering the market all the time; the reader should be aware that firms not listed below may exist which provide better or more economical services than the six we list.

http://www.ru/web.html	Russia
http://www.izhmark.udmurtia.su/WWW_list/jwz/other.html	Russia
http://www.ras.ru/map_list.html	Russia
http://www.cs.kiev.ua/library/pointer/ukr_www.html	Ukraine
http://www.best.be/InfoDesk/iap/Eastern_Europe.html	NIS
http://solar.rtd.utk.edu/~ccsi/emaildir.html	NIS

Relcom

ul. Raspletina 4/1
123060 Moscow
Tel: 194-2540, 194-3631, 943-4735
Fax: 194-3328, 198-9510
E-mail: office@office.relcom.msk.su
URL: http://www.kiae.su/

Relcom is the major e-mail and Internet access provider in the NIS, except in the Baltic countries. Its service is available in virtually every major city of the former Soviet Union. A clickable map of Relcom nodes is available at:

http://www.kiae.su/RELCOM/geography/geo_relcom.html

The map may be updated irregularly so it would be a good idea to contact Relcom (or, for that matter, any access provider) directly for the latest information on cities where it offers Internet access.

Demos
Ovchinnikovskaya nab. 6/1
113035 Moscow
Tel: 956-62-33, 956-60-80
Fax: 233-5016
E-mail: info@demos.su
URL: http://www.demos.su

Demos also offers e-mail access in a wide variety of NIS cities. It used to be part of Relcom.

Glasnet
ul. Sadovaya -Chernogryazskaya 4, kom. 16a
107078 Moscow
Tel: 207-0704
Fax: 207-0889
Email: support@glas.apc.org
URL: http://www.glasnet.ru/

Glasnet is a nonprofit organization offering e-mail and Internet access accounts. Many NGOs in the NIS have Glasnet accounts. Additionally Glasnet offers an electronic bulletin board system with news groups or "electronic conferences" devoted to specific themes, such as the environment or women's issues. (Relcom also offers an extensive list of news groups.)

Glasnet's online brochure includes information about Glasnet's service, prices, and cities which have local dial-up facilitites (**http://www.glasnet.ru/brochure.html**). Glasnet administers numerous accounts in the NIS which are sponsored by an organization in the U.S. For more information about this option contact David Caulkins or Barbara Loebner at: **glasadmin@igc.apc.org**

Glasnet–Ukraine
vul. Metrolgischeskaya 14b
252143 Kyiv
Tel: 266-9481
Fax: 266-9475
E-mail: support@gluk.apc.org

An affiliate of Glasnet, Gluk provides similar services in Ukraine.

SOVAM
ul. Nezhdanova 2a
103009 Moscow
Tel: 258-4170
Fax: 258-4160
E-mail: mosmarkt@sovam.com

URL: http://www.sovam.com/

SOVAM is available in most major NIS cities, although it is not as widely available as Relcom. Some users have found that SOVAM's service is more consistent and of higher quality than other service providers; however, the price can also be higher.

Sprint Russia
ul. Tverskaya 7-7
103375 Moscow
Tel: 201-6890
Fax: 923-2344
E-mail: sales@sovmail.rosprint.ru
URL: http://www.rosprint.ru/

Sprint has a reputation for offering high quality Internet access in major NIS cities, at a price.

II. Organizations Which Help with E-Mail Connections for NGOs

The Eurasia Foundation
1527 New Hampshire Avenue, NW
Washington, DC 20036-1206
Tel: (202) 234-7370
Fax: (202) 234-7377
E-mail: eurasia@eurasia.org

The Eurasia Foundation, which is funded by the United States Agency for International Development, provides small grants to NIS organizations for work in such fields as NGO development, media, and business. Eurasia has made a number of grants in the area of communications development, including funding for modems, e-mail accounts and Internet training.

Other Eurasia offices are located in:

Yerevan	**eferevan@arminco.com** *or* **armenia@eurasia.arminco.com**
Saratov	**ef@ef.saratov.su**
Moscow	**efmoscow@eurasia.msk.ru**
Vladivostok	**efvlad@sovam.com**
Kyiv	**eurasia@eurasia.kiev.ua** *or* **eurasia@eurasia.freenet.kiev.ua**
Tashkent	**eurasia@ef.silk.glas.apc.org**
Tbilisi	**eftbilis@iberiapac.ge**

IREX

1616 H Street NW
Washington, DC 20006
Tel: 628-8188
Fax: 628-8189
E-mail: tonyb@info.irex.org
Contact: Tony Byrne

IREX–Moscow

8 Khlebnyi Pereulok
121069 Moscow
Tel: 290-58-78
E-mail: irexog@glas.apc.org
fick@glas.apc.org
Contact: Olga Galkina or Bill Fick

In recent years IREX has launched a number of major programs to provide Internet access to universities, libraries, and civic organizations in the NIS. Information about all of IREX's Internet projects, including a list of the public access sites, is available at its Web site:

http://www.irex.org/internet.htm

In 1994 IREX launched a project to open public access e-mail stations at select universities in the NIS. The project, which includes providing training, is intended to encourage scholars to communicate with their colleagues abroad. However, e-mail access is also available to representatives of local NGOs and other non-commercial organizations. In late 1995 IREX announced plans to significantly expand the project.

IREX is also engaged in a project to help develop an e-mail network among NGOs in Russia which work in the areas of children's health and disabilities rehabilitation. The project involves contributing equipment, training, and e-mail access the NGO members of the network.

Kyiv Freenet

Klovskii uzviz
252010 Kyiv
Tel: 228-63-93
Email: webmaster@freenet.kiev.ua
commando@un.kiev.ua
URL: http://www.freenet.kiev.ua

Established by the United Nations office in Kyiv in November 1994, Freenet provides free Internet access to academic institutions, government agencies, and non-profit organizations in Kyiv. The project is funded by the U.N. for a minimum of five years. Within six months from start-up more than 300 organizations had opened accounts.

Network of East-West Women

1601 Connecticut Avenue, NW, Suite 302
Washington, DC 20009
Tel: (202) 265-3585

Fax: (202) 667-3291
E-mail: newwdc@igc.apc.org
URL: http://www.igc.apc.org/neww/

NEWW provides modems and computer training for women's organizations in Eastern Europe and the NIS.

Sacred Earth Network

267 East Street
Petersham, MA 01366
Tel: (508) 724-3443
Fax: (508) 724-3436
E-Mail: sacredearth@igc.apc.org
URL: http://www.igc.apc.org/sen/

SEN's Environmental Telecommunications Project, begun in 1989, provides computers, modems, and e-mail training to ecological groups in the NIS. See *U.S.-Based Organizations* section for SEN's coordinates.

SilkNet

PERDCA
ul. Furkat 1, kom. 524
Tashkent, Uzbekistan
Tel: (3712) 45-54-97/45-99-52
E-mail: root@silk.glas.apc.org

PERDCA
Central Asian Development Agency
Dushanbe, Tajikistan
Tel: (37372) 21-95-10
E-mail: aso@td.silk.glas.apc.org

PERDCA (Project on Economic Reform and Development in Central Asia) has established SilkNet, an e-mail network which offers free e-mail accounts for local NGOs. E-mail service is also available for others, but foreigners and businesses must pay. SilkNet, which has more than 700 users, has local dial-up facilities in a number of cities in Uzbekistan including Tashkent, Samarkand, Bukhara, Nukus, and Termez and also in Dushanbe and Khodjent, Tajikistan. It hopes to expand to other cities in Central Asia in the near future, including Bishkek, Kyrgyzstan. Local and foreign NGOs can also use a terminal in PERDCA's Tashkent office to send and receive e-mail.

Electronic Mailing Lists

lectronic mailing lists are one of the most fun, interesting, and easy-to-use resources on the Internet. They are so popular because they rely on the simplest Internet technology: e-mail. Virtually anyone with e-mail–from Atlanta to Almaty, from Zanesville to Zagorsk–can participate in an electronic mailing list.

Functionally, electronic mailing lists are a novel hybrid of a news service, a continual seminar, and an affinity group or special interest society. Technically speaking, an electronic mailing list is a software program installed on a host computer connected to the Internet with the following two features:

- an automatic mechanism whereby individuals may add or remove their name from the electronic mailing list;

- an automatic mechanism whereby a message posted to the list of subscribers is sent simultaneously to each subscriber.

Several software programs exist that automate this process. Three of the most common are Listserv, Listproc and Majordomo. The first has become so common that it has almost become a synonym for any electronic mailing list. In other words, a person might say, "I just signed up to a Listserv for fans of Tom Cruise."

Just as a good printed magazine creates a kind of community among its loyal readers and letters-to-the-editor writers, so do Listservs create "virtual communities." The advantage of the electronic version is that it can be supported by groups as small as 20 or 30 people, each living in a different nation or region of the world. There are no economies of scale that require a minimum subscriber base of thousands. As a result, today there are thousands of Listservs and news groups.

Like magazines, Listservs serve as a forum where subscribers share ideas in common or post announcements. Unlike magazines, something like a group discussion is also possible, and it can start within seconds of the posting of a message. Also, unlike a magazine, "clipping" and saving an item–or forwarding it to somebody else–is a matter of 10 or 12 keystrokes, and just as many seconds. No scissors, no filing, no addressing of envelopes, no stamps, no trip to the mailbox. When it is this easy to bounce information between people, you can imagine how many things get passed on that never made it out of the out-box in the past.

Posting questions is one of the most useful aspects of Listservs. At first it may take a bit of nerve to ask a question of so many faceless strangers. However, every list has a group of people who will help answer even the most elementary questions.

313

Besides, what better place is there to obtain information than from the hundreds, or thousands, of people interested in the same topic as you? Subscribing to the right Listserv is an excellent way to learn about Internet resources in your area of interest.

Some Simple Mailing List Rules

Electronic mailing lists are so efficient because they are automated. This means subscribers sign up and sign off from a list by themselves. The procedure is very simple, but it is important to be clear about one thing: all electronic mailing lists have two addresses: the List Subscription Address and the Message Posting Address.

The List Subscription Address

The List Subscription Address is the address to which you send a strictly prescribed message, requesting to sign on to (or to sign off of) a particular electronic mailing list. For Center for Civil Society International's CivilSoc list, this address is:

listproc@solar.rtd.utk.edu

Usually the first part of a List Subscription Address indicates which software program is being used by a particular electronic mailing list. For example, here are three List Subscription Addresses, representing three different electronic list administration software programs:

listserv@pucc.princeton.edu
listproc@solar.rtd.utk.edu
majordomo@rain.org

Sometimes one address can serve as the List Subscription Address for many different lists. (But *never* the Message Posting Address, which must be unique for each list.) For instance, the second address above, **listproc@solar.rtd.utk.edu,** serves as the List Subscription Address for both CivilSoc and another electronic mailing list known as Friends.

The Message Posting Address

The Message Posting Address is the address to which you submit messages for re-transmission to everyone else, *once you have subscribed to the list.* If you participate in your list only to read the messages of others and you never submit a message of your own, you will never use this address. However, if you do occasionally wish to submit messages for the entire list, you will use this address each time you submit a message for general posting.

Here is an example of a Message Posting Address: **civilsoc@solar.rtd.utk.edu**. It is the address of Center for Civil Society International's electronic mailing list. The first part of the address, the section before the **@** symbol, is usually the name by which the list is known, and generally offers a pretty good clue about the list's focus. In the above example, Civilsoc is a list that focuses on news related to the growth of civil society in Russia and the NIS.

Subscribing to a List

Despite the different softwares, the process and syntax of subscribing to most electronic mailing lists is very similar. Typically, you are asked to send a simple e-mail message to the List Subscription Address which says, *all on one line*, that you want to subscribe to a specific electronic mailing list:

subscribe list-name your-first-name your-last-name

For example, if Ivan Turgenev wanted to subscribe to the CivilSoc mailing list, he would send an e-mail message containing this sentence:

subscribe civilsoc Ivan Turgenev

to this address:

listproc@solar.rtd.utk.edu

Most e-mail software has a "Subject" line. Leave this line blank. Put your message in the "Message" area. It also usually does not matter whether you type letters in upper case or lower case.[1]

Once you have sent this message, you will receive a "welcome to the list" message acknowledging your subscription and a giving you directions for a variety of utilities, including how to post messages to the list and how to unsubscribe. **Save this message**. Once you are subscribed, you will begin to receive messages which always contain the Message Posting Address. But you won't see instructions again about how to unsubscribe. *So save them.*

Here's a typical electronic mailing list header:

Date: Wed, 4 July 1776
From: Benjamin Franklin <ben@poor.richard.almanac.com>
To: CivilSoc <civilsoc@solar.rtd.utk.edu>
Subject: Good news from Philadelphia–Declaration of Independence from the British!

---

[1] Majordomo software does not require that you give your name; thus, Turgenev's message to a Majordomo list processor would simply read: **subscribe civilsoc**

This header tells you that the message was posted to the CivilSoc list, of which you are now a member, and that it was sent by Benjamin Franklin.

Now suppose that you wanted to comment on this so-called "Declaration of Independence" that Franklin announced to everybody on the list. If you wanted to send a reply **only** to him, you would send your comment to:

ben@poor.richard.almanac.com

But if you wanted to open a discussion of Ben's Declaration, or invite comments on your opinion of Ben's Declaration from others on the list, then you would post your message to:

civilsoc@solar.rtd.utk.edu

This is basically how an electronic mailing list works. It's a powerful communications vehicle–as you will see if you sign up to some of the lists described belowand try them out for a time.

Some NIS-Related Electronic Mailing Lists

Balt-L

Balt-L is the only major electronic mailing list which focuses on the Baltic states. As a result it is a combination of both announcements and discussion. Balt-L subscribers are primarily ethnic Estonians, Latvians, and Lithuanians living in North America, Europe and Scandinavia. The list includes discussion of current events, travel information, genealogy, and official statements from the foreign ministries of the Baltic states. There is also regular discussion of events in Russia and how they pertain to the continued independence of the Baltic states.

Balt-L has 2-3 messages a day, one of which is a compilation of that day's reports from the Open Media Research Institute (formerly Radio Free Europe/Radio Liberty) that relate to the Baltic states. Often the messages come in digest format, which means that the moderator of Balt-L will combine several posts into a single message, which makes it easier to follow the current topics of discussion. The volume of messages posted in Balt-L in a recent month totaled nearly 500 kilobytes.

List address: **balt-l@ubvm.cc.buffalo.edu**

To subscribe, send the message: **subscribe balt-l firstname lastname**
to: **listserv@ubvm.cc.buffalo.edu**

BISNIS Briefs

A new electronic mailing list from the Business Information Service for the NIS (BISNIS) at the Department of Commerce. BISNIS Briefs provides weekly updates on Russian economic and financial developments, periodic market reports relating to the states of the former Soviet Union, and announcements of specific trade opportunities and promotional events. No more than five reports are distributed each week. This is a "distribution only" list, meaning that only BISNIS will be able to post messages. To be added to the list, send a request to: **bisnis@usita.gov**

CenAsia

People with projects in Central Asia, as well as those with a general interest in the region, will find the CenAsia list to be an excellent resource. CenAsia includes: announcements of meetings and job openings; news of organizations working in the region; leads to other Internet resources related to the region; and references to print materials, such as journals and dictionaries. Because the community of Westerners interested or working in Central Asia is relatively small, many members know each other and the ethic of sharing information is strong. A frequent use of the list involves queries about e-mail addresses and sources of connectivity in the region.

CenAsia is also a political discussion list, and unlike some discussion lists on the Internet, is distinguished by the high quality of discussion and the background and expertise of its participants. Academics such as James Critchlow and Edward Keenan of Harvard and Barnett Rubin of Columbia and the Council on Foreign Relations are joined by articulate people from the region, many of whom are also scholars.

List address: **cenasia@vm1.mcgill.ca**

To subscribe, send the message: **subscribe cenasia firstname lastname**
                              to: **listserv@vm1.mcgill.ca**

CivilSoc

Sponsored by the Center for Civil Society International, CivilSoc is a source of news and resources related to the development of civil society institutions in the NIS. It includes announcements about projects by U.S. organizations in the NIS, profiles of NIS NGOs (non-governmental organizations), grant announcements, and print and electronic resources. Many subscribers are active on NGO projects in the NIS.

CivilSoc averages 4-5 messages a week, with an average monthly volume of 50-70 kilobytes. Posts are kept concise so as to reduce cost for subscribers in the NIS. Many of the messages posted to CivilSoc are archived at CCSI's Web site: **http://solar.rtd.utk.edu/~ccsi/ccsihome.html**

List address: **civilsoc@solar.rtd.utk.edu**

To subscribe, send the message: **subscribe civilsoc firstname lastname**
to: **listproc@solar.rtd.utk.edu**

Civnet

Civnet is the companion listserv to the Civnet Internet site which focuses on civics education. Civnet contains announcements of new documents uploaded to the Civnet Internet site and discussion among teachers and organizations involved with civics education. Although not exclusively intended for an NIS audience, initially most of the non-U.S. subscribers have come from Eastern Europe and the former USSR. The list is not very active and probably averages 4-5 messages a month.

List address: **civnet@listserv.syr.edu**

To subscribe, send the message: **subscribe civnet firstname lastname**
to: **listserv@listserv.syr.edu**

E-Europe

Although its full title is Eastern Europe Business Network, postings on E-Europe also cover the NIS and include a wide variety of topics. Postings on E-Europe include new Internet resources, conference announcements, sample issues and subscription information for electronic journals, project information, and job announcements in such areas as agriculture, business, the environment, health, and law.

E-Europe used to be a modestly "heavy traffic" list with an average of 5-10 messages a day. At the end of 1995 the "owner" of the list was forced to move it to another computer. As a result the traffic on the list declined significantly. As of January 1996, it was too early to tell whether E-Europe would regain its robust character.

List address: **e-europe@cep.nonprofit.net**

To subscribe, send the message: **subscribe e-europe firstname lastname**
to: **listproc@cep.nonprofit.net**

EE & NIS lists from CEP

The Civic Education Project maintains 5 electronic mailing lists that focus on economics, higher education, employment opportunities, law, and women's issues in Eastern Europe and the NIS.

- **EE-Econ**

  ee-econ@cep.nonprofit.net

  Discussion of general economics issues related to Central and Eastern Europe and the NIS.

- **EE-Higher-Ed**

  ee-higher-ed@cep.nonprofit.net

  Discussion of issues related to higher education in Central and Eastern Europe and the NIS.

- **EE-Jobs**

  ee-jobs@cep.nonprofit.net

  For posting of employment opportunities in or related to Central and Eastern Europe and the NIS.

- **EE-Law**

  ee-law@cep.nonprofit.net

  Discussion of legal issues related to Central and Eastern Europe and the NIS.

- **EE-Women**

  ee-women@cep.nonprofit.net

  Discussion of women's issues related to Central and Eastern Europe and the NIS.

All of these lists are configured such that one must first subscribe to a list before one can post a message.

To subscribe, send the message: **sub listname firstname lastname**

to: **listproc@cep.nonprofit.net**

EnvCEE-L

An excellent source for news and announcements related to the environment in Eastern Europe and the NIS. EnvCEE-L is sponsored by The Regional Environmental Center for Central and Eastern Europe (REC), a non-profit foundation based in Budapest, Hungary. Each month EnvCEE-L includes a calendar of environment-related conferences and workshops. It also includes the monthly bulletin of EcoDefense, an environmental organization in Kaliningrad, Russia, and another environmental group in Chisinau, Moldova.

EnvCEE-L is an up-and-down list. Sometimes a week or more will pass without a posting, and then a flurry of five messages will appear in one day.

List address: **envcee-l@rec.hu**

To subscribe, send the message: **subscribe envcee-l firstname lastname** to: **listserv@rec.hu**

Friends

Companion of the innovative Friends and Partners Internet site established by Greg Cole in Knoxville, Tennessee, and Natasha Bulashova in Puschino, Russia, Friends is a great place to meet people and learn what is happening in a wide range of U.S.-NIS citizen activity. It includes many announcements which appear on other lists, but it also includes messages from individuals who introduce themselves or ask questions about where to find different types of information. The list is also used to announce additions to the Friends and Partners World Wide Web site.

Unlike most other electronic mailing lists which consist of messages posted by different people to the list, Friends is a "digested" list. This means messages posted to the list are combined into one file which is distributed to subscribers every two or three days. These "Digests" include a table of contents at the top that lists the sender of each message and the subject line. The Friends' Digests are usually around 30 kilobytes in size.

List address: **friends@solar.rtd.utk.edu**

To subscribe, send the message: **subscribe friends firstname lastname**
to: **listproc@solar.rtd.utk.edu**

FSUmedia

FSUmedia focuses on the media in the former Soviet Union and efforts by Western organizations to support the development of an independent media in the NIS. It is a project of Internews and is moderated by Eric Johnson, who is very knowledgeable about the Internet and has been a helpful member of a number of NIS-related listservs. Johnson has also traveled extensively in Central Asia, Ukraine, and elsewhere in the NIS and has done a good job of ensuring that FSUmedia has not become Russo-centric.

List subscribers include people from the West and NIS. In consideration of subscribers in the NIS who pay by-the-byte for their e-mail, postings are kept fairly short. FSUmedia averages 5-7 messages a week.

List address: **fsumedia@sovam.com**

To subscribe, send the message: **subscribe fsumedia firstname lastname**
to: **listproc@sovam.com**

Grants

Maintained by Marek Tiits of the Institute of Baltic Studies in Tartu, Estonia, Grants is of interest primarily to people in Eastern Europe and the NIS. The list consists solely of announcements about grant programs for which CEE and NIS residents can apply. The list averages 5-7 messages a month.

List address: **grants@ibs.ee**

To subscribe, send the message: **subscribe grants firstname lastname**
to: **listserv@ibs.ee**

Groong

Groong is the unofficial on-line network of the Armenian-American community. It includes announcements of events, conferences, and projects of various Armenian-American organizations both in the U.S. and in Armenia, and press releases from the Armenian National Committee of America and the Armenian Assembly of America. It also has extensive news of events in Armenia. Groong regularly includes: ASBAREZ-ON-LINE, an Armenian daily newspaper published in Glendale, California; and a weekly summary and daily headlines from the Aragil Electronic News Bulletin, which is a digest of the Armenian press.

Although Groong is restricted to announcements--there is a different list for discussion--the daily volume is pretty big: 50-70 kilobytes.

List address: **groong@usc.edu**

To subscribe, send the message: **subscribe groong your-email-address firstname lastname**
to: **groong-request@usc.edu**

Info-Russ

Info-Russ is primarily a place where emigrants from the former USSR can meet each other and share information. It was started in August 1991 by Alex Kaplan who collected e-mail addresses for 40 of his friends and has since grown to over 1,000 subscribers. Messages to Info-Russ are kept short and often consist of people seeking or providing information about job openings, visa and immigration requirements, means of communicating with people in the NIS, and contact information. Info-Russ is an excellent place to meet people who are knowledgeable about places in Russia that do not get covered by major news organizations.

List address: **info-russ@smarty.ece.jhu.edu**

To subscribe, send your e-mail address and name to:
info-russ-request@smarty.ece.jhu.edu

NISHEALTH

NISHEALTH is sponsored by the American International Health Alliance which manages hospital partnerships between health care institutions in the U.S. and NIS. The list carries news about AIHA hospital-to-hospital partnerships, but it also has a wide variety of health care information related to the NIS, including: assessments of health conditions in the NIS by the World Health Organization and other research organizations; announcements of health-related projects, conferences, and resources; and profiles of NIS NGOs. Many NISHEALTH subscribers have experience working on health projects in the NIS, which makes the list a good place to post questions.

NISHEALTH is not an automated list. If you want to subscribe or have questions about the list, you must--for some it's a relief--communicate directly with the list moderator. Often a post to NISHEALTH will consist of a synopsis of a longer document which the moderator will e-mail upon request.

List address: **nis-health@igc.apc.org**
To subscribe, send a message saying you want to subscribe to: **nphhi@igc.apc.org**

NISMEDINFO

The NISMEDINFO Weekly Bulletin profiles new resources made available online by the American International Health Alliance. The bulletin also includes annotated references to online health and medicine resources. AIHA hopes to use the list to help build up the library resources of the 25 U.S.-NIS hospital-to-hospital partnerships AIHA sponsors. The resources referenced are meant primarily for professionals.

To subscribe, send a message saying you want to subscribe to: **nphhi@igc.apc.org**

Okaziya

This is a list which brings together people traveling to and from Russia who are willing to carry letters and small packages for others and people who need to have such items delivered. Thus if you are traveling to Ekaterinburg and would be willing to carry some letters, you would simply send a message to Okaziya announcing when you will be traveling and what cities you will visit. If someone else on the list has a friend in Ekaterinburg to whom they want to send a letter, they would contact you and together you would work out a way to deliver the letter. In essence Okaziya is a "electronic cooperative of couriers."

List address: **okaziya@mitvma.mit.edu**

To subscribe, send the message: **subscribe okaziya firstname lastname**
                                          to: **listserv@mitvma.mit.edu**

RusTex-L

A technical discussion group that focuses on how to print and display Cyrillic on computers and to send Cyrillic text across the Internet. Many RusTex-L subscribers are computer experts and often the level of discussion is beyond most intermediate-level computer users. However, collectively RusTex-L subscribers are the single best source of information on how to use Cyrillic on computers, and some of them will respond to specific questions with very clear and helpful answers. RusTex-L averages 3-5 messages a week.

List address: **rustex-l@ubvm.cc.buffalo.edu**

To subscribe, send the message: **subscribe rustex-l firstname lastname**
                                          to: **listserv@ubvm.cc.buffalo.edu**

Ukes-news

Primarily the North American-Ukrainian community's on-line bulletin board. Many Ukes-news subscribers travel to Ukraine regularly and have projects or business deals there. Ukes-news includes announcements of Ukraine-related events in the U.S. and Canada, some discussion of current events in Ukraine, and occasional reports by Ukrainian organizations, including the *Ukrainian Arts Monitor* and *The Rukh Insider*. The list includes people who are very knowledgeable about e-mail and the Internet and who are also very willing to help--it is a good place to post questions about e-mail access in Ukraine. Although there is some discussion on Ukes-news, it is primarily a list for posting announcements. Discussion of Ukrainian related topics is done mostly on the other Ukes list, Ukes-social which is described in the materials you receive when you subscribe to Ukes-news.

   Ukes-news has an average of 3-7 messages a day. A recent month's messages totaled 750 kilobytes in volume.

List address: **ukes-news@soma.crl.mcmaster.ca**

To subscribe, send a message with the word **subscribe** in the Subject line
                                          to: **ukes-news-request@soma.crl.mcmaster.ca**

Women-East-West

Women-East-West is sponsored by the Network of East-West Women, which works to promote the formation of independent women's movements in Eastern Europe and the former USSR. NEWW has a project to distribute modems and provide e-mail training for women's organizations in Eastern Europe and the NIS. As a result, the Women-East-West list includes an interesting variety of messages from women in the region introducing themselves and their organizations. In the last couple of months the list has also included monthly reports from NIS NGOs, including "Femina" in Naberezhnye Chelny, Zonta International Tartu Club in Estonia, and the Association of Independent Women's Initiatives in Tver, Russia. The list averages 3-5 messages a week.

List address: **women-east-west@igc.apc.org**

To subscribe, send the message: **subscribe women-east-west**
                               to: **majordomo@igc.apc.org**

NIS-Related Internet Sites[1]

Azerbaijan Home Page

http://solar.rtd.utk.edu/friends/azerbaijan

Maintained by David Couchman of Southampton, England and located at the Friends and Partners WWW site in Knoxville, Tennessee, the Azerbaijan Home Page includes a list of links to Internet resources related to Azerbaijan in a variety of fields, including business, health care and human rights. Couchman has done a good job of finding and providing direct links to documents related to Azerbaijan that too often are lost on big Internet sites.

BISNIS

http://www.itaiep.doc.gov/bisnis/bisnis.html

BISNIS is the home page for the Department of Commerce's Business Information Service for the New Independent States. BISNIS includes a wealth of information about business opportunities, NIS companies seeking partners, analysis of market conditions and sectors, etc. Although primarily of interest to business firms, some of the practical information that interests them–telephone service, shipping companies, rules and regulations–also applies to NGOs. BISNIS is also of use to those American organizations, which in the course of working with NIS partners, have found themselves in the role of being a business consultant as their partners seek to improve their management techniques or look to commerce as a way of raising funds for their charitable activity.

Highlights

- **BISNIS Country Reports and Regional Commercial Information**
  http://www.itaiep.doc.gov/bisnis/country/country.html
  A set of three files for each country, including a file of Useful Contacts and Addresses.

- **Sources of Finance for Trade and Investment in the NIS**
  http://www.itaiep.doc.gov/bisnis/finance/finance.html

---

[1] All the resources listed are referred to by their URL (Uniform Resource Locator). URLs that begin with **http:** are World Wide Web documents. Those that begin with **gopher:** are obviously Gopher documents, and the same with **FTP**. When typing a URL remember: 1) Capitalization matters; and 2) URLs don't have any blank spaces.

Information on a variety of governmental and private sources for investment in
the NIS, including some funding sources for NIS businesses.

- **Forming a Russian Company**
  http://www.itaiep.doc.gov/bisnis/country/russin.html
  A clearly written introductory guide written by U.S. and Russian attorneys that
  includes Model Bylaws of a Not-Publicly-Traded Company.

Center for Civil Society International
http://solar.rtd.utk.edu/~ccsi/ccsihome.html

CCSI's Web site contains more than 450 documents of interest to people working in
a wide range of fields to support the development of nongovernmental organizations
and civil society institutions in the NIS. Documents at the site come from a number
of sources, including: CCSI's monthly newsletter, *Civil Society ... East and West*;
newsletters and announcements of other organizations; and messages posted to NIS-
related listservs. CCSI also formats and uploads documents for organizations that
do not have their own Internet site. Much of the information in *The Post-Soviet
Handbook* is available at CCSI's site.

CCSI uses the Friends and Partners Internet platform which is mirrored in Pushchino, Russia. The Friends and Partners WWW site is also accessible by "telnet."
For more information see the profile of Friends and Partners below.

Highlights

- **Announcements and News**
  http://solar.rtd.utk.edu/~ccsi/announce.html
  Announcements of grant programs, conferences, and some job opportunities.

- **Civil Society: USA**
  http://solar.rtd.utk.edu/~ccsi/csusa/cshome.html
  An electronic version of a CCSI publication produced to illustrate the large role
  that associations and private voluntary organizations play in America. "Civil Society: USA" contains an essay describing the third sector in America, followed by
  detailed profiles of over 140 organizations, selected for their range of functions as
  well as their possible interest to citizens of Russia and other countries in the region.

- **NIS-Oriented Projects**
  http://solar.rtd.utk.edu/~ccsi/usnisorg.html
  A collection of profiles of more than 50 U.S.-NIS projects.

- **NIS Third Sector Projects**
  http://solar.rtd.utk.edu/~ccsi/nisorgs.html
  Profiles and contact information for NIS NGOs.

- **Catalog of Resources and Materials in Print**
  http://solar.rtd.utk.edu/~ccsi/prnt-res.html
  Descriptions, with order information, of a wide variety of resources of interest to people working in the NIS, including: *Business and Economic Textbooks in Russian, Handbook for Journalists, Russian Edition, Kak Prosit Dengi (How to Ask for Money)*, and *Make Your Home Comfortable–If Age or Disability Require It, Russian Edition.*

Centers for Pluralism

The Centers for Pluralism is an informal network of NGOs in Central and Eastern Europe and, increasingly, the NIS, which work in the general field of civic education. The CfP office in Warsaw publishes a quarterly newsletter containing a great deal of information about NGO projects in the region. Beginning with the Winter 1995 issue, CfP started to upload the newsletter to the Internet. Unfortu-nately CfP does not have its own Web site and has had to rely on other organizations to upload its newsletter. The result is that the three copies which have been uploaded exist at different Internet sites. However, the quality of the information makes the effort to find it worthwhile.

- Winter 1995 newsletter: **http://sunsite.icm.edu.pl/poland/idee**

- Spring 1995 newsletter: **http://civnet.org/CEO/IDEE/pluralism.html**

- Summer 1995 newsletter (and probably subsequent issues) can be accessed from the Civnet WWW site at: **http://civnet.org/Teaching/civics.html**

Each issue has a section "Who is Who: Activities, Plans, SOS" which includes organizational profiles and project descriptions, and "Who is Offering What," an annotated list of resources and foundations. The newsletter also includes one or two feature articles. The last two issues have carried a series on "How to write a pro-posal."

The Summer 1995 issue includes a list of contact information for all the organizations mentioned in the current and previous issues of the newsletter (**http://civnet.org/Teaching/Journal/cfp9/addre/addre.htm**).

Civic Assistance–Committee to Aid Refugees and Forced Migrants
http://www.rshu.ru/eng/cca

Civiv Assistance announced the creation of its Web site in January 1996. The site is designed to contain the latest information on the refugee situation in Russia and the countries of the NIS, and on existing legislation and draft statutes regulating the status of refugees and forced migrants. Civic Assistance invites any proposals or remarks on the format and thematic contents of the site. E-mail addresses: rubin@rshu.ru (Cyrillic text must be encoded with the program Uuencode), or rubin@infao.rggu.msk.su, or gannushkina@infao.rggu.msk.su.

CivicNet
http://www.redline.ru/civicnet/

CivicNet is maintained by the Association for Civic Education in Moscow. It contains links to a variety of information sources and civic education organizations including: information about the association; governmental activity in civic education; important documents regarding civil rights; NGOs involved in civic education; and a bibliography of instructional, theoretical and methodological materials. It also provides schedules and news on the programs and activities of the association. The site is in Russian (KOI-8 fonts). To read some of the documents it is necessary to download them to your own computer and then apply Cyrillic fonts.

Civnet
http://civnet.org/

Civnet is a large collection of resources related to civic education. Civnet and its companion electronic mailing list are an outgrowth of an international conference on civics education, Civitas@Prague.1995, held in the Czech Republic in June 1995. Most of the participants at the conference were from the U.S., Eastern Europe, and the NIS. Civnet contains a large number of documents–in some cases, entire books– which can be downloaded and used by educators. Most of the documents available through Civnet are in English and have been prepared for use in the U.S. However, the maintainers of the site hope to collect materials developed in other countries and they make a point of offering to upload new materials that are sent to them.

Highlights

- **Organizations and Programs**
  http://civnet.org/CEO/index.html

  A collection of directories of organizations and programs related to civic education, civil society, civic participation, and civic journalism.

- **Civitas@Prague Participants**
  http://civnet.org/CEO/civitasorgs.html

  A list of more than 150 organizations which participated in Civnet conference, includes contact information and brief (one sentence) organizational profiles.

- **Education for Democracy International Directory**
  http://civnet.org/CEO/edid.html

  A directory of more than 300 civic education-related organizations worldwide. The directory is organized by country and includes contact information.

- **Civics Teaching Resource Library**
  http://civnet.org/Teaching/civics.html

  * "Basic Readings in Democracy:" A collection of (mostly American) historical documents, such as the U.S. Constitution. Also available here is a document titled National Standards for Civics and Government, which lists the concepts students should learn in civics education courses in the U.S.

  * "Civics Lesson Plans and Syllabi:" Available at the end of 1995 were three lesson plans on democracy and two English translations of curriculua developed for primary school children in Poland. These curricula and lesson plans are large electronic files ranging in size from 100-250 Kb.

  * Also available are some annotated bibliographies for civic education, research reports, and opinion pieces.

DemocracyNet

http://www.ned.org/

DemocracyNet is a project of the National Endowment for Democracy, a grant-making organization established and funded by the U.S. government to strengthen democratic institutions around the world through nongovernmental efforts. DemocracyNet is relatively new. However, in the coming months NED intends to upload a database of NED grantees, many of which have been organizations and projects in the NIS, and a catalog of its grantees' publications. NED also has assembled a good catalog of links to Internet resources related to democracy.

One of NED's grantees is the Center for International Private Enterprise. CIPE's quarterly publication Economic Reform Today is available from DemocracyNet (**http://www.ned.org/page_4/eco/eco_home.html**). A recent issue focused on business associations and includes articles on "Ensuring Quality of Local Chambers of Commerce" and "Better Business Bureaus: A Watchdog for the Private-Sector."

DUX

http://www.dux.ru/koi8/home.html

DUX is an e-mail and Internet access provider in St. Petersburg. The DUX Web site is home to three Russian-language newspapers and journals that focus on business. All three use KOI-8 fonts.

- **Business Law Journal**
  http://www.dux.ru/koi8/enpp/newspapers/blj/bljhome.html
  A bi-monthly journal which reports on national and local laws and regulations which affect businesses.

- **Business Petersburg**
  http://www.dux.ru/koi8/enpp/newspapers/dp/indexes/dp-160-index.html
  A weekly newspaper which reports on business events with a special emphasis on telecommunication firms.

- **Echo**
  http://www.dux.ru/koi8/enpp/newspapers/echo/echohome.html
  Another weekly business newspaper. Back issues are available through February 1995.

Environmental Technical Information Project

http://ecologia.nier.org/

The Environmental Technical Information Project is an excellent example of how the Internet can help in technical assistance work with NIS NGOs. A project of ECO-LOGIA, which has been working in the NIS since the mid-1980s, ETIP is a collection of links to Internet resources and online databases which contain technical information about environmental issues. It is divided into seven general categories:

- Toxic chemicals
- Radiation issues
- Waste management and pollution prevention
- Environmental legislation and treaties
- Energy-related technologies
- Global issues
- Environmental education

For each subject category ECOLOGIA has prepared a general introduction to the online resources available and how issues related to the specific category are approached in the U.S. (There are separate introductions for "those with little or no scientific background in the field" and for "those with a moderate to high level of scientific background in the field.") For each Internet resource to which ETIP provides a link there is also a document that describes the type of information provided and directions on how to navigate through the Internet site. As if ETIP was not user-friendly enough, ECOLOGIA has created three copies: one in English and two in Russian (using KOI-8 and Windows Cyrillic fonts).

Friends and Partners
http://solar.rtd.utk.edu/friends/home.html

If you were looking for information related to the NIS and you could only visit one site, Friends and Partners would be the place, because from there you can visit almost every other NIS-related Internet site. New documents and links to other Internet sites are added and updated every day.

F&P was started in January 1994 by Greg Cole, Director of the Center for International Networking Initiatives at the University of Tennessee, and Natasha Bulashova, who manages the Office of Grants and Special Information in the Institute of Biochemistry and Physiology of Microorganisms in the Russian Academy of Science in Pushchino, outside of Moscow. Greg and Natasha have used their computer expertise to create a place where others can collect and maintain information related to U.S.-NIS relations in a wide variety of fields, including art, education, health, history, literature, science, etc. The project has generated such great interest that Greg Cole reports he spends a significant amount of time everyday responding to people who want to help.

The Friends and Partners site is physically located in Knoxville, Tennessee. However, an exact duplicate (called a mirror site) exists on a computer in Pushchino. This is especially useful for people in the NIS, where connecting to computers located abroad is sometimes slow and more expensive than connecting to domestic computers. In 1996 F&P plans to establish mirror sites in other Russian cities. To reduce traffic congestion, the Pushchino site should only be visited from computers in the NIS. Its URL is: **http://alice.ibpm.serpukhov.su/friends/**

Friends and Partners is a World Wide Web site, which means that in order to view the files and navigate between them, you must have a World Wide Web browser. For users who do not currently have a Web browser, F&P has established a mechanism whereby people can "telnet" to its server and use the Web browser that is stored at F&P. You can "telnet" to either the main F&P computer in Knoxville or to the mirror site in Pushchino.

For the computer in Tennessee, "telnet" to: **solar.rtd.utk.edu**
     at the "log-in" prompt, type: **friends**

For the computer in Pushchino, "telnet" to: **alice.ibpm.serpukhov.su** at the "log-in" prompt, type: **friends**

Highlights

- **Center for Civil Society International**
  http://solar.rtd.utk.edu/~ccsi/ccsihome.html

- **Funding & Exchange Opportunities**
  http://solar.rtd.utk.edu/friends/funding/master.html

  Includes information about a variety of funding organizations, including The Eurasia Foundation, the International Science Foundation, the United States Information Agency, and The Global Fund for Women. Also listed are more than 20 funding programs for scholarly exchanges. Of special interest is a directory of foundations that support projects in the NIS compiled by World Learning **(http://solar.rtd.utk.edu/friends/funding/world.learning.funding.html)**.

- **NISHEALTH Clearinghouse** (see below)
  http://solar.rtd.utk.edu/friends/health/health.html

- **More Information Resources**
  http://solar.rtd.utk.edu/friends/info.html

  Contains descriptions and links to a wide variety of other Internet sites with information related to the NIS.

- **News**
  http://solar.rtd.utk.edu/friends/news/news.html

  Descriptions of and links to all the major online sources of news about the NIS.

- **Russian Legal Server**
  http://solar.rtd.utk.edu/friends/msanor/main.html

  A project of Mark Sanor, a U.S. attorney, and Ilya Nikiforov, an attorney in St. Petersburg, the Russian Legal Server includes the text of select NIS laws and constitutions, and a good collection of links to online sources of Russian laws, regulations and commentaries.

- **Telecommunications and Information Infrastructure Issues**
  http://solar.rtd.utk.edu/friends/telecomm/telecomm.html

  A good collection of files and links to other Internet sites with information on the telecommunication infrastructure in the NIS.

GlasNet

http://www.glasnet.ru/

GlasNet offers e-mail and Internet access primarily to individuals and nongovernmental organizations throughout Russia. Glasnet's WWW site serves as a home for a growing number of GlasNet subscribers, both individuals and organizations, who have created their own WWW home pages.

Highlights

- **GlasNet Edutainment Page**
  http://www.glasnet.ru/~asebrant/edut/edu_h.html
  This site helps teachers and students learn about the Internet.

- **Nezavisimaia gazeta**
  http://www.glasnet.ru/ng/index.html
  Summaries and occasionally full articles from this daily Russian-language newspaper (KOI-8 fonts required).

- **Electronic News and Mass Media**
  http://www.glasnet.ru/glasweb/rus/e-media1.html
  A good collection of links to NIS online newspapers.

- **Public Groups and NGOs**
  http://www.glasnet.ru/glasweb/rus/ngo_1.html
  Provides information in Russian and in English about groups such as IREX, Obschestvo Evreiskoe Nasledie (Jewish Heritage Society), Iudaika (Judaica), Al-Anon/Alateen and Envirolink.

GlasNews

http://solar.rtd.utk.edu/~aboyle/glasnews/master.html

GlasNews is a quarterly publication (available in print and online) which reports on East-West contacts in all aspects of communications, including: journalism, telecommunications, photography, opinion research, advertising, and public relations. GlasNews is edited by Alan Boyle, foreign editor of the *Seattle Post-Intelligencer* and is published by the Art Pattison Communications Exchange Program based in Seattle. *GlasNews* usually consists of three sections, two features and a section titled "Short Takes: Resources for East-West Communicators."

The feature articles mostly focus on developments in the media in Russia and the NIS. The section, Short Takes, includes brief descriptions of new East-West news sources, news of telecommunications developments, newsletters, electronic mailing lists, and Internet sites all related in some way to strengthening East-West contacts and the media in the NIS.

GlasNews is also available via e-mail. To add your name to the electronic distribution list, send an e-mail message with the words "**subscribe cepmail**" to **majordomo@eskimo.com**

International Rule of Law Clearinghouse Online
http://www.usdoj.gov/ojp/rol/docs/home.html

The Clearinghouse is a project maintained by Sergey Chapkey, formerly a senior assistant to the Procurator of the Odessa region in Ukraine and Visiting Fellow at the National Institute of Justice. It offers links to Internet resources of interest to those in the NIS working on reform of the legislative process and the criminal justice system. In addition to rule of law resources, the clearinghouse includes a good list of pointers to various U.N. organizations on the Internet.

Internews
http://red.path.net/internews/

Internews, a nonprofit organization based in Arcata, California, helps to develop independent broadcasting institutions in Eastern Europe and the former USSR. Of special interest at this site is "Independent Media in the NIS," a series of research reports that describe in detail the growth of independent media in the NIS. The reports written between 1992 and 1994 cover Georgia (15 Kb), Belarus (30 Kb), Central Asia (125 Kb), Siberia (90 Kb) and more. Each report includes a general overview of the conditions independent media (mostly television stations) face, and a brief description of the independent media outlets (with contact information) in the region (**http://red.path.net/internews/documents.html**).

IREX
http://www.irex.org or gopher://info.irex.org

IREX (International Research & Exchanges Board) has administered academic and research exchanges between the U.S. and NIS since 1968. Most of IREX's work on the Internet is in some way related to academic exchanges. For example, in 1993 IREX established a network of American scholars, IREXNet, which responds to inquiries from Russian or Eurasian counterparts. IREX has also established public access e-mail sites in select NIS cities to assist and encourage NIS scholars to use the Internet. These e-mail sites can also be used by NIS NGOs. (For more information see the section *Internet Access in the NIS*.) Recently IREX initiated a project to help develop an e-mail network among NGOs in Russia which work in the areas of children's health care and disabilities rehabilitation.

In 1995 IREX established a WWW site. It may be necessary to visit both its Web site and its Gopher site to find the full variety of information IREX has online. In time, however all of IREX's resources will probably be available at the WWW site.

Highlights

- **Computer Communications**
  gopher://info.irex.org/11/comp.comms

  Includes e-mail addresses for NIS scholars and academic institutes in Moscow, Kazan, and Novosibirsk.

- **Educational Advising Materials for NIS Scholars**
  gopher://info.irex.org/11/edu.adv

  A collection of files compiled by IREX and ACTR, both of whom maintain educational advising centers in the NIS. The collection includes such titles as: "Choosing a College or University," "How to Complete an Application to a U.S. University," and "How to Write a Statement of Purpose." It also has information about how postgraduate education is organized in the U.S. and how to find information about schools–in such fields as public administration, law, nursing, dentistry, medicine, and business.

- **FAQ: E-mail and Internet in the NIS and Baltics**
  http://www.irex.org/FAQ.htm

  FAQ, which stands for Frequently Asked Questions, is the Internet term for a "how-to" guide. This FAQ includes general background information on the Internet, a review of the major e-mail providers in the NIS, directions for hooking up a western modem to NIS telephone jacks, a glossary, and other useful information. The FAQ consists of six files which range in size from 9 to 12 Kb.

- **Fundraising Guide for NIS NGOs**
  gopher://info.irex.org/11/grant.writing/irex

  Materials prepared for a workshop in December 1993, which provide an overview of proposal writing and fundraising for Russian and other NIS nongovernmental organizations and educational institutes.

- **Guide to Foreign Affairs Research Organizations in Russia**
  gopher://info.irex.org/00/new_ceip/ceipdir.txt

  The guide includes contact information and (for most of the entries) a concise description of the research institute, most of which are located in Moscow. The file is 83 Kb.

- **Handbook for Working Journalists**
  gopher://info.irex.org/11/irex.reports/ceejour

  A Handbook for Working Journalists in the Baltics and Other Emerging Democracies is the final phase of a two-year project by IREX to strengthen business and economic journalism in Estonia, Latvia, and Lithuania. The online version includes sections on: beats, story ideas, interviewing, investigative reporting, writing, and ethics. It also includes ethics statements from the Washington Post and USA Today. The sections range in size from 7 to 14 Kb. The entire document is also available in a "zipped" file which can be downloaded (44 Kb).

Network of East-West Women
http://www.igc.apc.org/neww/

NEWW was founded in 1990 by women in the U.S. and USSR and now includes more than 800 women from 30 countries who work to improve tolerance, democracy, health, and other issues which affect the lives of women. The NEWW On-Line project has provided modems and e-mail training to women's organizations in Eastern Europe and the NIS. A list of people involved with project is also available at the site (http://www.igc.apc.org/neww/womenstext.html).

Highlights

- **Network of East-West Women's User Guide**
  gopher://info.irex.org/00/comp.comms/neww.txt

  The NEWW User's Guide was prepared as a manual to complement training sessions for women's organizations in Eastern Europe and the NIS. Although some of the information will only be relevant to participants in the NEWW training sessions, much of the Guide will be of interest to others. The Guide was written for e-mail beginners and includes introductory explanations of e-mail and Internet etiquette, a very useful glossary of electronic communication terms, and answers to frequently asked questions. The guide also includes an annotated list of electronic mailing lists and Internet resources "for the feminist activist."

- **Profiles of women's organizations**
  http://www.igc.apc.org/neww/ceewomen/ceewomen.html   (Eastern Europe)
  http://www.igc.apc.org/neww/fsuwomen/fsuwomen.html   (NIS)

NISHEALTH Clearinghouse
http://solar.rtd.utk.edu/friends/health/health.html

An extensive collection of files related to health care in the NIS and Eastern Europe. The clearinghouse is sponsored by the American International Health Alliance and is maintained by the same people who manage the NISHEALTH and NISMEDINFO electronic mailing lists. In 1996 the NISHEALTH Clearinghouse intends to make available on the Internet a directory of health resources that it has been compiling for health-care practitioners in Eastern Europe and the NIS.

The site is located at the Friends and Partners Internet site which means that it is accessible from within Russia at the Pushchino mirror site.

Highlights

- **NISHEALTH Clearinghouse Document Library**
  http://solar.rtd.utk.edu/friends/health/library.htm

  The NISHEALTH Clearinghouse maintains a library of more than 700 documents. As of this writing only some of the documents were available from the WWW site. However, a catalog of the 700+ documents exists and the site's manager will mail any documents from the catalog upon request. **(http://solar.rtd.utk.edu/friends/health/catalog.htm)**

  Most of the documents have also been posted to the NISHEALTH Listserv. Many of them are related in some way to the more than 20 U.S.-NIS hospital-to-hospital partnerships sponsored by AIHA, but there are also many descriptions of projects conducted by other organizations in the NIS. Also included are assessments of health care conditions in the NIS prepared by the World Health Organization and others. The catalog and the online document library are well categorized so it's relatively easy to search for information.

- **Directory of Health-Related Assistance Projects in the Former Soviet Union and Eastern Europe**
  http://solar.rtd.utk.edu/friends/health/proj/proj0005.htm
  A directory of more than 50 organizations with health-related projects in the NIS or Eastern Europe. The directory includes contact information and brief project descriptions.

- **Medical Matrix: Guide to Internet Clinical Medicine Resources**
  http://solar.rtd.utk.edu/friends/health/nismed/matrix/homepage.htm
  Medical Matrix is an online annotated guide to Internet resources of interest to physicians and health care workers. A project of the Internet Working Group of the American Medical Informatics Association, the Matrix's main subject categories include Medical Education, Medical Electronic Journals and Newsletters, Medical Software Databanks, and Patient Education and Support. AIHA is in the process of translating the Medical Matrix into Russian and making it available at the NISHEALTH Clearinghouse (Windows Cyrillic fonts). In 1996 AIHA in-

tends to upload a Breastfeeding manual (in Russian) and other Russian-language professional resources.

- **NISHEALTH Individuals Directory**
  http://solar.rtd.utk.edu/friends/health/edir/edir.htm

  E-mail directory of individuals involved with health in the former Soviet Union and Eastern Europe–includes contact information, areas of specialization, and projects with which individuals have worked. The directory is divided into four main files: the Technical Assistance Community, Western Health Professionals, NIS/CEE Health Professionals, and the Academic/Research Community.

- **Directory of Translated Materials**
  http://solar.rtd.utk.edu/friends/health/trns/trns0003.htm

  A directory of health-care related documents that have been translated into Russian or other languages of the NIS and Eastern Europe. Each entry includes the title and language, a brief description, and information on how to obtain copies. Documents range from detailed manuals for surgeons to public education brochures (140 Kb).

REESWeb: Russian and East European Studies Internet Resources
http://www.pitt.edu/~cjp/rees.html

REESWeb is a collection of links to a wide variety of Internet resources related to the NIS and Eastern Europe. (There are no documents or files located at this site, just links to other Internet sites.) As the title implies, many of the links are to academic Internet resources. There are also many links to business-related resources. The list of links is updated regularly by Karen Rondestvedt, Slavic Bibliographer at the University of Pittsburgh. With each link there is also a brief annotation about what the referenced Internet site includes. If you can't find what you are looking for anywhere else, try this site.

Highlights

- **New Items This Month**
  http://www.pitt.edu/~cjp/rees.html#New

  A good place to visit to keep up on Internet resources that have recently come online.

- **National Homepages and Major Sites**
  http://www.pitt.edu/~cjp/rees.html#Home

  A list of links to a major Internet site devoted to each country in Eastern Europe or the NIS. They are called National Homepages, although there is nothing official about them. Most of the sites are located in the country, but some are maintained by people in the U.S. From each of these sites you can visit almost all the Internet sites located within a specific country.

Regional Environmental Center
http://www.rec.hu

The Regional Environmental Center for Central and Eastern Europe was established in 1990 by the government of Hungary, the U.S. Environmental Protection Agency, and the European Commission to serve as a clearinghouse in support of environmental NGOs. Its site includes news of the REC's various grant and fellowship programs, its quarterly bulletin, and other publications. The REC's Information Exchange Team program provides library and information services to all its constituentcies–NGOs, governments, businesses, the media, international organizations, and academic institutions. The REC also maintains FTP and Gopher sites which include most of the information available at its Web site.

REC Gopher site: **gopher.rec.hu**   REC FTP site: **ftp.rec.hu**

Highlights

- **The Environmental Cooperation Bulletin**
  ftp://ftp.rec.hu/vol4/ftp/rec/kompass

  A monthly listing of announcements, brief project summaries, and other environmental activities in Eastern Europe and the NIS published by Kompass Resources International.

- **Environmental Events in Central and Eastern Europe**
  ftp://ftp.rec.hu/vol4/ftp/rec/events

  A list of upcoming conferences, seminars, and workshops compiled by the REC and published every three to four weeks.

- **NGO Directory for Central and Eastern Europe**
  http://www.rec.hu/REC/Databases/NGODirectory/NGOFind.html

  Contact information and brief project description for more than 1,000 organizations in Central and Eastern Europe and the Baltic states.

Russia-On-Line
http://www.online.ru/

In September 1995, Sovam Teleport, an Internet access provider in Russia, started a new service called Russia-On-Line. Similar to America Online and Compuserve in the U.S., Russia-On-Line offers e-mail accounts, access to the Internet, and online news services–some for free, some for a fee. The news services available include:

- *Dengi*   Daily. Issues from the most recent two weeks. In Russian.

- *Daily Digest of the Institute*   Daily. Issues from most recent two weeks. In
  of the Open Press   Russian.

- *Izvestia*   Daily. Issues from the most recent two weeks. In Russian.

- *Izvestia–Ekspertiza*   Daily. Issues from the most recent three months. In Russian.

- *Argumenty I Fakty*   Weekly. Issues from current month. In Russian.

- *Nezavisimaia Gazeta*   Daily. Issues from current month. In Russian.

- *St. Petersburg Press*   Daily. Current issues and archives of articles going back to July 1994. In English.

Russian Economy Resource Center

http://www.eskimo.com/~bwest/rerc.html

The Russian Economy Resource Center is an online reference guide to the Russian economy, maintained by Brenden West, a research economist in Seattle, WA. This project locates, organizes, and creates online resources that promote understanding of Russia and its economy. This site includes a comprehensive list of news sources, directories, and academic programs relating to Russia and the NIS.

Highlights

- **Directory of government contacts in Russia**
  http://mail.eskimo.com/~bwest/contacts.html

  Lists contact information for Russian federal and local government offices, and for all U.S. government offices and American Business Centers in Russia.

- **Comparison of Internet providers in the NIS**
  http://www.eskimo.com/~bwest/inetcomp.html

  Compares the prices and services of the major Internet Service Providers in the NIS. This table includes contact information (phone, fax, and WWW) for each company.

Russian Law Database

http://www.inforis.nnov.su/infobase.html.k

Contains full text versions of the Russian Federation Constitution and laws pertaining to Nizhnii Novgorod, the Nizhegorod Region, and the Commonwealth of Independent States. The menus and documents are in Russian KOI8 fonts. Unfortunately Netscape (at this writing) can't read the documents themselves with Cyrillic fonts so it is necessary to save the documents within Netscape to your local hard drive and then view them with your own word processor and KOI-8 Cyrillic fonts.

Russian Legislation from Garant-Service

http://garant.msu.ru

Databases available in Russian and English, including: Economic Legislation, Customs Legislation, Bank Legislation, Land and Environment Protection, and Moscow Municipal Legislation. Subscription prices are $10 per month for the Russian version. Charges for the English version are $25 for educational institutions and libraries and $50 for others. Garant-Service, a supplier of legal information, was established in 1991 by graduates of Moscow State University.

Russian Security Market Data

http://www.fe.msk.ru/infomarket/

A collection of Russian-language materials related to the emerging Russian securities market. Included here are daily news briefs from several Russian securities firms and REDGAR, an experimental database (46,217 records at present) of securities information from the Ministry of Finance. For more information send an e-mail message to: **webmaster@fe.msk.ru**

Sabre

http://www.sabre.org

The Sabre Foundation has two Internet projects related to the NIS. Under its Info-Disk project, Sabre receives an information request from one of its partners in the NIS and then Sabre staff collect electronic files that answer the question. The second project is the Ukraine FAQ+ project to collect electronic files related to Ukraine.

Initially the InfoDisk collections of files were available on computer diskette which Sabre sent, upon request and free of charge, to organizations and academic institutions in the NIS and to western nongovernmental organizations working in the NIS. Recently Sabre has begun to upload these collections to the Internet. To en-

sure the widest possible access to these electronic documents, Sabre uploads many
of these files to its:

–Gopher Site: **gopher.std.com** under the directories: **Nonprofit Organiza-
tions/Sabre Foundation.Inc**

and

–FTP Site: **ftp.std.com** under the directories: **Nonprofits/Sabre.Foundation.Inc**

Sabre has collected documents on:

- Basic Copyright Information
- Basic Internet and Internet By E-Mail
- Military Codes and Related Information (not yet available from the Internet)
- Parliamentary Reference Library Bibliography of Core Materials

In the future Sabre intends to collect documents on:

- Basic Business Information (2 Disk Set)
- Nongovernmental Organization Development
- Basic Trademark and Patent Information

The collection of electronic documents have been compiled by Sabre's staff librarian. Each collection includes a variety of documents which provide an in-depth
overview of the topic. Many of the files are suited for professionals in their respective fields. Some of the documents have copyright restrictions and are intended to
be used for nonprofit or educational purposes only. All of the documents are in
ASCII-text format so that they can be transferred easily via e-mail and can be
viewed and printed with most word-processing software.

Three of the InfoDisks (collections of documents) have been uploaded to the In-
ternet to date. Each collection is in a separate directory and each includes a
"ReadMe" file with an annotated list of the electronic documents in the collection.
The annotations include the URL for each document.

Sabre InfoDisks

- **Basic Copyright Information**
**gopher://ftp.std.com/11/nonprofits/Sabre.Foundation.Inc/Reference/Basic.Copyrig
ht.Information**

This includes the U.S. Copyright law and several files that provide background information to the U.S. law, information about copyright law as it relates to libraries
and academic institutions, information about copyright enforcement in Russia and

Ukraine, and a series of documents which address the question of international copyright protection.

- **Basic Internet and Internet by E-mail**
  gopher://ftp.std.com/11/nonprofits/Sabre.Foundation.Inc/Reference/Basic.Internet
  .and.Internet.by.E-mail

  This collection, which takes up two diskettes, has a number of big documents, including some general guides to the Internet, and lists of electronic journals and Listservs. There is also a collection of documents which describe various sophisticated techniques with which one can navigate the Internet by only using e-mail.

- **Parliamentary Reference Library Bibliography of Core Materials**
  gopher://ftp.std.com/11/nonprofits/Sabre.Foundation.Inc/Reference/Parliamentary.
  Library.Bibliography.of.Core.Materials

  The bibliography was prepared by the Congressional Research Service in 1991 as part of a project to identify resources that would be of interest to East European parliamentarians.

For more information about the InfoDisk project, contact:

Sabre Foundation Inc.
872 Massachusetts Avenue, Suite 2-1
Cambridge, MA 02139
Tel: (617) 868-3510
Fax: (617) 868-7916
E-mail: **sabre@sabre.org**

Sacred Earth Network
http://www.igc.apc.org/sen/

Since 1989 SEN has provided computers, modems, and e-mail training to more than 150 environmental NGOs in the NIS. For the past couple of years, SEN has also published a *Directory of Environmental E-Mail Users in the Former Soviet Union*. SEN's new WWW site includes back issues of its newsletter in English (the Russian edition will be available soon) and an abbreviated version of its print *Directory*. The *Directory* includes e-mail addresses and contact information for more than 300 NIS environmental activists, plus brief categorizations of their interests. SEN promises to add a search capability soon and also to upload detailed profiles of more than 60 NIS NGOs.

Sakharov Foundation

http://www.wdn.com/asf

The Andrei Sakharov Foundation was organized in Moscow shortly after Sakharov's death in December 1989 and a U.S. affiliate was established a year later. The Foundation's WWW site includes information about Sakharov and his wife, Elena Bonner. There are a number of documents related to the work of the Foundation in the fields of nuclear energy and human rights, including a useful list of links to human rights resources on the Internet (**http://www.wdn.com/asf/hrorg.html**).

Soros Foundations

http://www.soros.org

The family of foundations sponsored by George Soros, including the Open Society Foundation and the International Science Foundation, have funded a large number of projects in a wide variety of fields in Eastern Europe and the NIS. The Soros Foundation Internet site, titled "Open Society Home Page," includes detailed descriptions of Soros-funded programs in the region and project descriptions and contact information for all the Soros Foundation offices (**http://www.soros.org/found1.html**).

Most of the projects funded by the Soros foundations are administered by Soros Foundation offices in each country. Several of these national offices have their own Web sites, including:

- **Estonia:** http://www.oef.org.ee

  Includes: overview of projects supported by the Open Estonia Foundation; announcements of upcoming grants programs and deadlines (**http://www.oef.org.ee/news/index.html**); and 1994 Annual report (**http://www.oef.org.ee/annual/index.html**).
- **Lithuania:** http://www.osf.lt
- **Ukraine:** http://www.irf.kiev.ua

St. Petersburg Web Home Page

http://www.spb.su/

One of the first WWW sites in Russia, the St. Petersburg Web includes several online newspapers, information from travel agencies, and business publications.

Highlights:

- *The St. Petersburg Press*, an online version of the weekly English-language newspaper published in St. Petersburg (**http://www.spb.su/sppress/index.html**).

- *Prospects: The St. Petersburg Press Culture & Lifestyle Guide*, an English-language online publication which includes a regular listing of museums, cultural attractions, a metro map, etc., plus a weekly edition which includes feature articles and news briefs (**http://www.spb.su/lifestyl/index.html**).

- *BEAT?*, a Russian-language magazine on today's alternative cultural scene (**http://www.spb.su/beat/index.html**).

The St. Petersburg Web is also home to several business-related resources published in 1994, including:

- *Business Way '94*–St. Petersburg business profile, a guide for people interested in business opportunities in St. Petersburg.

- *St. Petersburg Business Journal*

- Back issues of *Rules and Regulations in Russia*, a quarterly magazine on local business regulations.

Tajikistan Home Page

http://www.soros.org/tajkstan.html

A project of the Soros Foundation, this Web site contains a wide variety of information related to Tajikistan. It includes an impressive list of links to documents which focus on such issues as the human rights situation in Tajikistan, the media, business climate, U.S. and UN policy, history, current news sources, etc. It also includes a directory of U.S. and European NGO projects in Tajikistan (**gopher://gopher.soros.org/0/Affiliated_Orgs/OSI_NY/Tajikistan_Project/list_of_NGO s.txt**) (60 Kb).

Ukraine FAQ+

http://world.std.com/~sabre/UKRAINE.html

An online library of information about Ukraine including the country's history, culture, current events, bibliographic resources, business information, and more. The site is a project of the Sabre Foundation.

Highlights:

- **Law**

  http://world.std.com/~sabre/UFPWWW_Etc/LAW.html

  Includes the full text, in English, of the constitutional agreement between the Supreme Rada of Ukraine and the President on the basic principles of the organization and function of state power and local government. Also available here are the text of the Ukrainian laws on joint venture registration and foreign investment.

- **Organizations, Institutions and Libraries**
  http://world.std.com/~sabre/UFPWWW_Etc/ORGANIZATIONS.html

  Homepages and links to homepages of more than a dozen organizations which work on issues related to Ukraine, including some in Ukraine itself such as the Ukrainian Legal Foundation and Kyiv-Mohyla Academy.

- **Ukrainian Weekly**
  http://www.tryzub.com/UFPWWW_Etc/Current/UkrWeekly/ABOUT.html

  Excerpts and full articles from the *Ukrainian Weekly*, one of the oldest Ukrainian-American newspapers.

Ukrainian Server

http://www.osc.edu/ukraine.html

Maintained by Max Pyziur, a Ukrainian-American who lives in St. Louis, this site is a rich collection of files related to Ukraine. There is also a version of the site available in Ukrainian (**http://www.osc.edu/ukraina.html**). The site includes general background information on Ukraine and its government, including: an annotated list of political parties with contact information; listings of companies and cooperatives (in Russian); Ukrainian language resources; and links to other Ukrainian-related Internet sites, including quite a number in Ukraine. Pyziur has also assembled a good collection of computer programs and files that are used to display and send electronic files written in Ukrainian Cyrillic.

Of special interest are the files Pyziur has collected which are lists of organizations and e-mail addresses. Included are:

- **E-mail Directory of Media in Ukraine**
  gopher://infomeister.osc.edu:74/00/ukrainian/media/mediaems.txt

- **Directory of Academic Institutions in Ukraine**
  http://www.osc.edu/ukraine_nonpubl/htmls/highed.html

- **Directory Ukrainian Émigré Organizations**
  http://www.osc.edu/ukraine_nonpubl/htmls/orgukr.html

  List of more than 120 (mostly) Ukrainian-North American organizations, with contact information.

Ukrainian WWW Links

http://soma.crl.mcmaster.ca/ukes/ua-links/Ukraine3/ukraine3.html

A list of nearly 3,000 links to Internet sites and documents related to Ukraine, including 1,000 in Ukraine itself. Although the list is not annotated it is easy to scan and see what is available.

Window-to-Russia Home Page

http://www.kiae.su/www/wtr/

Maintained by Relcom, Russia's largest Internet access provider, this site has links to a variety of other information sources on such topics as art, business, computers, science, and more. Relcom has made available materials which passed over the Relcom network during the August 1991 coup (**ftp://ftp.kiae.su/misc/politics/coup19-23aug91.tgz**–a very large file) and a log of events and news broadcasts during the October 1993 coup (**ftp://ftp.kiae.su/misc/politics/oct93.zip**). Also available here is a list of links to other WWW sites in Russia (**http://www.kiae.su/www/wtr/russ-web.html**).

World Wide Web sites in the NIS

Each of the sites listed below include a list of links to World Wide Web sites in the NIS. These are not the only lists, however most of them are regularly maintained and they are good places to start. Perhaps the single most complete list is available at REESWeb at: **http://www.pitt.edu/~cjp/rsfsu.html**

- **Estonia**

  http://www.nlib.ee/ESTONIA/list_WWW.html

- **Latvia**

  http://latvia.vernet.lv/www/list.html or
  http://www.nlib.ee/LATVIA/

- **Lithuania**

  http://www.nlib.ee/LITHUANIA/

- **Russia**

  http://www.izhmark.udmurtia.su/WWW_list/jwz/other.html
  http://www.ru/web.html
  http://www.ras.ru/map_list.html

- **Ukraine**

  http://www.cs.kiev.ua/library/pointer/ukr_www.html

Online News Sources

S ome of the references below are to non-interactive electronic mailing lists–
i.e., you can't send messages to other people on the list–others are to Web
sites. For example, complete issues of some major Russian newspapers, such
as *Izvestia* are available for free on the Web via "Russia-Online" on a daily basis.
Because of the difference in time zones, Americans can read on Wednesday, for
example, the Thursday edition of *Izvestia*.

Glasnet maintains a good collection of links to NIS newspapers online
(**http://www.glasnet.ru/glasweb/rus/e-media1.html**).

Some of these newspapers are formatted with Cyrillic fonts. For more
information about how to read Cyrillic fonts while using Netscape see the section
"Using Cyrillic on the Internet."

Acid Rain

This is the name of an ecological bulletin produced occasionally by a small
environmental organization formed in 1991 in the Lipetsk region. According to this
organization, Lipetsk was recently ranked by a Russian reference book, *The Towns
of Russia*, as belonging to a class of "catastrophically dirty" towns. To receive Acid
Rain, send e-mail requesting it to: **contact@green.lipetsk.su**

Aragil Electronic News Bulletin

Aragil offers a free weekly news summary of Armenian press headlines for
academic research or personal use only. Readers may subscribe to the complete
Aragil daily edition. It is also possible to establish an account with Aragil and
request the full transmission only for specific days. (Price for a single day's edition
is 50 cents U.S.) Send inquiries to: **request@aragil.arminco.com**, or to:
aragil@aragil.arminco.com.

Armenia News

http://office.aic.net/news.html

News Around Armenia offers a collection of links to online news sources about and
from Armenia. Another good source of Armenian news is also available from a
Web site in Germany (**http://wotan.wiwi.hu-berlin.de/~houssik/news.html**).

Baltic News Service

Baltic News Service is an online, English-language wire service, similar to Associated Press or Reuters, that covers the Baltic countries of Estonia, Latvia, and Lithuania. BNS covers international and domestic government, political, and economic news. It consists of one e-mail message per day, which averages 50-80 kilobytes. BNS also maintains a WWW site that contains contact information, archives of BNS daily reports in Estonian, and archives of other BNS Estonian-language reports, including its daily financial wire service (**http://www.digit.ee/ik/bns/Welcome.html**).

To subscribe, send the message: **sub bns**
                                                  to: **darba@mii.lu.lv**

Unlike most electronic mailing lists, when you subscribe you won't receive a confirmation or welcome message. The BNS daily reports will just start arriving in your mailbox.

Belarus Information Service Bulletin

News briefs (in English) published by the Minsk Mass-Media Center in Belarus. The Center was founded by a group of Belarussian journalists who wanted to improve the standards of journalism in their country. Several days worth of news briefs are compiled and e-mailed to subscribers every 3-5 days. The compilations can range in size from 10 to 25 kilobytes. To be added to the distribution list, send a message to the Mass-Media Center in Minsk: **mmc@glas.apc.org**

Business Law Journal

http://www.dux.ru/koi8/enpp/newspapers/blj/bljhome.html

A bi-monthly journal which reports on national and local laws and regulations which affect businesses.

Business Petersburg

http://www.dux.ru/koi8/enpp/newspapers/dp/indexes/dp-160-index.html

A weekly newspaper which reports on business events with a special emphasis on the telecommunications industry.

Economics and Life

http://solar.rtd.utk.edu/friends/economics/el/Economics.html

Economics and Life is a weekly Russian-language newspaper that reports on business and economics in Russia. The newspaper was founded in 1918 and now has more than 600,000 subscribers. The Internet edition includes articles on tax regulations, banking and finance, insurance, real estate, customs regulations, the stock market, and more. The online version is formatted in KOI-8 Cyrillic fonts.

Ecostan News

An English-language monthly bulletin which carries reports on the environment and environmental movements in Central Asia. A good source of information on nongovernmental organizations in the region. Back issues are available online at Friends & Partners
(**http://solar.rtd.utk.edu/friends/science/ecostan/ecostan.index.html**).

To subscribe, send a message asking to be added to the list to Eric Sievers at: **sievers@igc.apc.org**

Eesti Ringvaade

A weekly review of news from Estonia compiled from local news services and issued by Estonia's Ministry of Foreign Affairs. Each issue has sections on international, domestic, and business news.

To subscribe, send a message asking to be added to the list to: **vminfo@vm1.vm.ee**

Environmental Cooperation Bulletin

A monthly bulletin of environmental activities in Eastern Europe and the NIS compiled by Kompass Resources International in Washington, DC. The Bulletin comes in two parts: "Calendar" and News Briefs." Back issues of the Bulletin are available online (**ftp://ftp.rec.hu/vol4/ftp/rec/kompass**).

To subscribe, send a message asking to be added to the list to: **kri@igc.apc.org**

Express Khronika

Express Khronika, first issued in August 1987, is a daily Russian-language bulletin/news service that reports mostly on human/civil rights events and organizations. Express Khronika has a network of correspondents in Russia and the former republics of the USSR. The daily Russian-language edition is free and averages 15 to 25 kilobytes in size. It comes uuencoded. (See the section "Using Cyrillic on the Internet" for more information on how to decode the files.) There is also an English-language weekly summary which costs $30 per year.

To subscribe, send a message asking to be added to the list to:
chronicle@glas.apc.org

The Georgian Chronicle

Since December 1992 the Caucasian Institute for Peace, Democracy and
Development has issued a monthly bulletin in English, reviewing major trends in
political, social and economic life of Georgia. It is available by e-mail and
international mail, upon request. Send e-mail requests to: **cipdd@cipdd.ge**.

Health Cooperation Bulletin

A quarterly bulletin of health-care related projects in Eastern Europe and the NIS.
The bulletin, which is around 30 Kb in size, consists of concise, informative profiles
of health care projects, organizations, and studies. Each profile also includes
contact information. Kompass hopes to issue the bulletin monthly beginning
sometime in 1996.

To be added to the distribution list send a message to: **kri@igc.apc.org**

Izvestia

http://win.www.online.ru/providers/rrussica.xhtml

Links to three publications from Izvestia. All three are in Russian and require
Cyrillic fonts for Windows.

- *Izvestia*
  http://win.www.online.ru/mlists/izvestia/izvestia-izvestia/
- *Finansovye Izvestia*
  http://win.www.online.ru/mlists/izvestia/izvestia-finance/
- *Izvestia-Expertiza*
  http://win.www.online.ru/mlists/izvestia/izvestia-expert/

LETA: Latvian Telegraph Agency

Brief daily reports on government, political, and economic news in Latvia. The list
consists of one e-mail message a day that averages 10 kilobytes in size. Unlike most
other electronic mailing lists, when you subscribe to LETA you won't receive a
confirmation or welcome message. The daily reports will just start arriving in your
mailbox.

To subscribe, send the message: **sub leta**
to: **darba@mii.lu.lv**

Nezavisimaia gazeta
http://www.glasnet.ru/ng/index.html

Summaries and occasionally full articles from this daily Russian-language newspaper (KOI-8 fonts required).

Moscow News Confidential

In mid-1994 *Moscow News* announced a service of bi-weekly insider reports available by e-mail to subscribers. For more information, a price list, and a sample issue, send an e-mail message to: mosnex@sovamsu.sovusa.com

OMRI-L

The Open Media Research Institute is the successor of Radio Free Europe/Radio Liberty. The OMRI Daily Digest is probably the best single source for news of Eastern Europe and the former USSR. The Digest is a compilation of brief news stories by OMRI reporters in the region, and is sent in two parts, the first covering Russia and the CIS, and the second covering East Central Europe and the Baltics. It comes once a day and averages around 30 kilobytes. Past issues of the Daily Digest, going back to January 1994, are available online (http://www.omri.cz/Publications/Digests/DigestIndex.html).

To subscribe, send the message: **subscribe omri-l firstname lastname**
                               to: **listserv@ubvm.cc.buffalo.edu**

   A Russian-language edition of the Daily Digest is also available via e-mail. To learn more about this version visit the OMRI World Wide Web site (http://www.omri.cz/Publications/RussianDD/AboutRussianDD.html) or send an e-mail message to Pete Baumgartner at: **baumgartnerp@omri.cz**

Radio Free Europe/Radio Liberty
http://www.rferl.org/

For more than forty years RFE/RL has been broadcasting news to the countries of Eastern Europe and the NIS, In December 1995 RFE/RL joined the World Wide Web. Its WWW site includes selections of recent news briefs, plus longer analytical articles.

Rukh Insider

The Rukh Insider is a bi-monthly news bulletin which carries "in-depth information on political events in Ukraine, including behind-the-scenes coverage of significant current issues, the positions of policy-makers, tactics and strategy information on Ukraine's ongoing political struggle to leave behind its Soviet, communist past." Originally published by the secretariat of Rukh, one of Ukraine's first and largest democratic political parties, The Rukh Insider is now compiled by the Institute of Statehood and Democracy, a non-governmental, non-partisan research and educational institute in Kyiv. Usually it consists of one article and is around 5 kilobytes in size. Recent issues have focused on an in-depth look at the people who comprise the President's administration, the growth and influence of organized crime, and the attempted revival of the Communist Party of Ukraine. To be added to the electronic mail distribution list, send a request to: **lozowy@gluk.apc.org**

St. Petersburg Press
http://www.spb.su/sppress/index.html

An English-language newspaper in St. Petersburg, complete with classifieds, that is published weekly on the Internet.

Update on Ukraine
Ukraine in Numbers

The Council of Advisors in Kyiv provides this service free of charge to those who request it. The Council was set up in 1991 under the leadership of Dr. Bohdan Hawrylyshyn to provide an independent source of information and analysis to legislators in the Ukrainian Rada (parliament)–somewhat on the model of our Congressional Research Service. Update on Ukraine is published electronically monthly. The November 1995 issue, for example, carried news of Ukraine's admission to the Council of Europe, a review of recent progress in privatization, and an interesting analysis of Ukraine's proposed new Constitution, done by legal consultant Ihor Derkach.

The Council's macroeconomic review, *Ukraine in Numbers*, is available each quarter for free. It comes out on a timely basis (within 2-3 months after the end of a quarter). Other documents are also available for free, if requested by e-mail. These include an English-language translation of the "Constitutional Agreement" reached in June 1995 between the President and Parliament. The Agreement defines the division of powers in Ukraine, has "constitutional authority," and will remain in effect until a new constitution is adopted.

Send all requests to: **rada@carrier.kiev.ua**

You may also contact the Council at fax: (380-44) 296-1360.

UPRESA

gopher://kiev.sovam.com/11/UPRESA

The Ukraina Press Agency and Sovam-Teleport have joined forces to launch the "Ukrainian News Electronic Delivery" project. Part of the project consists of an excellent daily and weekly news service available from a Gopher site in Kyiv. The daily news usually consists of three or four stories about politics, the government, or foreign relations. The weekly news consists of an analytical article, an important public document, such as legislation or official statements, an interview, and a press digest. Each press digest is broken down into sections titled:

- The State
- Activity of Sociopolitical Parties and Organizations
- Foreign Contacts (Foreign relations)
- Economy
- Army, Interior Ministry, Security Service of Ukraine

Ukrainian Arts Monitor

A weekly bulletin that includes news and announcements of art and cultural events in Ukraine. Back issues are available online (**http://www.ukraine.org/UAMonitor/**).

To subscribe, send the message: **RFEED 30 ukrainet.eng.uam**
to: **newsserv@litech.lviv.ua**

Ukrainian Weekly

http://www.tryzub.com/UFPWWW_Etc/Current/UkrWeekly/ABOUT.html

Published by the Ukrainian National Association since 1933, the Ukrainian Weekly has full-time press bureaus in Kyiv and Toronto. The English-language newspaper reports news about Ukraine and Ukrainians around the world.

Vladivostok News

http://www.tribnet.com/vlad.htm

Stories from Vladivostok's English-language newspaper, provided by TribWeb, online service of *The News Tribune* in Tacoma, Washington.

Electronic Directories and Lists

Academic Institutes in Moscow

gopher://info.irex.org/11/comp.comms/whitepages/moscow

E-mail addresses and contact persons for 30 academic institutes in Moscow.

Baltic Journalists

http://www.irex.org/baltlist.htm

List of e-mail addresses for 20 Baltic journalists who participated in an economics and business journalism workshop in Jurmala, Latvia in spring 1994 organized by IREX.

Baltic Library E-mail Directory

gopher://info.irex.org/00/comp.comms/whitepages/baltarc.addresses

List of e-mail addresses for around 50 Baltic libraries and librarians.

Educational Advising Centers in the NIS

http://solar.rtd.utk.edu/~ccsi/csew/94-05/edadvis.html

Contact information for 45 educational advising centers operated by IREX, ACTR, and the Soros Foundations.

Environmental Directory for Central and Eastern Europe

http://www.rec.hu/REC/Databases/NGODirectory/NGOFind.html

Contact information and brief project description for more than 1,000 organizations in Eastern Europe and the Baltic states. The database is accessed through an on-line form (the user enters search criteria), which means you must have a World Wide Web browser to search it.

Estonian school address list

http://www.edu.ee/Koolid/KHM/index.html

A directory of schools in Estonia, with addresses and telephone numbers (in Estonian).

Estonia school e-mail addresses

http://www.edu.ee/Koolid/nimekiri/index.html

A list of e-mail addresses for nearly 150 schools in Estonia.

Eurasia Foundation Grantees:
Brief description of grants made by the Eurasia Foundation to NIS organizations and U.S. NGO projects in the NIS. Although there is no contact information, using other lists referenced in this section you can probably find contact information. If not, someone at the Eurasia Foundation can probably help: **eurasia@eurasia.org**.

- **First 100 Grants**
  http://solar.rtd.utk.edu/friends/funding/eurasia.first.100.grants.html

- **Summary of grants in Ukraine, Belarus, and Moldova**
  http://solar.rtd.utk.edu/friends/funding/eurasia.ukraine.html

Funding Sources for the NIS
http://solar.rtd.utk.edu/friends/funding/world.learning.funding.html

Contact information, with very brief descriptions, of foundations and U.S. government agencies funding NGO projects in the NIS. Compiled by World Learning.

Guide to Foreign Affairs Research Organizations in Russia
gopher://info.irex.org/00/new_ceip/ceipdir.txt

The guide includes contact information and (for most of the entries) a concise description of the research institute, most of which are located in Moscow.

Kazan State University E-mail Addresses
gopher://info.irex.org/00/comp.comms/whitepages/kazan.txt

Around 50 e-mail addresses, plus departmental affiliation, at Kazan State University

Kyiv Freenet Users
http://www.freenet.kiev.ua/FreeNet/yp.html

A listing of the more than 550 users (most of them NGOs) of the Kyiv Freenet, which provides free e-mail and Internet access to NGOs, educational institutes and government agencies in Kyiv. You can either view the entire list or the list of users divided by category, such as NGOs, governmental organizations, etc. For more information about the Kyiv Freenet see the section "Internet Access in the NIS" elsewhere in this guide.

The list itself is a list of links. All you see is the name of the organization. If you activate the link with a World Wide Web browser, a little program appears on your screen, called "MailTo," which enables you to send a message to that person immediately. If you do not want to send a message right then, you can cancel out of the program and return to the list. This is not the most convenient way to display a list of e-mail addresses. However, most World Wide Web browsers display the URL of the link you have highlighted before you activate the link. On the Kyiv Freenet list a link looks like this: **mailto:postmaster@some-org.freenet.kiev.ua.** From this you can tell that the e-mail address of this organization is: **postmaster@some-org.freenet.kiev.ua.**

Lithuania E-Mail Addresses

http://nemunas.sc-uni.ktu.lt/thomas/bluepgs.html

A list of hundreds of e-mail addresses at academic institutes and government ministries in Lithuania. (45 Kb)

Media List

gopher://ftp.std.com/00/periodicals/Middlesex-News/medialist or **gopher://gopher.std.com/00/periodicals/Middlesex-News/medialist** (45 Kb)

This is a listing of newspapers, magazines, TV stations and other media outlets that accept electronic submissions. The list, which is compiled and regularly updated by Adam Gaffin (**adamg@world.std.com**), includes the name of the media outlet and the e-mail address of one or more departments.

Millennium Report

http://www.Cdinet.com/Mill/Resource/resource.html

The Millennium Report was commissioned by the Rockefeller Foundation in April 1994 as a key component of the Foundation's The Common Enterprise initiative. The initiative seeks to revitalize citizenship at the local level by bringing collaborative problem-solving and conflict resolution techniques to diverse groups of community stakeholders. Includes profiles of 237 U.S. organizations, with contact information, divided into 14 categories such as conflict resolution, leadership development, national/community/voluntary service, citizen participation.

NGOs Projects in Eastern Europe and the NIS

http://civnet.org/Teaching/Journal/cfp9/addre/addre.htm

Contact information for 275 East European, NIS, U.S., and European organizations engaged in "broadly defined" civic education-related projects in Eastern Europe and the Western NIS. Compiled by the Centers for Pluralism in Warsaw, the list includes organizations in such fields as: media, human rights, education, youth, conflict resolution, women, ecology, civic participation, law, and more.

NGO Projects in Tajikistan

gopher://gopher.soros.org/0/Affiliated_Orgs/OSI_NY/Tajikistan_Project/list_of_
NGOs.txt

A directory of U.S. and European NGO projects in Tajikisatn.

NIS Environmental E-mail Directory:

http://www.igc.apc.org/sen/EurDB.html

E-mail directory of environmental organizations in the NIS compiled by Sacred Earth Network.

NISHEALTH Health-Related Assistance Projects in the NIS

http://solar.rtd.utk.edu/friends/health/proj/proj0005.htm

A directory of more than 50 organizations with health-related projects in the NIS or Eastern Europe. The directory includes contact information and brief project descriptions.

NISHEALTH Individuals Directory

http://solar.rtd.utk.edu/friends/health/edir/edir.htm

E-mail directory of individuals involved with health in the former Soviet Union and Eastern Europe--includes contact information, areas of specialization, and projects with which individuals have worked. The directory is divided into four main files: the Technical Assistance Community, Western Health Professionals, NIS/CEE Health Professionals, and the Academic/Research Community.

NIS Third Sector Projects

http://solar.rtd.utk.edu/~ccsi/nisorgs.html

Profiles and contact information for NIS NGOs. Includes list of more than 175 organizations in the Russian Far East compiled by COUNTERPART. (http://solar.rtd.utk.edu/~ccsi/nisorgs/vestindx.html)

Novosibirsk State University Addresses

gopher://info.irex.org/00/comp.comms/whitepages/novo.txt

Contact information, plus information on academic discipline and foreign language ability for around 30 academics at Novosibirsk State University

Rule of Law Database

ftp://ftp.fedworld.gov/pub/rol-nis/rol-nis.htm

An annotated directory of U.S. (and some Canadian and European) organizations which are engaged in "broadly defined" rule of law projects in the NIS. Some of the information is a little dated, but the annotations are very extensive. The database is compiled as part of the Rule of Law program administered by ARD/Checchi, which is funded by the U.S. Agency for International Development. The Directory is divided into separate files by country: Armenia (18 kilobytes), Azerbaijan (18kb), Belarus (45kb), Georgia (20kb), Moldova (32kb), Russia (163kb), Ukraine (86kb). As of the end of 1995, the files are only available in WordPerfect 5.1 DOS format. (When transferring the files, makes sure the settings are set for "binary" files.) ARD/Checchi intends to make the database available in World Wide Web format in 1996.

Russia and Ukraine Institutional Partnership Projects

http://www.irex.org/ipplist.htm

Contact information for 22 "Institutional Partnership Projects" between U.S. and Russian and Ukrainian organizations. The program is funded by USAID and administered by IREX.

Ukrainian Emigre Organizations

http://www.osc.edu/ukraine_nonpubl/htmls/orgukr.html

Contact information for more than 120 (mostly) Ukrainian-North American organizations. Categories of groups include: credit unions, general organizations, media, professional organizations, women's groups, and youth organizations.

Ukraine Media E-mail Directory

gopher://infomeister.osc.edu:74/00/ukrainian/media/mediaems.txt

E-mail addresses of 30 news agencies, newspapers, and magazines. The list was compiled in November 1994. A more detailed list of Ukrainian newspapers, with contact information is also available. The list is in Ukrainian (koi-8 font) and is around 90 kilobytes in size
(**gopher://infomeister.osc.edu:74/00/ukrainian/media/sprav.koi**).

Ukraine Offices of International Non-governmental Organizations

**gopher://ftp.std.com/00/nonprofits/Sabre.Foundation.Inc/Ukraine.FAQ.Plus/Busi
ness-**

Commerce.in.Ukraine/Directory.of.Business.Contacts.in.Ukraine/Contact.Organi zations

The list was compiled in late 1994 and many of the e-mail addresses have probably changed. Updated e-mail addresses for many of the organizations on this list can be found on the list of subscribers at the Kyiv Freenet.

Ukrainian Telephone Codes

http://www.gu.kiev.ua/utel/LocCodes_pre.html

A very useful list of area codes for cities and towns in Ukraine. In addition to the area codes this list also tells you how many digits local telephone numbers will have.

U.S.-NIS Oriented Projects

http://solar.rtd.utk.edu/~ccsi/usnisorg.html

A collection of profiles of more than 50 U.S.-NIS projects.

Sending and Receiving
in Cyrillic

The requirements for communicating in Cyrillic on the Internet can vary depending on which computers and what software are being used at each end. A single standard does not yet exist which allows anybody on the Internet, using a few simple keystrokes, to switch from Latin to Cyrillic characters and back. In this section we will demonstrate how to go back and forth between the two character sets for one of the common configurations: people using a Windows-based program (such as Microsoft Word) on a PC. Space does not allow us to give similar examples for Macintoshes or DOS-based systems. Readers with these configurations are urged to visit some of the Web sites indicated below and/or join the RusTex-L electronic mailing list. Its subscribers represent a wealth of know-how, and friendly assistance, on questions of configuring specific computer systems for sending and receiving in Cyrillic.

The challenge of using Cyrillic on the Internet breaks down into two separate problems:

- Being able to read documents at an Internet site that are written in Cyrillic characters;
- Being able to compose a message in Cyrillic and send it to the NIS or, vice-versa, being able to display a received message that was written in Cyrillic.

In a moment, we will discuss each of these challenges, in that order. But first, a brief digression is required about compressing and uncompressing files. If you are already familiar with utilities such as PkZip and know how to "zip" and "unzip" a file, skip the following section.

I. Pkzip

Pkunzip is a common utility for DOS and Windows that "zips" (compresses) files and unzips (decompresses or "extracts") them. By compressing a file, you can can sometimes reduce its size by a factor of as much as 50%.

Why is this important? Zipped files, of course, occupy less space in a computer's memory. If they are traveling on the Internet, where speeds can be as slow as 2,400 bits per second, they also arrive significantly faster. Zipped files can cost less to send or receive. This is important in the NIS, where many Internet users are charged not by the hours they are online *but by the kilobytes* of data they send or receive. Finally, if you intend to download any Cyrillic fonts from the Internet, they only come in zipped form. For these reasons, you need to know how to zip and unzip files if you intend to send and receive in Cyrillic on the Internet.

There are two ways to acquire PkZip software–the name of the most popular and accessible file-compression software. It is available as a commercial product in stores for a very reasonable price. It is also available as a shareware program that can be downloaded from the Internet. We have found a self-installing version of PkZip on the Internet that can be downloaded with Netscape. The file is around 200 Kb in size.

The name of this "self-extracting" file is **pkz204g.exe**. It can be downloaded from two places:

- **ftp://ftp.pkware.com/pub/pkware/**
- **http://wuarchive.wustl.edu/systems/ibmpc/simtel/msdos/zip/**

A. To download PkZip using Netscape

- Go to one of the two sites above and activate the link for **pkz204g.exe**.
- Netscape will display a message that it is an "Unknown File Type."
- Don't worry. Select "Save to Disk" from your "File" menu and Netscape will open a "Save As" dialog box.
- Choose the root directory on your hard drive "C:\" (or another directory if you prefer) and press Return.

You have just downloaded PkZip to your own hard drive. You will later be able to find it in the directory you specified. But it has arrived as a zipped or compressed file itself, so before you can use this utility to compress or uncompress other files, you must first unzip the file you just downloaded, **pkz204g.exe**. This is very easy to do, as **pkz204g.exe** is what is called a "self-extracting" file.

B. To install **pkz204g.exe** on your computer

- Open File Manager in Windows.
- Under the File menu select "Run."
- In the "Run" dialog box type: **C:\pkz204g.exe**
- Press Return.

Windows will briefly exit to the DOS prompt and you will see a message that the file is being "exploded" (meaning, extracted). Sixteen files will be created, including two named "pkunzip.exe" and "pkzip.exe". After the files are exploded you will be returned to File Manager in Windows. You are now ready to use your PkZip utility.

II. Reading documents at an Internet site that are written in Cyrillic

When we type text in English (or any Latin character-based language) on our computer, we are using what is called the "ASCII character set." Every time we strike a letter or symbol on our keyboard, this action is converted into a number corresponding to the ASCII character set. The range of numbers is from 1 to 126. The word "and," for example is represented by the numbers 97, 110, 100. (If it were all upper case "AND," the numbers would be 65, 78, 68.)

When writing in standard English, we are in effect sending strings of numbers ranging from 1 to 126 to the computer's processor, to be displayed on a screen, stored in memory–or transmitted on the Internet.

And here is the problem as far as communicating on the Internet in Russian is concerned. Computer users in Russia use numbers above 126 to represent the characters and symbols on a Cyrillic keyboard and, unfortunately, there is not yet a standard coding scheme that *always* assigns the same unique number to each Cyrillic character or symbol. In fact, there are *three* major Cyrillic character sets (sometimes called coding schemes) which correspond to the three major computer operating systems used in Russia and the NIS:

- AV (*Alternatyvni' Variant*) is the standard used for DOS computers. Sometimes called Code Page 866, AV has been the most commonly used character set for PCs in the NIS, since Windows has arrived there later than in the U.S.
- KOI-8 is the standard used for UNIX machines. Since the Internet is a UNIX-based system and most people in the NIS access their e-mail accounts from a UNIX machine, KOI-8 is probably the most commonly used standard for e-mail in the region. KOI-8 is also supported by Relcom, the major e-mail access provider in the NIS.
- Code Page 1251 is the standard used for Microsoft Windows software. This character set is gaining popularity as Windows spreads in the NIS.

There is also a separate Apple Macintosh standard, but space does not permit going into this.

In principle, any character set can be displayed on any operating system (DOS, UNIX, Windows) as long as a given computer has software on it that converts that character set to its operating system. The challenge of being able to read documents at an Internet site that were written in Cyrillic is:

1. to *know* what character set they were written in. (Normally, the authors of Cyrillic text clue the Internet user in Latin characters as to which character set they used. E.g., "the text below is in KOI8.")
2. to *have* downloaded and installed the fonts (or drivers) that can read that particular character set.

Below we provide a step-by-step example of how to load some Cyrillic fonts into your computer's Microsoft Windows operating sytem. This is the freebie method. You can also buy commercial software packages, which include AV, KOI-8, and Windows fonts, that have their own easy-to-use installation programs. (See the section, "Catalogs, Databases, Directories and Periodicals" for a listing of catalogs that sell a variety of Cyrillic fonts commercially.)

III. Installing Cyrillic Fonts in Windows

In the example below we will use Netscape to download a Cyrillic font from the Glasnet WWW site, unzip the file, and install the font in Windows. When we are finished, we will be able to read Internet documents formatted in KOI-8 Cyrillic fonts.

The Glasnet WWW site has two Cyrillic fonts that can be downloaded and offers brief directions for how to install them in Windows.

A. Downloading the fonts with Netscape

- In Netscape go to the Glasnet Web site whose URL is:

    http://www.glasnet.ru/glasweb/readrus1.html

- Activate the link to download the "ER Bukinist KOI-8" font. (ER Bukinist is the name of this particular Cyrillic font, perhaps given by its developer.)
- Netscape will display a message that it is an "Unknown File Type."
- Don't worry. Select "Save to Disk" from your "File" menu and Netscape will open a "Save As" dialog box.
- Choose a directory on your hard drive where you want to put the zipped file, **koi8buk.zip**. We created a directory named "C:\CYRFONTS" and saved the files to this directory.

B. Unzipping the files

- Activate File Manager in Windows.
- Under the File menu, select "Run."
- In the "Run" dialog box type "**pkunzip c:\cyrfonts\koi8buk.zip**" This commands the PkZip software to "extract" the file just downloaded from the Glasnet WWW site.
- Press Return. PkZip will unzip **koi8buk.zip** and create four new files: "buk_b.ttf;" "buk_bi.ttf;" "buk_i.ttf;" and "buk_n.ttf."

C. Installing the fonts in Windows

You have now downloaded the ER Bukinist Cyrillic fonts file and decompressed it into four different fonts (normal, bold, italic and bold-italic). You are two-thirds of the way to your goal. Now you must make sure that your Windows operating system "sees" these fonts and is able to access them when you need them. To do this, you must "install" your new Cyrillic fonts.

- In Program Manager, open the "Main" folder.
- Select "Control Panel," and then select "Fonts."
- In the "Fonts" dialog box, select "Add."
- In the "Add Fonts" dialog box, choose the directory where the unzipped files are located–in our case it was the "C:\CYRFONTS" directory.

- In the dialog box the name of the four font files you just unzipped will appear: ER Bukinist KOI-8; ER Bukinist KOI-8 Bold; ER Bukinist KOI-8 Bold Italic; and ER Bukinist KOI-8 Italic. (All of them are True Type fonts.)
- Highlight all four and select "OK."

Congratulations! You have just installed four new Cyrillic fonts on your computer. You now have the capability to read any World Wide Web documents formatted in the KOI-8 Cyrillic character set. Should you wish to download more Cyrillic fonts (e.g. for Ukrainian, or simply to have a greater variety of typefaces), there are a number of Internet sites which have Cyrillic fonts that can be downloaded with Netscape using the procedure described above. These include:

- **ftp://ftp.cs.umd.edu/pub/cyrillic/fonts_for_MS_windows/**

- **gopher://infomeister.osc.edu:74/11/ukrainian/software/windows/fonts**

- **gopher://infomeister.osc.edu:74/11/ukrainian/software/windows/fonts**

Each of these sites contains three or four different Cyrillic fonts. Each font is available in the three major character sets. Generally the name of the file provides a hint as to which character set the font is. For example:

- **bk1251.zip** is a Bukinist font for Windows
- **bk866.zip** is the font for AV/DOS
- **bkkoi8w.zip** is the same Koi8 font we got from Glasnet

There are a number of other Internet sites which contain useful information about how to configure a computer to read and write Cyrillic-based languages. At the end of this chapter, we list a number of them and describe what is available there. But now let us return to the original task: reading a document on the World Wide Web that is in Cyrillic.

Suppose you are "browsing the 'Net" and find a document on a server in Russia that was written in Cyrillic using the KOI8 character set. (As noted above, you are likely to see a phrase in English at the top of the document, indicating that "the following document is in the KOI8 Character set.") Now that you have installed some KOI8 Cyrillic fonts on your computer, reading this document is a snap.

- From the menu at the top of your Netscape screen, select "Options."
- Select "Preferences."
- Choose the "Fonts" screen.
- Select "Choose font."
- Scroll through the fonts dialogue box and select the font you want, e.g. "Bukinist KOI8."
- Select "OK."
- Select "OK" at the bottom of the screen which will bring you back to the Netscape main screen and the Cyrillic document you want to read.

That's it. When you are finished reading the Cyrillic document you may need to go back and choose your regular Netscape font, if the next "page" you visit on the Internet is all in Latin characters.

When you load the KOI8 fonts into Windows and use them with Netscape, you also load printer drivers for those fonts. You will be able to read *and print* any KOI8 Cyrillic documents you find on the Internet.

But what if your 'Net surfing leads you to Cyrillic documents written in another character set–say, AV/DOS or Code Page 1251 (the Windows-based Cyrillic font set)? The best way to deal with this situation is to have one font from each of the three Cyrillic character sets loaded into Windows. This way, if you encounter a document which does not tell you at the top in which character set it was written, and KOI8 does not clear up the garbage on your screen, you can try the two others and see if they work. However, you will do pretty well with just KOI8, since the great majority of Cyrillic documents on the Internet use the KOI-8 character set.

IV. Sending and Receiving E-mail in Cyrillic

There are three aspects to sending and receiving e-mail in Cyrillic: composing the message, coding and decoding the message, and reading the message.

A. Composing the Message

You can compose your message using some of the fonts you downloaded already. If you are composing in Word for Windows, select a KOI8 font from your menu of fonts. Then press the two "Shift" keys on your keyboard simultaneously. This toggles you between Cyrillic mode and Latin mode. You will have to figure out which keys on your keyboard correspond to which Cyrillic characters--one arrangement seeks to emulate a Russian keyboard; the other matches Cyrillic characters to English letters that sound, or look, the same--but you have essentially all the tools now on your computer to compose in Cyrillic.

Alternatively, you can purchase one of the variety of excellent software add-ons that give your word processing program a large selection of Cyrillic fonts and styles.

B. Coding the Message for Transmission over the Internet–and Decoding It

For reasons that need not concern us here, Cyrillic characters, which use the ASCII "upper register," cannot go over the Internet without first being coded in such a way that they appear to be Latin characters using the lower ASCII register. The most common program for coding and decoding Cyrillic text in this way for transmission on the Internet is a program known as "UUENCODE/UUDECODE."

Think of uuencode/uudecode as an envelope in which you put your Cyrillic message in order to e-mail it. The uuencoding protects the message during the transmission process. And, just as when you mail a letter to someone you must seal the envelope and the other person must open the envelope, so when sending an e-mail message written in Cyrillic you must uuencode it and the other person must uudecode it at the other end. Below is a complete example showing how to get the uuencode/uudecode utility, how to load it onto your personal computer, and how to use it.

uuencode/uudecode

1. Downloading UUENCODE/UUDECODE

Copies of the UUENCODE/UUDECODE program are available at many Internet sites. We got our copy[1] using Netscape from:

ftp://ftp.cic.net/pub/Software/pc/uudecode/

There are two versions of UUENCODE/UUDECODE available from this FTP site. One is a "zipped" file, **uudecode.zip**, and the other is a self-extracting file, **uudecode.exe**. Because we have PkZip, we downloaded **uudecode.zip**, as follows:

- Using Netscape, go to: **ftp://ftp.cic.net/pub/Software/pc/uudecode/**
- Activate the link for **uudecode.zip.**
- Netscape will display a message that it is an "Unknown File Type."
- Don't worry. Select "Save to Disk" from the "File" menu and Netscape will open a "Save As" dialog box.
- Choose a directory on your hard drive to save the program in. (We advise keeping your root directory as free as possible of other programs, so we created a directory called "C:\CODE," and saved **uudecode.zip** to this directory.)

2. Installing UUENCODE/UUDECODE

- Activate File Manager in Windows
- Under the File menu select "Run."
- In the "Run" dialog box type: **pkunzip C:\code\uudecode.zip**
PkZip will unzip **uudecode.zip** into three files: "uudecode.doc," "uudecode.exe," and "uuencode.exe."

3. Uuencoding a Document

We finally arrive at the nub of the problem! We have been wanting to send a Cyrillic e-mail message to our friend Sasha in Russia, but until now have not been able to do so. However now we have UUENCODE/UUDECODE installed, so we are ready to do this.

- First we compose the document in Cyrillic characters, using either the KOI8 fonts we downloaded, or a Cyrillic fonts software package that we purchased.

---

[1] This version will only work on files created in DOS or Windows. There are separate programs for Macintosh and UNIX files. A good version for the Mac is located at: **gopher://sumex-aim.Stanford.EDU:70/11/infomac/_Compress_and_Translate** The name of the file is: **uu-undo-10.hqx** It is a bin-hexed file.

- After composing the document, we give it a name, **sasha.doc**, and save it in the directory we created called C:\ CODE.
- Now we open File Manager in Windows.
- Under the File menu we select "Run."
- In the "Run" dialog box we type: **C:\code\uuencode sasha.doc**.

This command causes the program to code **sasha.doc** in the special way required to go across the Internet and save it as a separate file that it names **sasha.uue.** If we now tried to open the file in a word processor or saw it in an e-mail message, the beginning of the file would look like this:

section 1 of uuencode 5.24 of file sasha.doc   by R.E.M.

begin 644 sasha.doc
MT,\1X*&Q&N$```````````````````.P\`#'/[_[_0`&``````````!
M```0`````$```$```$``#_^A^#
M_____
M_____

It looks like nonsense, but it will go across the Internet to Russia this way, where Sasha, using his own copy of UUENCODE/UUDECODE, will be able to decode and read the file. To send the file we simply insert **sasha.uue** into an ordinary e-mail message, and send it off to Sasha's e-mail address.

4. Uudecoding a Document

So now Sasha in Russia has received a document that looks like garbage, but has the telltale line at the top, in English:

section 1 of uuencode 5.24 of file sasha.doc   by R.E.M.
begin 644 sasha.doc

This confirms for him that the message needs to be "uudecoded" before it can be read. To do this, Sasha carries out the following steps (let's assume he also has UUENCODE/UUDECODE on a directory named C:\CODE on his computer):

- First, he saves his e-mail message as a document and gives the document a name with the extension ".uue" (He does not need to name the document "sasha" but he *must* give it, whatever name he chooses, an extension of .uue. Let us assume he names and saves the document as **c:\code\ urgent.uue**)
- Next he activates File Manager in Windows.
- Under the File menu, choose the directory, C:\CODE, and then select "Run."
- In the "Run" dialog box type: **uudecode urgent.uue.**
- Press Return.

This commands the program to convert the file named **urgent.uue** back into the form it was in before being Uuencoded. The program recreates the file called **sasha.doc** which Sasha will be able to read using his standard Windows-based word processor.

That's it. It's really not difficult. The most daunting point is when you first see a screen full of garbage characters and you are not sure what you need to do to read them.

With regard to UUENCODE/UUDECODE, however, there are several important points to remember:

- When downloading a uuencoded file from your e-mail account you can name the file anything you want, so long as it ends with the extension **.uue**. Uudecode will work *only* on files that end with that extension.
- When you uudecode the file the program will automatically create a file with the original file name–in our example, **sasha.doc**. The original name is always listed at the beginning of a uuencoded file (see the example above.)

C. Reading a Cyrillic E-mail Message

Reading a Cyrillic e-mail message or printing it out with a Windows-based word processor involves the same steps as reading a Cyrillic document on the Internet with Netscape (discussed above). You must have Cyrillic fonts installed on your computer beforehand. Then use your favorite Windows word processor to apply the Cyrillic fonts to the message, just as you would to change the font when formatting a document. At the moment AV/DOS and KOI-8 are the most common fonts for composing e-mail in the NIS. However, as noted previously, it's always a good idea to have fonts from all three character sets loaded in Windows. The fonts you load will act as both screen fonts and printer drivers.

Addendum

Below we list five of the best Web sites for further investigation of issues related to using Cyrillic on the Internet. In addition to providing links to other sites, where you can find Cyrillic fonts for downloading, these sites also include information about more complicated issues such as how to install and configure different keyboard drivers for composing in Cyrillic.

Friends & Partners
http://solar.rtd.utk.edu/friends/cyrillic/cyrillic.html
A regularly updated collection of links to other Internet sites which contain Cyrillic fonts for all types of computers and directions for how to use them.

REESWeb Software Resources
http://www.pitt.edu/~cjp/rssoft.html
An excellent collection of links to Internet resources for using Cyrillic. It includes links to a number of companies which sell Cyrillic fonts and keyboard drivers.

Russification of Mac
http://www.pitt.edu/~mapst57/rus/russian.html

A well organized collection of documents which explain how to use Cyrillic fonts on Macintosh computers. The site includes a step-by-step guide to installing fonts on your Mac that is very clear and simple to use. Apple Computer, Inc. is scheduled to release a Cyrillic Language Kit in early 1996. For more information on the Kit visit: **http://product.info.apple.com/productinfo/datasheets/as/cyrillic.html**

SovInform Bureau
http://www.cs.umd.edu/ftp/pub/cyrillic/
A good collection of fonts and software utilities for using Cyrillic.

Ukrainian Server
http://www.osc.edu/ukraine.html#SOFTWARE
Maintained by Max Pyziur who does a good job of explaining the myriad of issues involved with using Cyrillic fonts and provides links to fonts for DOS, Windows and Macintosh. Of special interest is the information available on getting Cyrillic fonts for Ukrainian.

Appendices

Additional Resources

One measure of the growth of the third sector in the NIS lies in the number of large databases of organizations that have been developed, as well as the high quality of various books, magazines and directories–all related to the third sector–that have been published in the NIS in recent years.

The list below describes some of those that have come to the attention of Center for Civil Society International.

Access Russia Catalog

Russian Information Services, Inc.
89 Main Street
Montpelier, VT 05602
Sales: (800) 639-4301

Russian Information Services began in 1990. It offers a semi-annual catalog of "books, audio, maps, accessories, periodicals and software" related to Russia, plus the Baltics, Central Asia, the Caucasus and Ukraine. "Accessories" include such items as a Russian telephone adapter for a laptop modem and keytop Cyrillic character labels for attachment to a standard American computer keyboard. The Books section features a very interesting selection of books, not least among them those described as "Armchair Travel" books. These include, for example, *Fifty Russian Winters: An American Woman's Life in the Soviet Union* by Margaret Wettlin.

Azerbaijan International

PO Box 5217
Sherman Oaks, CA 91413
Tel: (818) 785-0077
Fax: (818) 997-7337
E-mail: azerintl@aol.com
Contact: Judith Scott, Circulation

This quarterly magazine describes itself as "an independent publication which seeks to provide a forum for discussion and though related to Azerbaijanis throughout the world on a wide range of subects." It is a bi-lingual publication, averaging 80 pages or more and featuring articles on art, business, culture, history, etc. Each issue has a theme–e.g. "Crisis in the Arts" in the Spring 1995 edition–and each issue also carries information on various international relief and humanitarian agencies active in Azerbaijan. Subscriptions are $28/year in the U.S.

Azerbaijan Newsletter

Azerbaijan Embassy
PO Box 28790
Washington, DC 20038-8790
Tel: (202) 842-0001
Fax: (202) 842-0004

This is a bi-weekly publication of the embassy, providing news of recent events in Azerbaijan.

The BEARR Trust Newsletter
Information About NGO Links with the former Soviet Union

The BEARR Trust
Chichester House
278 High Holborn
London WC1V 7ER
Tel: (0171) 404-7081
Fax: (0171) 404-7103
E-mail: bearr@gn.apc.org

BEARR stands for British Emergency Action in Russia and the Republics. The trust is a registered British charity formed in 1991 to act as a bridge between the welfare and health sectors of Britain and those of the former Soviet Union. It operates a small grants program in the NIS, serves as a clearinghouse and publishes this quarterly newsletter, which costs £20/year in the UK.

Business and Economic Textbooks in Russian

Sol System
Ostuzeza 12/2, room 6, K-104
103104 Moscow
Tel/Fax: 202-6026
E-mail: foyle@solsys.msk.su.
Contact: Michael Foyle

In March 1994, Sol System published the first edition of its catalog, *Книги по экономике и бизнесу (Books on Economics and Business),* consisting of 282 annotated entries of Russian, American, German, French and Canadian sources. Among these were titles such as:
- Кузнецов и Малиничева, *Финансовые фьючерсы*–МГУ (Kuznetsov and Malinicheva, *Financial Futures*–Moscow State University)
- Philip Kotler, *Marketing Essentials*
- Drucker, *Innovation and Entrepreneurship: Practice and Principles*
- Мялков, *Малые предприятия* (P. A. Myalkov, *Small Enterprise)*

With support from the Eurasia Foundation, Sol System has updated its catalogue to cover 1,000 books. In 1994 it distributed approximately 3,500 copies of the revised edition to teaching and training institutions across Russia.

The CCET Register

Centre for Co-operation with Economies in Transition
OECD, 2, rue Andre Pascal
75775 Paris Cedex 16
France
Tel.   (33 1) 45 24 83 60
Fax: (33 1) 45 24 91 77
Contact: Mrs. Jean Gomm, Principal Administrator

The Centre for Co-Operation with Economies in Transition (CCET) was created by the OECD (Organization for Economic Cooperation and Development) in October 1991. Its purpose is to provide up-to-date information on the range of OECD member-sponsored technical and humanitarian assistance programs in the NIS and the Central and Eastern European countries.

The Register is a database whose information can be provided either in print, on computer disk, or on-line. An "energy section" in the database is regularly updated by the International Energy Administration (IEA). There is also a User's Manual for the Register, available in English, French and Russian. In 1994 the Register contained information on approximately 6,600 assistance activities, of which over 2,200 concerned the NIS.

Central Asia Monitor

Institute for Democratic Development
RR 2, Box 6880
Fair Haven, VT 05743
Tel: (802) 537-4361
Fax: (802) 537-4362
Contact: Valery Chalidze, Editor-in-chief; David Nalle, Washington Editor

E-mail: DavidN5512@AOL.COM

The *Monitor* comes out six times a year. Cost is $96/year for institutions, $60 for individuals. Price of sample issue: $16.

Charities Aid Foundation
ul. Elizarovoi, 10
103064 Moscow
Tel: 928-0557, 917-2514, 917-0971, 921-0219
Fax: 298-5694
E-mail: lenay@glas.apc.org
caftacis@glas.apc.org
Contact: Lena Yang, Executive Director

CAF is a rich source of publications and reference materials for those involved in third sector work in the NIS. Following are examples of their publications, some of which were co-published with other agencies. All are in Russian.

- Алексеева, Ольга. *Благотворительное Движение: Регионы России Кто Помогает Детяам? О Работе Благотворительных Организаций.* 1995. *(Charitable Activities: Russian Regions)* Gives contact information and describes the work of 157 nonprofit organizations throughout Russia.
- Алексеева, Ольга. *Кто Помогает Детяам?* 1994. *(Who Helps the Children?)* Describes in detail the work of 79 organizations in Moscow dedicated to addressing the social, economic and medical problems of children. It also features two essays, one surveying the range of social problems Russian children encounter today, the other giving a historical review of charitable activities in

Russia from the 17th century to the present.
- Абросимова, Е. А., Бочарова, С. Н., Бурцева, Н. Ф. *Юристы Некоммерческого Сектопа России.* A guide to law firms in various cities of Russia that assist nonprofit organizations.
- *Роццийская Благотворительность (Историа в Материалах Прессы).* Published in two volumes (1987-92 and 1993-94), this is an annotated guide to articles published in the mass media on third sector issues during an eight-year period. Each entry gives the article's title and date of publication and summarizes its contents. Referenced articles come from more than 100 newspapers. CAF and Charitable Fund "Soprichastnost" are the co-publishers.
- *Основы Деятельности и Успеха Чекоммерческих Организаций.* 1995. *(Main Activities and Programs of Nonprofit Organizations.)* A comprehensive, well-organized manual for use in seminars and workshops on NGO management training.

Civic Organizations and Ecology
ISAR–Ukraine
a/ya 47
252006 Kiev
Tel/Fax: 269-2157
E-mail: isar@isar.freenet.kiev.ua
or
Echo-Vostok
a/ya 56
253192 Kiev
Tel: 544-1780
Fax: 543-5852
E-mail: echo@echo-vostok.kiev.ua

This is a directory in English and Russian of NGOs in Belarus, Moldova, and Ukraine, with a focus on environmental groups.

Connections: Russia News

Public Information and Media Outreach Office
U.S. Embassy in Moscow
B. Devyatinsky per. 6, room 60
Tel: 956-4281, -4282
Fax: 956-7092, -7093
E-mail: usis@glas.apc.org
Contact: Anna Lawton, Editor

The purpose of the monthly magazine, *Connections,* is "to disseminate information on U.S. assistance programs to Russia, and publicize results," but it is far from being a dry or propagandistic product. Items often feature the work of various third sector organizations and U.S. collaborations.

In Russia, the magazine is available for free, in English or in Russian (*Sviazi*). It is also available in electronic form from the Glasnet conferences: glas.connect (English) or glas.sviazi (Russian).

Culture Review

ul. Kuybysheva 96
443099 Samara
Tel: 33-67-25
Contact: Natalya Ogudina, Editor

Culture Review has been published in Samara since March 1993. The newsletter provides information on third sector activities in Russia and abroad, as well as information on associations, educational programs and academic institutions.

Directory of Institutions in the New Independent States and Baltic Republics

Compiled by Erika Popovych
Published by Projects in International Education Research (PIER)
PIER Publications
Box 231
Annapolis Junction
Maryland 20701
Tel: (301) 317-6588
Fax: (301) 206-9789

PIER is a committee comprised of members of the American Association of Collegial Registrars and Admissions Officers and NAFSA: Association of International Educators with the participation of the College Board. This directory was published in 1995 and includes listings for universities, polytechnics, institutes and academies, pedagogical institutes, specialized *uchilishcha*, and conservatories. Each listing includes the name of the institution in both English and Russian (in Cyrillic), address, phone, when established, and fields of study. The cost is $35 for members of NAFSA or AACRAO and $50.00 for non-members. When ordering, please include with your check the amount for shipping and handling: $5.00 for U.S. addresses and $7.50 for addresses outside the U.S.

Database of Ukrainian NGOs

COUNTERPART
WESTNIS Regional Representative
Staronavodnytska 8B, kv. 71
Kyiv
Tel: (044) 296-3913
Fax: (044) 295-8961

In June 1993 COUNTERPART, an international development organization based in Washington, DC, opened a Service Center in Kiev, as part of a 3-year project funded by USAID. Its purpose was to serve a clearinghouse and coordinating function for USAID missions and local and international NGOs. The office has offered training programs in project design and implementation, hosted monthly meetings for USAID grantees, promoted partnerships between U.S. and Ukrainian NGOs, and helped co-ordinate USAID-provided disaster relief in the region.

Directory of Programs in Russian, Eurasian, and East European Studies
American Association for the Advancement of Slavic Studies
8 Storey Street
Cambridge, MA 02138
Tel: (617) 495-0677
Fax: (617) 495-0680
E-mail: aaass@hcs.harvard.edu
Contact: Carol R. Saivetz, Executive Director

Published bi-annually. Includes information on academic departments, faculty and their research interests, summer language programs and overseas programs at over 300 North American institutions of higher education. $30 prepaid for non-AAASS members, plus $3 for postage and handling.

East European Constitutional Review
CSCEE
The University of Chicago Law School
1111 East 60th Street
Chicago, IL 60637

Published quarterly by the Center for the Study of Constitutionalism in Eastern Europe at the University of Chicago Law School in partnership with the Central European University (CEU). The CEU was founded by George Soros and provides facilities, resources, and funding for the Center for the Study of Constitutionalism's network of correspondents and affiliates in Eastern Europe.

The Spring 1995 issue of the *Review,* for example, contained five essays on the theme of the political consequences of parliamentary rule in five countries: Russia, Czech Republic, Slovakia, Romania and Belarus. A regular department, "Constitution Watch," provides country-by-country updates on constitutional politics in Eastern Europe and the ex-USSR.

Subscriptions to the *East European Constitutional Review* are free. The *Review* is also published in Russian as *Конституционное Право: Восточноевропейское Обозрение.* Copies may be obtained from Olga Sidorovich at the Russian Science Foundation, 8/7 B. Zlatoustinsky Lane (formerly Bolshoi Komsomolsky per.), 103982 Moscow, Russia. **Fax:** (095) 206-8774. **E-mail:** olga@glas.apc.org

Возможности Телекоммуникаций в России (Electronic Networking Options in Russia)
Е. В. Якышев, под редакцией А. О. Макеева и Д. Н. Дурманова
Moscow, 1995, 68 pp.
Moscow State University
Faculty of Soil Science, room 598B
Vorobyevy Hills
119899 Moscow
Tel/Fax: 932-1182

E-mail: yakushev@fadr.msk.ru
Contact: Evgeniy V. Yakushev

This little booklet was written by Evgeniy Yakushev of the Foundation for Agrarian Development Research (FADR) in Moscow, with the editorial assistance of A. O. Makeeva and D. N. Durmanova. The project was carried out under a contract between FADR, the Russian Foundation for Basic Research, and World Learning, with funds from USAID.

Возможности Телекоммуникаций в России is a clearly written and well-organized introduction to the Internet. Its author, who is deputy director of FADR, covers all the important aspects of the Internet and includes eight pages on the development of telecommunications in Russia. One learns that as of the summer of 1994 Russia had 206 computer networks linked to the Internet, in comparison to 304 for the Czech Republic and 19,689 for the U.S. There is also a table comparing the prices and levels of service offered by seven different Internet access providers in Russia. Although prices are changing rapidly in Russia–those in the table were as of early 1995–the table still can help a resident of Russia compare the relative costs of different services and decide which access provider is most suited to his or her needs.

To obtain copies of *Возможности Телекоммуникаций в России,* contact either Dr. Yakushev at the address above, or the offices of World Learning in Moscow.

Environmental Directory of the Newly Independent States and the Baltic Nations

Kompass Resources International
1635 17th Street NW, Suite 22
Washington, DC 20009
Tel: (202) 332-1145
Fax: (202) 234-4953

This directory, now a bit dated, includes contact information, year founded, and a description of academic, governmental, media, political, and non-governmental organizations working on environmental issues. 1992. $25.

Eurasian Environmental Electronic Mail Users: A Comprehensive Directory

The Sacred Earth Network
267 East Street
Petersham, MA 01366
E-mail: sacredearth@igc.apc.org

SEN is a networking service among the Western and Eurasian environmental activist communities. It has provided equipment and training that has directly enabled more than 150 Eurasian environmental groups to communicate via electronic mail. In September 1995 SEN published the third edition of its directory–"a comprehensive resource designed to help organizations and individuals communicate with Eurasians who are working to protect and heal their beautiful land."

It is divided into two parts: a detailed list of 377 active electronic mail users and in-depth profiles of 112 groups. The paper used is tree-free, made entirely from the kenaf plant.

The *Directory* costs $20, which includes domestic shipping. To order, send check or money order and address envelope, "Attn: Dave Camoirano." Add $5 for international shipping.

Geneza Expert

Geneza Political Science Center
a/ya 8475
290058 Lviv
Tel: (0322) 52-74-97
Tel/Fax: (0322) 52-18-81
E-mail: igor@geneza.lviv.ua

This is a new monthly magazine, produced by a group of young Ukrainian social scientists at the Geneza Political Science Center. The magazine has 64 pages and four regular sections: politics, economics, religion, and "socioinform" (e.g., results of survey research). It is available in Ukrainian and English editions. Subscription rates for the latter are $180/year for individuals, $240/year for institutions. To see a free sample issue, write to the address above.

Guide to Foreign Affairs Research Organizations in Russia

IREX—International Research & Exchanges Board
1616 H Street NW
Washington, DC 20006
Tel: (202) 628-8188
Fax: (202) 628-8189
E-mail: irex@info.irex.org
Contact: Keith Burner, Public Information Officer

The *Guide to Foreign Affairs Research Organizations in Russia* was produced by IREX and the Carnegie Endowment for International Peace and lists 87 different organizations. The *Guide* "is intended to serve as a tool for all institutions and individuals attempting to establish contacts with partners in Russia." In selecting organizations for the *Guide*, the authors did not restrict themselves to organizations primarily focused on foreign affairs. They included some institutes whose primary fields of concern were different–e.g., economics, ethnography, and nuclear physics–but were deemed important or relevant to issues of international relations. Thus the *Guide* profiles not only the Center for Strategic and Global Studies, but also the Institute of Economic Transition (founded by Egor Gaidar, a former Prime Minister of the Russian Federation); the Public Opinion Foundation; and the International Charitable Foundation for Political and Legal Research (Interlegal).

All the information in the *Guide* is available electronically at IREX's Gopher site (*info.irex.org*). Carnegie and IREX also plan to publish expanded and updated versions of the *Guide* in the future and they encourage users of this *Guide* to submit updates and information for future editions. April, 1995. 85 pp.

Handbook for Journalists

Russian edition
World Press Freedom Committee
The Newspaper Center
11600 Sunrise Valley Drive
Reston, VA 22091
Tel: (703) 648-1000
Fax: (703) 620-4557
Contact: Dana R. Bullen, Executive Director

This is a Russian-language edition of the World Press Freedom Committee's *Handbook for Journalists of Central and Eastern Europe*, edited by Malcolm F. Mallette. The 160-page book was first prepared in 1990 in response to a request from Stefan Bratkowski, president of the Polish

Journalists Association, to help the numerous small local papers then coming into existence in Poland. The handbook is based primarily on American journalism experience and relates mostly to print journalism, although its principles apply also to the broadcast media. It includes chapters on:

- Interviewing
- Writing the Lead
- Modifiers: Beware a wobbly crutch
- Attribution and Sourcing
- Newsroom Planning
- Crime and Courts
- Newspaper Credibility: How to make readers believe
- Typography and Design
- Writing for Broadcast
- Starting a Small Newspaper
- Selling Newspaper Advertising
- Classified Advertising: Tiny ads with big clout
- Circulation's Tasks

Copies of the Russian-language edition of the *Handbook* are available from:
Russian PEN Center
Neglinnaya 18/2
103031 Moscow
Tel: 7 (095) 209-45-89
Fax: 7 (095) 200-02-93
or
Russian-American Press and Information Center
2/3 Khlebny Pereulok
a/ya 229, Novy Arbat
121019 Moscow
Fax: 203-6831

International Center for Foreign Journalists
11690-A Sunrise Valley Drive
Reston, VA 22091
Tel: (703) 620-5745
Fax: (703) 620-6790

E-mail: editor@cfj.org
Contact: Whayne Dillehay, Vice President and Executive Director

CFJ publishes a monthly newsletter, *CFJ Clearinghouse on the Central & East European Press,* which carries information about U.S. media-assistance programs in the NIS, institutional and legal developments that affect the media, and an extensive calendar of upcoming events. Subscriptions are free upon request. ICFJ also has an extensive collection of media training materials, both print and video, some of which are available in Russian.

Как Просит Деньги *(How to Ask for Money)*
World Learning
Volkov per. 13, suite 8
123242 Moscow
Tel/Fax: 255-9724, 255-9001, 956-5003
E-mail: wldlearn@glas.apc.org

This is a 60-page booklet in Russian on how to write grant proposals. The main elements of the table of contents are: search for and choice of financial sources; project composition; principles of grant proposal writing; additional documents; other sources of information and lists of organizations and foundations making grants.

Правозащитник *(Human Rights Defender)*
a/ya 207 Glavpochtamt
101000 Moscow
or
Zubovskii bulvar 17, kom. 30
119847 Moscow
Tel: 246-9720
206-0923 (subscription information)

Contact: Vladimir Vedrashko, Editor-in-Chief

This highly professional quarterly, averaging more than 100 pages per edition, contains essays by leaders of the human rights movement in Russia and the NIS, profiles of significant new organizations, analysis of legal developments, and progress reports on active projects. It is supported in part by the association:

> Liberty Road
> 18 Chemin Briquet
> 1209 Geneva
> Tel/Fax: 41 22 733-8266
> Contact: Mr. K. Ermichine

Subscription information is also available from:

> Book Service Agency
> Krzhizhanovskogo 14/1
> 117168 Moscow
> **Tel:** 129-2909, 124-9449, 129-7212
> **Fax:** 129-0154

International Exchange and Training Activities of the U.S. Government

Bureau of Educational and Cultural Affairs
United States Information Agency
Washington, DC 20547
Tel. (202) 619-5307
Contact: Gloria Simms, Office of Policy and Evaluation (E/Z)

USIA's Bureau of Educational and Cultural Affairs prepares an annual report to inform Congress, institutions in the public and private sectors, and interested individuals of the status of U.S.-government funded exchange activity. The report summarizes the work of roughly 23 federal departments and agencies that conduct international exchange and training programs. It includes descriptions of over 100 programs involving more than 105,000 exchange participants, and costing $1.4 billion in federal funding. Among the programs described is the Citizen Exchanges Program, which coordinated the NIS Secondary School Initiative, under which 5,500 high school students were ex-changed in FY1993—"the largest youth exchange ever attempted."

The Report gives the names and telephone numbers of officials to contact in reference to each particular program.

ISRE Newsletter On Russian and Eurasian Education

Institute for the Study of Russian Education
Indiana University
Smith Research Center 102
Bloomington, IN 47405-2301

This newsletter is published quarterly by ISRE at Indiana University and is a bargain for those interested in the field of education. Subscriptions are $10 annually for individuals and $20 for institutions. The Spring 1995 issue, for example, was 48 pages long and contained the following articles or sections, among others:

- Polish School Days: Observations of a Peace Corps Volunteer
- Selected statistical tables from *The Development of Education: National Report of the Russian Federation* (Moscow, 1994)
- The Soros Foundation's 'Transformation of Humanities Program in Central Asia'

- Electronic Resources for Studying Russian, Eurasian and East European Education

Law Library of Congress

James Madison Memorial Bldg, LM-240
101 Independence Ave. SE
Washington, DC 20540
Tel: (202) 707-5088
Fax: (202) 707-1820
Contact: Ivan Sipkov, Chief, European Law Division

The Law Library of Congress provides a wide range of research and references in a variety of formats on foreign, comparative and international law. Services offered to the public include reference assistance on a limited basis, legal research studies, bibliographies on legal topics, and guides to the law and legal literature of foreign countries. The countries of Central and Eastern Europe are covered by legal specialists.

Maximov's Companion to Who Governs the Russian Federation: A Reference Book and Telephone Directory (Кто правит в Российской Федерации: Справочник с телефонной книгой)

85 Liberty Ship Way, Suite 201
Sausalito, CA 94965
Tel: (415) 331-6785
Fax: (415) 331-8609
E-mail: maximov@mckinley.com

This directory contains over 6,000 telephone, fax and local telex numbers, plus the addresses of over 450 federal, regional and local government officials. All entries are bi-lingual and updated every six months. The least expensive

subscription (one year, two editions of the pocket size version) is $225/year.

For information in Moscow, contact Maximov Publications at:
12 Rozhdestvenka Street
Moscow 103031
Russian Federation
Tel: (095) 925-5696
Fax: (095) 925-8523

Media Developments: News on Media Development and Technical Assistance in the Russian Federation

The USIA Media Assistance Clearinghouse
Russian-American Press and Information Center
P. O. Box 229
Moscow, Russia 121019
Tel: (7095) 290-4016
Fax: (7095) 203-6831
Contact: Nicholas W. Pilugin, Clearinghouse Coordinator

This is an excellent resource for those interested in U.S.-Russian projects involving the mass media. It is written by the coordinator of the USIA Media Assistance Clearinghouse in Moscow. Pilugin is an experienced journalist of Russian-American background, who works out of the Russian-American Press Information Center.

Funding for the MAC comes from the United States Information Agency under a two-year program grant intended to "foster communications between Russian and foreign organizations working to build a free and commercially viable mass media."

Pilugin's 8-page monthly newsletter is available in both Russian and English editions, free of charge, either by post or through the Internet. It often features stories about the formation of important new associations or organizations in the Russian print and broadcast media. It also offers a regular calendar of upcoming events and an interesting collection of brief items in its "News Notes" section.

Pacific BVL Corporation

1329 Sixth Ave.
San Francisco, CA 94122
Tel/Fax: (415) 753-6961

This publisher offers a "Russian Business and Law Library by Mail." Titles (in Russian) include: *Marketing Essentials* by Northwestern University Professor Philip Kotler and *Essentials of Accounting* by Harvard Business School Professor R. Anthony. Among the reference works Pacific BVL publishes is an *English-Russian Medical Dictionary*. For the would-be entrepreneur, in the U.S. or NIS, there is the bi-lingual *Are You Ready to Start Your Private Business?* by Khersonski and Tennison.

Raduga Publishers

3-ya Frunzenskaya ul. 1-73
119270 Moscow
Tel: 268-4035
E-mail: raduga@glas.apc.org
Contact: Andrei Vakulenko, President

Either working with Western organizations based in Moscow, or on its own behalf, Raduga has published numerous books and reference materials for the nonprofit sector in Russia. In 1994, for example, Raduga published, together with the Vancouver (Canada) Volunteer Centre and United Way International, *Добровольцы: Как их Найти, Как их Удержать*

(Volunteers: How to Find Them, How to Keep Them).

Russian Info & Business Center, Inc., USA

731 Eighth Street, SE
Washington, DC 20003
Tel/Fax: (202) 546-3275
or
1400 S. Joyce Street, suite 1232
Arlington, VA 22202
Tel/Fax: (703) 521-6238
E-mail: ric@DGS.dgsys.com

This firm sells a large variety of industrial directories, atlases, and business guides on Russia and the NIS. It also offers a directory of *Russian Universities and Research Institutions* and a volume titled *Russian Charity: Religious and Non-Profit Organizations*.

Русский Инвалид (Russian Invalid)

ul. 1905 Goda, dom 7
Moscow
Tel: 299-7981
Contact: Nikolai Zhukov, Editor in Chief

According to the editor, *Russkii Invalid* is a resurrection of the respected newspaper founded in the aftermath of the Napoleonic Wars by Pavel P. Pesarovius. Until closed by the Bolsheviks one hundred years later, the newspaper not only published about disability issues, but also managed a large program of donations and other support for disabled veterans, orphans, schools and almshouses

Sabre Foundation, Inc.
872 Massachusetts Ave., suite 2-1
Cambridge, MA 02139
Tel: (617) 868-3510
Fax: (617) 868-7916
E-mail: sabre@sabre.org

Sabre Foundation, working through affiliates in the region, has translated a number of useful books into Ukrainian and other languages of the NIS. For example, *Your Small Business Made Simple*, by Richard Gallagher, and several other books oriented to the small entrepreneur have been translated into Ukrainian and published by Sabre-Svitlo of L'viv. For more information about Sabre's translation and publication-support programs, send e-mail or visit their World Wide Web site at http://www.sabre.org/

Transition: The Newsletter About Reforming Economies
World Bank
Room 11023X
1818 H Street, NW
Washington, DC 20433
Tel: (202) 473-7466
Fax: (202) 522-1152
E-mail:
    jprochnowwalker@worldbank.org
Contact: Jennifer Prochnow-Walker

Of all the countries formerly in the Communist bloc, did you know that Hungary and Romania as of 1994 had received 25 times more aid per capita from institutions like the World Bank and IMF than Ukraine and the Baltic countries had received? Despite this, did you know that Estonia led all the so-called "transition economies" in the success of its privatization program?

This and much more can be learned from the World Bank's newsletter,

Transition: The Newsletter About Reforming Economies. Articles are not technical, and each issue includes a calendar of upcoming events, interesting charts and graphs, and reviews of other resources. Free.

The Ukrainian Weekly
30 Montgomery St.
Jersey City, NJ 07302
Tel: (201) 434-0237, -0807, -3036
Contact: Roma Hadzewycz, Editor-in-chief

Founded in 1933, this newspaper is a premier, inexpensive source of information about both events in Ukraine and in the U.S. that affect U.S.-Ukrainian relations. Coverage is especially strong in cultural areas. An annual subscription costs $60. ($40 for members of the Ukrainian National Association.)

United States Information Agency
Regional Program Office
Schmidgasse 14
A-1082 Vienna, Austria
Tel: (43-1) 405-3347
Fax: (43-1) 408-8288
E-mail: rpo@usia.co.at

USIA's RPO is funded by the Office of East European and NIS Affairs to provide services and products to 33 Posts in the region. RPO offers a catalog, *1995 List of Publications in Translation*, which lists "pamphlets and books on democracy, market economics, aspects of civl society, United States historyr, geography, economics, politics and society." The number of publications translated into Russian and other languages of the NIS is considerable. To obtain the catalog, contact the RPO in Vienna.

Separately, USIA has for a number of years also operated a Book Translation Program, under which the agency partially subsidizes the translation and printing of a range of American books by an in-country publishing house. More than 75 titles that have been translated into Russian or other languages of the NIS. (Book translation programs exist not only for Russia but also Armenia, Kazakstan and Ukraine.)

Some print runs have numbered 50,000 copies or more. For help in obtaining a list of titles in translation and their publishers, contact any USIS officer at a U.S. embassy in the NIS. The Moscow USIS office e-mail address is: usis@glas.apc.org

Some of the titles published in Russian under the Book Translation program include:

- *The Federalist Papers*, James Madison
- *How American Laws Are Made,* by Edward Willet
- *Democracy in America*, Alexis de Tocqueville
- *Born for Liberty: A History of Women in America*, Sara M. Evans
- *Economic History and the History of Economics*, Mark Blaug
- *Economics of the Public Sector*, Joseph E. Stiglitz
- *American Government: A Brief Introduction*, Max J. Skidmore
- *How Washington Works: The Executive's Guide to Government*, A. Lee Fritschler and Bernard H. Ross
- *Macroeconomics in the Global Economy*, Jeffrey D. Sachs

- *International Business: Environments and Operations*, John D. Daniels and Lee H. Radebaugh
- *Mastering the Politics of Planning: Crafting Credible Plans and Policies That Make a Difference*, Guy Benveniste
- *Controlling Corruption*, Robert E. Klitgaard
- *The Theory of Democracy Revisited*, Giovanni Sartori
- *Fundamentals of Financial Management*, Eugene F. Brigham
- *Managing Local Government: Public Administration in Practice*, Richard D. Bingham

World Learning

1015 15th Street, NW suite 911
Washington, DC 20005
Tel: (202) 408-5420
Fax: (202) 898-1920
E-mail: 5663077@MCIMail.com
Contact: Kathy Kalinowski, Editor

World Learning publishes occasional "PVO/NIS Project Bulletins." The last one, on the theme of NGO law in the NIS, was 28 pages in length. It included an interesting historical essay by Professor Galina Ulianova on patterns of charitable giving in Moscow from the 1860s to World War I. To receive copies of the Bulletin, contact Ms. Kalinowski.

Writing Tools from Russia Catalog

Smartlink Corporation
4695 Macarthur Court, Suite 230
Newport Beach, CA 92660
Sales: (800) 256-4814
Tel: (714) 552-1599

Fax: (714) 552-1699

This is a catalog of fonts and drivers, proofing tools (spelling and grammar checkers), OCR software, translation software, electronic dictionaries, and CD-ROM-based language learning aids for Russian and other languages of the NIS. The ParaType Library of fonts offers a collection of typefaces developed by Russian type designers over the past 50 years and furnished by the highly-regarded Paragraph Company in Moscow. There is also a set of Windows-based fonts and drivers for Turkish and East European languages.

Yellow Pages Moscow
MARVOL USA
1925 Century Park East, 10th Floor
Los Angeles, CA 90067
Sales: (800) 4-MARVOL
Tel: (310) 553-6100
Fax: (310) 553-9340

The latest edition claims to include 27,000 up-to-date phone numbers, fax numbers and addresses for Moscow's commercial, industrial, and government enterprises. A combination of a business-to-business and consumer directory, it contains hundreds of standard Yellow Pages categories, including: hotels, embassies and consulates, joint ventures, interpreters, travel agencies, schools, restaurants, newspapers, legal services, and shipping agents. In English. 421 pp., $45, plus $4.50 postage and handling.

Yevshan Ukrainian Catalog
Yevshan Corporation
Box 325
Beaconsfield, Quebec
Canada H9W 5T8
Tel: 1-800-265-9858
Fax: (514) 630-9960
E-mail: info@yevshan.com

Yevshan Communications describes its catalog as North America's "#1 source of Ukrainian books, music and videos." In addition, the catalog offers maps, flags, holiday cards, Cyrillic font programs for computers, subscriptions to popular Ukrainian newspapers and periodicals, and even a food parcel service to Ukraine. Yevshan's specialty is Ukrainian music production and distribution.

Index of NIS Cities with Grassroots Organizations

Index of U.S.-Based Organizations

Center for Civil Society International

Center for Civil Society International (CCSI) supports activities by American voluntary organizations and independent associations—our so-called "third sector"—that strengthen institutions of pluralism, law, and market economies worldwide. The focus of CCSI's activities is on publishing resources, both in print and electronically, that foster contacts and relationships between America's "third sector" (professional associations, charitable organizations, mutual aid societies, special interest groups, educational and health organizations, etc.) and the third sector that has emerged in recent years in Russia, Ukraine, and other states of the former Soviet Union. Informational products of CCSI include its newsletter *Civil Society: East and West; NetTalk*, a monthly bulletin of tips and news related to the Internet; and occasional special publications such as *Civil Society: USA* and *Интернет Для Журналистов (The Internet for Journalists,* in Russian). CCSI also maintains an extensive World Wide Web site on the Friends and Partners platform[1], containing more than 450 documents, and operates an electronic mailing list named *CivilSoc.*

On the Board of Advisors of CCSI are Elena Bonner, Herbert J. Ellison, Richard Greene, John Miller, Yale Richmond, S. Frederick Starr, Witold Sulimirski, and Sharon Tennison. Members of CCSI's Board of Directors are Ronald S. Bemis, Allan Blackman, Larry Ehl, Neil Elgee, Michael D. Evans, Catherine A. Fitzpatrick, Dennis McConnell and Daniel C. Waugh. Chairman of the Board is John Hamer.

CCSI is a private, nonpartisan educational organization, based in Seattle, Washington, USA. It is registered as tax-exempt under section 501(c)(3) of the U.S. Internal Revenue Code and receives its funding from voluntary donations and foundation grants.

Principal staff of Center for Civil Society International are Holt Ruffin and Richard Upjohn. For more information, contact:

Center for Civil Society International
2929 NE Blakeley Street
Seattle, WA 98105-3120 USA

Tel: (206) 523-4755
Fax: (206) 523-1974
E-mail: ccsi@u.washington.edu

---

[1] The URL is http://solar.rtd.utk.edu/~ccsi/ccsihome.html